# PUBLIC RELATIONS
## The Profession and the Practice

# PUBLIC RELATIONS
## The Profession and the Practice

Craig E. Aronoff
Georgia State University

Otis W. Baskin
University of Houston at Clear Lake City

**WEST PUBLISHING COMPANY**
St. Paul   New York   Los Angeles   San Francisco

SECTION OPENING CREDITS

**Section I.** Photo by Hella Hammid, Photo Researchers, Inc. **Section II.** Courtesy of the American Public Radio Network. "A Prairie Home Companion" is a production of Minnesota Public Radio. **Section III.** Photo by Cary Wolinsky, Stock, Boston. **Section IV.** Logos courtesy of American Cancer Society; American Heart Association; American Public Radio Network; Goodwill Industries of America; Lutheran Social Services of Minnesota; March of Dimes Birth Defects Foundation; National Federation of the Blind; United Way of America. **Section V.** Logos courtesy of Burlington Northern Railroad; Dana Corporation; Ford Motor Company; General Mills; Munsingwear Inc.; National Car Rental; NCR Corporation; Northwestern Bell. **Section VI.** Logos courtesy of Better Business Bureau; Cargill; Environmental Protection Agency; International Business Machines; Minnesota Public Interest Research Group; Nissen (subsidiary of Kidde, Inc.); United States Department of Labor; World Health Organization.

*Copy editing:* Louise Lincoln
*Interior design:* James Buddenbaum
*Cover design:* Barbara Redmond
*Composition:* Parkwood Composition Services, Inc.

COPYRIGHT © 1983 By WEST PUBLISHING CO.
50 West Kellogg Boulevard
P.O. Box 3526
St. Paul, Minnesota 55165

Printed in the United States of America

**Library of Congress Cataloging in Publication Data**

Aronoff, Craig E.
   Public relations.

   Includes index.
     1. Public Relations.  I. Baskin, Otis W.  II. Title.
HM263.A7863 1983     659.2     82-10852
ISBN 0-314-63154-2

*To Lara Lorena and the next generation*

# CONTENTS

## SECTION VI  CRITICAL ISSUES    373

# A QUICK GUIDE TO PUBLIC RELATIONS IN ACTION

# PREFACE

Public relations is a profession in transition. In an environment of rapid social change, every organization must change or die. Public relations practitioners possess the communications expertise and social sensitivity necessary to help organizations adapt to their changing environments.

In many ways, this is a new role for public relations practitioners. No longer are they mere technicians who shape and transmit messages from organizations to their publics. Rather, public relations has become a critical dimension of management itself. All managers now recognize that they themselves practice public relations. They are also recognizing that public relations practitioners should be part of the management mainstream.

To this broadened role, the public relations practitioner must bring all of the traditional skills of the craft. The ability to understand public opinion, to plan public relations programs, to create effective messages in all media for all organizational publics, and to evaluate public relations effectiveness, remain crucial talents and techniques. But public relations as it is practiced today demands much more. A full understanding of all communication processes is essential. A complete acquaintance with the methods of management is critical to the successful practice of public relations. Thorough knowledge of the environment of the organization in which the practitioner works is a prerequisite to public relations effectiveness.

*Public Relations: The Profession and the Practice* is the first realistic guide to the practice of public relations in the 1980s. It covers all of the basic materials developed in the practice of public relations during this century, but it goes much further than any previous text. It deals with public relations in the overall context of organizational communications. It stresses the practitioner's role in organizational and societal communication systems. It comes to grips with challenges to the profession from within organizations and from organizations' surrounding environments. It views public relations from the perspective of overall organizational decision making, examining how public relations affects and is affected by decisions that are made.

Our goals in writing this book were quite ambitious. We feel we have probed the deepest issues of public relations and fully explored them for the first time. It is a book for a profession that has come of age. We have attempted to give the public relations student and practitioner the necessary tools and knowledge they need. We hope we have provided these in ways that reflect the reality of the public relations world. Moreover, we have consistently attempted to provide that information in a direct, interesting, and highly readable fashion. In short, we have made every effort to make *Public Relations: The Profession and the Practice* the public relations textbook for today—and tomorrow. We believe that we have created a new standard in the field.

**ACKNOWLEDGMENTS**   Our thanks are due to many people: colleagues with whom we have worked in the public relations field, leading practitioners with whom we have spent hours in rewarding conversation, students and fellow teachers on whom we tested concepts contained in this book. They are too numerous to name, but all have our gratidude.

We owe a particular debt to Alan Scott, our public relations mentor, who helped to shape our understanding of the field. We also would single out Mary McCleary Posner, president of Posner Public Relations, for helping to ground us in the real world of public relations. Gene Donner and Darrel Alexander gave us our first public relations jobs and perhaps started us on the course that led to this book. Frederick C. Teahan, Vice President—Education for the Public Relations Society of America, was especially helpful in our preparation and research.

The following professors reviewed our manuscript and helped us to make it as useful as possible to students and teachers:

R. Ferrell Ervin, Norfolk State University
Hunter McCartney, West Virginia University
Dulcie Murdock, Virginia Commonwealth University
Greg Phifer, Florida State University
Walt Seifert, The Ohio State University
David Siegal, Los Angeles Pierce College
Nancy Somerick, University of Akron
Dennis Wilcox, San Jose State University

We are deeply appreciative to those who distilled from their professional and teaching experience the cases which appear after each chapter. Our thanks to:

James Anderson, University of Florida
J. Carroll Bateman, University of Tennessee
S. Carlton Caldwell, University of Maryland
Carolyn Cline, University of Alabama
R. Ferrell Ervin, Norfolk State University
Betsy Graham, Georgia State University
Art Guillermo, University of Northern Iowa
Charlotte Hatfield, Ball State University
Dulcie Murdock, Virginia Commonwealth University
Walt Seifert, The Ohio State University
Melvin Sharpe, Ball State University
Nancy Somerick, University of Akron
Robert Taylor, University of Wisconsin
Jim VanLeuven, Washington State University
Thomas W. Zimmerer, Clemson University

Our love and thanks go to our wives, Kathy and Maryan, who have suffered with us through this and our other collaborations. Our appreciation goes to our universities and departments for support, services, and resources. We are especially grateful to George Crowling and Howard Feldman, research assistants, and to Diane Exum, Deborah Lawson, Marjorie Hudson, Kathy Holland, and Louise Kelly, who have been so helpful in the preparation of our manuscript. Finally, we give our sincere thanks to the professionals at West Publishing Company, particularly our editor, Gary Woodruff, who worked so hard and long with us.

Craig E. Aronoff, Ph.D.
Georgia State University

Otis W. Baskin, Ph.D.
University of Houston at Clear Lake City

# PUBLIC RELATIONS
## The Profession and the Practice

# SECTION I PUBLIC RELATIONS: THE PROFESSION

This book deals with *Public Relations: The Profession and the Practice*—its process, its publics, the kinds of organizations in which it is practiced, and the critical issues that confront it. The book takes a practical approach, drawing on the experience of many practitioners and executives. It also incorporates the theoretical perspectives of researchers and scholars from various disciplines including communications, business, and psychology. It is intended to provide students with a thorough understanding of public relations and a basis for successful practice today and in the future.

The first section of *Public Relations* covers fundamentals of the practice. Chapter 1 develops a working definition of public relations, reviewing and refining the definitions of previous studies. The history of public relations, which provides a useful perspective on the field, is described in Chapter 2. Chapter 3 deals with communications theory and process. The most important application of public relations— its contribution to organizational decision making—is explained in Chapter 4. Chapter 5 looks at careers in public relations—where the jobs are, what they pay, and what to expect when you get one.

# CHAPTER 1   WHAT IS PUBLIC RELATIONS?

**PREVIEW**   Public relations is a management function that helps to define organizational objectives and philosophy.

Public relations practitioners communicate with all relevant internal and external publics in the effort to create consistency between organizational goals and societal expectations.

Public relations practitioners develop, execute, and evaluate organizational programs that promote the exchange of influence and understanding among organizations' constituent parts and publics.

The phone rings. You answer it. A voice says, "Hi. I'm Pamela Roberts, Director of Public Relations for . . . ."

You are thinking, "Why would the Director of Public Relations be calling me?"

". . . We would like you to stop by our showroom to take advantage of our grand opening specials. . . ."

"Public relations?" you are thinking. "This doesn't sound like public relations to me. The *Director* of Public Relations is doing telephone solicitation?"

You are reading the classified employment ads. Two jobs are listed under "Public Relations." One requires modeling experience. The other reads:

**MAKING ENOUGH MONEY?**
**If you are a dependable worker with an outgoing personality and a reliable car, you can earn an additional $100 to $200 weekly, working 4 hours nightly, Monday through Friday. We will train. Serious inquiries. Call . . . .**[1]

By this time you are wondering: "What is this thing called public relations? Public relations classes talk about corporate images and decision makers, but in the real world, it looks like marketing gimmicks and telephone sales."

So like any good college student seeking a definition, you go to the dictionary—the biggest one you can find. And there on pages 1456–7 of *Webster's New Twentieth Century Dictionary of the English Language,* unabridged, you read:

*Public relations;* **relations with the general public through publicity; those functions of a corporation, organization, branch of military service, etc. concerned with informing the public of its activities, policies, etc. and attempting to create favorable public opinion.**[2]

And somehow you are still unsatisfied. The definition deals only with sending information, not with receiving it. Surely public relations is more than "publicity." If you consult the Yellow Pages of your telephone directory, you will be further confused. In one major city's phone book, 88 entries were to be found under "Public Relations," ranging from "International Association of Pacemaker Patients Inc." to "Peterson J. Chandler Financial Planning Wealth Management."

By now it is quite obvious that the term "public relations" is used and misused in many different ways. Public relations is not telephone sales, nor modeling, nor door-to-door peddling, nor financial planning, nor even simply developing messages to inform the public and gain its favorable opinion. Many have asked: What is public relations? But as veteran public relations scholar Rex Harlow found in his comprehensive review of public relations definitions:

**Unfortunately, the answers to these questions have been so diverse and conflicting, so affected by the opposing demands of theory and practice, so uncertain and inadequate, that hardly any two of them have been alike or even similar.**[3]

Dr. Harlow overstates his case; by considering many definitions from many sources, it becomes possible to make some generalizations about what public relations is and what it does. Consistently, these definitions include the following components: management function; communications; influencing public opinion; relations with publics; interpreting public opinion; and social responsibility.

## PUBLIC RELATIONS: A MANAGEMENT FUNCTION

In attempting to understand the nature of public relations, it is probably first necessary to recognize that public relations is a management function. While it may support or facilitate production or sales, public relations is not merely an adjunct of personnel, marketing or advertising.

The managerial responsibilities associated with the public relations function are both general and specific. Some public relations functions are shared by all managers; others are the particular job of public relations specialists. All managers spend much of their time developing and communicating various messages to various external or internal publics. All managers, indeed virtually all employees, represent their organization to some public and thus help to shape public responses to their organization. Public relations also contributes to general management. Ideally, public relations within an organization can help establish organizational objectives and philosophy, and helps that organization to adapt to a changing environment.

## Defining Objectives and Philosophy

Public relations can make important contributions in forming an organization's ideas about what it is, what it should do, and what society wants and expects it to do. Charles Steinberg describes this aspect of public relations as "structuring of company philosophy and carrying out of that philosophy in practice so that what the institution says is not at variance with what it does."[4]

Other public relations authorities make a similar point: "The first constructive step in public relations is to advise management in development of sound policies which are in the public interest as well as company interest."[5] Of course, public relations practitioners within organizations do not have final authority in creating objectives, policies or philosophy. But in many modern organizational structures, they are important members of policy-making groups.

The role of public relations is critically important in such situations for two reasons. First, because public relations is charged with monitoring public opinion, practitioners can represent the public interest and predict public reaction to institutional decisions. Second, public relations must communicate decisions to the organization's publics, and the commitment and understanding gained by participating in making decisions are tremendous assets when the time comes to communicate them.

**Helping Organizations to Change**

While all managers are concerned with adapting organizations to changing environments, those with specific responsibilities for public relations play a particularly important role in this area as well. Indeed, facilitating organizational change has become a frequently mentioned part of public relations definitions.

Again, public relations managers do not make the decisions that lead to change within organizations. But because they constantly monitor and interact with the organizational environment, public relations managers frequently possess information that suggests a need for change and indicates the directions that change should take. Public relations practitioners often can discover a problem when it is still managable. Thus, unnecessary crises can be avoided.

Harlow's historical review of public relations definitions indicates that emphasis on change has grown steadily since the 1940s, when *PR News's* oft-quoted definition was suggested: "Public relations is the activities of a corporation . . . building and maintaining sound and productive relations . . . so as to adapt itself to the environment."[6]

In the 1950s, public relations practitioner Thomas Gonser stressed acceptance of change as a necessary attitude of public relations: ". . . A willingness to make the business what the public wants it to be, rather than trying to convince them that they should like the business for what it is."[7]

The turbulent 1960s brought forth a flood of change-oriented definitions. Charles B. Coates, a leading professional, called public relations "a kind of pilot . . . it knows the rocks, the shoals . . . and it can gauge the probable consequences of the choice of one direction as against the other." Others identified public relations as "an engineer of change," and claimed that it "senses, even anticipates, the changing temper of the times before a problem or crisis stage is reached."[8]

By the 1970s, some leaders in the public relations field sounded panic-stricken. David Finn, board chairman of Ruder & Finn, Inc., one of the world's leading public relations firms, suggests that public relations tries:

**to prevent the crisis from getting out of hand . . . to help clients conduct their business in a way that is responsive to the new demands made by concerned scientists, environmentalists, consumerists, minority leaders, underprivileged segments of the community, the young generation.**[9]

The 1980s may prove somewhat calmer than the two decades just past, but public relations will undoubtedly continue to help harmonize organizations with their environments and to promote positive organizational change. The process of defining goals and facilitating change is further discussed in Chapter 4.

**PUBLIC RELATIONS AS COMMUNICATION**

Between the general and specific aspects of public relations lies a rather gray area. All managers are involved in and responsible for communication. But public relations managers have additional, more specific responsibilities in this regard. The nature of communication is treated more extensively in Chapter 3, while specific problems in communicating to external and internal audiences are covered in Chapters 8 and 10 respectively. *Communication,* here, applies to the definition of the public relations role in at least four specific ways. It refers to *skills* possessed by public relations practitioners; to *tasks* performed; to *systems* established; and to *operation* of established systems.

**Skills**

Many authors point to the need for public relations practitioners to be excellent writers and speakers. Some now call for expertise in graphics or audiovisual communication. Allen Center, co-author of a leading public relations textbook, calling public relations people "technicians in communication," adds to the list a "knack for persuasion."[10] Practitioners also need to be able to conduct research.

**Tasks**

Many commentators on public relations point out the tasks and goals of communication. Frank Jefkins, a British public relations authority, defines the process as "planned, pervasive communication designed to influence significant publics."[11] Public relations scholars Gene Harlan and Alan Scott in their early work also stress manipulation in their definition: "skilled communication of ideas to various publics with the object of producing desired results."[12]

**Systems**

Rather than stressing individual skills or tasks, some public relations writers have advocated the establishment of systems for ongoing communications. Thus, Jefkins describes "a system of communications to create goodwill,"[13] while Harlow emphasizes establishment and maintenance of mutual lines of communication.[14]

**Operations**

Finally, several observers concentrate on how such systems should be used once established. Most who carry the definitions to this extent hold that public relations is responsible for maintaining systematic two-way communication.

**PUBLIC RELATIONS AS A MEANS OF INFLUENCING PUBLIC OPINION**

As we have already mentioned, exerting influence on public opinion is often considered a part of the public relations mission. Just how public relations should deal with public opinion, however, is a matter of considerable debate. The opinions of scholars in the field range from simple discussions of pumping up corporate prestige and ensuring public awareness of organizational performance to complex prescriptions for the establishment of mutual understanding between an organization's management and its publics.

Perhaps the simplest definitions deal with the enhancement of an organization's prestige. Harlow and Jefkins touch on this aspect of public relations. Another simple and widely quoted conception of public relations is "good performance publicly appreciated." [15] Indeed, effective public relations depends upon the effective performance of the organization being represented. Another theme holds that it is simply the task of public relations to supply accurate information concerning subjects of value to the public.

Beyond touting the organization or dispassionately dispensing information, several scholars and practitioners maintain, public relations should be an active process of interpreting the organization to its publics or to society as a whole. This interpretation leads directly to a public relations definition which stresses pursuit of public understanding and acceptance of the organization as a mission of public relations.

Thus far, our attempts to define public relations have dealt with informing, promoting, understanding, and interpreting. Affecting public opinion, however, implies conscious efforts to exert influence. A number of public relations textbook authors describe influence as an important component when defining the field. Public relations textbook author Howard Stephenson says that public relations is "convincing people that they should adopt a certain attitude." [16] *Fortune* magazine writer Irwin Ross calls it the "attempt, by information and persuasion, to engineer public support." [17] Similarly, in the late 1940s, Philip Lesly, chairman of his own public relations firm for over 30 years, defined public relations as "all activities and attitudes intended to judge, influence and control the opinion of any group or groups of persons in the interest of any individual, group or institution." [18] William Nielander and Raymond Miller, in their 1968 public relations book, are less blunt; they call public relations "the gentle art of letting the other fellow have your way." [19]

Effective influence or persuasion inevitably rests upon an understanding of those to whom the effort is directed. The price of influence is being influenced. Not surprisingly, certain writers suggest that communication must not go only in one direction. In his 1947 textbook, Verne Burnett stresses that public relations means "trying to understand other people . . . and then trying to influence them." [20] Edward Stan calls it a "planned effort to influence opinion through acceptable performance and two-way communication." [21] Once the recognition of two-way communication has been established, it becomes possible to define public relations in literal terms; that is, in terms of *relations with publics*.

**Relations with Publics**   The cumulative experience of public relations practitioners suggests that public opinion is an ornery beast, nearly impossible to push or prod. It will move, however, if you understand its needs and cater to them. Rather than seeking to "engineer," or "control," or "convince" the public, public relations is a means by which common ground is sought. It is the linking pin in a relationship that looks past short-term goals and interests toward the kind of long-term success that requires positive public opinion. Author and practitioner Charles S. Steinberg's 1958 definition of public relations exemplifies this train of thought:

Public relations is that specific operating philosophy by which management sets up policies designed to serve both in the company's and the public's interest.   .   .   . (The) long-range, carefully nurtured effort to develop and maintain a strong, resilient and positive consensus from all of the publics upon whom the activities of the institution impinge.[22]

While certain aggressive corporations still seek to create their own public opinion climates, most perceive public opinion as a significant environment which needs constant attention and active response. A primary aim of public relations, rather than attempting to manipulate various publics, is to sensitize the organization to public images and expectations. Public relations staffs effectively link institutions and assist organizations in their efforts to harmonize behavior with the expectations of various external and internal publics.

## INTERPRETING PUBLIC OPINION

Many thoughtful observers of the contemporary world now maintain that adaptability is an organization's greatest asset. With regard to public relations, this view suggests that emphasis should be placed on gathering and interpreting information from the organization's relevant publics and disseminating it to management, thus reversing the traditional direction of the flow of information. This idea is closely related to the general function of facilitating organizational change.

Such an approach to public relations suggests that some of the most important messages communicated by public relations practitioners are aimed neither at the media, nor at customers and the general public, nor even at employees. The most important messages, rather, are developed with management in mind and deal with fundamental aspects of organizational direction, decision making, and coordination. Thus public relations is established as an integral part of organizational management. Those public relations definitions stressing interpretation of public opinion vary. Opinion research and management consultation are the most commonly mentioned activities. Alan Scott sums it up best by placing emphasis "upon the sensitive interpretation of the human scene to management .   .   . evaluating and interpreting public opinion, public issues and public demands."[23] Further discussion of the nature of public opinion, and the public relations issues involved in influencing it, reacting to it, and interpreting it, can be found in Chapter 6.

## SOCIAL RESPONSIBILITY

During the past twenty-five years, social responsibility has become a major concern in American society. It is felt by many that institutions should assume responsibility for the consequences of their actions. Within the context of public relations, according to Donald Wright, this implies that "public relations people .   .   . should act at all times with the best interests of society in mind."[24]

Rex Harlow makes much of the social responsibility theme, maintaining that the public relations practitioner "defines and emphasizes the responsibility of management to serve the public interest." [25] Moreover, the practitioner:

suggests adjustment of the organization's behavior to meet the social, political and economic responsibility and the needs created by shifting human standards and attitudes . . . tries to help the organization demonstrate a keen sense of social responsibility along with profit responsibility.[26]

The logical extreme of this position, suggesting that public relations be defined as representing the public and attempting to influence management, has been argued by Scott Cutlip, who claims that public relations gives the public "a voice at policy making tables." [27]

Despite the wide discussion of social responsibility as an aspect of public relations, Wright's research indicates that at the present time:

Professionalism and social responsibility are not the same thing in public relations. . . . It's possible to be a professional without being very socially responsible. . . . Some socially responsible PR people are not very professional.[28]

Although the exercise of social responsibility thus may not always be visible in practice, it nonetheless remains vitally important as a public relations ideal. As we shall see in Section 6, social responsibility will be increasingly perceived as an integral aspect of the public relations function.

**SO WHAT IS PUBLIC RELATIONS?**

Existing attempts to define the field include many factors that we have not dealt with in our discussion. Some concern themselves with listing the kinds of organizations which utilize public relations (all kinds); the media used in public relations communications (all media); and the publics with which public relations communicates (all publics). Others give exhaustive lists of what public relations is not. A few even claim that public relations as such no longer exists, preferring some other name referring to the same general process.

For the purposes of this book, however—and to establish a broad, realistic, and accurate description of the public relations function—we can summarize this chapter's discussion with the following working definition:

Public relations is a management function that helps to define organizational objectives and philosophy and facilitate organizational change. Public relations practitioners communicate with all relevant internal and external publics in the effort to create consistency between organizational goals and societal expectations. Public relations practitioners develop, execute, and evaluate organizational programs that promote the exchange of influence and understanding among organizations' constituent parts and publics.

Not all people who say they practice public relations do all that is implied by this definition. Some interpret their jobs even more broadly. But for now and for the foreseeable future, this description captures the essential aspects of public relations practice. Our next chapter demonstrates that this definition is valid for much of the past as well.

---

**CASE STUDY:**     **By Nancy M. Somerick**
**"DOING PR"**      **Department of Mass Media-**
                    **Communication,**
                    **The University of Akron, Akron, Ohio**

---

You have applied for a public relations position with a $10.2 million savings and loan association, a conservative financial institution that has been in existence for over fifty years. The organization has never employed a public relations person before. Now that its assets have risen above $10 million, however, the president of the institution feels it is time to hire someone to "do the PR."

During an interview, the president admits he is not sure what public relations is, but he is fairly sure that he wants the person he hires to plan promotions and stage events that will attract new customers, write stories that will get free space and time in the local media, and start an employee publication. The president also states that he is open to suggestions about the position and asks you to explain how you would establish a professional, effective public relations program if you were hired.

**Questions**   1. Do the responsibilities outlined by the president indicate that he understands how the public relations function can be utilized most effectively?

2. What would you tell the president about your plans for establishing an effective PR program for the financial institution?

---

**NOTES**   [1] *Atlanta Journal,* 29 October 1979, p. 6.

[2] 2nd edition, (Cleveland: World Publishing Co.), 1970.

[3] Rex F. Harlow, "Building a Public Relations Definition," *Public Relations Review* (Winter 1976): 34.

[4] Charles S. Steinberg, *The Creation of Consent: Public Relations in Practice* (New York: Hastings House, 1975), p. 19.

[5] Richard W. Darrow, Dan J. Forrestal and Aubrey Cookman, *The Cantrell Public Relations Handbook* (Chicago: Dartnell, 1967), p. 30.

[6] Rex F. Harlow, "Public Relations Definitions Through the Years," *Public Relations Review* (Spring 1977): 56.

[7] Ibid., p. 56.

[8] Ibid., p. 58.

[9] Ibid., p. 61.

[10] Allen H. Center, "What About the State of the Art?" *Public Relations Journal* (January 1976): 30–31.

[11] Frank, Jefkins, *Planned Press and Public Relations* (London: International Textbook Co., 1977), p. 2.

[12] Gene Harlan and Alan Scott, *Contemporary Public Relations: Principles and Cases* (New York: Prentice-Hall, 1955), p. 3.

[13] Frank Jefkins, *Public Relations in World Marketing* (London: Crosby, Lockwood and Son, 1966), p. 4.

[14] Harlow, "Public Relations Definitions," p. 56.

[15] See, for instance, Harlow, "Public Relations Definitions," p. 56; Irwin Ross, *The Image Merchants* (New York: Doubleday, 1958), p. 16; and Raymond Simon, *Perspectives in Public Relations* (Norman, OK: University of Oklahoma Press, 1966), p. 63.

[16] Howard Stephenson, *Handbook of Public Relations* (New York: McGraw-Hill, 1960), p. 9.

[17] Ross, *Image Merchants,* p. 15.

[18] Philip Lesly, *Public Relations in Action* (Chicago: Ziff-Davis, 1947), p. 280.

[19] William A. Nielander and Raymond W. Miller, *Public Relations* (New York: The Ronald Press, 1951), p. 5.

[20] Verne Burnett, *You and Your Public* (New York: Harper, 1947), p. 4.

[21] Edward Stan, *What You Should Know About Public Relations* (New York: Oceana Publications, 1968), p. 1.

[22] Charles S. Steinberg, *The Mass Communicators: Public Relations, Public Opinion and Mass Media* (New York: Harper, 1958), pp. 16, 198.

[23] Allan W. Scott, "Does PR Need Redefinition?" *Public Relations Journal* (July 1970): 23–24.

[24] Donald K. Wright, "Professionalism and Social Responsibility in Public Relations," *Public Relations Review* (Fall, 1979): 23.

[25] Harlow, "Building a Definition," p. 36.

[26] Ibid., p. 35.

[27] Ibid., p. 37.

[28] Wright, "Professionalism and Social Responsibility," p. 31.

# CHAPTER 2  A BRIEF HISTORY OF PUBLIC RELATIONS

**PREVIEW**  Public relations is an outgrowth of the recognition of the power of public opinion, continuous competition among institutions for public support, and the development of media through which the public could be readily reached.

Public relations historically has had three stages: manipulation; information; and mutual influence and understanding. While their development has been sequential, all three continue to exist.

Public relations has generally moved from a role of using whatever means were available to achieve desired public opinion toward one of informing the public and providing information and counsel to management.

Vox populi, vox Dei.
The voice of the people is the voice of God.
    —Ancient Roman Proverb

Public opinion has always been a force in human events. Leaders have always courted the sentiments of their people to sustain their power and to gain support for their actions. Only those rulers who were believed to be gods, or chosen by gods, could afford to ignore public attitudes, and even they usually took pains to assure their subjects that their faith was well placed. Many despots who believed that they held absolute power and were thus immune from public opinion nevertheless lost their heads.

Because public opinion has been a powerful and important factor throughout human history, it is easy to claim that public relations has similarly ancient antecedents. However attractive such a pedigree might be to the public relations historian, it would be erroneous. Public relations as such is a fairly recent development, a product of the recognition of the power of public opinion combined with competition among institutions for public support and the development of media by which that public could be reached. In short, the United States with its republican government, its democratic sensibilities, its free markets, its various systems of checks and balances, and its independent population forever voting with ballots and dollars while increasing their levels of affluence and education, was the perfect crucible from which public relations could emerge.

**AMERICAN ANTECEDENTS TO PUBLIC RELATIONS**

It has been said that public relations prospers under adverse circumstances—when power is threatened or when public support is needed. Such were the circumstances preceding the American Revolutionary War, when Samuel Adams initiated what can be called a public relations campaign. Adams recognized the value of using symbols that were easily identifiable and aroused the emotions. He used slogans remembered to this day: "Taxation without representation is tyranny." He staged the Boston Tea Party to influence public opinion. Because he got his side of the story to the public first, shots fired into a group of rowdies became known as "the Boston Massacre." Adams directed a sustained-saturation public relations campaign using all available media. In the Sons of Liberty and Committees of Correspondence, he maintained mechanisms to implement the actions made possible by his public relations campaign.[1]

During the 1820s and 1830s, the franchise was granted to a larger portion of the population, expanding public education increased literacy, and the mass medium of the penny press was developing. The campaign that brought Andrew Jackson to the White House was the first to go past the elite and appeal directly to the public. Amos Kendall, a member of the famous Kitchen

Cabinet, served as Jackson's pollster, counselor, ghost writer, and publicist. Although he did not hold the title, Kendall effectively served as the first presidential press secretary and congressional liaison. Jackson, who did not express himself terribly well, used Kendall as a specialist to convey his ideas to Congress and the American people.

Jackson's foes were forced to adopt similar tactics in the effort to gain public favor. In March, 1831, the Bank of the United States, locked in a life-or-death struggle with President Jackson, decided "to cause to be prepared and circulated such documents and papers as may communicate to the people information in regard to the nature and operations of the bank."[2] Jackson and Kendall, however, prevailed.

Through the better part of the nineteenth century, public relations remained a rudimentary adjunct to political activities. The vigorous expansion of American business was tremendously popular and faced few challenges. In its early days, big business played its cards close to the vest—the less the public knew, the better. By the latter part of the century, however, it had perhaps overplayed its hand.

The 1880s saw government's first major steps into the marketplace. Markets and capital were growing rapidly. Simultaneously, there were dramatic shifts in public attitudes toward business and in the roles played by social institutions. Workers were beginning to organize themselves into unions, and they perceived their interests in many cases as directly opposed to those of management. Business was at once highly successful and increasingly besieged. It is therefore not surprising that at this time the term *public relations* came into use; its earliest appearance was probably that in Dorman B. Eaton's 1882 address to the graduating class of the Yale Law School. The concept, as we have noted, was not new, but the coining of the term suggests a new level of importance and consciousness. As historian Marc Bloch has noted, "the advent of a name is a great event even when the object named is not new, for the act of naming signifies conscious awareness."[3]

By 1889 George Westinghouse, founder of the industrial giant that still bears his name, had seen the light; he established the first corporate public relations department, hiring Pittsburgh newspaperman E. H. Heinrichs to direct a fierce struggle with Thomas A. Edison over alternating and direct electric current. Westinghouse won, and consequently, you use alternating current today. Other businesses followed the example of Westinghouse.

According to historian Marie Curti:

**Corporations gradually began to realize the importance of combating hostility and courting public favor. The expert in the field of public relations was an inevitable phenomenon in view of the need for the services he could provide.**

Curti draws attention to George Harvey, a newspaperman and publisher who was an early practitioner of public relations for financiers Thomas Fortune Ryan and Harry Payne Whitney in the 1890s.[4]

The massive social and economic changes of the late nineteenth century and the resulting pressures upon business forced a change in the attitudes of businessmen. A philosophy of pure competition gave way to different concerns. Social as well as economic benefits had to be taken into consideration. Public relations practitioners, as the twentieth century began, concentrated increasingly on this aspect of corporate legitimacy.

**PUBLIC RELATIONS: THREE STAGES OF DEVELOPMENT**

The development of public relations in the United States can be divided into three stages. To some degree, their progression is sequential, but all have existed simultaneously and, indeed, do so today. Moreover, while the three stages evolved rapidly on intellectual and theoretical bases during the first quarter of this century, in practice the most advanced stage has only recently gone beyond the point of novelty. The three stages are:

1. *Manipulation.* Public relations is assumed to use whatever means are available to achieve desired public opinion and action. Practitioners of this type of public relations were called "press agents."
2. *Information.* Public relations is regarded as a conduit for information flowing from organizations to the public so that the public will understand, sympathize with, and patronize the organization. Practitioners of this form of public relations were called "publicity agents."
3. *Mutual influence and understanding.* Public relations continues to accept the responsibilities of stage two, but in addition sees its role as providing information and counsel to management on the nature and realities of public opinion and methods by which the organization can establish policy, make decisions, and take actions in light of public opinion. Practitioners who practice public relations following this approach are called "public relations counselors." Not everyone who takes this title, however, deserves it.

**Stage 1: Manipulation**

Manipulation was the technique of nineteenth-century press agents who served political campaigns and carnival shows more than mainstream business. The frequently quoted remark, "There's a sucker born every minute," exemplifies the manipulative approach.

In their efforts to promote land sales in the American west or attract attention for politicians, early publicists did not hesitate to embellish the truth. Press agents made exaggeration into a high art. The myth of Davy Crockett was a creation of the political enemies of Andrew Jackson. Matthew St. Clair Clarke, Crockett's press agent, was attempting to lure the frontier vote away from Jackson.[5]

The success of the press agents in attracting attention and public response, coupled with their blatantly manipulative aims, inevitably aroused hostility from the press and public. Press agentry gave public relations an odor that persists to this day.

**Stage 2: Information**

By the early 1900s business, increasingly forced to submit to governmental pressures, encountered increasingly hostile criticism from newspapers. Because of the social forces that gathered against business at the turn of the twentieth century, public relations became a specialized function broadly accepted in major corporations. Furthermore, it was rapidly recognized that deception, manipulation, and self-serving half-truths were inappropriate responses to challenges raised by media and government. Edward L. Bernays, practitioner, first teacher of public relations at the college level, and author of the first book on the subject, explained the emergence of the public relations function in this way:

**The first recognition of distinct functions of the public relations counsel arose, perhaps, in the early years of the present century as a result of the insurance scandals coincident with the muckraking of corporate finance in the popular magazines. The interests thus attacked suddenly realized that they were completely out of touch with the public they were professing to serve, and required expert advice to show them how they could understand the public and interpret themselves to it.[6]**

Former journalists began to find it possible to make a living in the public relations business. In 1900, George V. S. Michaelis established The Publicity Bureau in Boston. His job, as he saw it, was to gather factual information about his clients for distribution to newspapers. By 1906 his major clients were the nation's railroads. Two years later William W. Smith established a publicity office in Washington, D.C. He sought employment from anyone who had business with Congress.

The father of public relations, however, and the man who nurtured the fledgling profession, was Ivy Ledbetter Lee, son of a Georgia preacher. Lee was a reporter who saw better prospects in the publicity arena. After working in New York's mayoral campaign and for the Democratic National Committee, Lee combined with George Packor, another newspaper veteran, to form the nation's third agency. In 1906, coal operators George F. Baer and Associates hired the partnership to represent them in an anthracite coal strike. Lee took the assignment and promptly issued a "Declaration of Principles" to all newspaper city editors. The sentiments expressed in this document clearly indicated that public relations had entered its second stage. As Eric Goldman observes: "The public was no longer to be ignored, in the traditional manner of business, nor fooled, in the continuing manner of the press agent."[7] Lee declared that the public was to be informed. The declaration read:

**This is not a secret press bureau. All our work is done in the open. We aim to supply news. This is not an advertising agency; if you think any of our matter ought properly to go to your business office, do not use it. Our matter is accurate. Further details on any subject treated will be supplied promptly, and any editor will be assisted most cheerfully in verifying directly any statement of fact.   .   .   . In brief, our plan is, frankly and openly, on behalf of business concerns and public institutions, to supply to the press and public of the United States prompt and accurate information concerning subjects which it is of value and interest to the public to know about.[8]**

Railroads were among the early users of public relations consultants. In 1906, the Pennsylvania Railroad retained Lee as publicity counselor. From 1897 on, the term *public relations* was frequently used in railroad trade publications. Indeed, publications of the day maintained that as early as 1893 railroads had begun "to reach and study the social condition of its public."[9] Lee's activities for the Pennsylvania included publicizing employee benefits and railroad safety. He also emphasized the large numbers of people who owned the railroad's stock (not mentioning that a very few people held the vast majority of stock). He urged executives to accept public exposure and to cooperate fully with community projects. Most controversially, Lee released complete, factual information about accidents; traditionally, such news had been suppressed.

The railroad industry was convinced of the value of public relations. By 1909, an industry leader called on all major companies to create a:

**Vice President in charge of public relations [a man] . . . of mature years and judgment, skilled in railway affairs and human affairs as well, and carrying enough weight in the councils of his company so that his suggestions would be apt to be carried out.**[10]

Such an adviser, it was held, could reveal and eliminate the unpopularity of the railroad industry by evaluating and improving customer service.

In a similar vein, a 1912 article stressed that "real publicity" goes beyond appointment of a special agent to court journalists. "It should be inground [*sic*] in the entire staff from top to bottom. . . ."[11] And an early textbook entitled *Railroad Administration* included a chapter devoted to "Public Relations of a Railroad."[12] Despite their early adoption of public relations techniques, the railroads were notably unsuccessful in lobbying their cause before government bodies.

Over 2,000 laws affecting railroads were passed by Congress and the various state legislatures in the period between 1908 and 1913.

By 1908, universities, churches, charitable causes, health groups, and even the military were using the services of public relations specialists. The New York Orphan Asylum was paying a publicity man $75 per month. Most importantly, however, business leaders were convinced of the legitimacy and importance of public relations. In the 1911 AT & T annual report, corporation president Theodore Vail advocated a policy of absolute truthfulness, not even withholding unfavorable information from the public:

**In all times, in all lands, public opinion has had control at the last word— public opinion is but the concert of individual opinion, and is as much subject to change or to education.**

Another business leader who spoke out on public relations was U.S. Steel Board Chairman Elbert H. Gary. In 1909 he maintained, "I believe thoroughly in publicity. . . . The surest and wisest of all regulations is public opinion."[13]

**Stage 3: Mutual
Influence and
Understanding**

To dedicated and thoughtful public relations professionals it became increasing obvious in the decade following 1910 that corporations communicate with the public not only by words released through the press, but by their policies and actions as well. Consequently, they sought to advise business executives in such matters, attempting to gain a place in the heart of business organization—decision-making and operational aspects of enterprise. Ivy Lee was again in the vanguard, by recognizing that good words had to be supported by good deeds. Lee sought to elevate his own status to that of "brain trust" for his clients.

N. W. Ayer & Son published a booklet in 1912 recommending that businessmen discuss with their advertising agents ". . . if conditions in the business are in harmony with an advertising program." Like Lee, Ayer wanted businessmen to understand that the successful publicity campaign involved their companies' basic policies as much as the procedures for telling the public about their companies' goods or services.[14] These basic policies included not only external concerns, but internal ones as well. Following this theme, it was perhaps not so surprising that George Michaelis, who had founded The Publicity Bureau in Boston, would be advising Westinghouse in 1914 to pay more attention to internal "human relations."[15]

A protracted and violent strike against Colorado Fuel and Iron Company gave Ivy Lee the opportunity to become a consultant on the internal workings of a business. John D. Rockefeller, Jr., the company's principal stockholder, employed Lee in 1914 after savage criticism for his handling of the strike. Lee publicized management's position in the strike (without revealing himself as the source of the information). He also persuaded Rockefeller to visit the stricken area. Beyond these traditional actions, however, Lee strongly recommended to management that they improve communication from workers to management and establish mechanisms to redress workers' grievances.[16] Thus, Lee became an advisor to Rockefeller not only in relation to dealings with the press and the public, but in relation to the actual operation of the business.

In addition to its outward focus, then, public relations was gaining an inward focus. This had several results. Employees came to be recognized as a significant public and an appropriate, important audience for public relations efforts. By 1925, more than half of all major manufacturing companies were publishing employee magazines.[17] Textbooks of the day stressed the integration of public relations with general business activities. Samuel Kennedy maintained that from the viewpoint of companies, which person had immediate responsibility for directing publicity and giving out news was of little importance. What mattered was that the policies of the organization be guided by executives aware of political considerations.[18]

By the 1920s, the vanguard of public relations practitioners considered themselves responsible not only for informing the press and the public, but also for educating management about public opinion and advising managerial decisions and actions in terms of public response. Only rarely, however, were public relations men actually allowed to play such roles.

This third stage in the development of public relations became established at American Telephone & Telegraph during the career of Arthur W. Page. A successful businessman, public servant, writer and editor, Page was approached with an offer to become vice-president of AT&T, succeeding the pioneer public relations specialist James D. Ellsworth. Page agreed to accept the position only on the condition that he would not be restricted in his responsibilities to publicity in the traditional sense. He demanded and received a voice in company policy and insisted that the company's performance be the determinant of its public reputation.[19] Page practiced the stage-two, informative approach to public relations. He maintained:

**All business in a democratic country begins with public permission and exists by public approval. If that be true, it follows that business should be cheerfully willing to tell the public what its policies are, what it is doing, and what it hopes to do. This seems practically a duty.[20]**

Under Page's leadership, however, the company recognized that winning public confidence required not merely ad hoc attempts to answer criticism, but rather a continuous and planned program of positive public relations using institutional advertising, the usual stream of information flowing through press releases, and other methods. Bypassing the conventional print media, the company went directly to the public, establishing, for instance, a film program to be shown to schools and civic groups.

AT&T sought to maintain direct contact with as many of its clients as it possibly could. The company made a total commitment to customer service. Moreover, deposits were broadly distributed among banks; legal business was given to attorneys throughout the country; contracts for supplies and insurance were made with many local agencies. AT&T paid fees for employees to join outside organizations, knowing that through their presence the company would be constantly represented in many forums. Finally, the company sought to have as many people as possible own its stock. Today, AT&T is the most widely held of all securities.

What truly set Page apart and established him as a pioneer, however, was his insistence that the publicity department should act as an interpreter of the public to the company, drawing on a systematic and accurate diagnosis of public opinion. Page wanted data, not hunches. Under his direction, the AT&T publicity department (as it was still called) kept close check on company policies, assessing their impact on the public. Thus, Page caused the company "to act all the time from the public point of view, even when that seems in conflict with the operating point of view."[21]

---

**Public Relations Pioneers**   *Samuel Adams*. Most active prior to and during the Revolutionary War, Adams organized the Sons of Liberty, used the liberty tree symbol, minted slogans like "Taxation Without Representation is Tyranny," staged the Boston Tea Party, named the Boston Massacre, and mounted a sustained propaganda compaign.

*Amos Kendall.* During the 1820s and 1830s, Kendall served candidate and President Andrew Jackson as public relations counselor, pollster, and speechwriter. He spearheaded the successful campaign against the Bank of the United States.

*Mathew St. Clair Clarke.* As publicist for the Bank of the United States in the 1830s, Clarke saturated the press with releases, reports, and pamphlets in the most extensive, albeit unsuccessful, public relations campaign to that date. In an effort to develop a politician to oppose Andrew Jackson, he created the myths surrounding the historical figure Davy Crockett.

*P. T. Barnum.* A consummate showman during the middle and late 1800s, Barnum originated many methods for attracting public attention.

*E. H. Heinrichs.* As press secretary to George Westinghouse from the late 1880s through 1914, Heinrichs prevailed over Thomas Edison's forces and established for Westinghouse the use of alternating electric current.

*George Michaelis.* Organizer of the nation's first publicity firm, The Publicity Bureau of Boston, in 1900, Michaelis used fact-finding, publicity, and personal contact to saturate the nation's press.

*Ivy Lee.* Often called the father of modern public relations, Lee believed that the public should be informed. He recognized that good words had to be supported by positive actions on the part of individuals and organizations. His career spanned thirty-one years from its beginning in 1906.

*James D. Ellsworth.* Working with Theodore N. Vail in the early 1900s, Ellsworth established the public relations program of the American Telephone and Telegraph Company. His activities led to public support for the regulated private monopoly concept that has resulted in the world's best communications system.

*George Creel.* As head of the Committee on Public Information during World War I, Creel used public relations techniques to sell Liberty Bonds, build the Red Cross, promote food conservation, and other war-related activities. In so doing, he proved the power of public relations and trained a host of the twentieth century's most influential practitioners.

*Edward Bernays.* An intellectual leader in the field, Bernays coined the phrase "public relations counsel," wrote *Crystallizing Public Opinion,* the first book on public relations, and taught the first college-level public relations course at New York University in 1923.

*Arthur Page*. When offered a vice-presidency at AT&T, Page insisted that he have a voice in shaping corporate policy. He maintained that business in a democratic country depends on public permission and approval.

---

**PUBLIC RELATIONS: THE 1930s TO THE PRESENT**

From the 1930s on, the theory and practice of public relations has centered around variations on the three themes or stages we have discussed. More and more, public relations has become continuous rather than episodic, positive rather than defensive, and accepted as a legitimate function within virtually all institutions and organizations.

Other trends are less clear. The argument over professionalism of public relations practitioners continues. While the practice of public relations often calls for sophisticated technical skills and capabilities, public relations within organizations is frequently practiced, if not directed, by managers with training in other fields. Public relations practitioners as a group are probably more professionally ethical today than in the early years, when the residue of press agentry still tainted the practice. But instances of laundering press releases through subsidized agencies, manipulation of statistics, selective reporting, staging events, and even the attempted use of advertising clout to influence editorial content are still uncomfortably common. Perhaps for this reason, the term public relations still has an unsavory connotation in some circles.

As the 1970s began, public relations seemed to be enjoying a renaissance of sorts. Corporations again felt themselves beset by adverse circumstances. Some have compared the 1970s with the muckraking era, and maintain that public relations has now become more concerned with helping corporations to avoid destructive attacks than with attempting to get the company positive attention. "The public relations man now is far less of an ingenious producer of marvelous editorial gifts for his clients," says David Finn, "and far more of an experienced counselor in relating to potential or actual media attacks." [22]

Indeed, with the importance of business's traditional technological and economic criteria increasingly challenged on social and political grounds, corporations are expanding public relations staffs, budgets, and programs, and elevating the function to a higher status in the organizational hierarchy. [23] Chief executives are assuming more and more public relations responsibility as their own. At companies like McGraw-Edison (where public relations convinced top management to abandon the use of the chemical PCB in electrical capacitors), public relations has reached the third stage of development. But in return, the results-oriented approach of top management demands of public relations demonstrable achievements similar to those expected of all other corporate functions.

William A. Durbin, former chairman of Hill and Knowlton Public Relations, recently stated:

**The PR function is about to cross the threshold from a primarily communications function to a management function participating systematically in the formation of policy and the decision-making process itself.** [24]

Durbin sees the profession at the same threshold seen by Michaelis, Lee, and Bernays—the threshold that was crossed over half a century ago by Arthur W. Page. How things change and remain the same.

The precise role public relations will play in the post-industrial America of the twenty-first century is impossible to predict. With ever more information and voices competing for attention, acceptance, approval, and support, however, it is a safe bet that public relations in all its stages will prosper for some years to come.

**NOTES**

[1] Philip Davidson, *Propaganda and the American Revolution, 1763–1783* (Chapel Hill, N.C.: University of North Carolina Press, 1941), p. 3.

[2] Quoted in James L. Crouthamel, "Did the Second Bank of the United States Bribe the Press?" *Journalism Quarterly* 36 (Winter, 1959): 372.

[3] Marc Bloch, *The Historian's Craft* (New York: Knopf, 1953), p. 168.

[4] Marie Curti, *The Growth of American Thought,* 3rd ed. (New York: Harper & Row, 1964), p. 634.

[5] Marshall Fishwick, *American Heroes: Myths and Realities* (Washington, D.C., 1954) pp. 70–71.

[6] Edward L. Bernays, *Propaganda* (New York: Horace Liveright, 1928), p. 41.

[7] Eric F. Goldman, *Two-Way Street* (Boston: Bellman Publishing Co., 1948), p. 21.

[8] Quoted in Sherman Morse, "An Awakening on Wall Street," *American Magazine* 62 (Sept. 1906): 460.

[9] Theodore Dreiser, "The Railroads and the People," *Harper's Monthly* 100 (Feb. 1900): 479–480.

[10] Ray Morris, "Wanted, A Diplomatic Corps," *Railroad Age Gazette* (27 Jan. 1909): 196.

[11] James H. McGraw, "Publicity." *Electric Railway Journal* 39 (27 Jan. 1912): 154.

[12] Ray Morris, *Railroad Administration* (New York: Appleton & Company, 1910).

[13] N. S. B. Gras, "Shifts in Public Relations," *Bulletin of the Business Historical Society* 19, no. 4 (October 1945): 120.

[14] Alan R. Raucher, *Public Relations and Business, 1900–1929* (Baltimore: The Johns Hopkins Press, 1968), pp. 4–5.

[15] George V. S. Michaelis, "The Westinghouse Strike," *Survey* 32 (1 August 1914): 463–465.

[16] Ray E. Hiebert, *Courtier to the Crowd: The Story of Ivy Lee and the Development of Public Relations* (Ames: Iowa State University Press, 1966).

[17] National Industrial Conference Board, *Employee Magazines in the United States* (New York: National Industrial Conference Board, Inc., 1925).

[18] Samuel M. Kennedy, *Winning the Public* (New York: McGraw-Hill, 1920).

[19] Scott M. Cutlip and Allen H. Center, *Effective Public Relations,* 5th ed. (Englewood Cliffs, N.J.: Prentice-Hall, Inc., 1978), p. 87.

[20] George Griswold, Jr., "How AT&T Public Relations Policies Developed," *Public Relations Quarterly* 12 (Fall 1967): 13.

[21] Raucher, *Public Relations and Business*, pp. 80–81.

[22] David Finn, "The Media as Monitor of Corporate Behavior," in *Business and the Media,* Craig E. Aronoff, ed. (Santa Monica: Goodyear Publishing Company, 1979), pp. 117–121.

[23] "The Corporate Image: PR to the Rescue," *Business Week,* 22 January 1979, p. 47.

[24] Ibid., p. 60.

# CHAPTER 3  UNDERSTANDING COMMUNICATION

**PREVIEW**  Communication problems are as often a symptom as they are a disease. Because public relations practitioners are called upon to deal with what are perceived to be communication problems, they must have a thorough understanding of all aspects of communications processes.

Most of us have developed "common sense theories" of communication. While of some value, these theories lack scientific objectivity.

Public relations professionals deal with communication on many levels, most importantly in terms of individual communicators, interpersonal communication, communication within and between organizations, and public communication.

Public relations personnel play at least four specific communication roles for the organizations for which they work. These roles are: gatekeeper, liaison, opinion leader, and external boundary spanner.

"What we have here is a problem of communications." This may be the single most widely used sentence in organizations today. Inefficiency, waste, conflict, laziness, and many other problems are seen as the result of communication failures, blockages, and breakdowns.

Lack of communication is an easy thing to point to when things go wrong. And since communication is involved in all human interaction, it is always around to take the blame. But in fact, communication often gets a bum rap. Poor communication is as often a result of a problem as it is the problem's cause; it is as often a symptom as it is the actual disease.

Public relations practitioners are often called upon to deal with communication problems. Sometimes they are blamed for the problem or for not fixing the problem. When the citizens of a community are enraged about smells from a factory; when customers are incensed because prices have doubled; when voters turn incumbents out of office because they have failed to serve; when employees strike; when investors sell; when the media expose questionable practices—all of these things may be labeled problems of communication, and public relations professionals may be called to help find the solution. It is essential, then, that public relations people have a thorough understanding of the communication process as it relates to individuals, groups, organizations, and the public. Both communication practice and theory must be understood. Most of the rest of this book deals with the practice of communications. This chapter deals with some communication theories and models in the effort to broaden and deepen your understanding of communication.

## SOME "COMMON SENSE" THEORIES OF COMMUNICATION

Because we are all experienced communicators (and often miscommunicators as well), most of us have developed communication theories of our own. Experienced public relations people often give theoretical advice to youngsters just entering the field, some of them similar to the theories listed below. These ideas are quite common outside the profession as well, and when challenged, they are defended on the grounds of "common sense."

### The "Decibel" Theory

According to the Decibel Theory, the best way to get your message across is to state it frequently and loudly. Public relations practitioners subscribing to this theory exaggerate the importance of events, flood the media with news releases, and generally seek to attract attention by making lots of noise. While repetition of messages can be very important to assure message penetration, advocates of the Decibel Theory need reminding that shouting only makes poor communication louder.

**The "Sell" Theory**

The Sell Theory assumes that one person "sells" information and the other person "buys." Communication is seen as a one-way street. The object of communication is thought to be manipulation of an audience so that it will accept the message. Public relations people with this theory are always trying to "sell" story ideas or "sell" ideas to the public. While an occasional sale might be made, fundamental relationships are often injured by the approach. Communication based on the Sell Theory increases distrust and raises barriers between groups. Consequently, the chances of achieving mutual understanding are reduced.

**The "Minimal Information" Theory**

The Minimal Information Theory stresses secrecy, keeping a low profile, and playing it close to the vest. Public relations practitioners rarely subscribe to this communication theory, but the organizations they work for sometimes do. When what are supposed to be public meetings go behind closed doors, when questions consistently are answered with "no comment," when cover-ups are normal operating procedure, the Minimal Information Theory is at work. Operating on the notion that "what they don't know can't hurt us," proponents of minimal information fail to recognize the harm done by a lack of trust, commitment, and openness.

**The "If-I-Were-Them" Theory**

The "If-I-Were-Them" Theory assumes communication will be successful if senders of information can place themselves in the position of the receivers of information and communicate appropriately. Actually, this is one of the better informal communication theories, growing as it does from the Golden Rule: "Do unto others as you would have them do unto you." George Bernard Shaw, however, found it necessary to rewrite the Golden Rule: "Don't do unto others as you would have them do unto you because their tastes may be different." Shaw's revision lends insight into the major problem with the "If-I-Were-Them" Theory. While it is often helpful to place oneself in the situations faced by receivers of one's messages, this theory overlooks the fact that different people respond in different ways to the same information. There are many other "commonsense" communication theories. Most are similarly flawed. To better understand communication, let us look at some theories and models developed by those who deal with communication from the perspective of scientific research.

**COMMUNICATION THEORIES AND MODELS**

Researchers have studied communication at many levels. Five of them are immediately relevant to public relations practitioners: individual communicators; interpersonal communication; organizational communication; inter-organizational communication; and public communication.

**Individual Communicators**

Communication flows through individuals. You cannot communicate with a newspaper, you must deal with reporters or editors. You cannot talk with a government, you must deal with a mayor or a commissioner, an alderman or representative. You cannot correspond with a business; some individual is answering the mail (or has programmed a computer to respond). To understand communication processes, you must understand how individuals communicate.

Individuals simultaneously send and receive messages which are filtered through perceptual screens comprised of their needs, values, attitudes, expectations, and experiences. Figure 3-1 shows that stimuli (or messages) are received and interpreted in terms of individuals' personal expectations. Similarly, individuals create messages in terms of their needs, perceptions, and values.

No matter what role an individual is playing at a given time, the process remains the same. Employees, stockholders, editors, voters, customers, taxpayers, neighbors, contributors, regulators, and all others comprehend and send messages according to the psychological factors mentioned above. The ability to understand these factors in one's self or in others enhances the ability to predict behavior. However, because meaning is derived from messages only through perceptual screens, communicators cannot control the way in which their messages will be understood.

For the public relations practitioner, perhaps the most crucial aspect of individual communication is the process of perception. Its importance is well illustrated by a discussion that took place among three baseball umpires. "Some's balls and some's strikes and I calls 'em as they is," claimed the first umpire. The second umpire made a subtle but important distinction: "Some's balls and some's strikes," he said, "and I calls 'em as I sees 'em." The third umpire disagreed with both his colleagues: "Some's balls and some's strikes," he maintained, "but they ain't nothing till I calls 'em."

**Figure 3-1**
The Individual
Communicator

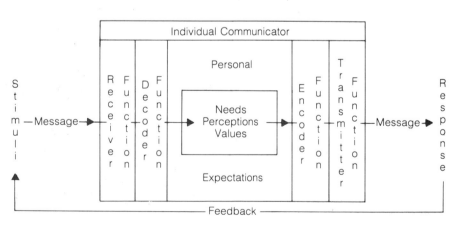

Reprinted from Otis W. Baskin and Craig E. Aronoff, *Interpersonal Communication in Organizations* (Santa Monica, CA: Goodyear Publishing Company, Inc., 1980), p. 7. Copyright © by Goodyear Publishing Co., 1980. Reprinted by permission.

Like umpire number three, it is the receiver of the message who decides its meaning. The editor who receives the news release decides whether it is actually news or not. The stockholder who receives an annual report decides whether or not the information contained therein bodes good or ill. The announcement of cutbacks in government programs will be seen as positive or negative depending on the needs, experiences, and attitudes of those hearing the announcement.

Since communicators cannot assume that messages will be understood as intended, effective communication requires a knowledge of one's audience, a means of receiving feedback from the audience, consistency of messages provided by words and deeds, and mutual responsiveness and understanding in a climate of trust between communicators and those with whom they share messages.

**Interpersonal Communication**

As individual communicators exchange messages, they also share their needs, perceptions, and values. This sharing leads to the development of mutual ideas and expectations. Figure 3-2 shows such a communication situation between two individuals. The source of messages and their destination are able to communicate about a given thing to the extent that their experiences with that thing overlap—to the extent to which they have developed mutual understanding.

As individuals exchange more messages, they build upon their mutual understanding and expand their range of constructive interaction. When similar stimuli evoke markedly different images, however, the opportunity to develop constructive action is restricted severely. If an organization thinks of itself as a friendly giant while its public considers it a fierce dragon, communication problems inevitably result.

**Organizational Communication**

Most public relations texts, taking their cue from the importance of the mass media to public relations practice, use public communication as a model to understand the communication process. While not denying the necessity of addressing mass communication, we feel that new understandings of the organizational communication and the public relations function in organizations point to the even greater importance of communication processes *within* and *between* organizations.

**Figure 3-2**
An Interpersonal Model
of Communication

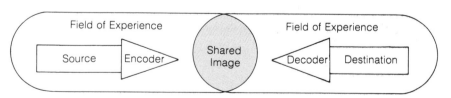

Adapted from Wilbur Schramm, "How Communication Works," in *The Process and Effects of Mass Communication*, ed. Wilbur Schramm (Urbana, Ill.: University of Illinois Press, 1954) pp. 3–10.

Gerald Goldhaber, a leading organizational communication scholar, identifies three propositions common to most organizational communication studies:

1. Organizational communication occurs within a complex open system which is influenced by and influences its environment.
2. Organizational communication involves messages, their flow, purpose, direction and media.
3. Organizational communication involves people, their attitudes, feelings, relationships and skills.[1]

Communication within the organization is influenced by information and messages that originate in the organization's environment. Within the organization, communication flows in the form of messages within networks of interdependent relationships. People are the linking pins of the organizational communication process and thus their attitudes, feelings, needs, perceptions, and values have an effect on message flows. This process is represented in Figure 3-3.

**Interorganizational Communication**   While the importance of organizations' environments is made clear in our discussion of communication within organizations, we must now recognize that environments also encompass other organizations. These organizations, of course, communicate with each other. Corporations, for example, communicate with government, media, labor, consumer, community, and educational organizations, as well as other businesses.

Like communication within organizations, communication among organizations is structured. Various employees within organizations are assigned responsibility for receiving information from and sending it to other organizations. Individuals occupying such positions have been termed "boundary spanners,"[2] "cosmopolites,"[3] or "liaisons." These individuals act as the doors and windows of organizations. (*Figure 3-4*). Through them, organizational communication systems link their organizations with their environments.

**Figure 3-3**
A Model of
Organizational
Communication

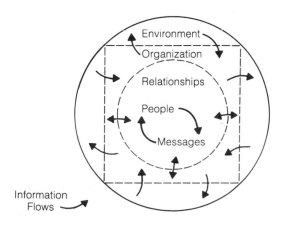

**Figure 3-4**
Boundary Spanners:
Doors and Windows of
Organizations

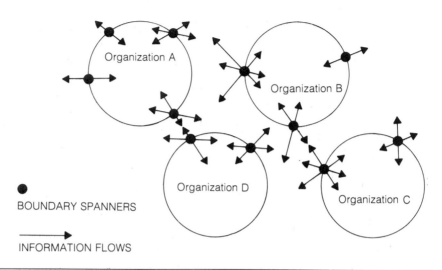

Those who function as external boundary spanners pay a substantial price for their efforts. Social psychologist David Kahn and his associates found in studies of individuals occupying boundary positions that:

. . . as a person's job-required contacts outside his company increase, there is a corresponding increase in the extent to which he feels caught between the demands of the outsiders and the requirements of his own management.[4]

Public relations practitioners working with media are a perfect example of boundary spanners caught between the demands of editors and reporters, on one hand, and their own management on the other. While management may wish to say things in a particular way or want to release only selected bits of information, public relations practitioners, knowing the demands of media personnel, will be forced to argue the position of reporters or editors against their own bosses. Bosses well may inquire: "Which side are you on?" When practitioners present the information to reporters or editors, the response may well be "This stuff is self-serving—whose side are you on?" Public relations practitioners in this situation must seek harmony between the needs and values of their constituents. Their paychecks may depend on it.

**Public Communication**

Before we examine the process of public or mass communication, we must note that it is closely related to interpersonal and organizational communication. As Paul Lazarsfeld points out: "The closer one observes the working of the mass media, the more it turns out that their effects depend on a complex network of specialized personal and social influences."[5] Research on public communication has been carried on for about fifty years. In the early period it was assumed that mass media acted like hypodermic needles, injecting information into members of the public who would respond in particular ways to messages. We now know that mass communication is a far more complicated process than was realized at that time. Since 1930, many models of mass communication have been developed, only to be proven inaccurate or overly simplistic. It is clear, however, that public communication is a *multi-step, multi-directional* process. We know that messages move through complex networks of active transmitters who select, distort, amplify, or otherwise affect messages in passing them on. We also know that meanings ascribed to messages by members of the public, and indeed whether these messages will be perceived at all, depend upon those who receive those messages.

**INTEGRATING THE MODELS**

As should be clear by now, the communication process can be viewed from several perspectives. To fully appreciate the process, it must be considered from individual, interpersonal, organizational, interorganizational, and public viewpoints. Like Jerry Koehler and his colleagues, we come to see communication as:

**The internal and external processes by which all of the organization's informing, adjusting, and coordinating activities take place to a dense network of signals and responses, actions and reactions, effects and countereffects . . . (embracing) the ongoing exchange of information, opinion and attitude by which adjustments are made as required in order to coordinate activities within the organization and interface effectively with the exterior environment.**[6]

Through individual and organizational interaction, communication builds upon itself in a continuous stream. Senders and receivers are transmission stations; messages and meanings are the currency of the ongoing system of coadaptation by which society and its organizations are sustained.

**COMMUNICATING IMAGES**

An organization's image is a composite of people's attitudes and beliefs about the organization. Images cannot be communicated directly. They are built over time, developed through the cumulative effect of many messages. Such messages, which take many forms, are frequently not transmitted intentionally. The image of an organization is formed in the minds of customers, citizens, employees, volunteers, investors, or regulators not simply through the official statements of the organization, but through all of its activities.

Of course, all formal organizations attempt to document their public images for people inside and outside of their boundaries. Budgets, media releases, advertising, even corporate architecture and interior decor are planned and executed with the organizational image in mind. But as public relations veteran Robert Ross points out:

The quality of performance communicates eloquently . . . interest or lack of interest in the quality of work and in the customer . . . good management or poor management and a host of other things (communicate) more eloquently than words can.[7]

In many cases it is not what a person hears or reads but what she or he actually experiences that determines a particular image. The image of oil companies as price-gouging profitmongers in the second half of 1979 was not a function of ranting politicians or raving mass media. *Time* magazine and other media went to great lengths to explain why oil industry actions and profits were justified. Noted economists made substantially the same point on national television, as did oil industry executives on televised news clips of congressional hearings. But many people said, in effect: "Don't confuse me with the facts." Their minds were made up by their experiences at the gasoline station, where the cost of filling the tank went from $12.00 to $25.00. William Weston makes the point very well:

When institutions encounter hostile attitudes or find support melting away, it is not necessarily because their constituents and others don't understand what they are hearing. It is also possible that they don't like what they are experiencing.

The way people experience an institution has its origins in the institution's policies, which are in turn grounded in purpose.[8]

All actions, all products, all pronouncements of an organization generate messages that contribute to perceptions of the corporation. These, in turn, are products of organizational policy based on organizational purpose. With so many variables involved, how can organizations hope to manage the process of communication?

## MANAGING COMMUNICATION

Managing information and communication is a responsibility of executives or supervisors at every level of an organization. As David K. Berlo suggests, "Management of information systems has become one of the central competencies needed in modern society."[9]

Organizational communication researchers R. V. Farace, P. R. Monge, and H. M. Russell propose a specialized position of communication manager within organizations. They describe the position as follows:

In general, the communication manager should be located at the center of the message flow in the organization. This means that the manager has knowledge of all important types of message flow. . . . By operating in or near the center of the organization's message flow, the manager is able to serve as a bridge or liaison to the other units in the organization. . . .[10]

As a management generalist or a communication specialist, a communication manager assumes at least four specific roles: gatekeeper, liaison, opinion leader, and external boundary spanner.[11]

Gatekeepers are people who are positioned within a communication network so as to control the messages flowing through communication channels. They can filter, screen, block or modify messages and determine the overall volume of message flow. Public relations practitioners function as gatekeepers when they determine what and how much information will be transmitted to various external or internal publics, including management itself.

Liaisons are linking pins that connect two or more groups within the organizational network. In this role, communication managers integrate the various parts of the overall system. They help different groups to develop shared expectations. Practitioners consistently play this role within the organization, bringing together organizational functions like advertising or consumer affairs with marketing and production.

Opinion leaders are those who often, formally or informally, influence other peoples' attitudes or actions. Public relations professionals not only seek to influence opinion leaders, but can play this role themselves within the organization. In fulfilling this role, communication managers facilitate decision making within the organization. They may exert some control in selecting actions consistent with the goals of the organization. Public relations practitioners frequently take this role on issues related to social responsibility or organizational responses to public opinion.

The external boundary spanner, as we discussed previously in this chapter, relates the organizational system to its environment. Thus, the communication manager assesses the behavior of the organization in relation to its environment, assesses the environment to provide direction for the organization and generally provides the means by which an organization can adapt to meet public expectations.

**PUBLIC RELATIONS AND ORGANIZATIONAL COMMUNICATION**

As we seek to understand the responsibility of public relations for organizational communication, we must regard it in terms of all of the roles discussed above. As gatekeepers, public relations managers must evaluate and anticipate the effect of every proposed policy, plan and implement action in relation to each organizational public. They can do this because of their experience as external boundary spanners. As liaisons, public relations people help various groups to produce coordinated, purposeful action. As opinion leaders, they influence the creation of organizational policy and strategy.

A Conference Board survey of major corporations showed that these functions are served in practice as well as theory. Phyllis McGrath, who produced the survey report, suggested the following categories:

1. *Advice and counsel.* Internal consulting to operating and functional units and the chief executive.
2. *Service.* Conceiving, conducting and carrying out programs relating to various corporate publics.
3. *Control.* Involvement in formulation of policy and guidelines that determine the corporation's relations with its various publics, as well as monitoring the implementation of such policy and guidelines.[12]

The reality of these functions is also demonstrated by corporate descriptions of the role of public relations manager. Figure 3-5 shows how Panhandle

**Figure 3-5**
Interdepartmental
Coordination—
Panhandle Eastern
Pipeline Company

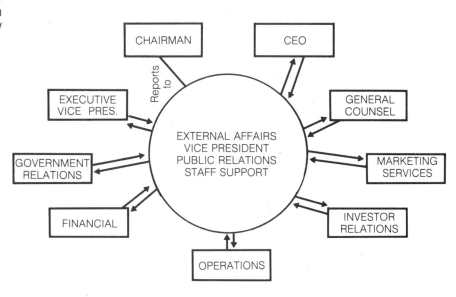

Phyllis S. McGrath, *Managing Corporate External Relations: Changing Perspectives and Responses.*New York: The Conference Board, 1976, p. 28. Reprinted by permission.

Eastern Pipeline Company conceives the role of its chief communications officer. Centrality, interaction, and influence on all organizational functions is the clear message of this diagram.

The following is a job description of General Telephone and Electric's (GTE) vice president-public affairs, its chief communications officer.[13] It too stresses evaluating environments, counseling management, developing and communicating policy, and assuring effectiveness.

**Job Description for
GTE Vice President,
Public Affairs**

1. Identifying and evaluating current situations and future trends having major public affairs implications for the overall organization.
2. Advising and counseling management on methods for acting upon these situations and trends.
3. Developing formal statements of policy on various public affairs matters, and assuring adequate communication of the approved policies throughout the organization.
4. Developing specific programs and procedures to implement these policies.

5. Auditing and reviewing the effectiveness of these
   activities to assure their maximum possible and
   practicable effectiveness.

---

The attitudes and ideas held toward an organization by all who interact with
it in any capacity are the result of all of the complex interactions between
an organization and its environment. This is the arena where public relations
is practiced, where its activities are defined, and where its contributions are
counted.

---

| | |
|---|---|
| **CASE STUDY: THE DIFFERENCE BETWEEN PUBLIC RELATIONS AND JOURNALISM** | **By Melvin L. Sharpe Ball State University, Muncie, Indiana** |

---

Public relations practitioners must understand the basic messages an organization is seeking to project and develop corresponding news-information
programs designed to maintain and contribute to an organization's image.
The importance of this to successful media relations is all too frequently
overlooked.

Communication management can maintain sound media relations through
well-planned programs. Such programs provide access by the media to information and information sources within the organization. They identify and
define goals and objectives clearly understood by top management as well
as the media relations staff. Finally, these programs establish a schedule for
media releases so that practitioners' time can be best used and media acceptance (and public awareness) can increase.

Achievement of the goals and objectives in a sound communications management program is not measured in terms of news space, but in terms of
increased public awareness and understanding of the organization.

The importance of the mutual understanding of communication goals and
objectives by an organization's top management and its media relations staff
became clear when a major southeastern state university found itself under
increasing criticism by black students for what they viewed as inadequate
efforts for recruitment of black students and faculty. University administrators
readily agreed that more needed to be done, but they were also aware that
much had been done, that the faculty and the administration shared a commitment to progress in that area, and that progress had been made in spite
of funding limitations. Therefore, the university's information officer was
instructed to develop a series of feature articles designed to inform the public

as to the steps the university had taken and was taking to improve recruitment efforts.

Although the information officer was a competent journalist, he failed to understand or explain to the staff member to whom the task was assigned that the objective of the articles was to show the "progress" the university had made in its minority recruitment. Instead, the articles approached the subject from the students' point of view as well as that of the university. The coverage was defended as an attempt to present both sides of the issue. Although balancing news is a major responsibility of the press, the university's objectives should have been to educate the public about the progress achieved. The media would have been responsible for including the opposing view. The articles were never used, the information officer was replaced because of his inability to attune his media relations program to the organization's goal and image objectives, and black student unrest increased. Accurate information might have helped to create a climate for positive progress and dialogue without disruption.

**Questions**   1. What are the differences in responsibility of reporting members of the press and members of the media relations staff of an organization?

2. In a period of economic recession, "stability" could be an important message to project to employees, stockholders, the business community and the public. Make a list of the type of news and feature stories that a media relations program might include in order to project an image of stability provided, of course, that the facts exist to support the image projection.

3. Using simple one- or two-word descriptions such as "stability," "progress," and "achievement," develop a list of other messages an organization may need and want to project. Agreement on the part of management and an understanding on the part of the media relations staff as to the emphasis and importance to be given each message projection during a given year will result in the focus needed for the development or maintenance of a sound media relations program.

**NOTES**   [1] Gerald H. Goldhaber, *Organizational Communication* (Dubuque, Iowa: Wm. C. Brown Co., 1971), p. 11.

[2] D. Katz and R. Kahn, *The Social Psychology of Organizations* (New York: John Wiley and Sons, 1966).

[3] E. M. Rogers & R. Agrwala-Rogers, *Communication in Organizations* (New York: The Free Press, 1976).

[4] R. Kahn et al, *Organizational Stress* (New York: John Wiley, 1964), p. 103.

[5] P. Lazarsfeld and H. Menzel, "Mass Media and Personal Influence," in *Science of Human Communication*, ed. Wilbur Schramm, (New York: Basic Books, 1963), p. 95.

[6] J. W. Koehler, K. W. E. Anatol, & R. L. Applbaum, *Organizational Communication* (New York: Holt, Rinehart and Winston, 1976), pp. 4–5.

[7] R. D. Ross, *The Management of Public Relations* (New York: John Wiley and Sons, 1977), p. 111.

[8] W. W. Weston, "Public Relations: Trustee of a Free Society," *Public Relations Review* (Fall 1975): 12.

[9] David K. Berlo, "The Context for Communication," in *Communication and Behavior*, ed. J. Hanneman and W. J. McEwen (Reading, MA: Addison-Wesley, 1975), p. 10.

[10] R. V. Farace, P. R. Monge and H. M. Russell, *Communicating and Organizing* (Reading, MA: Addison-Wesley, 1977), p. 252.

[11] Rogers and Agrwala-Rogers, *Communication in Organizations*, pp. 132–133.

[12] Phyllis S. McGrath, *Managing Corporate External Relations: Changing Perspectives and Responses* (New York: The Conference Board, 1976), p. 54–55.

[13] Ibid, pp. 56–57.

# CHAPTER 4 PUBLIC RELATIONS IN ORGANIZATIONAL DECISION MAKING

**PREVIEW** To play a serious role in organizational decision making, public relations practitioners must gain management support and understanding; be more than technicians, broaden their knowledge, interests, and perspectives; become issue-oriented; and learn to think like managers while retaining an independent perspective.

Throughout this book we stress that the contribution of public relations to organizational decision making is among its most important aspects. We do not claim that public relations practitioners actually make the decisions through which managers provide organizations with purpose, direction, co-ordination, and control. We do maintain, however, that all managers can and should take public relations considerations into account when making decisions, and that public relations practitioners can and should make direct contributions to fundamental organizational decisions.

In earlier chapters we discussed the public relations roles of gatekeeper, liaison and external boundary spanner. All of these serve the organization with information and insight essential to its decision making. We noted that the public relations specialist as opinion leader directly facilitates decision making within organizational systems and helps to provide organizational direction. We also described how public relations practitioners represent the public interest and predict public reaction to organizational decisions; by active participation in managerial decision making, they can gain the commitment and understanding necessary for effective communication.

In future chapters we will discuss how contributions of public relations to organizational decision making affect employee relations, local community opinion, financial activities, and dealings with the government. We will also look at how public relations affects organizational decisions about such issues as pollution, consumerism, urban problems, and international operations.

In a sense, then, this chapter is a pivotal one in the book. It deals with decision making, the essence of the managerial process, and the position of public relations in that process. The chapter explains the role and function of public relations in relation to organizational decision making. It discusses the nature of public relations inputs, and the constraints on those inputs. It tells how public relations can be most influential in organizational decision making. Finally, this chapter deals with the interrelationships between public relations and other organizational functions including legal, personnel, advertising, and marketing.

**STAFF AND LINE: WHERE PUBLIC RELATIONS FITS IN DECISION-MAKING STRUCTURES**

The most common type of organizational structure is called line organization. In its most basic form, it can be thought of as a sequence of ascending levels of responsibility, connected by direct vertical links. All functions and activities are directly involved in producing goods or services. Line organizations can be found in churches, charities, museums, and not-for-profit clinics, as well as business organizations.

As line organizations grow in size, however, various specialists are added, creating a "line and staff" organization. These staff functions provide advice and support to line management and are designed to contribute to the efficiency and maintenance of the organization. Staff functions might include research and development, personnel management and training, accounting, legal services, and public relations.

As a staff function, public relations must be supportive of management. The entire reason for the existence of public relations is to help create an environment of public opinion in which *management* can function most effectively. Moreover, as staff, public relations has an advisory function. It provides counsel which management may ignore or consider, follow or reject. Part of being an effective adviser, however, is taking actions to assure that your advice is heard, heeded, and frequently acted upon. In this way, public relations makes its contribution to organizational objectives and prosperity and earns management's support. Bob Thompson, public relations director of Spring Mills, Inc., points to the bottom line: "In the end, public relations in an organization is what top management says it is."[1]

## THE ROLE OF PUBLIC RELATIONS IN ORGANIZATIONAL DECISION MAKING

The need for public relations to become more thoroughly integrated into the organizational decision-making process cannot be questioned in the environment faced by all organizations in the 1980s. Government agencies at all levels retrench as tax cuts limit revenues. Hospitals struggle with regulations, rising costs, new technologies, and changing customer demands. Arts organizations seek new sources of funds. Businesses deal with global competition, gyrating interest rates, and a skeptical public. Successful managers in today's environment are those who maintain "a high batting average in accurately assessing the forces that determine [the] most appropriate behavior at any given time . . . and in actually being able to behave accordingly.[2] The contributions of a public relations specialist often enable managers to assess such forces accurately.

Even the initiation of organizational decision making can depend on public relations input. "The organizational decision-making process is activated when information is received indicating changes in an organization's internal or external environment calling for an organizational response."[3] Information gathered by the public relations staff can promote the organization's ability to adapt to changing political, social, economic, and cultural conditions. "Public relations should occupy one of the most strategic positions in the corporate [organizational] structure," James N. Sites explains, "if for no other reason than that it sits squarely astride the communication channels that are absolutely vital to the effective operation of an organization."[4]

Chief executive officers of major corporations are well aware of public relations' contribution to decision making. Consider their statements:

*Walter Wriston, Citibank chairman.* "The principal mission of the public affairs departments . . . is to make sure that when senior officers make important business decisions they do so with a clear understanding of how their action or inaction is likely to be perceived by the public. . . . Our director of public affairs . . . attends all meetings of our senior management policy committee."

***Thomas Murphy, General Motors former chairman.*** "The public relations staff is charged with two-way responsibility at GM: determining and explaining public demands on the corporation to management; and the more usual job of communicating corporate policy and positions to the public."

***William E. Wall, Kansas Power and Light president.*** "The best public relations person is impotent and wasted unless used and supported by the company. The way to do this is to bring public relations to the heights of management, where public relations advice can be regularly and easily inserted into the development and evolution of the company's policies and practices. The public relations executive can't explain, interpret or defend company policy unless he has seen it at its conception and birth, and participated in both."

Perhaps the most important task of public relations is to ensure the public-relations-mindedness of management officials. To blend public relations goals with organizational goals, public relations information must be part and parcel of the organizational decision-making process, and must include intelligence regarding likely reactions and response to decisions by relevant publics. Moreover, the commitment and understanding that come through participating in organizational decision making are invaluable assets when communicating decisions to the organization's publics.

## ENTERING THE MANAGEMENT MAINSTREAM

Acknowledging the importance of public relations in organizational decision making is one thing. Ensuring that public relations is part of the management mainstream[5] is quite another. If public relations is to be an effective part of the decision-making process in any organization, and if the practitioner is to be taken seriously in a decision-making role, five interrelated steps must be taken:

1. Gain management support and understanding.
2. Be more than a technician.
3. Broaden your knowledge, interests and perspectives.
4. Become issue-oriented.
5. Learn to think like a manager while retaining an independent perspective.

### Gain Management Support

"Early in his career every public relations practitioner finds to his surprise—and often distress—that he must . . . communicate . . . with those key centers of influence and power within his own organization."[6] Management is one of public relations' key publics. Like that of any other public, the support of management must be earned. Like those of any other audience, their needs, wants, attitudes, values, and perceptions must be considered.

The public relations function cannot be taken as a given by those who practice it, for assuredly management generally does not view the communications function in that light. Public relations was traditionally first on the budgetary chopping block, precisely because management does not perceive that it is essential to long-term organizational health. Only in the recession of 1981–82 did this tendency begin to fade.

Like all other staff specialists within organizations, public relations practitioners must be prepared to explain and justify their existence to managers, and to lead them to realize that public relations "is an investment in the privilege to operate . . . perhaps more an investment in the future than an operating expenditure for the present."[7] Most importantly, public relations can influence organizational action by demonstrating the ability to produce results in accordance with the organization's goals.

**Be More Than A Technician**

Many communicators conceive of themselves as communicators, first, last and always. They think of their relationship to management of "tell me what you want to say and I'll tell you how to say it." Communication skills are essential to effective public relations. But if your attitude is like that described above, you simply encourage management to think of public relations as a tool with which to implement policy rather than a crucial part of the policy-making process.

Even if your title is "staff writer," "editor," "speechwriter," or "audiovisual specialist," you must learn to think of yourself as more than a technician and your job as more than a communication medium. A writer writes, but a public relations practitioner helps to solve problems. An editor reacts to management requests, but a public relations practitioner helps to diagnose problems and opportunities while planning solutions and strategies. Writers and editors are typically concerned with the content and techniques of communication; public relations practitioners are concerned with results.

These differing perspectives will lead individuals working in public relations jobs to ask different questions in the performance of their jobs, to seek different insights, and ultimately, to offer different kinds of programs and solutions. One reacts, the other anticipates. One responds to decisions after they are made; the other is an essential part of decision making.

Communication consultant Ron Weiser tells of an incident that illustrates the distinction we are making. Early in his career, when he was an editor at a factory in Pennsylvania, Weiser was told to communicate a change in safety policy to plant employees. Everyone in the plant would have to wear safety glasses at all times and in all locations. Instead of simply writing a memo to announce the change, Weiser started asking questions. Why everyone? Why everywhere? How was the policy decided? What prompted the change? What was management's objective? It became clear that management had not really thought the policy through—that the main consideration was ease in administering the rule.

In response to the questions, management decided to rethink the policy and invited Weiser to help out. The newly-formulated policy required safety glasses in areas of the plant where specific hazards justified the requirement. Instead of a memo, a six-week multi-media program introduced the change. The policy was implemented smoothly, and Weiser gained the respect of management, allowing him to take part in future decisions.

**Broaden Your Knowledge**

To be valuable to management in a decision-making role, the public relations practitioner must have the appropriate knowledge, background, interests, and perspectives. Public relations practitioners no matter what their training or background must learn everything they can about business and government in general, the specific industry (or areas) in which their corporation (or agency) operates, and the organization itself. To be successful, public relations practitioners should know the functions, viewpoints, and problems of all parts of the organization. More than any other executives except the chief executive officer, public relations people must know what is going on inside the organization and how all of its activities and functions interrelate. They must do their homework and know the why, who, what, where, when, and how of whatever comes up for managerial consideration. They must also be prepared to present and evaluate a variety of alternatives and contingencies related to organizational problems and opportunities.

Drawing on such knowledge, the public relations practitioner is in a position to contribute creative ideas and sound judgment to the process of clarifying and accomplishing organizational objectives.

**Become Issue-Oriented**

This broadened base of knowledge and perspective helps elevate public relations to a central role in the identification and management of key issues confronting the organization. Issues management is an important means of integrating public relations into organizational planning and operations. The management of issues involves early identification of controversies, ranking of issues in terms of importance to the organization, developing policy related to issues, developing programs to carry out policies, implementing programs, communicating with appropriate publics about organizational policies and programs, and evaluating the results of such efforts.[8] Such issues may range from ethical standards for organizational behavior to energy conservation, from solid waste disposal to immigration policy.

Spring Mills board chairman H. W. Close explains:

**Meeting issues head-on is perhaps the biggest challenge facing management today. . . . If misunderstandings about the motives for business damage our freedom to run our businesses in the best interests of everyone concerned, then we won't be in business long and everyone loses. That's why this area of issue identification and response is so important. And it's why top management is looking to public relations pros for assistance.[9]**

Public relations practitioners must develop the formal and informal research skills to survey their organizations' internal and external environments to determine what issues their organizations must confront and how those issues can be successfully dealt with. Section 6 of this book deals with some of the issues confronting many organizations, but each organization must determine for itself which issues are most crucial at any given time. The issues-management process, however, is one of the areas in which public relations can make its greatest contributions to managerial decision making.

**Think Like A Manager**   In order to influence management, public relations practitioners must learn to understand the managerial point of view, at the same time realizing that public relations' greatest asset in decision making is its access to viewpoints not traditionally included in managerial deliberations. In other words, the public relations practitioner must think in terms of results, accountability, and accomplishments necessary to achieve organizational objectives while retaining a broader perspective that considers social as well as economic variables.

Former *Fortune* editor Max Ways points to what he calls the "danger inherent in any kind of concentrated framework of decision." He explains:

**"The public" cannot decide . . . where to put a paper mill. For that decision special competence in pursuit of narrowly defined goals is necessary. Yet if this power is not somehow related to interests outside the framework of competent action, the results will reflect a larger incompetence.**[10]

To use Way's example, the public relations practitioner involved in deciding where to locate a paper mill must understand the economic and geographic considerations of such a decision. But he or she must also understand social considerations, such as displacement of existing houses and pollution of waterways, and effectively communicate these concerns to other decision makers. If these issues are not considered early in the process, the mill might be built on a site appropriate by economic criteria, but might be prevented from operating by community protests.

Similarly, when planning communication strategy, managers are often faced with the question of how truthful and open they wish to be about a given matter. In such circumstances, the public relations practitioner who does not think like a manager typically will counsel openness, honesty, and the people's right to know. In short order, such individuals are labeled "Johnny-one-notes" who really do not understand the big picture. Their advice and counsel are rejected as impractical or preachy.

The public relations practitioner who thinks like a manager seeks the same goals of openness and honesty, but takes a different approach. Instead of preaching, he or she helps management weigh the pragmatic risks of communicating or not communicating. By pointing out the costs and benefits resulting from choices concerning what should be said and how this practitioner is much more likely to provide constructive and acceptable advice, to retain credibility in a decision-making role, and to steer the organization toward the course of openness and honesty.

William W. Weston, public relations director of Sun Oil Company, has observed, "How well the public relations practitioner succeeds in retaining some distance and objectivity, resisting the almost irresistable pull toward total absorption into the view of the world held by the leadership of his institution, will critically affect his ability to be truly useful."[11]

All of this suggests that effective public relations practitioners who take part in organizational decision making must frequently tell their executives what they do not want to hear. They must ask the hard, probing questions and raise the points that may not have been considered. To do so takes a certain amount of assertiveness and guts. It is a role that, while essential, may certainly lead to alienation and ineffectiveness if it is not tempered by understanding of managerial thinking and commitment to organizational goals.

**ETHICAL AND LEGAL CONSIDERATIONS OF PUBLIC RELATIONS PRACTICE**

The contribution of public relations to decision making is constrained by ethical and legal as well as practical and tactical considerations. Professional standards of public relations, and legal matters pertaining to sensitive aspects of the communication process, affect the practitioner's role and counsel.

**Ethics**

Ethics is an area of particular concern for public relations for three reasons: practitioners are aware that public relations has a reputation for unethical behavior; practitioners have struggled to create a suitable code of ethics for themselves; and public relations is often considered a source of ethical standards within an organization.

Public relations practitioners are very sensitive, even defensive, about allegations of unethical behavior. The term public relations is sometimes used as a synonym for lying, distortion, selective disclosure, or cover-ups. A recent *Wall Street Journal* article points to the ethical shortcomings of public relations, quoting the former public relations vice president for United Brands. "The more I thought about it, and the more I looked at events around me, the more certain I became that PR was helping to screw up the world," he said. "I could see the hand of the PR man pulling the strings, making things happen, covering things up. . . . Everywhere I looked it seemed as if image and style had taken the place of substance."[12]

Amelia Lobsenz, then co-chair of the Public Relations Society of America's National Task Force on Public Relations, writing in *Public Relations Journal,* responded to the article. She claimed that the article was one-sided, concentrating on the unethical practices of a handful of public relations persons who bowed to managerial pressure. To refute the charges, she offered a list of ethical corporate actions taken by organizations with the assistance of public relations practitioners.

Charges and counter-charges do not offer much clarification in such matters. In fact, as with any other profession, public relations contains both ethical and unethical practitioners. Because public relations practitioners often claim to represent the public in organizational decision making while at the same time they are accused of misleading the public, they are in a particularly difficult position.

The Public Relations Society of America has established a Code of Professional Standards for the Practice of Public Relations (*Figure 4-1*). In general, this voluntary code calls for truth, accuracy, good taste, fairness, and responsibility to the public. The question of personal ethics, however, is less controversial than the general issue of business ethics. Although business practices have been bitterly attacked and staunchly defended since the late nineteenth century, as we saw in Chapter 2, the debate continues, varying only with the public issues and concerns of the day.

## Declaration of Principles

Members of the Public Relations Society of America base their professional principles on the fundamental value and dignity of the individual, holding that the free exercise of human rights, especially freedom of speech, freedom of assembly and freedom of the press, is essential to the practice of public relations.

In serving the interests of clients and employers, we dedicate ourselves to the goals of better communication, understanding and cooperation among the diverse individuals, groups and institutions of society, and to equal opportunity of employment in the public relations profession.

We pledge:

To conduct ourselves professionally, with truth, accuracy, fairness and responsibility to the public;

To improve our individual competence and advance the knowledge and proficiency of the profession through continuing research and education;

And to adhere to the articles of the Code of Professional Standards for the Practice of Public Relations as adopted by the governing Assembly of the Society.

### Code of Professional Standards for the Practice of Public Relations

These articles have been adopted by the Public Relations Society of America to promote and maintain high standards of public service and ethical conduct among its members.

1. A member shall deal fairly with clients or employers, past and present, with fellow practitioners and the general public.
2. A member shall conduct his or her professional life in accord with the public interest.
3. A member shall adhere to truth and accuracy and to generally accepted standards of good taste.
4. A member shall not represent conflicting or competing interests without the express consent of those involved, given after a full disclosure of the facts, nor place himself or herself in a position where the member's interest is or may be in conflict with a duty to a client, or others, without a full disclosure of such interests to all involved.
5. A member shall safeguard the confidences of both present and former clients or employers and shall not accept retainers or employment which may involve the disclosure or use of these confidences to the disadvantage or prejudice of such clients or employers.
6. A member shall not engage in any practice which tends to corrupt the integrity of channels of communication or the processes of government.
7. A member shall not intentionally communicate false or misleading information and is obligated to use care to avoid communication of false or misleading information.

8. A member shall be prepared to identify publicly the name of the client or employer on whose behalf any public communication is made.
9. A member shall not make use of any individual or organization purporting to serve or represent an announced cause, or purporting to be independent or unbiased, but actually serving an undisclosed special or private interest of a member, client or employer.
10. A member shall not intentionally injure the professional reputation or practice of another practitioner. However, if a member has evidence that another member has been guilty of unethical, illegal or unfair practices, including those in violation of this Code, the member shall present the information promptly to the proper authorities of the Society for action in accordance with the procedure set forth in Article XII of the Bylaws.
11. A member called as a witness in a proceeding for the enforcement of this Code shall be bound to appear, unless excused for sufficient reason by the Judicial Panel.
12. A member, in performing services for a client or employer, shall not accept fees, commissions or any other valuable consideration from anyone other than the client or employer in connection with those services without the express consent of the client or employer, given after a full disclosure of the facts.
13. A member shall not guarantee the achievement of specified results beyond the member's direct control.
14. A member shall, as soon as possible, sever relations with any organization or individual if such relationship requires conduct contrary to the articles of this Code.

Reprinted by permission of the Public Relations Society of America.

According to David Finn, public relations may perform the role of keeping management in line. "When functioning well, (public relations) acts as the anvil against which management's moral problems can be hammered." When executives are establishing a public relations policy for their organization, Finn maintains, "They are really concerned with significant ethical questions." [13]

When public relations practitioners participate in organizational decisions, they carry a heavy ethical responsibility. Their responsibilities are not only to themselves and their organizations, but to their profession and to the public as well. All these considerations must be weighed when helping to make organizational decisions and communicating decisions once made.

**Law**  Many laws affect the practice of public relations; the most important of these is the First Amendment. Indeed, protection of corporate speech has been recently expanded by the Supreme Court which held that corporations may take positions on issues not directly related to their business. Other laws relating to public relations practice include the Sherman Anti-Trust Act, the Federal Regulation of Lobbying Act, the Freedom of Information Act, and the Copyright Act. Public relations activities may violate regulations of the Securities and Exchange Commission (SEC), the Federal Trade Commission (FTC) or the National Labor Relations Board (NLRB). Public relations practitioners have been taken to court in cases of civil libel, slander, invasion of privacy, and contempt of court.

How can public relations run afoul of the Sherman Act? A court maintained:

**There may be situations in which a publicity campaign, ostensibly directly toward influencing governmental action, is a mere sham to cover what is actually nothing more than an attempt to interfere directly with the business relationships of a competitor and the application of the Sherman Act would be justified.**[14]

Media releases may violate SEC regulations regarding adequate disclosure of corporate information affecting investment decisions (for further discussion see Chapter 17). The NLRB comes into play if the corporation threatens employees seeking a union (for further discussion see Chapter 10). The FTC will take action against false claims in publicity releases as well as in advertising.

Public relations practitioners have faced charges of libel for malicious publication defaming a living person. They have been accused of invasion of privacy for using pictures or names without consent. They have been found in contempt of court for attempting to influence the court through the use of publicity in an active case.

If public relations practitioners have a general knowledge of law as it affects their profession, take reasonable care to fulfill obligations and avoid legal transgressions, follow organizational procedures in the handling of sensitive information, and consult corporate counsel when any question or doubt emerges, legal troubles can be avoided. A complete discussion of law as it relates to public relations is obviously impossible within the limits of this textbook. The most comprehensive (albeit dated in some areas) book and one that should be available to all public relations practitioners, is Morton J. Simon's *Public Relations Law* (New York: Appleton-Century-Crofts, 1969).

## PUBLIC RELATIONS AND OTHER ORGANIZATIONAL FUNCTIONS

Public relations practitioners work not only with organizational decision makers to develop policies and actions affecting the entire organization, but also with staff members in other organizational functions. Most important in this regard are public relations and marketing, advertising, personnel, and the legal department.

### Public Relations and Marketing

A few old-timers in the public relations game still maintain that the main reason for public relations is to help sell products. In their opinion public relations should be an adjunct to sales efforts, concerned primarily with product publicity and with the objective of getting "free advertising."

Back in the 1950s, a noncommercial page in *Life* magazine devoted to a company's product was considered to be worth tens of thousands of dollars. To believe that a feature in *Life* could instantly magnify a product's sales showed misunderstanding of how products are sold.

In some corporations misunderstanding of differing natures of marketing and public relations continue to make cooperation difficult between the two. When marketing fails to understand public relations,

**public relations may be brought in belatedly at advanced stages in the marketing process. With marketing unmistakably dominant, there may be a decided inclination to disseminate messages heavily promotional in nature by means of publicity techniques. As a result, the full scope of public relations may never be utilized or communications circuits may be over-powered by heavy-handedness.[15]**

By the same token, some public relations specialists resent or misunderstand marketing. As a result,

**they may have .   .   . secondary interest in furnishing marketing support. Or, because he undervalues the product publicity function, the public relations specialist may simply try to help carry out a marketing plan without making a full contribution.[16]**

Fortunately, such animosity does not exist in most organizations. Indeed, marketing people increasingly appreciate the integral contributions of public relations and specifically incorporate public relations into the marketing mix.[17] Marketing specialists have come to understand that what a company does about pollution, equal rights, or urban renewal is just as much as part of a company's ability to sell as are advertising, merchandising, or sales training. Hill and Knowlton vice president Douglas G. Hearle cites studies documenting "that shoppers in department stores, or purchasing agents, are strongly influenced by what they know .   .   . about a company's policies and practices.   .   .   ."[18] The influence of public relations on organizational policies and practices, and its role in communicating these, affect the marketing process.

Public relations also can increase sales-force efficiency. Sales people spend a great deal of time, especially on first calls, explaining the company to the customer. If a prospective client already knows of the company, the salesperson's chances of getting in the door and making the sale are greatly increased.

When public relations and marketing work together effectively, public relations makes three important contributions.

1. Product publicity and other forms of communication that serve to support sales;
2. Conceptual contributions to marketing strategy;
3. Assistance in maintaining the integrity of product claims and promotion and thereby in safeguarding the survival of the firm.[19]

Product publicity is the traditional role of public relations in marketing. The second and third contributions listed above, however, are relatively recent developments. They are symptoms of more general trends in the development of public relations, including the tendency to become involved in planning and decision making, the new emphasis on inwardly-directed public relations communication, and the concern for social responsibility. In this regard, P. Kotler and W. Mindak report:

**Public relations people are growing increasingly concerned with their company's marketing practices, questioning whether they "square" with the company's social responsibility. They seek more influence over marketing and more of a counseling and policy-making role.[20]**

The new relationship between public relations and marketing has had dramatic effects. Some organizations have created "marketing teams" consisting of a marketing manager, a public relations manager, a brand manager, and representatives of sales promotion and the advertising agency. A major food company established a product review board to judge the nutritional content of planned new products before they are brought to market. The board must be convinced of nutritional worth of the item, and had absolute authority to approve projects. The review procedure was conceived by the company's public relations director, who also heads the board.[21] Examples of public relations' conceptual contributions to marketing strategy abound. Once the creative juices are flowing, it is not surprising that fresh promotional ideas and insights are generated.

For example, a major problem facing the toy business is its seasonality. Marketing people at Kenner Products asked their public relations counsel to suggest ways to promote toys at times other than the Christmas season. The answer was "workshops for baby-sitters," a response to parental desires for babysitters who could both look after children and use the time in constructive and interesting ways. Kenner Products conducted hour-long seminars, designed to help junior high school students become baby-sitters. Held in New York, Houston, and Los Angeles in conjunction with public school systems, the sessions dealt with safety and first aid, keeping children's interest, and earning more money. The programs also suggested that if baby-sitters came to their jobs with a bag of toys—Kenner Products' toys—the children's interest and attention would be improved. Through this program and the media coverage it generated, Kenner Products' toys were brought to the attention of nearly 2 million TV viewers, over 2 million radio listeners and over 32 million newspaper readers. The program cost was only $5,500 per city.[22]

An even more dramatic example of public relations' contributions to marketing strategy occurred at Beech-Nut Foods Corporation. Beech-Nut and other baby food manufacturers had been criticized for adding sugar and salt to their products. Nutritional experts demonstrated that these additives established an unwholesome preference for sugary, salty food in babies, and could also affect their health adversely. The companies feared, however, that mothers would not buy baby food that did not satisfy adult tastes. Beech-Nut nevertheless announced the removal of salt and the reduction of sugar in their products. According to Beech-Nut marketing manager Charles Lanktree, public relations provided:

complete repositioning of our one-product company; a national product introduction in one day where Beech-Nut received more publicity than any consumer package goods product in history; complete change in morale within the company all the way from our top executive to our plant union personnel, and a springboard for all of our other marketing programs.[23]

Through a coordinated public relations program, the company presented itself as responsive, credible, and trustworthy. The response from the public was overwhelmingly favorable, and although other baby food manufacturers quickly followed suit, Beech-Nut has gained a larger share of the market while the competition slipped.[24]

Public relations can become a vital part of the marketing effort, not only in terms of product publicity but in relation to the entire marketing process from product development to final sale.

**Public Relations and Advertising**

Public relations and advertising work together as members of marketing teams, but the hottest area of cooperation between the two does not relate to sales or products. Rather, advertising is coming to be seen as part of the overall corporate communication program, and on some occasions is recognized as a public relations tool.

This is particularly true of advocacy advertising, which promotes ideas and images rather than products. Such advertising also allows the organization to project its message as it wishes to selected audiences, because advertising permits an element of control that publicity lacks. The use of advertising to convey corporate messages, ideas, positions, and policies has led to "the increasing realization that corporate advertising is not a separate discipline . . . but rather an integral element of the total communications program."[25] This suggests that overall corporate communications must be coordinated, generally through the public relations department. Moreover, such advertising rests on the public relations efforts preceding it. "Only (an organization) that devotes its communications consistently to projecting its own unique identity in a believable way can derive maximum benefit from issues-type advertising."[26]

The growing use of such advertising represents important new responsibilities for public relations practitioners. Given public relations' traditional responsibilities and its emerging role in management decision making, public relations managers are called upon to shape corporate image and response through advertising and to take an increasing share of the decision making and creative effort in this area.[27]

Thomas A. Kindre, director of Hill and Knowlton's advertising division, outlines a seven-step communicator-manager exercise to make public relations advertising programs work.

1. Begin with organizational objectives. Who are we? What business are we in? What are we trying to accomplish?
2. Define the problems that face the organization as it tries to achieve those objectives. Make sure to deal with the real problem, not just its symptoms.

3. Develop organizational policy positions on the problems, the solutions and all matters of public concern that bear on the organization's objective.
4. Research the supporting data that demonstrate why the positions the organization is taking are sound and in the public interest.
5. Prepare detailed position papers on every policy position. These should include support data and present the organization's case for its position.
6. Get the position papers to all organizational communication specialists— speech writers, release writers, editors of booklets, brochures and newsletters, and advertisers. Let their creativity work within the bounds of what they have been given. Let the objectives be used as the standard against which to measure results.
7. Constantly evaluate and update programs in relation to evolving environments while maintaining contact with both policy makers and creative staffs.[28]

**Public Relations and Personnel**

The example of implementing safety policies cited earlier in this chapter shows how public relations staff can become involved in matters related to personnel. Indeed, because equal-opportunity employment is an issue of public concern, who is hired or promoted and how can be a critically important matter for public relations. Moreover, responsibility for employee communications such as newsletters, brochures, training manuals, benefit booklets, and employment literature, while often assigned to the personnel department, can benefit from the inputs and expertise of public relations.

Chapter 10 is devoted to employee communication, so we will not belabor the issue here. It is crucial, however, that public relations establish a sound working relationship with the personnel department so that employment policies and practice are consistent with the organization's image and its ideas of social responsibility.

**Public Relations and the Legal Department**

In our earlier discussion of law as it affects public relations practice, we showed how useful lawyers can be to public relations professionals. Were that the extent of the dealings between the two, relative peace would undoubtedly prevail. Unfortunately, such is not the case. Lawyers and public relations practitioners often find themselves in competition for the ear of top management, and find that their advice is often contradictory.

Public relations practitioners are sometimes envious of the status enjoyed by lawyers in the corporate world. Indeed, the term "public relations counsel" emulates the term "legal counsel." Early public relations specialists specifically compared their role to that of lawyers—one specializing in representing organizations before the court of law; the other performing similar services before the court of public opinion.

These "courts," however, are not as distinct in practice as they are in theory. What an organization does in the name of public relations may well affect its legal position. Likewise, corporate behavior in court may affect public opinion. Consequently, legal and public relations counsels often find themselves at loggerheads. As Ivy Lee put it, "I have seen more situations which the public ought to understand . . . spoiled by the intervention of a lawyer than in any other way."[29]

David Finn, discussing problems that occur between business and the media, suggests that disclosure of information is frequently impeded by legal counsel. According to Finn, this is "the least-known aspect of corporate communications, yet, it is in all probability the most troublesome in achieving an open, constructive communication between business and the media."[30]

Lawyers generally advise their clients to avoid making any public statements that could prove troublesome in future legal actions. Usually they recommend saying nothing; when an executive tersely says "no comment," it is usually on the advice of his lawyer rather than his public relations counsel.

Finn comments:

**For the most part, I find that business executives would like to be open and candid about their affairs. They repeatedly make the point that they want the truth to be known, and that they would like to cooperate with the press as much as possible. . . . When public relations advisors tell their clients that the only way to avoid distortions is to answer all questions as fully as possible, the instinct of most businessmen is to do so. But when there are critical issues involved, legal counsel usually has a greater influence on business executives by making it clear that speaking too freely about matters that may have to be litigated can cause a great deal of trouble for the corporation and even for the executives personally.[31]**

The damages that lawyers anticipate are very real. So are the damages when a corporation appears unresponsive, unfeeling, defensive, or irresponsible and consequently loses the respect and trust of its publics. In either case, millions of dollars can be lost. Careers can be ruined.

There are no simple answers to how the differences between lawyers and public relations practitioners can be solved. Our earlier admonition that public relations should speak in terms of practical potential consequences of various communication strategies and rather than merely preaching truth and openness certainly applies to this case. Our discussions of Procter & Gamble's Rely tampon case in Chapter 18, and Firestone's 500 radial tire case in Chapter 15, illustrate this point.

In this chapter, we have looked at how public relations specialists fit into the organizational decision-making process. We found that they are playing an increasingly important role in all areas of organizational decision making. We examined ethical and legal constraints on public relations input and practice. Finally, we looked into the relationships between the public relations function and the marketing, advertising, personnel, and legal functions.

As we continue now to consider public relations careers in the next chapter, the process of public relations in Section II, communication with organizational publics in Section III, how public relations is practiced in specific kinds of organizations in Sections IV and V, and critical issues for public relations in Section VI, think of the public relations practitioner not in the narrow terms of one who writes media releases or who plans publicity stunts. Think instead of someone who harmonizes organizations with their environments by analyzing those environments, advising management and participating in decisions affecting all areas of organizational activity, as well as communicating with various corporate publics concerning policy, programs, activities, ideas, and images. In the fullest sense, public relations practitioners are not only communication technicians. They are an integral part of the management team, with special skills, training, and sensitivities in the area of communication.

| | |
|---|---|
| **CASE STUDY: NEIGHBORS** | **By Dulcie Murdock**<br>**Virginia Commonwealth University,**<br>**Richmond, Virginia** |

You are public information director for a city mental health and mental retardation department. Your department plans to open a group home for eight mentally retarded adults. Group homes, in which a small number of clients live together with counselors, are designed to serve as an alternative to institutional living for some mentally retarded people. A house located in a middle-class subdivision was privately donated to the city for use as a group home. This is to be the first group home in your state; other states have been using the group home system for years; others have not begun community care programs.

The mentally retarded people (four men and four women) will live in the group home with a married couple who are trained counselors. All eight residents have full-time jobs in the city at places such as McDonald's. The money they earn working will go towards food bills, their clothing, and pocket money.

A few months ago some general stories about the concept of group home care for mentally retarded people appeared in the local newspaper. One story had a statement by the city director (your boss) that said a group home was planned in the city "at a future date." After this article appeared in the paper, the director received a few letters from citizens objecting to the idea of mentally retarded persons living in group homes. One concern was that property values would be lowered in neighborhoods where group homes were located.

The director, fearing negative reactions from residents in the neighborhood where the group home is to be located, tells you he wants to keep a low profile about the opening of the group home. In a memo, he tells you not to generate any publicity about the group home's opening. When the counselors and residents arrive at the group home a few days later to move in, they find hand-lettered signs posted on the trees in the yard, saying that they are not welcomed in the neighborhood.

The counselors call the director, who calls you, to say that something has to be done before the situation gets out of hand. He asks for your advice.

**Questions**   1.  Do you think the city director made the right decision in deciding not to generate any publicity about the group home? What would you, as public information director, suggest be done now?
2.  How would the situation been different had the public information director been involved in the original decision rather than being brought in after the fact?

---

**NOTES**   [1] H. W. Close, "Public Relations As a Management Function," *Public Relations Journal* (March 1980): 12.

[2] R. Tannenbaum and W. H. Schmidt, "How to Choose a Leadership Pattern," *Harvard Business Review* (May–June 1973): 162–180.

[3] O. W. Baskin and C. E. Aronoff, *Interpersonal Communication in Organizations* (Santa Monica, CA: Goodyear Publishing Co., 1980), p. 118.

[4] James N. Sites, "Solving Problems That Keep Your Boss Awake at Night," *Public Relations Journal* (August 1974): 6.

[5] The authors are indebted in Ron Weiser of the consulting firm Meidinger, Inc., for the phrase "Management mainstream" and for some of the ideas contained in this section.

[6] Sites, "Solving Problems," p. 5.

[7] Robert D. Ross, *The Management of Public Relations* (New York: John Wiley and Sons, 1977), p. 10.

[8] R. P. Ewing, "Issues," *Public Relations Journal* (June 1980): 14–16.

[9] Close, "Public Relations as a Management Function," p. 13.

[10] Hill and Knowlton Executives, "Critical Issues", *Public Relations* (Englewood Cliffs, NJ: Prentice-Hall, Inc., 1975) p. xxv.

[11] William W. Weston, "Public Relations: Trustee of a Free Society," *Public Relations Review* (Fall 1975): 13.

[12] J. Montgomery, "The Image Makers," *Wall Street Journal*, Aug. 1, 1978, p. 1.

[13] David Finn, "Struggle for Ethics in Public," *Harvard Business Review* January–February 1959): 9–11.

[14] Noerr Motor Freight, Inc. et al. v. Eastern Railroad Presidents Conference et al., 365 U.S. 127, 144 (1961).

[15] E. E. Weck, "Challenge to Management: Blending Public Relations Into the Marketing Mix," *Public Relations Journal* (January 1973): 6.

[16] Ibid.

[17] P. Kotler and W. Mindak, "Marketing and Public Relations," *Journal of Marketing* (October 1978): 13.

[18] D. G. Hearle, "The Effective Use of Public Relations in Marketing," *Public Relations Journal* (January 1973): 8.

[19] Weck, "Challenge to Management," p. 7.

[20] Kotler and Mindak, "Marketing and Public Relations," p. 13.

[21] Ibid., p. 14.

[22] V. W. Wigotsky, "How PR Can Fill Marketing's Black Holdes," *Sales and Marketing Management*, August 20, 1979, pp. 43–44.

[23] Quoted in J. Gumin, "PR Is Primary Element in Beech-Nut Foods Marketing Program," *Advertising Age*, February 6, 1978, p. 39.

[24] Ibid.,

[25] T. A. Kindre, "Corporate Advertising—Now or Never" in *Critical Issues*, Hill and Knowlton Executives, ed., p. 188.

[26] Ibid.

[27] F. P. Seitel, *The Practice of Public Relations* (Columbus, O.: Charles E. Merrill Publishing Co., 1980), p. 168.

[28] Kindre, "Corporate Advertising," pp. 191–192.

[29] Ivy Lee, *Publicity: Some of the Things It Is and Is Not* (New York: Industrial Publishing, 1925), p. 58.

[30] David Finn, "Media as Monitor of Corporate Behavior," in *Business and the Media*, Craig E. Aronoff, ed. (Santa Monica: Goodyear Publishing Company, 1979) pp. 120–121.

[31] Ibid., p. 122.

# CHAPTER 5  PUBLIC RELATIONS AS A CAREER

**PREVIEW**   The demand for public relations practitioners is growing at a faster rate than ever before. This growth is due primarily to the need in organizations of all types to maintain effective relationships with their constituents.

Public relations practitioners are gaining more influence in policy-level decisions in their organizations.

Women represent a significant portion of the total number of public relations professionals in practice today.

More practitioners are employed in corporations than any other type of public relations. The latest research indicates that two-thirds of all public relations graduates find their first job in business organizations.

While communication skills and media knowledge are still the backbone of professional public relations practice, the need for new training in business and the social and behavioral sciences is evident.

Perhaps the most important message we would like to communicate in this book is that public relations is a complex and changing field. Therefore, those who earn their living through public relations must be able to apply a variety of skills to many new and unique situations. Public relations practitioners cannot be stamped out of a common mold or trained to perform routine functions. The field is changing so rapidly that tried and true approaches may no longer be successful. Instead, each practitioner must approach his or her career with a knowledge of what has happened in the past and the skill to find new solutions to the problems of the present and the future.

**THE EXPANDING SCOPE OF PUBLIC RELATIONS PRACTICE**

The 1980 edition of the *Occupational Outlook Handbook* listed the number of workers employed in the field of public relations as 31,000;[1] as we discussed in Chapter 1, however, the term public relations covers a variety of occupations. The *Handbook* also predicted that the demand for public relations workers will grow at a faster pace than the average demand for all occupations in the 1980s. Competition for starting positions will remain keen, but the rewards for those who are prepared to meet the challenges of a rapidly changing environment will be great. As *Business Week* points out, the practice of public relations is feeling tremendous pressure as the result of a changing business and societal environment:

**As the tempo of corporate PR activities rises, the very nature of the profession is changing profoundly. What was once scorned as press agentry and flackery and dismissed as a peripheral function of management is becoming a more consequential endeavor worthy of serious attention by senior management.[2]**

Because management is increasingly aware of the importance of effective public relations, public relations staffs will continue to grow both in number and in influence. The search for appropriate responses to contemporary issues has already led to an unprecedented emphasis upon public relations in most major organizations. A 1981 study conducted by the International Association of Business Communicators (IABC) shows that nearly one-third of the practitioners surveyed reported having significant influence on the policy-making process in their organization. Eighty percent of the same respondents said they had direct access to the top executive. The same study shows that the number of practitioners at vice-presidential levels has increased more than seventy percent since a similar survey in 1972.[3]

Broad social and economic problems cannot be solved with a quick fix of publicity; they are deep and complex components of our modern culture that will not go away if ignored or allowed to run their course. The riots in Miami and Chattanooga in the summer of 1980 served as painful reminders that the problems that produced similar occurrences in other major cities nearly twenty years before are still with us. Environmental and consumer issues may shift focus from time to time, but they will continue to have a major impact on the way organizations function. With the growth of multinational organizations, the importance of relationships between business and the federal government will become even more crucial than they are today.

If there are changes apparent in the ways that public relations has traditionally been practiced within a corporate setting, there are also major new directions opening up for public relations outside of business and industry. The same pressures that are providing challenges to public relations in the corporate world have opened up new fields for public relations employment. Although public relations has long been part of the operations of not-for-profit undertakings like hospitals and universities, public relations practitioners may now be found working for consumer groups, labor unions, government agencies, television stations, and numerous other types of organizations, all of which now recognize the need to approach their dealings with the public in an organized and coherent fashion.

**Public Relations Practitioner Profiles**

One of the most comprehensive studies of public relations practitioners ever conducted was a 1978 survey of 4,500 members of the Public Relations Society of America (PRSA).[4] The results of this study showed that only thirty-nine percent of the practitioners responding had formal training in public relations. More than seventy-five percent were male and fewer than six percent were minority group members (*Table 5-1*). Although the average income of the respondents was reported at $26,000 for 1977, it should be noted that forty-five percent fell below that figure. Table 5-2 presents a comparison of income data by type of organization for professionals included in this survey. Practitioners employed in corporations, counseling firms, and investor relations reported the highest median incomes. While this study is important because of its large number of respondents, it must be remembered that it was conducted only among members of PRSA and that only 2.4 percent had two or fewer years of experience. Therefore, it is clear that the data in this survey are primarily representative of well-established professionals.

Descriptions of the "average" practitioner from data such as these can be misleading. No one is "average," and extremes at either or both ends of the range of reported information can distort median and mean figures. For example, the fact that fewer than twenty-five percent of those who responded to the PRSA survey were female does not mean that public relations is not a good career field for women. In fact, public relations was one of the earlier areas of professional or managerial employment to be open to women. What this study does not show is that the ratio of women to men entering the public relations field has improved significantly. The International Association

**Table 5-1**
Basic Profile of Public
Relations Professionals

| Classification | | Percent |
|---|---|---|
| Age | Under 30 | 10 |
| | 30–40 | 26 |
| | 40–50 | 28 |
| | 50–60 | 26 |
| | Over 60 | 10 |
| Salary | | |
| | Up to $15,000 | 13 |
| | $16,000 to $20,000 | 16 |
| | $21,000 to $25,000 | 19 |
| | $26,000 to $35,000 | 26 |
| | $36,000 to $50,000 | 17 |
| | $51,000 to $75,000 | 7 |
| | Over $75,000 | 3 |
| Sphere of Work | | |
| | National | 39 |
| | Regional | 35 |
| | Local | 25 |
| | International | 19 |
| Years Practiced | | |
| | 15 or more | 47.1 |
| | 10–15 | 18.5 |
| | 5–10 | 20.0 |
| | 3–5 | 12.0 |
| | 2 or less | 2.4 |

James A. Morrissey, "Will the Real Public Relations Professional Please Stand Up," *Public Relations Journal*, December 1978, p. 26. Reprinted with permission of the *Public Relations Journal* © 1978.

**Table 5-2**
Income of Public
Relations Professionals:
Overall and by
Employment

| Organization/Profession | Median Income |
|---|---|
| Association | $26,000 |
| Corporation | $30,000 |
| Counselor | $35,000 |
| Educational Institution | $20,000 |
| Financial Institution | $24,000 |
| Government | $23,000 |
| Health | $20,000 |
| Investor Relations | $30,000 |
| Utility | $26,000 |
| Overall | $26,000 |

James A. Morrissey, "Will the Real Public Relations Professional Please Stand Up," *Public Relations Journal*, December, 1978, p. 27. Reprinted with permission of the *Public Relations Journal* © 1978.

of Business Communicators, which has a broader-based membership among organizational communication practitioners, reports that almost seventy percent of its members are female.

IABC's *Profile/81* reports that nearly fifty percent of the 1500 practitioners responding work for a corporation; eleven percent work for an association

|  | | |
|---|---|---|
| **Table 5-3**<br>IABC Profile/81 Survey<br>of 1500 Practitioners:<br>Summary of Findings | **Age (median–32 years)** | Under 30 years ............... 36.7%<br>30–39 years ............... 37.8%<br>40–49 years ............. 15.4%<br>50–59 years ................ 8.3%<br>Over 60 years ............... 1.8% |
|  | **Experience (median–5 years)** | 0–2 years ................... 21.2%<br>3–4 years .................... 21.4%<br>5–6 years ................... 15.7%<br>7–10 years ................. 18.3%<br>11 or more .................. 23.4% |
|  | **Salary Distribution (1981)** | $10,000–$12,499 ............. 4.2%<br>$12,500–$14,999 ............. 5.4%<br>$15,000–$17,499 ........... 16.0%<br>$17,500–$19,999 ........... 11.9%<br>$20,000–$29,999 ........... 38.2%<br>$30,000–$39,000 ........... 14.0%<br>$40,000–$49,999 ............. 6.0%<br>$50,000 or more ............. 4.3% |
|  | **Type of Organization (1981)** | Corporation .................. 48.5%<br>Association or<br>  nonprofit .................. 11.0%<br>Hospital/medical<br>  institution ................. 7.8%<br>Financial<br>  institution ................. 7.3%<br>Government .................. 5.9%<br>Educational<br>  institution .................. 4.7%<br>Public relations/<br>  Communication<br>  counseling firm ............ 3.7%<br>Self-employed ............... 1.3%<br>State-owned<br>  corp. (UK) ................. .4%<br>Labor union .................. .3%<br>Other ....................... 9.1% |
|  | **Department in which<br>Communicator Works (1981)** | Public relations .............. 25.0%<br>Communication .............. 17.2%<br>Public affairs ................ 9.3%<br>Personnel/<br>  Human resources .......... 9.1%<br>Marketing/Advertising ........ 7.8%<br>Internal communication ....... 6.6%<br>Public information ............ 4.3%<br>Administration ............... 4.1%<br>Video/AV .................... .4%<br>Other ....................... 12.5% |

Used by permission: Profile/81—International Association of Business Communicators.

or other nonprofit organization. "The balance of the respondents work for hospital and medical institutions (7.8 percent); financial institutions (7.3 percent); government (5.9 percent); educational institutions (4.7 percent); public relations or communication counseling firms (3.7 percent)."[5] The typical practitioner in the IABC study was thirty-two years old, female, a college graduate in journalism/news editorial, and had been working in the profession for about five years. Table 5-3 summarizes some of the findings from the IABC study that can be compared with data from the 1978 PRSA survey. The average salary reported for IABC practitioners in 1981 was $30,000 for men and $20,900 for women.

While the IABC survey represents the broad spectrum of public relations practice, it does not focus on entry level positions. A 1981 survey of 100 former members of the Public Relations Student Society of America who had just accepted their first job is reported in Table 5-4.[6] The respondents, recent graduates from fifty-two universities and colleges, reported average starting salaries of $11,999 for women and $13,717 for men with B.A. degrees; with a master's degree, women earned an average of $13,914 while men were paid $15,600. As in the previous two surveys we have discussed, the PRSSA recent graduates found the largest number of jobs available in corporations. It should also be noted that eighty-six percent of the PRSSA recent graduates surveyed were women. This data combined with the fact that the majority of IABC members are women suggests that large numbers of women have entered the profession and are continuing to do so. Therefore, we could expect that future surveys of more established public relations professionals like the 1978 PRSA survey will reflect this trend.

To help overcome the impersonal quality of statistical profiles it is useful to take a closer look at some individuals who have been recognized for their success in the field of public relations. Therefore, we have reprinted some brief biographical sketches of ten public relations executives singled out by *Business Week* magazine as the top names in corporate public relations.

| **Table 5-4** Average Beginning Salaries, by Public Relations Sector, of 22 Male and 78 Female Respondents. | **Men** | **Women** |
|---|---|---|
| Corporate | $14,110 (8, or 36%) | $13,207 (27, or 35%) |
| Counseling | $14,050 (4, or 18%) | $10,793 (14, or 18%) |
| Non-Profit | $14,500 (3, or 14%) | $10,904 (13, or 17%) |
| Association | $14,500 (2, or 9%) | $13,667 (6, or 8%) |
| Government | — | $12,476 (6, or 8%) |
| Hospital | $13,600 (2, or 9%) | $11,251 (5, or 6%) |
| Education | $11,000 (2, or 9%) | $11,667 (3, or 4%) |
| Banking | — | $11,000 (2, or 3%) |
| Resort | — | $12,000 (1, or .5%) |
| Broadcasting | — | $14,400 (1, or .5%) |
| Entertainment | $13,000 (1, or 5%) | — |

"1980 Graduates: Where Did They Go? What Did They Earn?" *Public Relations Journal*, February, 1982. Reprinted with permission of the *Public Relations Journal*, © 1982.

**The Top 10 Names** The pioneers of the public relations business during the
**in Corporate PR** 1920s and 1930s were a handful of ex-newspapermen and
press agents who set up their own agencies and became as
well-known personally as the corporate clients they served:
men such as Edward L. Bernays, Ben Sonnenberg, Ivy Lee,
John Hill, Carl Byoir, and Pendleton Dudley. As the PR
agencies continue to flourish, a new generation of PR leaders
has grown up within the corporate structure itself. Lacking
the exposure of the men who own and run the agencies, the
corporate PR practitioners are largely anonymous executives
whose managerial feats are not always visible to outsiders.

Basing its selections on such criteria as the respect of
professional peers inside and outside their companies, the
confidence of their companies' top management, their PR
accomplishments, the degree of corporate influence they
wield, and the depth of experience they have in dealing with
major policy issues, BUSINESS WEEK rates the following
executives as the nation's top 10 corporate PR practitioners:

**John J. Bell,** senior-vice president, Bank of America, San
Francisco. Worked as a radio-TV news writer while at the
University of Detroit, became a General Motors Corp. PR man
and helped set up its first community affairs department.
Held top-slot PR jobs at B.F. Goodrich Co., where he
handled the vinyl chloride problem, and Bendix Corp.
Recruited by BofA in June, 1977, he has revitalized its PR
program and made it a top-priority matter for the world's
largest bank.

**Edward M. Block,** vice-president, American Telephone &
Telegraph Co., New York City. Has been in PR and
advertising for the Bell System since 1952. Presides over a
PR program that is expanding as AT&T adopts a more
aggressive marketing orientation.

**Donald J. Colen,** vice-president, Citicorp, New York City.
Was a Research Institute of America editor, GE public affairs
analyst, and vice-president of Ruder & Finn before joining the
company in 1965. Is credited with blunting consumer
advocate Ralph Nader's attack on Citibank, the company's
primary subsidiary, and with building the bank's solid image.

**Richard J. Davis,** vice-president, McDonnell Douglas Corp.,
St. Louis. Former military affairs correspondent for
*Newsweek*. Became Washington PR representative for
Douglas Aircraft Co. in 1958, was made a vice-president
seven years later. Was one of a handful of Douglas corporate

officers to survive the merger with McDonnell Aircraft. Has created a strong PR image for what had been a low-profile, publicity-shy corporation.

**Robert L. Fegley,** staff executive to the CEO for communications, General Electric Co., Fairfield, Conn. His influence does not show up in GE's organization chart. Adviser on public policy issues and speechwriter for Chairman Reginald H. Jones, oversees planning for the company's annual top management conference. Joined the company 37 years ago in advertising and sales promotion, later headed institutional advertising and public issue analysis.

**John H. F. Hoving,** senior vice-president, Federated Department Stores Inc., Cincinnati. Former Wisconsin newsman, has solid Washington credentials as presidential campaign executive, Democratic National Committee executive, White House official, vice-president of Air Transport Assn. Joined Federated in 1972.

**Joseph T. Nolan,** vice-president, Monsanto Co., St. Louis. Former UPI Washington correspondent and *New York Times* writer and editor. Joined RCA Corp. as manager of editorial services in 1955, was later senior vice-president for public affairs at Chase Manhattan Bank. Earned PhD in economics, was college journalism professor for two years, joined Monsanto in 1976. Developed its highly touted "Chemical Facts of Life" campaign to counter activist criticism of the industry.

**Willis Player,** senior vice-president, Pan American World Airways Inc., New York City. Former reporter for *The Wall Street Journal, Chicago Daily News,* and Booth Newspapers. Joined Pan Am as PR man in 1946, later headed PR for Northwest Airlines, Air Transport Assn., and American Airlines before rejoining Pan Am in 1964. Displayed considerable Washington clout in protecting Pan Am's fuel allotments during the 1974 energy crisis.

**Herbert Schmertz,** vice-president, Mobil Corp., New York City. Former general counsel of Federal Mediation and Conciliation Service, joined Mobil in 1966 to handle labor relations, took charge of all public affairs when the company's program was expanded three years later. Has strong Democratic ties in Washington.

**William H. Shepard,** vice-president, Aluminum Co. of America, Pittsburgh. Awarded master's degree in journalism from Boston University in 1949, immediately joined the

company as PR man. Architect of aluminum industry's energy
conservation program and congenial relationship with
Washington (in contrast to steel's), which has helped
aluminum price increases to pass through with a minimum of
fuss from the bureaucrats.

**Qualifications for
Public Relations
Careers**

The 1978 survey of members of the Public Relations Society of America found
that only thirty-nine percent of those responding had received any formal
public relations training while attending college. It should be noted, however,
that the average age of survey respondents was forty-five, and they had an
average of fifteen years of experience; older practitioners would be less likely
to have had college training since public relations as a course of study is a
recent phenomenon. However, the 1981 IABC survey of practitioners found
that most had earned at least an undergraduate degree, with journalism being
the most frequent major for men and women (*Table 5-5*).

In fact, public relations has become the leading career objective in schools
of journalism, according to a survey taken in the fall of 1980.[7] Another study,
*Status and Trends in Public Relations Education 1981,* reported that the
growth in public relations education at the college level is exceeded only
by growth in the areas of business and computer sciences.[8] This study, sponsored by the Foundation for Public Relations Research and Education, found
that in almost one half of the 256 colleges and universities surveyed, public
relations was taught as part of a journalism curriculum.

**Table 5-5**
**IABC Profile/81 Survey
of 1500 Practitioners**

**Education Level of Communicators**

|  | Overall 1981 |
|---|---|
| High school | 1.2% |
| Some college/university | 10.6% |
| College degree/certificate | 46.9% |
| Some post-grad | 19.8% |
| Master's degree | 19.0% |
| Doctoral degree | .7% |
| A/O level, matric (UK) | .7% |
| Other | 1.0% |

**Majors of Communicators**

|  | % | Men | Women |
|---|---|---|---|
| Journalism | 33.6% | 31.5% | 31.5% |
| English/speech | 19.5% | 17.9% | 20.4% |
| Communication/pr | 12.2% | 10.7% | 13.5% |
| Business/economics | 9.7% | 12.6% | 7.5% |
| Social science | 8.4% | 10.7% | 7.0% |
| Other | 16.7% | 3.6% | 6.2% |

Thus, there is an increasing tendency for public relations practitioners to prepare for their careers through academic training in the field. But as the responsibilities of public relations increase, so too will the requirements for job entry. Some organizations express a desire for practitioners to have training in fields related to business or finance in addition to public relations. Pat Jackson, a former president of the Public Relations Society of America, has predicted some major changes in the practice of public relations for the 1980s. He anticipates a role for practitioners as "managers of change rather than defenders of the faith."[9] To make this important transition, he believes, public relations practitioners will need to go beyond traditional preparation. They will need the interpersonal skills that can be learned in courses in group psychology, organizational development, and applied behavioral sciences. Solid writing ability and an understanding of media functions will remain important for public relations jobs. But, as Jackson observes, public relations seems to be moving beyond a total emphasis on journalism toward more preparation in management, sociology, and psychology.

While there has been a great deal of progress in expanding public relations curricula to include more than traditional journalism, some feel more needs to be done. The Foundation for Public Relations Research and Education concludes in its 1981 survey report: "Although public relations students today are graduating with strong backgrounds in the social and behavioral sciences, they still appear to be weak in business."[10] This point is supported by Table 5-6 which shows that budgeting and general business practice were two of the three areas in which recent public relations graduates felt least qualified. Nevertheless, the need for skills and knowledge of various types must be balanced with a firm commitment to excellence in the art and science of communication. The expansion of public relations curricula must not be accomplished at the expense of the writing and media skills that have long been the hallmark of professionals.

Regardless of the academic background a public relations practitioner possesses, the most important qualifications for a career in this field can be summed up as follows:

**People who choose public relations as a career need an outgoing personality, self-confidence, and an understanding of human psychology. They**

| Table 5-6 Public Relations Functions New Professionals Felt Least Prepared for Academically | Men | Women |
|---|---|---|
| Budgeting for PR Programs | 30% | 32% |
| General Business Practice | 20% | 23% |
| Graphics | 22% | 20% |
| Print Technology | 15% | 17% |
| Photography | 6% | 4% |
| Writing/Editing | 5% | 2% |
| Financial Public Relations | 2% | — |
| Fund Raising | — | 2% |

"1980 Graduates: Where Did They Go? What Did They Earn?" *Public Relations Journal*, February, 1982. Reprinted with permission of the *Public Relations Journal* © 1982.

should have the enthusiasm necessary to motivate people. Public relations workers need a highly developed sense of competitiveness and the ability to function as part of a team.[11]

## The Nature of Public Relations Work

Practitioners of public relations apply their skills and knowledge in many different ways. The *Occupational Outlook Handbook* suggests that public relations specialists are responsible for maintaining positive relationships with the press, employees, community, consumers, investors, regulatory agencies, contributors, constituents, and a number of other publics. They must be involved in activities as diverse as sales promotion, political campaigning, interest group representation, fund raising, and employee recruitment. As we pointed out in Chapter 4, those who practice public relations have the opportunity to contribute to better understanding and increased cooperation among the diverse segments that exist in our society.

An organization's success in communicating its goals, operations, and policies affects its public standing, profitability, and ability to survive. Public relations practitioners help organizations build and maintain positive reputations. This, however, involves more than telling the organization's story the way management wants it told. Public relations specialists must be capable of understanding the concerns and attitudes of customers, employees, investors, managers, special interest groups, and a vast array of other publics. But the job cannot stop at an understanding of these complex issues; public relations practitioners must be able to integrate this information into the organization's managerial decision-making process.

There can never be a precise definition of public relations work itself because it must be adapted to each type of organization in which it is employed. Public relations is practiced in organizations that range in type from giant multinational oil companies to small human-service agencies. A public relations manager for a private university may devote most of his or her efforts to fund raising and student recruitment. On the other hand, the public relations staff of a large multinational corporation will be responsible for the organization's relationships with customers, suppliers, investors, employees, and the governments of several countries.

## The Duties of the Job

Public relations practitioners are basically responsible for assimilating and communicating information between an organization and its environments. Public relations employees span the boundaries of an organization, attempting to relate to the needs and interests of its publics, and to inform them about the organization's impact on their lives, thereby building positive relationships. As they perform these services for their organizations, public relations practitioners must maintain effective relationships with media representatives who may be interested in publishing or broadcasting information about the organization and its publics. Public relations departments are frequently the source of information for special reports, news and feature articles for television, radio, newspapers, and magazines. These messages do not always advertise the organization or its services and products directly. Instead, the information contained in publicity releases may be designed to aid consumers or some other public, and only indirectly contribute to a positive image for the organization. Information about health, nutrition, energy, and the environment may be researched and communicated because the organization recognizes an obligation to respond to the needs of its publics in socially responsible ways.

Public relations duties may also include arranging for company representatives to make direct contact with members of various publics. Speakers' bureaus, which arrange for members of the organization to speak to civic and social groups on topics of current interest, frequently come under the umbrella of public relations.

In addition to arranging such events, public relation specialists may write speeches for various members of the organization, or even serve as representatives themselves. Other activities common to public relations jobs include editing in-house publications, producing and distributing films, slides, and other audio-visual programs, and managing fund-raising campaigns and community activities.

**Carrying Out the Job**   Public relations departments range in size from more than 200 members in large organizations to one or two individuals in small companies. Large corporations frequently have an officer at the vice-presidential level in charge of the public relations function, who develops overall policy as a member of the organization's top management. In addition, large organizations typically include various other levels of public relations managers at both corporate and division levels, and may also employ a number of public relations specialists such as writers, researchers, and representatives to the media. On the other hand, practitioners who work for individuals or small organizations may handle all these responsibilities. Within public relations counseling firms, there may be specialists in a particular area, such as merger or takeover campaigns, or generalists who advise management on a wide range of matters.

This great diversity in the job duties of public relations practitioners is illustrated by the latest list of public relations functions published by PRSA in their booklet entitled *Careers in Public Relations*:

1. *Programming.* This involves analyzing problems and opportunities, defining goals and the publics (or groups of people whose support or understanding is needed), and recommending and planning activities. It may include budgeting and assignment of responsibilities to the appropriate people, including non-public relations personnel. For example, an organization's president or executive director is often a key figure in public relations activities.

2. *Relationships.* Successful public relations people develop skill in personally gathering information from management, from colleagues in their organizations and from external sources. Continually evaluating what they learn, they formulate recommendations and gain approval for them from their managements.

    Many public relations activities require working with and sometimes through other functions, including personnel, legal and marketing staffs.

The practitioner who learns to be persuasive with others will be most effective.

Public relations people also represent their organizations. Sometimes this is formal, in which they are an official representative to a trade or professional association. But in all their relationships with others—including people in industry groups, regulatory agencies and government, educational institutions and the general public—public relations personnel are "at work" in behalf of their organizations.

3. *Writing and Editing*. Since the public relations worker is often trying to reach large groups of people, the tool most often used is the printed word. Examples of its use are found in reports, news releases, booklets, speeches, film scripts, trade magazine articles, product information and technical material, employee publications, newsletters, shareholder reports and other management communications, directed to both organization personnel and external groups. A sound, clear style of writing which effectively communicates, is virtually a must for public relations work.

4. *Information*. Setting up channels of dissemination of material to appropriate newspaper, broadcast, general and trade publication editors, and contact with them with a view toward enlisting their interest in publishing an organization's news and features are normal public relations activities. This requires a knowledge of how newspapers and other media operate, the areas of specialization of publications and the interests of individual editors. Competition is keen for the attention of editors and broadcasters who have a limited amount of space and time at their disposal. As one public relations practitioner puts it, "You have to get to the right editor of the right publication with the right story at the right time." Although ideas are accepted on the basis of news and other readership value, an ability to develop relationships of mutual respect and cooperation with the press can be useful to both the practitioner and the newsperson.

5. *Production*. Brochures, special reports, films and multi-media programs are important ways of communicating. The public relations practitioner need not be an expert in art, layout, typography and photography, but background knowledge of the techniques of preparation is needed for intelligent planning and supervision of their use.

6. *Special Events*. News conferences, convention exhibits and special showings, new facility and anniversary celebrations, contest and award programs, tours and special meetings make up a partial list of special events used to gain attention and acceptance of groups of people. They involve careful planning and coordination, attention to detail, preparation of special booklets, publicity and reports.

7. *Speaking*. Public relations work often requires skill in face-to-face communication—finding appropriate platforms, the preparation of speeches for others and the delivery of speeches. The person who can effectively address individuals and groups will enjoy an advantage over those whose facility of expression is limited to writing.

8. *Research and Evaluation.* The first activity undertaken by a public relations practitioner is always fact gathering. As previously indicated, this can be highly personal, through interviews, review of library materials and informal conversations. It can also involve the use of survey techniques and firms specializing in designing and conducting opinion research.

After a program is completed, the public relations practitioner should study its results and make an evaluation about the program's implementation and effectiveness. More and more managements expect research and evaluation from their public relations advisers.[12]

A revealing look at the changing nature of public relations work can be seen in the results of the 1978 PRSA survey. Table 5-7 lists these results of the survey according to the percentage of practitioners that identified each activity as a part of their jobs. The first three activities—media relations, public relations management, and publicity—are reported far more frequently than are the remaining nine. It should be noted that the activities of media relations and public relations management are managerial functions of the practice of public relations. Public relations management and media relations do not depend only upon hands-on skills that enable an individual to complete a piece of work from start to finish. Instead they emphasize the ability of the practitioner to accomplish his or her job through the cooperation of other people.

Philip Lesly has identified "the trend . . . toward putting non-public relations people into the top public relations positions . . ." as cause for concern in the decade of the '80s.[13] This development suggests that public relations practitioners have not been as competent in the managerial functions of their profession as they have in the more traditional activities. In a recent survey of fifty chief executive officers of major corporations, thirty said they did not have confidence in their top public relations managers.

**Table 5-7**
**Public Relations**
**Activities Reported**

| Activity | Percent* |
| --- | --- |
| Media relations | 64.0 |
| PR management or administration | 60.4 |
| Publicity | 60.0 |
| Community relations | 45.8 |
| PR counseling | 40.9 |
| Editor of publications | 33.9 |
| Employee relations | 27.8 |
| Government relations | 24.3 |
| Investor relations | 16.3 |
| Consumer affairs | 14.2 |
| PR teaching | 7.9 |
| Advertising/sales promotion | 4.4 |

*Multiple responses were invited on this question.

James A. Morrissey, "Will the Real Public Relations Professional Please Stand Up," *Public Relations Journal,* December 1978, p. 25. Reprinted with permission from the *Public Relations Journal* © 1978.

Only fifty percent of these chief executive officers reported that they were satisfied with their corporate communication efforts.[14] If organizations are looking outside their public relations staff for people to fill their top public relations positions, there is apparently a need for more emphasis on managerial as well as traditional skills in the preparation of public relations practitioners. Public relations professionals, in addition to being skilled practitioners of the more traditional roles, must also be competent managers who can integrate public relations issues into the top decision-making levels of an organization.

**Where Public Relations Jobs Are Found**

As we have already discussed, public relations practitioners are employed in a variety of organizations such as business firms, hospitals, schools, state, local and federal government, and consulting or counseling firms. Jobs in corporate public relations departments appear to be the most plentiful, however, especially at the entry level. The 1981 survey of 256 colleges and universities sponsored by the Foundation for Public Relations Research and Education concluded that two-thirds of public relations graduates enter corporate public relations.[15] In addition, opportunities for advancement and reward appear to be increasing faster in private industry as greater recognition is given to changing business, political and social conditions. Larry Marshall, an executive search consultant for major corporations, recently reported a trend toward more communication-related jobs in the upper levels of management.[16] Table 5-8 shows the percentage of practitioners and their

**Table 5-8**
IABC Profile/81
Survey of 1500
Practitioners

| Percentage of Communicators and Average Salaries by Product or Service of Organization, 1981 | | |
|---|---|---|
| Aerospace | 2.4% | $32,000 |
| Agriculture | 1.2% | $24,300 |
| Automotive | 1.6% | $26,300 |
| Chemical | 1.9% | $22,700 |
| Computer technology | 3.0% | $26,800 |
| Education | 6.1% | $19,500 |
| Engineering/construction | 2.5% | $24,900 |
| Finance/banking | 6.1% | $19,600 |
| Food/beverage | 2.8% | $23,900 |
| Forest products/paper | 1.6% | $31,300 |
| Graphic arts/printing | 1.8% | $27,300 |
| Insurance | 5.9% | $24,300 |
| Manufacturing | 9.1% | $24,800 |
| Medical/hospital | 9.7% | $22,400 |
| Metals/mining | 1.8% | $30,500 |
| Petroleum | 4.2% | $26,700 |
| Pharmaceutical | 2.9% | $27,100 |
| Public relations | 2.1% | $28,200 |
| Publishing | 1.3% | $25,000 |
| Retail sales | 2.7% | $24,000 |
| Transportation | 1.3% | $32,100 |
| Utility: communication | 3.3% | $29,100 |
| Utility: water/power/gas | 5.3% | $25,900 |
| Other | 21.4% | $25,300 |

Reprinted by permission: Profile/81—International Association of Business Communicators.

average salaries according to the type of organization in which they are employed. This illustrates the widespread nature of public relations practice.

In terms of what is most helpful in getting the first job in public relations, both the PRSSA and IABC surveys agree. More than seventy percent of the practitioners responding to IABC's *Profile/81* said that internship programs were the most beneficial in helping them get their first job.[17] Table 5-9 shows that undergraduate internships were the best source for first jobs among the PRSSA graduates surveyed. Referrals by friends and personal mail campaigns were tied for second place.

## Relationships Between Corporate Departments and Counseling Firms

Even in organizations which have an exceptionally large public relations staff it may be useful to contract for the services of a counseling firm. Chester Burger has provided six reasons for hiring the services of outside consultants:

1. Management has not previously conducted a formal public relations program and lacks experience in organizing one.
2. Headquarters may be located away from New York City, the communications and financial center of the nation.
3. A wide range of up-to-date contacts is maintained by an agency.
4. An outside agency can provide services of experienced executives who would be unwilling to move to other cities or whose salaries could not be afforded by a single firm.
5. An organization with its own PR department may be in need of highly specialized services that it cannot afford on a permanent basis.
6. Crucial matters of overall outside policy dictate a need for the independent judgment of an outsider.[18]

Basically, an organization may decide to retain the services of a counseling firm because of some special needs that they cannot meet internally. The same reasons may prompt an organization to turn to external sources for management, legal, or financial counseling, or a variety of other services that may not be needed frequently enough to justify a permanent staff position.

In addition to supplementing their own talent, organizations frequently employ outside public relations consultants to provide a third-party opinion. The principal advantages of an in-house public relations staff—familiarity with issues, loyalty, team membership—may also be important drawbacks in some decision-making situations. Like all managers, public relations ex-

| **Table 5-9**<br>PRSSA Survey of Recent Graduates Sources of First Jobs, By Percentage of Respondents | **Men** | **Women** |
|---|---|---|
| Undergraduate Internship Sponsor | 22% | 22% |
| Friend's Reference | 17% | 16% |
| Personal Mail Campaign | 16% | 17% |
| Teacher's Reference | 14% | 11% |
| College Placement Office | 14% | 8% |
| Classified Advertisement | 11% | 14% |
| Employment Agency | 3% | 9% |
| "Knocking on Doors" | 3% | 3% |

"1980 Graduates: Where Did They Go? What Did They Earn?" *Public Relations Journal*, February, 1982. Reprinted with permission of the *Public Relations Journal* © 1982.

ecutives are so intimately involved in their organization that it is difficult for them to maintain an objective point of view. Public relations consultants can often bring a startlingly fresh approach to the problems and programs of an organization. Most often they are used to help in the assessment of effectiveness and planning phases of an organization's public relations function.

Although the use of public relations counseling firms is expected to continue, organizations appear to be enlarging their public relations staffs and relying more on them for the majority of the services they need. This trend is due in large part to the greater need for public relations services that has made it more economical to employ full-time specialists in a variety of areas. Also the increased need for public relations expertise in all levels of management has necessitated the internalization of many functions that were once contracted.

Public relations jobs both in organizational departments and counseling firms are concentrated in the larger cities because of access to government, media, corporate, union, and trade association headquarters. For example, more than half of the approximately 2,000 public relations counseling firms are located in New York, Los Angeles, Chicago, and Washington, D.C. However, a major trend toward the dispersal of public relations jobs throughout the country has been reported.[19]

**PROFESSIONAL ORGANIZATIONS AND LICENSURE**

The discussion of whether or not public relations can legitimately be considered a profession has been continuing for years. Essentially, those involved in the discussion agree that public relations should be considered an area of professional endeavor, but they are divided on what characteristics should be attributed to a profession. It has been suggested that a profession can be distinguished from an occupation if it imposes the following three requirements on its practitioners: membership in a professional organization, licensure, and adherence to a code of ethics.

Although only about half of all those classified as public relations workers actually belong to a professional organization, this has been the most widely accepted form of professionalization. Organizations that promote professional standards for public relations practitioners are:

Agricultural Relations Council
American Society for Hospital Public Relations Directors
Bank Marketing Association (formerly the Financial Public
   Relations Association)
Council for the Advancement and Support of Education
   (CASE)
Chemical Public Relations Association
International Association of Business Communicators
Library Public Relations Council
National Association of Government Communicators
National School Public Relations Association
Public Relations Society of America
Railroad Public Relations Association
Religious Public Relations Council

The largest of these are the Public Relations Society of America and the International Association of Business Communicators with about 10,000 members each. PRSA was founded in 1948 through the merger of the National Association of Public Relations Council and the American Council on Public Relations. In 1961 the American Public Relations Association also joined PRSA to make it one of the dominant professional organizations in the field. Both PRSA and IABC have accreditation programs for experienced practitioners who pass a comprehensive examination. These programs are the closest anyone has come to licensing procedures. Less than one-half the memberships of both associations are accredited; however, the 4,500 PRSA members who responded to Morrissey's 1978 survey ranked their desire to promote professional status for public relations third behind "association with peers" and "development of practical skills." [20] IABC members ranked accreditation fourteenth in importance out of sixteen services offered by the association.[21]

Those who argue for licensure believe that it is the only effective method of enforcing professional standards, but efforts to impose this standard have been highly controversial. Even if licensure were to be implemented, however, many practitioners would probably not be affected because they work in corporate departments. In the legal and accounting professions, many trained practitioners never sit for their bar or CPA examinations because they do not have to represent their firms in official capacities. Thus, licensing standards would probably not result in significant change.

The establishment of ethical guidelines is an obvious requirement for professionalization. One such attempt, the code of professional standards of practice that we discussed in Chapter 4, is difficult to enforce without a formal licensing procedure, and attempts to censure members who violate the PRSA code have been rare.

Some have suggested that the entire controversy over professionalization is more damaging than helpful to the field of public relations. William Agee, president of the Bendix Corporation, concluded that:

.   .   . the continued debate over whether public relations is a profession, trade, occupation, science, or art is a futile and needless exercise when public relations achievements speak so well for themselves .   .   .

If my colleagues in the business world and I did not know the value of public relations advice, we would not spend millions of dollars on corporate public relations departments and programs. Nor would public relations counsel be sought by all those needing expert communication advice.[22]

Those who agree with this point of view would urge public relations practitioners to let their skills and programs meet the kind of high standards which are expected of professionals and leave licensing legislation alone.

The practice of public relations has come a long way since its early beginnings. While the early pioneers of public relations could rely on their creativity and knowledge of communication media, today's professionals must have the broad skills to admit them to the top executive levels of modern organizations. Practitioners must help their organizations respond to the challenges of a rapidly changing environment by promoting more sophisticated decision-making practices in management. To meet these new challenges and opportunities, practitioners of the future will need all the skills of communication for which their forerunners were known, plus the knowledge and skill necessary to influence decision making in the complex organizations of today.

---

| CASE STUDY: PUBLIC RELATIONS FOR EVERYONE? | By R. Ferrell Ervin Norfolk State University, Norfolk Virginia |
| --- | --- |

---

The caller to your public relations counseling firm says that an organization he represents is having difficulties and has decided that it needs professional help to clear the air. There is nothing unusual here; most of your clients have problems and you do not really become interested until the speaker identifies himself. He is a member of the American Nazi Party.

He says "Our organization has not been receiving the type of exposure that we need or deserve. In fact, many American citizens think that the group folded with the assassination of George Lincoln Rockwell—and you know how long ago that was."

"You know," he continues, "We are not the same group we used to be. Is there anything we can do to improve our image and thus increase membership in the party?"

You realize that the speaker is asking for help and you are unsettled about accepting the client. When he asks you to work up a proposal, you stall and suggest that you will have to get back with him tomorrow after you have reviewed needs of your present clients.

Should you accept the client?

**Questions**   1. The American Nazi Party is a militaristic organization. Does it have the right to receive an open presentation to the public just as any other organization might?

2. Although each client is separated from all others, what might be the ultimate backlash to your agency or other firms should you decide to accept the Party? Be specific.

3. How important is it that you believe in the client's cause to do a good job for him?

---

**NOTES**   [1] U.S. Department of Labor, Bureau of Labor Statistics, Bulletin 1978, *Occupational Outlook Handbook*, 1980 ed., pp. 476–478.

[2] "The Corporate Image: PR to the Rescue," *Business Week*, 22 January 1979, p. 48.

[3] *Profile/81: Special Report* (San Francisco: International Association of Business Communicators, 1981,) p. 2.

[4] James A. Morrissey, "Will the Real Public Relations Professional Please Stand Up," *Public Relations Journal* (December 1978): 22.

[5] *Profile/81: Special Report,* p. 2.

[6] Frederick H. Teahan, "1980 Graduates: Where Did They Go? What Did They Earn?" *Public Relations Journal* (February 1982).

[7] Paul V. Peterson, *Today's Journalism Students: Who They Are and What They Want To Do* (Columbus, Ohio: School of Journalism, The Ohio State University, 1981), p. 3.

[8] Albert Walker, *Status and Trends in Public Relations Education in U.S. Senior Colleges and Universities 1981* (New York: Foundation for Public Relations Research and Education, 1981), p. 12.

[9] Quoted in "What is the Best Preparation for a Career in Public Relations?" *The Houston Post,* 18 April 1980, Section C, p. 7.

[10] Walker, *Status and Trends in Public Relations Education,* p. 12.

[11] U.S. Department of Labor, *Occupational Outlook Handbook,* p. 478.

[12] *Careers in Public Relations,* Public Relations Society of America, © 1979.

[13] Philip Lesly, "New Dimensions," *Public Relations Journal* (December 1979): 25.

[14] "The Corporate Image: PR to the Rescue," p. 61.

[15] Walker, *Status and Trends in Public Relations Education,* p. 12.

[16] Larry Marshall, "The New Breed of PR Executive," *Public Relations Journal* (July 1980): 9–13.

[17] *Profile/81: Special Report,* p. 13.

[18] Chester Burger, *Primer of Public Relations Counseling,* (Counselors Section of the Public Relations Society of America, 1972), p. 81.

[19] U.S. Department of Labor, *Occupational Outlook Handbook,* p. 477.

[20] Morrissey, "Real Public Relations Professional," p. 26.

[21] *Profile/81: Special Report,* p. 14.

[22] William Agee, "The Role of Public Relations," *Public Relations Journal* (September 1979): 54.

PRACTICING
PUBLIC
RELATIONS

# STRATEGIES FOR GETTING YOUR FIRST JOB IN PUBLIC RELATIONS

Even with the growing number of jobs available for people with public relations skills and knowledge, it still takes some doing to get your first job—especially the one that is right for you. As we discussed earlier in this chapter, the best sources of initial positions appear to be internships and other work experiences while in school. In addition to this, however, there are several strategies that can help you get not only your first job in public relations, but subsequent ones as well.

**SELECTING THE RIGHT EMPLOYER**  Job hunting should be organized and carefully executed to achieve the desired results. If you start in a panic to apply for any job available, you may get some kind of job. But to get the right job, you should begin your efforts with some careful research.

*Know Yourself.* Getting a job is essentially a process of selling yourself, so get to know the product. Begin by making a list of your unique qualifications. Remember that all prospective employers will be asking themselves the same question: What does this person have that my organization needs? You have to be prepared to answer that question.

Begin by gathering together all documents, transcripts, awards, current and former job descriptions, old resumés, and anything else that may apply. With this information in hand, you are ready to start your self-analysis.

Begin to write down brief descriptions of all your strengths and weaknesses. Organize these personal assets and liabilities into two lists. No item is too old, small, or insignificant to be included. Try to recall everything that may be of some help in your own analysis of the situation; even small items may trigger other more important facts. Write everything down and then begin to eliminate trivial items.

Next reflect on your past experiences at school, work, or in other organizations. Take each experience singly, answering such questions as: What were my accomplishments, achievements, or contributions? What specific responsibilities did I have? What did I learn that can be applied in other situations? It is also important to ask yourself what you disliked about your experiences. This list of negative factors can help you identify the types of jobs that you would not enjoy regardless of the salary.

Material in this section taken from Aronoff et al. *Getting Your Message Across.* St. Paul: West Publishing Company, 1981. Reproduced by permission of the publisher.

# PRACTICING PUBLIC RELATIONS

*Organize Your Selling Points.* After you have made your two lists, examine the strengths in more detail. Look for common themes or threads that seem to appear over and over. Frequently skills and knowledge can be organized into one of four categories: people, ideas, data, things. Sort out all of the experiences you have had that relate to these four and any other categories you feel are important. Once you have them distributed under these various headings, go through each list and weight each strength according to its importance. Some skills are more highly developed than others; some knowledge is more complete. This will give you two methods of comparison between your categories: quantity (number of items per list) and quality (significance of items).

A final step in deciding which strengths may be attractive to a potential employer is to review your list of weaknesses. Compare the experiences that you feel were unrewarding or negative to your categories of strengths. Don't be surprised if you find some similarities. We often develop skills and knowledge in areas that we do not particularly enjoy. Circumstances may have forced us to pursue a field in which we had little interest. Frequently we don't realize that we will not enjoy an experience until we have had it.

*Selecting the Proper Target.* The key is *research*—research about the area of the country in which you would like to work; research about the kinds of organizations that need your skills and knowledge; and research about the prospective organizations themselves. This is one of the most important and most frequently skipped phases of the job search process. It is important because research is the best way to screen and choose your new public relations career, geographical area, and employer.

The things you need to research are:

1. Your skills and knowledge.
2. Your selected geographical area.
3. The organizations for which you may wish to work.

Researching areas of the country where you do not live now may present an extra challenge. There are several helpful sources of information including the Chamber of Commerce in the area you are considering. Ask for a list of local organizations that may employ people in the job categories you have identified, as well as other information about climate and economic conditions. Several sources will be available at your local library including a yearbook of newspaper advertising compiled by *Editor and Publisher* magazine. In addition to great quantities of other information, this yearbook will provide profiles of major U.S. communities. Also, if the town you are considering has a library, you can write directly to the librarian for information you cannot obtain locally.

# PRACTICING PUBLIC RELATIONS

Next, try to find out about specific organizations in the communities you are interested in. You should answer the following questions: Which organizations are most likely to need my skills and knowledge? What problems do they face that my particular abilities could help solve? Who has the power to hire in my job classification at each of these organizations (usually not in the personnel department)? Again, your local library is a good place to start. Some helpful sources are:

1. O'Dwyer's Directory of Public Relations Firms, J. R. O'Dwyer Co., Inc., New York.
2. PR Blue Book (4th ed.) PR Publishing Co., Meriden, New Hampshire.
3. *Dun and Bradstreet Million Dollar Directory.*
4. *Dun and Bradstreet Middle Market Directory.*
5. *Standard and Poor's Register of Corporations, Directors, and Executives.*
6. *Thomas' Register of American Manufacturers.*
7. *Fortune* Magazine's "Directory of Largest Corporations."
8. *Fortune* Magazine's "Annual Directory Issue."
9. *Black Enterprise* Magazine's "The Top 100."
10. *College Placement Annual.*
11. Membership directories of professional and trade organizations.
12. Annual reports and other publications of the organizations.

Naturally, you can write or call the organization and ask for information. Thorough research on your part will assure that you will have the right questions when the time comes.

The results of this process should provide you with a specific plan of action for getting the job that is right for you. You should now be able to compile a list of jobs that use your skills and knowledge, geographical areas in which those jobs can be found and in which you would like to live, prospective employers who meet your criteria, and individuals within those organizations who have the authority to hire you.

**STRATEGIC JOB HUNTING**

Now you must develop an organized plan of attack. Organization is important. You will probably want to establish a file for each prospective employer. This will help you keep track of the jobs you are applying for and the progress you are making toward each. Every piece of correspondence should be filed along with basic information about the company and individuals who make employment decisions. Also, it is a good idea to keep a record of the following steps of Strategic Job Hunting:

*Resumé and Letter of Application.* Once the target organizations and persons have been identified, you should prepare a resumé and letter of application for each. This step is an initial screening to identify organizations that may have an interest in you. Early elimination of organizations that are

not interested will save you time, money, and frustration. We will discuss
letters and resumés later. At present it is sufficient to say that they must
be personalized and directed toward a specific job. Keep a record of when
you sent your first letter of application and resumé, as well as copies of
them. You may wish to send a follow-up later.

*Initial Interview.* In response to your letter and resumé you may receive
an invitation to be interviewed by someone in the target organization. Reply
immediately by telephone to the person who issued the invitation. When
setting the date for this initial interview, try to leave yourself enough time
to prepare and yet not appear too eager. Follow your telephone conversation with a letter of confirmation. This two-step approach allows you to
(1) make a personal contact with the interviewer before the interview and
(2) remind the interviewer of your interest just before the interview. After
the interview, jot down your impressions and other information you obtained for future reference. Always follow this initial interview with a letter
to the interviewer thanking him or her for their time and consideration.
This is a good opportunity to reinforce your expression of interest in the
job.

Of course, you may receive a rejection letter instead of an invitation for
an interview. If you do, it is usually best to take this organization out of
your file and forget it. It is not likely that they will contact you again, even
though they did promise to keep your resumé. If you do not hear anything,
a follow-up letter and another resumé will be in order after sufficient time
has passed. Use this opportunity to restate your interest in the organization.
A follow-up phone call can be substituted if you have a specific person to
contact.

*Handling Job Offers.* Handling job offers is not a problem when you know
you have already been offered the best position of all those for which you
applied. However, it is frequently impossible to know if a better offer may
result from one of your other inquiries until everyone has had an opportunity to review your qualifications. Therefore, if you receive an early job
offer that you feel may not be the best possible opportunity, it is appropriate
to request a reasonable delay before you accept. You may do this either
by letter, telephone, or both. If you do ask for more time to take care of
unfinished business and consider the offer thoroughly, be certain your
request is reasonable. An employer may be able to wait a few days or even
a week, but a longer delay would disregard his or her need to fill the position.
On the other hand, you must be careful not to accept a job you really do
not want, just because it was the first one offered to you.

When you determine which job offer you wish to accept, make your
acceptance in writing, even if you were notified and have already accepted
by telephone. If you receive other offers after you have accepted a position,

# PRACTICING
# PUBLIC
# RELATIONS

promptly respond with a letter of refusal thanking the person who made the offer for his or her consideration. If you have asked for time to consider other offers, respond to them with similar letters as soon as you have accepted a job and received confirmation of your employment in writing.

Now that we have outlined the basic job-seeking strategies, we will discuss several key elements in the process. In the remainder of this section we shall consider letters of application, resumés, and interviews.

**Application Letters**  A letter of application for a job is often the first step in the job-getting process. A good letter will not usually *get* you the job. It will get you an interview; at the interview, you must present yourself as qualified, energetic, reliable, and enthusiastic. Few companies hire without an interview.

Even so, the application letter is crucial to you. Sometimes you make a telephone call to a company you are interested in, and the personnel manager or some other official suggests that you send a resumé or data sheet. (These are sometimes called the vita, qualification sheets, or personal profiles.) You will, of course, send it in response to this invitation.

Many letters of application are *solicited.* Most solicited letters, however, are sent in response to advertisements. The United States Congress has passed laws regulating equal employment opportunity. As part of their efforts to comply, companies use advertisements much more than they used to. Although many of these ads run in newspapers and in magazines of general circulation, most run in specialized newspapers, magazines, and publications.

It is also proper for you to send letters of application that are *unsolicited.* Analyze your qualifications carefully, pick out companies or institutions that you wish to work for, and send the strongest letter you can. It is not uncommon for persons graduating from college to send twenty or twenty-five such unsolicited letters. Usually, some of these will be answered, and a chance for an interview can develop. Mass mailing of unsolicited letters, however, is expensive and takes a lot of time. It is often better to narrow your sights and write only to companies or institutions in which you have a real interest. Follow the suggestions for selecting the right employer we discussed earlier.

*In preparing a letter of application, what general rules should you follow?*

1. Present the strongest case favorable to yourself. Emphasize your strong points. In one sense, you are writing a sales letter. Do not exaggerate.
2. Remember that each time a company hires somebody, it takes a risk. Think about what the company wants and take it into account in preparing your letter. If you have done your research properly, this will be easy to do.

3. Never say critical things about other places you have worked, or other people you have worked for. Most potential employers believe that if you were unhappy elsewhere, you will be unhappy with them.

4. Do not talk about what you want in salary and benefits. Normally these subjects will come up in the interview.

5. See that your letter is perfectly prepared. A smudgy letter could ruin you. A typographical error or an incorrect spelling will be spotted at once. Use good quality bond paper. Never send a carbon or photocopy of a letter.

6. Where possible, address your letter to a person, not to "Personnel Manager" or "Vice-President" or "President."

7. Remember that there is no one format for your letter. People are different, and so are letters of application.

A few years ago, there would have been an eighth rule: send a photograph. This no longer applies. A photograph will usually identify you by race and sex (if your name has not already done so), and some employers are not comfortable receiving this information. Many do not wish to know the race of the applicants or the sex. The general rule about photographs now is to send one *if you wish.* It will do no harm. But do not be surprised if some potential employers send it back.

Most job applications are in two parts—the letter itself and an attachment or enclosure. The attachment or enclosure is the resumé/vita/data sheet/ qualification sheet/personal profile. Although all five titles are correct, we shall hereafter refer to the resumé. Both letter and resumé are important; neither should be slighted.

The letter usually should be typed. You often see letters of application that are printed, but they suggest a mass mailing, which means that they will be taken less seriously than individually typed ones.

**Resumé**    Several general statements may be made about resumés. They are a kind of tabulation of a candidate's qualifications. There are no wasted words and few personal words, because the resumé is an impersonal document. The contents are balanced on the page so that they look good. When it is necessary to carry the resumé over to a second page, a carry-over tag goes on the top of the second page. "Resumé of Elena Vastakis," or some such.

Most resumés have several parts, although the order in which they come is not fixed (except for the heading), and the exact form in which the information is placed on the page is flexible. Resumés do not all look alike. The heading, however, always comes first. It gives the name of the person applying, the address, and the telephone number, where appropriate. It may give the name of the company to which application is being made, but it may omit it if the resumé is being sent to many companies after being mass-

# PRACTICING PUBLIC RELATIONS

produced. (Resumés may be mass-produced in any attractive way, but should never be mimeographed.)

After the heading, the applicant should put the strongest part of the resumé: education, experience, personal details, activities and achievements, references (sometimes). As a general rule, personal data sections of resumés used to be considerably longer and were always placed first. However, much of this information is not important to the hiring decision for most jobs. Indeed, it is unlawful to consider several of these factors in hiring. Some personal data probably should be included, although not first, because employers will expect to read something about you as a person that will help them visualize you. What data you include depends on what you feel is most helpful to your chances of being selected. Activities and Achievements could include youth organizations, religious organizations, and others. Applicants seldom give fewer than three references, unless they give none at all and simply include the statement that references will be furnished upon request.

Remember that a resumé needs constant updating, even when you are not in the job market, so that it will be ready whenever needed. Resumés are frequently used for more than just job hunting. If you are asked to speak at a meeting, the chairperson may ask for a resumé to use in the preparation of introductory remarks. Frequently organizations ask that personal data in one form or another be submitted when a person is being considered for promotion. Perhaps most importantly, keeping an up-to-date resumé helps you maintain a healthy view of the way your career is progressing.

## Communicating in the Job Interview

As we indicated earlier, job interviews are an important part of the hiring process in American industry. Even organizations that do a poor job of interviewing seem to place a great deal of emphasis upon the process. When you are invited for an interview, remember that you are an active participant in this interaction, just as you would be in any other person-to-person encounter. Therefore, you must be prepared and willing to do your part to make the interview a success.

**Planning for the Interview.** Now that you have been invited to an interview, refer back to your files for helpful information. From the organization's file you can develop a data sheet that will help you prepare for the interview. Your research should have yielded certain information about the organization, such as: major products or services, names and facts about top executives, other locations, gross sales, assets, number of employees, market share, financial position, history, closest competitors, problems—especially those that need your public relations skills and knowledge.

This data sheet should also help you identify the gaps in your knowledge about the organization. Recognition of such gaps can help you to prepare questions that you want to ask during the interview. In addition, be sure that you have the name of the interviewer and can pronounce it. If you have any doubts, check with the secretary or receptionist before you go into the interviewer's office. (Also get the secretary's name; you may find it useful later.)

While you are preparing for the interview, refer back to your original self-analysis inventory and identify the particular strengths that you think would be appropriate for this job. You will want to think back over your educational and job experiences and single out examples of the skills and knowledge you have to offer. Organize these examples in your mind so that you can describe each and make your point—a valuable skill, etc.— quickly and effectively. These personal success stories are ammunition you can use during the interview to sell yourself.

It is also useful to attempt to predict what questions an interviewer may ask you. David Gootnick, in his book *Getting a Better Job,* lists twenty questions that are likely to come up in most interviews:

1. Tell me about yourself!
2. Why are you interested in working for this company?
3. Why do you want to leave your job?
4. Why have you chosen this particular field?
5. Why should we hire you?
6. What are your long-range goals?
7. What is your greatest strength?
8. What is your greatest weakness?
9. What is your current salary?
10. What salary do you require?
11. What do you expect to earn five years from now, ten years from now?
12. Tell me about your boss, your company.
13. In your opinion, what are the characteristics of the person filling this job?
15. What do you do in your spare time?
16. Which feature of the job interests you most?
17. Which feature of the job interests you least?
18. How do others describe you?
19. What are your plans for continued study?
20. Tell me about your schooling!

Your answers to questions like these can appear more direct and sincere if you think through them before you go to the interview.

**Strategy for the Interview.** Remember, you are not a passive object in this selection process. You must take an active role in directing and shaping the interview. Although the interviewer expects to control the interaction— you should not violate this expectation—you do have considerable latitude in your responses to his or her questions. Make the most of these oppor-

# PRACTICING
# PUBLIC
# RELATIONS

tunities to showcase your experience, education, skills, and knowledge. Most skilled interviewers will ask you broad open-ended questions that require more than a brief reply. This is done to find out what you think is important. Then the interviewer will follow up with more specific questions about areas that interest him. Use these questions to mention as many of your unique selling points as you can.

Good interviewers want you to talk more than they do; be sure you have something to say. However, you must be aware that not all interviewers are good at their job. If an interviewer does not encourage you to talk and seems to prefer to do the talking, do not get in the way. You must be prepared to take the role of active listener. Sometimes people are hired as interviewers because they enjoy talking to others and have outgoing personalities. However, if they do not understand the function of the employment interview, they may end up giving far more information than they receive.

The best way to handle such interviewers is to let them talk, even encourage them. It is not your place to teach the talkative interviewer his or her job. Even though you have prepared all of your selling points in advance, do not try to force them in when they are not wanted. Instead, be attentive, respond with positive feedback such as: "isn't that interesting," "I see your point," "please tell me more," etc. Remember that this person enjoys the sound of his or her own voice and will like you if you seem to enjoy it as well.

Have some questions ready to ask that are based on what you have heard. Questions indicate your interest and perceptiveness. You will want to make notes about some details. Take brief notes during the interview unless it bothers your interviewer. As soon as possible after the interview, write out all of the facts and impressions you have gained for future reference.

**Nonverbal Communication in the Interview.** Nonverbal cues take on great importance in an interview situation. Interviewers are usually very sensitive to these signals; so give some thought to them. Eye contact is very important to establishing a climate of trust between you and the interviewer. Be sure to look him or her in the eye when you talk. Do not stare, but indicate that you feel comfortable looking directly at the interviewer. Do not let your facial expressions give away thoughts you may not want known. If you are disappointed or even thrilled by something you hear, it may not be to your advantage to show your feelings.

Hands and legs can betray nervousness and anxiety. Control your motions at all times to give a confident impression. Avoid habitual or nervous gestures, swinging your foot, toe tapping, and other possibly irritating movements.

Dress is important in job interviews. No matter how strongly you feel that you should be hired for your talents rather than your clothes, you must consider the interviewer's initial impression. If you are in doubt, visit the interviewer's office unannounced ahead of time and observe the way people there dress, wear their hair, etc. Personal features should not get in the way of the interviewer's perception of your ability.

Getting the first public relations job is a matter of careful planning and preparation. There are no magical tricks or easy formulas, but if you are willing to follow the suggestions presented here, you will be well on your way to finding the job that is right for you.

Press kit for the Prairie Home Companion courtesy of the American Public Radio Network.

# SECTION II PUBLIC RELATIONS: THE PROCESS

Now that we know what public relations is and what purposes it serves, we will consider the process by which public relations is practiced. As we have already discussed, public relations is a process that goes far beyond the task of producing messages. An effective organizational image is the result of mutual understanding between an organization and its publics. The development of this understanding can be regarded as a four-step process:

1. *Understanding Public Opinion.* An initial fact-finding stage to define the problem areas and differentiate between publics.
2. *Planning for Effectiveness.* Once the facts have been gathered from the various publics, decisions have to be made regarding their importance and potential impact on the organization. Then strategies must be developed that will allow the organization to achieve its goals.
3. *Building Messages.* Plans are then translated into communication strategies and messages are constructed to meet these specifications.
4. *Evaluating Effectiveness.* Once a public relations campaign has been developed and implemented, it should be followed with an evaluation of its effectiveness in meeting the criteria that were set. The results of this step must then be channeled back into the initial fact-finding step for the next campaign.

These four steps are essential to any effective public relations campaign. They are not, however, four independent functions. Rather each step overlaps the others in such a way that if any one of them is neglected the entire process will be affected. Figure 6-1 illustrates the interdependence of the three functions that are necessary to this four-step process. Research is both the start and finish of an effective public relations campaign. The *research process* provides the facts about the organization and its publics that are necessary to plan an effective campaign. The *planning process* transforms the raw data of research into specific strategies for developing an effective public image. These strategies are then implemented through the *communication process* by the development of messages for the various publics involved. Finally, the *research process* once again takes over by evaluating the effectiveness of the campaign and providing new facts that can be used in planning the next campaign.

# CHAPTER 6  UNDERSTANDING PUBLIC OPINION

**PREVIEW**     Research is an important part of the public relations process. Information gained through careful research can be used to guide planning, pre-test messages, evaluate results, and guide follow-up efforts.

The use of research data to forecast future events and evaluate current practice is well accepted in most organizations today. Public relations practitioners must be able to evaluate their efforts and demonstrate effectiveness.

Good public opinion research must be sensitive enough to identify publics as definable groups rather than unrelated masses.

Public relations audits, social audits, communications audits, and environmental monitoring are effective research methods for public relations planning and evaluation.

**Mini Case 6-1**
**The Need to**
**Understand Public**
**Opinion**

Management at the Research and Development Division of a major oil company began to receive numerous complaints about the quality of food and service in the cafeteria. These, along with a statement from the union stewards' committee describing the need for a shorter working day, led the site manager, a noted scientist, to issue the following directive to all employees:

> Beginning March 22 the following changes become effective:
> 1) Regular work hours for all employees will be 7:30 a.m. to 4:00 p.m. This is the overwhelming recommendation of the majority of our employees.
> 2) The lunch period will be one-half hour compared to the current one hour.
> The cafeteria has been newly remodeled and will be open from 11:00 a.m. until 1:00 p.m. Each employee should select a 30-minute lunch period between 11:00 a.m. and 12:30 p.m. to accommodate these hours. Because of the increased traffic this new schedule will cause in the cafeteria, you must show your I.D. badge to enter. No outside personnel will be served.

Instead of the favorable response the plant manager had expected, the new policy provoked further complaints. The manager, perplexed, called in various management personnel, all of whom assured him that they had heard employees asking for shorter hours and improved cafeteria service. Finally he asked the public relations manager, "What went wrong, why are the employees complaining about the new working hours and cafeteria policies when I gave them what they asked for?"

The public relations manager responded with a series of questions about the opinions of this important public:

What percentage of the total group wanted shorter working hours?
What did they mean by shorter hours?

Did they prefer earlier or later hours?
Did they want shorter hours strongly enough to give up half
  of their lunch hour?
Did the new cafeteria policies correct the problems about
  which employees complained?

---

Of course, the answer to each of the above questions was that no one really knew. The site manager thought he had acted in response to the desires and needs of the employee public, but no one stopped to ask the public relations manager's questions before action was taken. As a result, the strength and quantity of opinions about working hours and the cafeteria were unknown. A little research concerning the opinions of this very important public could have saved management a great deal of wasted effort.

**THE NEED FOR RESEARCH IN PUBLIC RELATIONS**

As we noted at the beginning of Section II, research is a vitally important function in the process of public relations, in that it provides the initial information necessary to plan a campaign and performs the important role of evaluating the campaign's effectiveness (*Figure 6-1*). It is no longer possible for public relations practitioners to rely on their hunches and past experience to tell them what communication messages and strategies will be most effective. Management demands hard facts, not intuition or guesswork. Public relations practitioners, like all their colleagues in every area of management, must be able to demonstrate convincingly their contribution to the goals and objectives of the organizations in which they work. The economic realities of modern organizations have made it necessary for public relations to incorporate data-gathering techniques into every phase of the process.

Because public relations professionals have traditionally been doers rather than researchers, they too often assume others see the value of their actions. Therefore, their programs are often thought of as expendable and have always been among the first to go when budgets became tight. Even when economic conditions are not critical, public relations is often perceived as "window dressing." Media, regulatory agencies, consumer groups, and many managers doubt that public relations has a useful purpose in American business. Typically, public relations professionals have responded with the claim that they contribute to a process of better understanding between publics and organizations.

Practitioners must be able to speak with authority when asked to prove their value to business and society. This authority can only come through an ability to conduct research and apply those results to public relations campaigns. The public relations professional, to survive in today's corporate environment, must be able to do more than maintain good media relations, produce employee publications, release financial information, and conduct community relations programs. Those who succeed must also be able to measure the effects of their programs and provide sound forecasts of future needs. Even those who hire others to do their research must be able to understand and evaluate the process in order to know what they need.

**Figure 6-1**
Interdependent
Functions of the Public
Relations Process

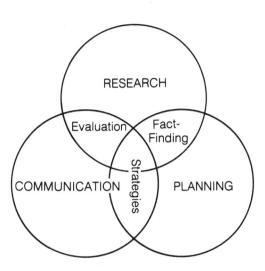

## THE MEASUREMENT OF PUBLIC OPINION

### Opinion Sampling

Most organizational goals and objectives dealing with public relations depend to some extent upon the concept of public opinion. Therefore, the first step in public relations research is *sampling public opinion*. It is important to understand at the outset that an organization does not have a single undistinguishable public. The public relations practitioner who relies on so-called public-opinion polls to provide insight into the characteristics of his or her potential audience may be operating with erroneous data. Most polls of this type are not very useful from a public relations point of view, because they actually measure mass opinion rather than public opinion. The difference is that public opinion involves carefully targeted populations.

Mass opinion represents an average taken from a group with heterogeneous opinions. Averages tend to blur the strength of some attitudes, however. When opinions that are substantially different are averaged together the result may be very different from the actual opinions of the people you are trying to find out about. For example, if we conduct a poll asking people about the image of a particular organization we might find that sixty percent of our sample gave them very high marks and forty percent felt very negative about the organization. Looking at these responses all together, we might deduce that the organization in question had a moderately positive image. While this might cause them to seek ways to make their image more positive, it would hide some crucial facts.

Our survey has actually uncovered *two publics*—one that has a very positive image of the organization and another that has a very negative image. In fact, no one in our sample held the moderately positive view of the organization that the poll suggested. Therefore, instead of planning a public relations campaign directed toward people who hold a somewhat favorable opinion of the organization, we should be constructing communication strategies for two groups of people with very strong, but opposite, opinions. As in our opening example, public relations must be concerned with the strength as well as the direction of public attitudes. The employees mentioned may have wanted shorter working hours, but they also wanted a full hour for lunch, and the latter attitude prove to be the stronger.

While the measurement of public opinion is critical to the practice of public relations, many mass opinion polls are useful for little more than predicting voting in political contests. They shed little light on the complexities of public opinion that an effective public relations program must address. The public relations professional must break the audience down into meaningful subgroups and design a specific communication campaign for each segment. Public opinion sampling is not useful unless it reflects accurately the feelings of each significant audience group and provides some insight into why these opinions are held.

**Publics**  John Dewey in his 1927 book *The Public and Its Problems* defines a public as a group of people who:

1. face a similar indeterminate situation
2. recognize what is indeterminate in that situation
3. organize to do something about the problem[1]

A public, then, is a group of people who share a common problem or goal and recognize their common interest. In the remainder of this chapter we will discuss specific methods for measuring public opinion more effectively for public relations applications.

Traditional public-opinion polling methods typically break their results down into demographic categories that seldom identify groups of people with common interests. Because of this inadequacy, James Grunig has proposed and tested three categories for the identification of publics based on Dewey's definition:

*Latent Public.* A group faces an indeterminate situation
   but does not recognize the situation as problematic.
*Aware Public.* The group recognizes a problem—what is
   missing in the situation—and the latent public becomes
   aware.
*Active Public.* The group organizes to discuss and to do
   something about the situation.[2]

Such categories group together people who are likely to behave in similar ways. This makes it possible for public relations practitioners to communicate with each group regarding their needs and concerns rather than attempting to communicate with some mythical "average" public. Researching public opinion in appropriate categories can help direct the public relations process. For example, it may be possible to classify the primary audience for a public relations campaign in one of the three categories listed above and develop specific messages for them.

## USES OF RESEARCH IN PUBLIC RELATIONS

A recent study funded by the Foundation for Public Relations Research and Education concluded that "the use of public relations research by corporations is on the rise and its function and contribution are becoming better defined and recognized."[3] The study points out that the term public relations research is descriptive no longer of specific types of research methodology such as content analysis, public opinion polls, or readership surveys. Instead the term as it is now being employed in the twenty-eight public- and private-sector organizations surveyed refers to any type of research that may yield data that can be used in planning and evaluating communication efforts. Four basic categories of research activities in public relations were found to be most common: environmental monitoring, public relations audits, communications audits, and social audits. These four categories may incorporate any or all of the methodologies mentioned above to furnish public relations practitioners with information that is useful in every phase of the public relations task. Table 6-1 illustrates the areas of public relations practice for which these categories of research provide useful information.

### Environmental Monitoring

Results of the survey by the Foundation for Public Relations Research and Education revealed environmental monitoring to be the fastest growing category of public relations research.[4] Because organizations today recognize themselves to be dynamic open systems that must react to changes in their environment, keeping track of the changes that are taking place around them is important.

These formal systems for observing trends and changes in public opinion and other areas of the environment can be used to guide many phases of organizational planning including public relations.

Liam Fahey and W. R. King have described three basic scanning models employed by various organizations to keep track of environmental changes.

---

**Table 6-1**
Categories of Public
Relations Research

| External Environment | Organization | Publics | Message | Media | Effects |
|---|---|---|---|---|---|
| I. ENVIRONMENTAL MONITORING | | | | | |
| | II. PUBLIC RELATIONS AUDIT | | | | |
| | A. Audience Identification | | | | |
| | B. Corporate Image | | | | |
| | III. COMMUNICATIONS AUDIT | | | | |
| | | 1. Readership Survey | | | |
| | | | 2. Content Analysis | | |
| | | | 3. Readability Survey | | |
| IV. SOCIAL AUDITS | | | | | |

Otto Lerbinger, "Corporate Use of Public Relations Research," *Public Relations Review* 3 (Winter 1977). 13.

Table 6-2 lists some of the characteristics of each of the three models. These techniques of environmental scanning can be described as follows:[5]

**The Irregular Model.** This form of environmental study is an ad hoc approach. Generally this type of study is precipitated by a crisis situation such as the introduction of a significant new product by a competitor or an oil embargo. Once the unanticipated event occurs, the scanning process begins with its focus on past events that may help to explain what has happened. The model is useful for identifying immediate reactions to problem situations and can provide input for short-range planning. However, it does not provide input which would help to identify crises before they occur or form long-range plans for future occurrences.

**The Regular Model.** More comprehensive and systematic than the first model, the regular model generally employs an annual appraisal of environmental situations. Typically the focus is on specific issues or decisions facing the organization. For example, automobile companies use this model when they conduct annual research on consumer attitudes about auto safety and economy to help them develop advertising appeals for the models they have already designed for the next year. Obviously the regular model is still retrospective because attention is directed to the recent past and the current situation to develop limited plans for the near future. However, this approach is an improvement over the irregular model in that current issues and de-

**Table 6-2**
**Scanning Model Framework**

**Scanning Models**

|                                    | Irregular                        | Regular                                | Continuous                                            |
| ---------------------------------- | -------------------------------- | -------------------------------------- | ----------------------------------------------------- |
| Media for scanning activity        | Ad hoc studies                   | Periodically updated studies           | Structured data collection and processing systems     |
| Scope of scanning                  | Specific events                  | Selected events                        | Broad range of environmental systems                  |
| Motivation for activity            | Crisis initiated                 | Decision and issue oriented            | Planning process oriented                             |
| Temporal nature of activity        | Reactive                         | Proactive                              | Proactive                                             |
| Time frame for data                | Restrospective                   | Primarily current and retrospective    | Prospective                                           |
| Time frame for decision impact     | Current and near-term future     | Near-term                              | Long-term                                             |
| Organizational makeup              | Various staff agencies           | Various staff agencies                 | Environmental scanning unit                           |

cisions are examined in reference to the environment and predictions about future impacts on these issues and decisions are made. Basically the difference between the regular and irregular models is a matter of degree and regularity.

**The Continuous Model.** This third model emphasizes the continuous monitoring of a variety of environmental elements rather than being limited to specific issues and decisions. Any number of environmental segments may have input into this model including political, regulatory, and competitive systems. Auto companies that conduct consumer research to analyze preference trends among different market segments are using continuous environmental scanning when the data collected becomes input for future automotive designs. The nature of continuous scanning requires that the system be designed into the organization. Irregular and to some extent regular scanning methods can be managed by the particular division or department involved. However, an agency such as the public relations department or some subunit is needed to function as a clearinghouse for environmental data that may be appropriate for several divisions or departments of the organization. In addition computerized management information systems (MIS) are generally needed to store, evaluate and integrate the vast amounts of information generated.

The continuous scanning model provides support for the strategic planning efforts of organizations. Other models provide data to support specific issues or decisions. But, the continuous model provides data support for a variety of issues and decisions that an organization may face. For example, the American Council of Life Insurance has developed a Trend Analysis Program (TAP). TAP "seeks to identify the direction of major social and economic trends so that companies may plan for the years ahead with greater confidence."[6] The program operates as a cooperative effort with over 100 life insurance executives involved in the process of monitoring the speciality press and other publications where evidence of emerging social and economics trends may first appear. Reports are issued whenever the data in a particular area are sufficient. For example, one report issued by TAP provided an in-depth survey of possible changes in American culture for the coming years.

**The Public Relations Audit**

The most frequently used type of public relations research is the audit. The public relations audit is essentially a broad-scale study that examines the internal and external public relations of an organization. Its purpose is to provide information for planning future public relations efforts. Carl Byoir and Associates, one of the pioneers of public relations auditing, describe it as follows: "The Public Relations Audit, as the name implies, involves a comprehensive study of the public relations position of an organization: how it stands in the opinion of its various 'publics' . . . ."[7]"

The survey of public relations research practices sponsored by the Foundation for Public Relations Research and Education lists four basic elements of a comprehensive audit:

**Relevant Publics.** A list of the organization's relevant publics is made describing each according to its function—stockholders, employees, customers, suppliers, and the like. It may also include publics with no direct functional relationship which may nevertheless be in a position to affect the organization—consumer, environmental, community, and other social action groups. The procedure is basically one of audience identification to aid in the planning of public relations messages. Some audits stop at this step.

**Organization's Standing with Publics.** Each public's view of the organization is determined through various research methods, such as image studies and content analysis of newspapers, magazines, and other print media. Both of these research methods are discussed later in this chapter. Most public relations audits incorporate these first two elements. Because of the increase in public-affairs concerns brought on by social action groups and governmental regulation, two additional elements are becoming common to public relations audits.

**Issues of Concern to Publics.** Environmental monitoring is used to construct an issue agenda for each of the organization's relevant publics. These data help identify publics according to issues of interest and their stand on those issues, so that these can be compared to the organization's own policies. This becomes a vital step in planning public relations campaigns for various audiences.

**Power of Publics.** Publics are rated according to the amount of economic and political (and therefore regulatory) influence they have. Interest groups and other activist organizations are evaluated by size of membership, size of their constituency, budget size and source of income, and staff size and number and qualifications of specialists (lobbyist, attorneys, public relations professionals, etc.).

Public relations audits are becoming regular components of many public relations programs. They provide input data for planning future public relations programs and help to evaluate the effectiveness of previous efforts. Several public relations counseling firms offer audit services to their clients. Joyce F. Jones of the Ruder and Finn agency describes the audit process in four steps:[8]

1. *Finding out what "we" think.* Interviews with key management at the top and middle strata of an organization to determine: company strengths and weaknesses, relevant publics, issues and topics to be explored.
2. *Finding out what "they" think.* Researching key publics to determine how closely their views match those of company management.
3. *Evaluating the disparity.* A public relations balance sheet of assets, liabilities, strengths, weaknesses, etc. is prepared based on an analysis of the differences found between steps 1 and 2.
4. *Recommending.* A comprehensive public relations program is planned to fill in the gap between steps 1 and 2 and correct deficits of the balance sheet prepared in step 3.

**Organizational Image Surveys**

Attitude surveys that determine the perceptions publics have about an organizational entity help public relations managers obtain an overall view of its image. Generally such research seeks to measure: 1) How familiar the public is with the organization, its officers, products, policies, and other facets of the corporation; 2) degrees of positive and negative perceptions; and 3) the characteristics various publics attribute to the organization. Frequently organizations use image surveys as planning tools to compare existing images with desired images. Once the differences are assessed, image goals can be set and strategic plans can be made to overcome problems that have been identified.

Although several organizations conduct their own image studies, many employ outside consultants or research organizations to supply them with data. Some of the major organizations that provide this type of data are Opinion Research Corporation, Roper Public Opinion Research Center, Inc., Louis Harris and Associates, and Yankolovich, Skelly and White.[9]

**Communication Audit**

The communication audit procedure, like the public relations audit, is applied in many different ways. Generally it is an attempt to monitor and evaluate the channels, messages, and communication climate of an organization. Sometimes audits are applied only to internal organizational communication systems; the same technique, however, can be used to evaluate external systems as well. Frequently the results of a communication audit will reveal problems such as executive isolation, filtering of upward communication, dysfunctional gatekeeping, and groups or individuals who are isolated from communication.

The research methods listed below are used in appropriate combination to audit organizational communication.

1. *Communication Climate Surveys.* These attitudinal measurements are designed to reveal how open and adequate publics perceive the communication channels to be.
2. *Network Analysis.* Generally done with the aid of a computer, this research method observes the frequency and importance of interactions within an organization, and maps out an interaction network based on the most frequent linkages. These patterns can be compared to official organizational charts and communication policies to determine disparities between theory and practice.
3. *Readership Surveys.* These identify which articles or sections of publications are read most frequently. While this method is strictly quantitative, it is an excellent method for determining the reading patterns of various publics.
4. *Content Analysis.* This quantitative tool measures the content of messages of any type. Content analysis plots the frequency with which selected topics appear in selected messages. This technique is frequently used to describe the amount of favorable and unfavorable news coverage an organization receives.
5. *Readability Studies.* There are several methods employed to assess how readily written messages can be understood. Most of these methods are

based on the number of syllables contained in the words and the length of the sentences used in the message. These formulas will be discussed in more detail in Chapter 9, when we discuss evaluation techniques. For now we shall only note that they can help determine the clarity of a written message and the appropriateness of the message for the educational level of its audience.

A complete audit of all organizational communication systems applies each of these research methods to both internal and external publics to assess the entire communication function. Various combinations of these methods may be used to investigate specific problem areas.

**Social Audits**  The concept of organizations performing audits of their social activities was first proposed by Howard R. Bowen about thirty years ago:

**Just as businesses subject themselves to audits of their accounts by independent public accountant firms, they might also subject themselves to periodic examination by independent outside experts who would evaluate the performance of the business from the social point of view.[10]**

The idea, however, lay dormant until the late 1960s, when pressure for corporations to be socially responsible reached a peak. There have been numerous calls for organizations to be required to prepare social audits for public distribution. Although some forms of social audits are required by certain government agencies, most remain voluntary.

At present, federal regulations only call for partial or limited audits specific to a particular industry and the agency to which the report is sent. The Federal Drug Administration and Federal Trade Commission require companies to report on certain characteristics of products, such as flammability of textiles and side effects of drugs. The Environmental Protection Agency requires that organizations report their compliance with pollution-control standards. The Occupational Health and Safety Administration requires periodic reports regarding working conditions for employees, and the Equal Employment Opportunity Commission requires the submission of information about affirmative-action employment procedures.

Although no agency requires a comprehensive report covering all these areas, many organizations have found it beneficial from a public relations and planning point of view to conduct major audits in these areas and in many other non-regulated areas of social action. These comprehensive social audits seek to determine the effects an organization has on its publics. The question of how to measure best an organization's social performance is still unsettled. Some audits amount to little more than a catalog of the social action programs an organization has sponsored or participated in over a period of time. Most go a step further and attempt to evaluate the effectiveness of these programs, and some make recommendations regarding future activities. Only a few, however, have actually adopted Bowen's proposal of public disclosure of an evaluation by an objective third party.

In a report published by the Committee for Economic Development, Corson and Steiner recommended a five-step model for social auditing (*Table*

6-3).[11] Frequently, attitudinal measurements are used to quantify the response of an organization's publics to various dimensions of its operation. Robert Hay in a report of a social audit of the Sanitation Department of the City of Fayetteville, Arkansas concluded:

**We have examined how well the Sanitation Department of the City of Fayetteville has satisfied the objectives of its customers, creditors, community, government, management, employees, suppliers, and society in general. Our examination was made using internal and external sources of information. We used different methodologies in determining how well the Sanitation Department satisfied the needs of its various contributors.**

**In our opinion the accompanying charts present fairly the degree of the social responsibility of the Sanitation Department of the City of Fayetteville in discharging its obligations to its contributors and to society in general. The charts present the strengths and weaknesses of the Department in improving the quality of life of the members of society with whom it comes in contact.[12]**

Figure 6-2 presents a graphic summary of the evaluation of the department by its various publics regarding its social responsibility. Figure 6-3 presents

**Table 6-3**
**A Model for Social Auditing/Reporting**

| | |
|---|---|
| 1. An enumeration of social expectations and the corporation's response | A summary and candid enumeration, by program areas (e.g., consumer affairs, employee relations, physical environment, local community development), of what is expected and the corporation's reasoning as to why it has undertaken certain activities and not others. |
| 2. A statement of the corporate social objectives and the priorities attached to specific activities | For each program area the corporation would report what it will strive to accomplish and what priority it places on various activities. |
| 3. A description of the corporation's goals in each program area and of the activities it will carry on | For each priority activity, the corporation will state a specific goal (in quantitative terms when possible) and describe how it is striving to reach that goal (e.g., to better educational facilities in the community, it will make available qualified teachers from among members of its staff). |
| 4. Statement indicating the resources committed to achieve objectives and goals | A summary report, in quantitative terms, by program area and activity of the costs, direct and indirect, assumed by the corporation. |
| 5. A statement of the accomplishments and/or progress made in achieving each objective and each goal | A summary, describing in quantitative measures when feasible and through objective, narrative statement when quantification is impracticable, the extent of achievement of each objective and each goal. |

John J. Corson and George A. Steiner, *Measuring Business Social Performance: The Corporate Social Audit.* New York: Committee for Economic Development, 1974. Reprinted by permission.

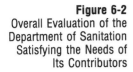

**Figure 6-2**
Overall Evaluation of the
Department of Sanitation
Satisfying the Needs of
Its Contributors

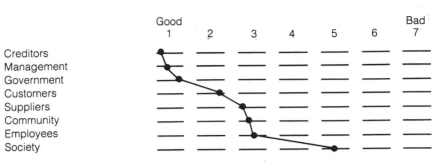

Overall average 2.85

Robert D. Hay, "Social Auditing: An Experimental Approach," *Academy of Management Journal*
December 1975, pp. 873-874. Reprinted by permission.

**Figure 6-3**
Overall Evaluation of the
Department of Sanitation
Satisfying the Needs of:

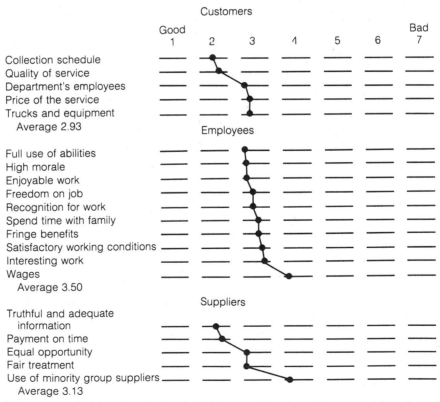

Robert D. Hay, "Social Auditing: An Experimental Approach," *Academy of Management Journal*
December 1975, pp. 873–874. Reprinted by permission.

some of the individual categories on which the various publics were asked to evaluate the sanitation department. Public relations practitioners, along with accountants, economists, and social scientists, are helping to develop more comprehensive and accurate social audit procedures. The public-relations management of an organization is particularly involved in decisions regarding which publics should be included and how the audit report should be distributed. Audit results can be particularly important for long-range corporate planning. The expertise of public relations management is needed in the interpretation of these data and in the planning of future social action programs designed to meet any deficiencies discovered.

Research is an important part of any public relations effort. It provides the initial inputs to guide strategy and message development and provides a method for predicting effectiveness and assessing the results. Public relations professionals must be able to measure the effects of their work and make reasonable predictions about future success to influence managerial decisions in most organizations today.

Many public-opinion surveys may not be useful in public relations planning and evaluation because they tend to average responses to the point that the relative strengths of attitudes present are disguised. Good public-opinion research must be sensitive enough to segment publics according to the strength of their opinions. Four basic categories of research in public relations appear to be sufficiently sensitive: environmental monitoring, public relations audits, communications audits, and social audits.

| CASE STUDY: DESIGNING THE STUDENT UNION | By Jim VanLeuven Associate Professor of Communications, Washington State University, Pullman, Washington |
|---|---|

Before hiring an architect to design a new student union building, University of Idaho student leaders commissioned an attitude study of student leisure interests. The student leaders wanted to know which kinds of students used which kinds of facilities. Study the following data and then answer the questions.

**SAMPLING METHODOLOGY**

384 students were selected from a student body of 7,000 by taking every 17th name in the student directory. Each respondent was asked to complete a four-page mail questionnaire that utilized several question formats. Some 225 students, or roughly 60%, completed the procedure.

|  | Respondents | Actual Student Body |
|---|---|---|
| Year in school: |  |  |
| Freshman | 21.9 | 21.3 |
| Sophomore | 18.3 | 19.0 |
| Junior | 21.0 | 20.2 |
| Senior | 17.9 | 18.6 |
| Graduate/Law | 20.9 | 20.9 |

Residence:
|  |  |  |
|---|---|---|
| Fraternity | 12.1 | 12.0 |
| Men's hall | 22.9 | 20.6 |
| Sorority | 4.0 | 5.2 |
| Women's hall | 5.4 | 8.2 |
| UI married housing | 1.3 | 1.4 |
| Off-campus | 54.3 | 52.6 |

Sex:
|  |  |  |
|---|---|---|
| Male | 68.4 | 59.2 |
| Female | 31.6 | 40.8 |

| Participation in Activities | Involved: 4/more hrs/wk | Slightly Involved: Up to 4 hrs/wk | Not Involved: No time | Groups Most Involved |
|---|---|---|---|---|
| ASUI committees | 0.9 | 1.4 | 97.7 | f,s,m,2,3 |
| ASUI senate | 0.0 | 0.9 | 99.1 | f,m,s,3,4 |
| ASUI communications (Arg, KUOI, etc.) | 2.3 | 3.7 | 94.0 | m,w,2,3,4 |
| Other ASUI activity | 1.5 | 2.0 | 96.5 | f,s,2,3 |
| Living group officer | 6.9 | 7.8 | 85.3 | f,s,m,w,3 |
| Living group social activity | 17.9 | 25.5 | 56.5 | f,s,w,1,2,3 |
| Living group recreation activity | 11.8 | 28.4 | 59.7 | f,s,w,m,1,2 |
| Visiting with members of living group | 31.4 | 17.6 | 51.0 | f,s,1,2,3,4 |
| Live off-campus, still take part liv. gr. | 3.3 | 10.6 | 86.1 | f,1,2,3,4,5 |
| Campus religious organization | 5.2 | 10.0 | 84.8 | s,w,m,1,2 |
| Religious study group | 5.7 | 12.7 | 87.3 | s,w,m,1,2,3 |
| Campus/community craft groups | 0.5 | 3.8 | 95.8 | o,4,5 |
| Music performance group | 3.8 | 2.3 | 93.9 | m,w,1,2,3 |
| International student organization | 0.0 | 2.5 | 97.5 | m,3,4,5 |
| Other cultural group | 11.4 | 8.9 | 79.7 | m,w,o,3,4 |
| Hunting and fishing | 23.0 | 35.7 | 41.3 | m,f,0,3,4,5 |
| Camping and backpacking | 19.3 | 41.5 | 39.2 | m,o,3,4,5 |
| Campus intramural sports | 16.2 | 25.0 | 58.8 | f,m,s,w,1,2 |
| Swimming and water sports | 7.3 | 38.0 | 54.6 | w,o,3,4,5 |
| Golf and tennis | 8.7 | 33.0 | 58.3 | f,0,2,3,4,5 |
| Handball and gym sports | 13.6 | 28.8 | 57.6 | m,o,4,5 |
| Bowling | 4.1 | 19.8 | 76.1 | m,w,1,2 |
| Skiing | 19.5 | 30.2 | 50.3 | f,s,o,1,2,3 |
| Other sports | 31.5 | 24.3 | 44.1 |  |
| Television viewing | 30.7 | 42.7 | 26.6 | u,m,w,o, 1,2,3,4 |
| Movies and films | 8.9 | 59.8 | 31.3 | u,f,m,s,w,o, 1,2,3 |
| Bowling and billiards | 8.1 | 29.9 | 62.0 | m,1 |
| Visiting over coffee or soft drinks | 37.7 | 47.0 | 15.3 | f,s,w,1,2,3 |

| | | | | |
|---|---|---|---|---|
| Service clubs and organizations | 3.5 | 12.4 | 84.2 | f,s,o,2,3,4 |
| Honoraries, clubs in my major | 7.2 | 22.5 | 70.3 | u,o,4,5 |
| Political organizations | 0.0 | 8.0 | 92.0 | f,m,w,1,2,3 |
| Other organizations | 21.4 | 14.3 | 64.3 | m,o,3,4 |

| Participation key: | 1 = freshman | 4 = senior | m = men's hall | u = UI married student |
|---|---|---|---|---|
| | 2 = sophomore | 5 = graduate law | s = sorority | housing |
| | 3 = junior | f = fraternity | w = women's hall | o = off-campus |

**Questions**

1. In which eight activities are nearly half or more than half of the respondents involved?

2. How representative are the respondents of the total campus population?

3. If this were your survey, would you feel comfortable suggesting to the management that they act on these findings?

4. In general, what is the relationship between a student's year in school, his or her living arrangement, and participation in student activities?

**NOTES**

[1] John Dewey, *The Public and Its Problems* (Chicago: Swallow, 1927).

[2] James E. Grunig, "A New Measure of Public Opinions on Corporate Social Responsibility," *Academy of Management Journal* 22 (December 1979): 740–41.

[3] Otto Lerbinger, "Corporate Use of Research in Public Relations," *Public Relations Review* 3 (Winter 1977): 11.

[4] Ibid., p. 12.

[5] Liam Fahey and William R. King, "Environmental Scanning for Corporate Planning," *Business Horizons* 20 (August 1977).

[6] Lerbinger, "Corporate Use of Research," p. 15.

[7] Ibid., p. 16.

[8] Joyce F. Jones, "The Public Relations Audit: Its Purpose and Uses," *R & F Papers, Number 3* [New York: Ruder and Finn, Inc., 1975, reprinted in *Public Relations Journal* 31 (July 1975): 6–8].

[9] Lerbinger, "Corporate Use of Research," p. 12.

[10] Howard R. Bowen, *Social Responsibilities of the Businessman* (New York: Harper and Brothers, 1953), p. 155.

[11] John J. Corson and George A. Steiner, *Measuring Business Social Performance: The Corporate Social Audit* (New York: Committee on Economic Development, 1974).

[12] Robert D. Hay, "Social Auditing: An Experimental Approach," *Academy of Management Journal* (December 1975): 872.

PRACTICING
PUBLIC
RELATIONS

# FORMAL AND INFORMAL
# TECHNIQUES OF RESEARCH

The term *research* has come to mean the collection of information directly
from primary sources, for example, subjects in a survey. But research is
not always elaborate or highly structured. We want to begin this section
by considering a few informal research methods that practitioners should
always have available.

**PERSONAL AND
ORGANIZATIONAL
SOURCES OF
INFORMATION**
One of the most important skills necessary to the successful practice of
public relations is the ability to keep comprehensive and accurate records.
Practitioners are frequently asked to produce critical information at a moment's notice for use inside and outside their organizations. Thus when an
editor or a manager calls for information, the public relations practitioners
must be able to produce the needed data within a relatively short time
span or suffer some loss of credibility. By earning a reputation as a source
of valuable information, the public relations practitioner can develop a
network of internal and external information contacts.

**Committees**
To help obtain the information necessary to function as a public relations
professional, many practitioners organize special committees. Internal and
external committees of key communicators, decision makers, and opinion
leaders can help identify issues before they become problems. Some practitioners find the screening of printed material helpful. Monitoring news
reports in both print and broadcast media should be done in a systematic
way that will allow consideration of the quality as well as quantity of
coverage. Carefully watching the incoming mail, telephone calls, and salespeople's reports can also provide valuable information. Like all information
collected through informal research methods, however, these techniques
have built-in biases because the data are not collected from representative
samples of the target publics.

**Photo and Future
Files**
Photo files and future files can also help to accumulate information that
may be useful in future public relations efforts. Photos of major executives
and others who may frequently be the subject of news releases and media
inquiries should be kept up-to-date. Photos of products, buildings, equipment, and a variety of other things can also be helpful. Quarterly and annual
reports, both for your organization and its competitors, can be important
sources of information for future use. Newspapers and magazine articles
can provide background information for future releases and speeches that
a practitioner may write. In addition, all types of brochures and other
publications that provide good ideas for layout, design, and typography
should be filed. Besides these types of information, a public relations prac-

titioner should be able to locate key people when they are needed; therefore, a number of directories for you own organization, media, government
offices, community organizations, etc., should be kept up-to-date.

**LIBRARY SOURCES
OF INFORMATION**

Libraries are important and convenient sources of all types of information.
Public and private libraries can be sources of data that it would be impossible for the practitioner to collect personally. Reference libraries can be
helpful in finding sources for your information needs and many libraries
now subscribe to computerized data retrieval networks that can obtain
information from anywhere in the world. Census data and other types of
public information are available at libraries that have been designated as
government depositories. In addition, a number of independent research
organizations, such as the Survey Research Center at the University of
Michigan, publish information that may be valuable to the public relations
practitioner.

Besides the media guides, trade and professional journals, and reference
books which you may keep as a personal library there are some further
sources that should be noted. The following list can be useful in researching
a future employer or a competing organization:

Dun and Bradstreet Million Dollar Directory
Dun and Bradstreet Middle Market Directory
Standard and Poors Register of Corporations, Directors,
    and Executives
Thomas' Register of American Manufacturers
Fortune Magazine's "Directory of Largest Corporation"
Fortune Magazine's "Annual Directory Issue"
Black Enterprise Magazine's "The Top 100"

As you read the next section on formal or primary research, keep in mind
that secondary sources such as those discussed here should be exhausted
before a primary research effort is planned. A good review of information
available should precede every major research effort to be certain that the
questions asked have not already been answered by others. Secondary research can also be valuable in the identification and definition of topics for
primary research.

**FORMAL RESEARCH
IN PUBLIC
RELATIONS**

**Survey Research**

While the practice of public relations in one way or another employs all
types of research processes, the survey method is the most common. Laboratory and field experiments as well as various types of simulations can
have a place (such as pretesting a message) in a public relations research
effort. However, surveys are the most effective method for assessing the

# PRACTICING
# PUBLIC
# RELATIONS

characteristics of publics in a form that will allow the data to be used in planning and evaluating public relations efforts. Before using a survey, the practitioner should be aware of the difference between measuring mass opinion and public opinion described earlier in this chapter. Surveys should provide a means of differentiating between publics rather than lumping them all together into one amorphous mass.

The term survey as it is applied in public relations research refers to careful, detailed examinations of the perceptions, attitudes, and opinions of members of various publics. The general purpose of a survey is to obtain a better understanding of the reactions and preferences of a specific public or publics so that public relations efforts can be targeted to them. Most surveys collect two types of information (data): demographic and opinion. Opinion data are responses to those questions a practitioner raises concerning the attitudes and perceptions of certain publics about critical issues. Demographic data are those characteristics (age, sex, occupation, etc.) of the people responding to the survey that help a practitioner classify them into one or more publics. Thus the key to measuring public rather than mass opinion is the careful collection of good demographic data to use in subdividing and understanding the responses to a survey. For example, a survey among the employees of a hospital about the quality of working life in that organization might be very useful for internal public relations planning. However, the data obtained would be meaningful only if it was possible to differentiate the opinions of nurses, doctors, lab technicians, dietary technicians, laundry workers, etc., into separate publics rather than looking at them as one employee mass.

**Experimental Research**

Experimental research is generally divided into two categories: laboratory and field experiments. Laboratory experiments take place in carefully controlled environments designed to minimize outside effects on the research. Field experiments take place in real world settings such as an organization. The trade-off between field and laboratory experiments is essentially one of authenticity versus purity. In a field experiment, the researcher sacrifices a great deal of control over the experimental setting to obtain reactions in a real environment. In a laboratory setting, however, the researcher can control any outside stimuli that might contaminate the results of the study. A public relations practitioner might decide to pretest a particular message in several forms by inviting people into a room to view the messages and then measuring their reactions. This laboratory setting would insure that the responses of the subjects were based upon the message being studied and not other stimuli that might be available in a "real" environment. On the other hand, if this practitioner wanted to test the effects of a message in a more authentic setting a test-market study could be arranged using a specific group of people in their normal environment.

**COLLECTING
FORMAL RESEARCH
DATA**

**Descriptive and
Inferential Methods**

Formal research information can be obtained in a variety of ways which can basically be classified as either descriptive or inferential. Descriptive data are used to describe something such as a particular group of people (public). If a public relations practitioner in an organization asks the personnel department to prepare a demographic profile (average age, sex breakdown, years of education, experience level, etc.) of employees, he or she would be asking for descriptive data. Such studies use averages, percentages, actual numbers or other descriptive statistics to summarize the characteristics of a group or public.

Inferential data do more than describe the particular group or public from which they were collected. Inferential data can be used to describe ("infer") the characteristics of people not included in the group from which the information was obtained. Through the process of sampling, which we will discuss later in this section, it is possible to select a relatively small number of people who are representative of a larger population. Through the use of inferential statistics, a public relations practitioner can infer the characteristics of a very large public such as a consumer group from a relatively small but representative sample of that population.

**Sampling Methods**

A *sample* is a subset of a population or public. Public relations researchers use samples because in most instances it is impractical to collect information from every person in the target public. There are numerous sampling techniques, but the best methods rely on the theory of probability to provide a miniature version of the target public. While the theory of probability is too complex for our discussion here, it should be noted that it is the basis of all inferential statistics. The following sampling methods rely on the theory of probability to assure a sample that is representative of the public from which it is drawn:

*Simple random sampling* is a technique that allows each member of a public to have an equal chance of being selected. As long as the sample is large enough (some experts say at least thirty to sixty people) it will accurately reflect the characteristics of its public if it is selected totally at random. Probably the most common example of simple random selection is drawing a name from a basket. If the slips of paper have been mixed up adequately, each slip has an equal chance of being selected at the time of the drawing.

*Systematic sampling* uses a list, such as a telephone directory or mailing list, to select a sample at random. Generally a table of random numbers is used to find a starting point on the list along with a selection interval. For example, a researcher might pick at random the number 293006 from a table of random numbers. Using the first three digits the researcher could start on page 293 of the telephone directory and then using the last three digits he or she would select every sixth name for the sample. This method

# PRACTICING
# PUBLIC
# RELATIONS

is more practical than pure simple random sampling in most public relations research.

*Stratified random sampling* is a two-stage process which first divides the public into two or more mutually exclusive categories (such as males and females) and then randomly selects samples from each stratum. This method is used to insure that each subgroup of a particular public was adequately represented in the sample.

*Cluster sampling* involves the random selection of groups rather than individuals for a sample. For example, if we wanted to measure the attitudes of United Auto Worker's members, we could randomly select union locals to include in our study rather than individual U.A.W. members.

*Quota sampling* involves randomly selecting a fixed number of people from each of several distinguishable subsets of a public. For example, a researcher may decide to select fifty subjects from each of the following groups by sex and age regardless of what proportion of the actual public they account for: males 18–25, males 26–40, males over 40, females 18–25, females 26–40, and females over 40. This would allow accurate assessments of the opinions of each subgroup.

## Methods for Obtaining Information

Whether the research is classified as descriptive or inferential, survey or experimental, and regardless of the sampling technique employed, there are three basic means for collecting research data: observations, interviews, and questionnaires.

*Observational techniques* are easily misused in public relations research because of the informal nature of many observations about publics. The personal observations of a practitioner are severely limited by his or her own perceptions, experience, and sensitivity. These problems can lead to decisions made more from "gut feeling" than reliable information. The limitations of personal observations can be reduced through the use of structural techniques. Observers can be trained within established rules for the systematic observation and recording of data, however, this is normally an expensive and complex process.

*Interviews* can be a successful way to gain information from a public. The use of skilled interviewers can yield information that subjects might not otherwise volunteer. Interviews can occur in person as well as over the telephone, and are generally classified as structured or unstructured. Unstructured interviews allow subjects to respond to an open-ended question however they wish, while a structured interview uses a schedule of questions with specific response choices ranging from yes/no to multiple choice. Although interviews are frequently employed, they have disadvantages: For example, the personality, dress, and nonverbal cues of the interviewer may bias the response. To minimize such problems, it is necessary to have expertly trained interviewers, and the cost of this process can be prohibitive.

*Questionnaires* are the most common form of data collection because they are stable in presentation and inexpensive to use. Once a questionnaire has been printed, each subject will be asked the same questions in exactly the same way. Questionnaires are generally designed to measure one or more of the following: attitudes, opinions, and demographic characteristics of the sample. Figure 6-4 is an example of a questionnaire used to measure the effects of certain messages on the public images of political candidates; note that it seeks information in all three categories.

**Figure 6-4**
Sample Questionnaire
Used to Measure Effects
of Political
Advertisements on
Candidate Images

INSTRUCTIONS—Please Read Carefully

We would like to know how you feel about the political candidates whose T.V. advertisements you are about to view. Please judge the candidates in terms of what the descriptive scales mean to you. There are, of course, no "right" or "wrong" answers and we urge you to be as accurate as possible in your ratings. Try to imagine yourself as a potential voter for each of the candidates when viewing the advertisements and checking the scales.

For purposes of illustration, suppose you were asked to evaluate John Doe using the "attractive-ugly" scale. If you judged him to be extremely "ugly" you would check the scale as follows:

_____**3**_____        Ugly  ✓_:__:__:__:__:___  Attractive

If you judged him to be substantially "ethical," you would check the scale as follows: ____**1**____        Unethical  __:__:__:__:__:✓:___  Ethical

If you judged him to be moderately "harmful," you would check the scale as follows: ____**2**____        Beneficial  __:__:__:✓:__:___  Harmful

In the far left column please rank in order the three scales which mean the most to you in describing each candidate.

In summary.  .   .    .

1. Be sure you mark every adjective-pair for all candidates. Never fill in more than one box on a single scale.

2. Make each item a separate and independent judgment.

3. Work at a fairly high speed through this survey; we want your first impressions—the way you actually feel at the present time toward the candidates.

# PRACTICING
# PUBLIC
# RELATIONS

(Do not write in spaces on right margin.)

| _____ | _____ | _____ | _____ |
|---|---|---|---|
| 1 | 2 | 3 | 4 |

Sequence ID

Your response to *every* item is important to the success of this research.

Please check each of the items below.

Sex: _____ Male _____ Female

$$\overline{\phantom{xxxxxxxx}}$$
5

Age (check one):

_____18–20 _____21–25 _____26–35 _____over 35

$$\overline{\phantom{xxxxxxxx}}$$
6

Are you a registered voter? _____ Yes _____ No

$$\overline{\phantom{xxxxxxxx}}$$
7

How many local, state or national elections have you voted in since becoming eligible to vote?

_____1–2 _____3–5 _____6–10 _____over 10

$$\overline{\phantom{xxxxxxxx}}$$
8

Please indicate your political party preference:

_____ Democrat _____ Republican _____ Other

$$\overline{\phantom{xxxxxxxx}}$$
9

Please indicate your parents' political party preference:

_____ Democrat _____ Republican _____ Other

$$\overline{\phantom{xxxxxxxx}}$$
10

How strongly do you feel about the political party you prefer?

Very                    ___:___:___:___:___:___      Not Very
Strongly                                             Strongly

$$\overline{\phantom{xxxxxxxx}}$$
11

| | | | _____ | _____ | _____ | _____ |
|---|---|---|---|---|---|---|
| | | | 1 | 2 | 3 | 4 |

| _____ | _____ | _____ | _____ | _____ | _____ | _____ |
|---|---|---|---|---|---|---|
| 5 | 6 | 7 | 8 | 9 | 10 | 11 |

| Rank Top 3 Here | John Olson-Republican | | Do not write in this column |
|---|---|---|---|
| _____ 26 | Direct | _:_:_:_:_:_ Evasive | _____ 12 |
| _____ 27 | Uninspiring | _:_:_:_:_:_ Inspiring | _____ 13 |
| _____ 28 | Frightening | _::_:_:_:_:_ Reassuring | _____ 14 |
| _____ 29 | Qualified for Politial Office | _:_:_:_:_:_ Not Qualified for Political Office | _____ 15 |
| _____ 30 | Ugly | _:_:_:_:_:_ Attractive | _____ 16 |
| _____ 31 | Knowledgeable | _:_:_:_:_:_ Ignorant | _____ 17 |
| _____ 32 | Beneficial | _:_:_:_:_:_ Harmful | _____ 18 |
| _____ 33 | Ethical | _:_:_:_:_:_ Unethical | _____ 19 |
| _____ 34 | Powerless | _:_:_:_:_:_ Powerful | _____ 20 |
| _____ 35 | Genuine Image | _:_:_:_:_:_ Artificial Image | _____ 21 |
| _____ 36 | Wrong Political Party | _:_:_:_:_:_ Right Political Party | _____ 22 |
| _____ 37 | Our Kind of Man | _:_:_:_:_:_ Not Our Kind of Man | _____ 23 |
| _____ 38 | Competent | _:_:_:_:_:_ Incompetent | _____ 24 |
| _____ 39 | Represents the Interests of the Few | _:_:_:_:_:_ Represents the Interests of the Many | _____ 25 |

_____        _____
   40              41

From Otis W. Baskin, "Perceptions of Advertisement Effectiveness and Party Affiliation as Predictors of Candidate Image." Presented at the 1976 meeting of the Association for Education in Journalism, College Park, Maryland.

Whether a researcher is preparing a questionnaire or a schedule of interview items there are certain dimensions to consider, such as degree of structure, scales and scale of anchors, and method of administration. To illustrate how the structure of questionnaire items may vary, consider the measurement of publication readership (*Figure 6-5*). Note that the most structured response is required in Item 1 of Figure 6-5. Here the respondent

# PRACTICING PUBLIC RELATIONS

must simply answer *yes* or *no*. To an extent this may be the most straight-forward data a researcher could collect; it might also be the least infor-mative. Notice that Item 3 allows the subject more freedom in selecting a response among the six choices and provides more information than Item 1. Still more freedom of response and potential information are provided by Item 6. At the opposite end of the structure continuum, Item 7 simply asks the respondents to tell the researcher anything they wish about why they read the publication. Notice that as the degree of structure decreases the potential for information and error both increase. The researcher must carefully balance the need for information richness in the data of a study with the need to provide a structure for the comparison of responses.

For any given questionnaire item scale points, continuity, and anchors may vary. The number of scale points can range from two as in the yes/no response of Item 1 (*Figure 6-5*) to almost any number that may represent logical choices to the subject. Most experts advise that seven to ten choices represent the maximum number of responses that a subject can be expected to perceive as distinct choices. The inclusion of too many choices in a question can confuse a respondent, while too few choices will not distin-guish adequately between different points of view.

The continuity of a scale can range from discrete steps like those in Item 3 (*Figure 6-5*) to a continuous scale such as Item 4. The appropriate degree of scale continuity depends upon the nature of the information being sought and the ability of subjects to understand the relevance of the choices. The labels associated with scale points are called scale anchors. These can vary from an anchor for each step to scales that are anchored only at their extreme points (*Figure 6-5*). The use of scale anchors depends upon what is being asked and the ability of subjects to distinguish between the points on the scale.

The decision about whether to use a questionnaire or interview in gath-ering data for public relations research must take into account the study's budget, purpose, subjects, and a variety of other considerations. Question-naires can be sent in the mail, and can be administered to individuals or groups. They provide anonymity, and present a uniform stimulus to all subjects. Interviews, on the other hand, are more flexible, get a higher percentage of responses in some situations, and can be used with relatively uneducated publics.

**The Practitioner as Researcher**   Although many practitioners may never actually conduct their own formal research, the practice of public relations today requires familiarity with the concepts discussed here. Research has become a fact of life in all types of organizations. Even organizations that hire outside consulting firms to do their research need practitioners of public relations who understand the research process enough to decide between the proposals of various re-search firms, provide guidance to the project, interpret results to manage-

**Figure 6-5**
Sample Questionnaire
Items for the
Assessment of
Readership

1. All things considered, do you like to read *Update?*

   _____          _____
   Yes               No

2. How often do you read *Update?*

   _____     _____     _____     _____     _____
   Never            Rarely          Sometimes         Often           Always

3. All things considered, I like to read *Update.*

   _____     _____     _____     _____     _____     _____
   Strongly         Moderately       Slightly         Slightly        Moderately       Strongly
   Disagree         Disagree         Disagree          Agree            Agree            Agree

4. What percentage of *Update* do you read?

   ____/____/____/____/____/____/____/____/____/____/____
   0%   10%   20%   30%   40%   50%   60%   70%   80%   90%  100%

6. All things considered, I think *Update* is:

   Boring        __:__:__:__:__:__      Interesting
   Informative   __:__:__:__:__:__      Uninformative

7. What are your reasons for reading or not reading *Update?*

ment, and apply those results to public relations efforts. In addition, public relations practitioners must be able to supply information obtained from research to the media. Editors will be interested in:

The sponsor of the research;
The nature of the sample (who, how selected);
The recentness of the data;
The possibility of bias by those who conducted the
   study;
The methods used to arrive at interpretations and
   comparisons.

Public relations practitioners must be prepared to use and interpret research results internally and externally for their organizations and clients.

# CHAPTER 7 PLANNING FOR
## PUBLIC RELATIONS EFFECTIVENESS

**PREVIEW**    Public relations practitioners must be able to plan adequately to be effective in an organizational environment. Good planning is the best way to practice "preventive" rather than "remedial" public relations.

Tactical and strategic plans for an organization must include a variety of functions in addition to public relations. Likewise, public relations practitioners must be able to affect the various components of organizational goals in order to have any long term effects.

Public relations units in organizations are generally considered expense centers when budgets are prepared because only the inputs or expenditures can be adequately measured from a financial point of view. Therefore, in order to secure an appropriate share of the organization's resources, the public relations unit must do a good job of "selling" its activities to managerial decision-makers.

Public relations practitioners can apply the basic four-step planning model discussed in this chapter to increase their effectiveness in organizational settings.

Public relations practitioners, like most other managers, tend to be action-oriented. The constant changes that take place both inside and outside of any organization produce an endless procession of public relations problems. Too often, because of the number of pressing problems with which managers are confronted, they find themselves responding only to exceptional situations. Such situations usually are negative in that they require the practitioner to intervene after a problem has gotten out of control. Thus, public relations managers frequently find themselves so busy putting out fires that they do not have time to prevent them from starting.

While putting out fires is certainly a part of the job of public relations and of every other manager as well, it cannot be allowed to dominate all other functions. Otherwise, the practitioner becomes a victim of circumstances, and is only able to react to the situation at hand. Perhaps the most frequent complaint of public relations practitioners is that other managers ask for their services only after the problem has become unmanageable (see minicase 6-1). When damage to the organization's image has already been done, the public relations manager is often given the responsibility of "fixing it." These generally prove to be no-win situations both for the organization and for the practitioner, who must engage in usually fruitless "remedial public relations."

For a long time public relations practitioners have been advocating "preventive public relations" to avoid such problems. Part of this approach involves the type of fact-finding research we have already discussed in Chapter 6. If practitioners can detect potential problems before they erupt into damaging situations, management can be given early warning and advice. Sometimes even the early detection provided by research methods like those discussed in Chapter 6 cannot forestall some negative impact. When advanced warning is coupled with adequate planning, however, negative effects can be minimized and public relations management can provide well-designed positive actions rather than hastily conceived reactions.

Only through continuous advance planning can public relations practitioners find relief from the burden of reacting after the damage has been done. Even though many public relations managers feel they have no time to plan, the opposite is actually true. The more time managers devote to planning based on adequate research information, the less time they will need to spend putting out fires. Planning actually creates the time needed to plan. Planning permits the development of integrated public relations efforts that support the goals of an organization in a positive rather than a defensive manner. Planning provides the opportunity to involve management from other relevant areas of the organization, and thus helps insure their cooperation and support. One important cause of ineffective public relations efforts is a lack of planning. Through careful, detailed planning, more efficient use can be made of the resources allocated to the public relations function of any organization.

**TYPES OF PLANS**   Managerial planning is generally classified into two broad categories: strategic and tactical. *Strategic* plans are long-range plans, usually made by higher levels of management. This type of planning involves decisions concerning the major goals of an organization and the policies for their implementation. *Tactical* plans are specific decisions about what will be done at every level of the organization to accomplish the strategic plans. Strategic planners typically deal with future events and must therefore rely on data that is relatively uncertain. The use of forecasting techniques to predict what effects economic and technical changes will have on an organization five years from now is an example of strategic planning. Tactical planners, on the other hand, are more concerned with the day-to-day operation of an organization and its immediate future.

Public relations plans may be both strategic and tactical. Decisions concerning the long-range future of an organization are made by top management. These plans, however, are not concerned solely with public relations. Because of the broad nature of strategic plans, they may include several organizational functions. At the tactical level these broad plans are translated into designs for specific action in each area involved. Therefore a strategic plan to control a certain share of a product market leads to tactical plans for production, marketing, and advertising as well as public relations. This results in a hierarchy of plans that can be divided into three broad groups, as illustrated in Figure 7-1: goals, single-use plans, and standing plans.[1]

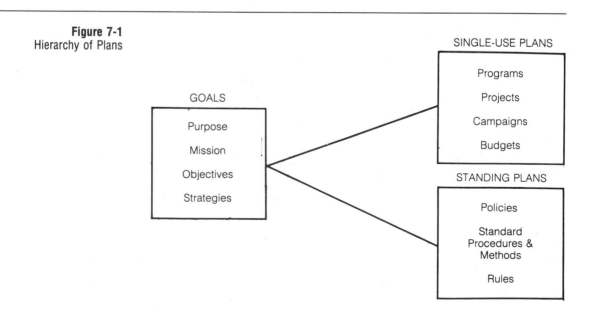

**Figure 7-1**
Hierarchy of Plans

**Goals**   Goals refer to the basic direction in which an organization is heading. The purpose, mission, objectives, and strategies of an organization are all component parts of its goals. While these terms are frequently used interchangeably, we have chosen to adopt a narrower scope of meaning to define specific concepts. There appears to be no universally accepted line of demarcation between these terms, however.[2]

**Purpose.** This term will be used to describe an organization's role as it is defined by the society in which it exists. It is broadly descriptive of all organizations of a certain type in a particular society. Generally speaking, the purpose of the following types of organizations in American society can be defined in the following way:

1. *Private sector business.* To make profit through the production of goods and services within certain limits set by society.
2. *Public or charitable hospitals.* To provide health care for their patients.
3. *Government.* To provide services necessary for the well-being of its citizens.
4. *Universities.* To provide environments for learning, teaching, and discovering knowledge.

These purposes are not directly chosen by the organizations themselves, but instead are set by the expectations of society.

**Mission.** While the purpose of an organization groups it with other similar organizations according to the expectations of society, the mission of an organization distinguishes it from others in the same category. An organization's mission is the unique role it defines for itself within the general limitations that society places on all organizations of its type. Therefore, the purpose of General Motors is to produce goods and services at a profit, but its mission is to produce automobiles and related products at a profit.

From a public relations point of view the distinction between purpose and mission can be a crucial one. If management does not understand the subtle but important difference between these concepts, they may select a mission for their organization that is in conflict with the expectations of society. An oil company that continued to view its mission as selling as much refined petroleum as possible in the face of worldwide shortages and higher prices might have its purpose and mission confused. The purpose of oil companies has changed in the view of society to include conservation and environmental concerns as well as the discovery, processing, and distribution of energy sources. Likewise, missions of individual organizations must be adjusted to communicate their efforts and concerns for these new issues. As society changes, the purposes of various types of organization change; frequently missions must be adjusted to meet these changes. For example, many believe that the problems of railroad companies are the result of their failure to adjust their missions after the introduction of the automobile. The radio and motion-picture industries, however, were successful in adapting their missions to the changes in purpose society set for them after the introduction of television. The March of Dimes, a charitable organization whose original mission was to fund research to find a cure for polio and to aid its victims, was forced to change its mission after the discovery of the Salk vaccine. The organization's purpose—to function as a nonprofit charitable group—remained unchanged; its mission, however, was broadened to include birth defects.

**Objectives.** Objectives are specific results that must be achieved in order for the organization to accomplish its mission. The broad mission can be translated into several parts that are sufficiently clear to make measurement possible. By dividing its broad mission statement into more specific objectives, an organization is able to devise plans for action that will lead to their accomplishment. Some objectives are relatively short-range, others require more time to achieve. An organization must therefore constantly review its objectives, replacing those that have been achieved and measuring long-range progress.

Frequently mission statements are broken down into objectives that relate to subunits of the organization. Public relations objectives are examples of subunit objectives, although the public-relations subunit frequently has responsibilities associated with the accomplishment of objectives from other subunits.

Peter Drucker, a renowned management expert, has listed eight general areas in which organizational objectives are typically found: market standing, innovation, productivity, physical and financial resources, profitability, manager performance and development, worker performance and attitude, and public responsibility.[3] Public relations could have a role in the accomplishment of objectives in each of these areas. Product publicity, for example, is frequently used to help improve market standing; the process of innovation can be aided through the intelligence-gathering function of public relations; manager and worker performance are affected by the internal communication systems often operated as part of the public relations function. Chapter 9 makes it clear that objectives must be measurable, whether they are solely those of the public relations department or include organizational objectives. Specific, measurable objectives are the first crucial step in an evaluation process that can demonstrate public relations effectiveness.

**Strategies.** Strategies are the overall guiding principles that help the organization establish action plans. The strategic plans of an organization are usually carried out through one of two types of plans: *single-use* and *standing plans*.

**SINGLE-USE PLANS**   Any plan that is used to accomplish some action that is unlikely to be repeated is a single-use plan. Public relations campaigns are frequently plans of this type because the particular events that exist at the time the effort is planned will never be duplicated. Public relations activities that are frequently repeated and can be operated by routine procedures and programmed decisions do not fall in this category. Because campaigns are usually designed to accomplish unique objectives, they must be planned with nonroutine procedures and unprogrammable decisions.

**Programs and Projects**

Managing programs and related projects is a regular part of the job of many public relations professionals. Preparing for a proxy fight, meeting consumer-advocate attacks, and dealing with environmental protests over the construction of a new plant are all examples of public relations activities that should be handled as nonroutine programs. A program typically consists of (1) the major steps that will be used to reach the objective, (2) the persons or organization responsible for each step, and (3) the order and time schedules of completion.[4] Frequently a budget is added as a fourth component. While a program is a broad plan with a relatively large set of activities, a project is a smaller plan that usually covers only one activity. Therefore, a program generally consists of several projects.

Mark P. McElreath proposes a planning system for dealing with these unprogrammable decisions designed to generate innovative solutions to complex problems.[5] McElreath believes that public relations can benefit from the use of six steps in the process for program management which have been defined by André Delbecq and Andrew Van de Ven: obtaining a mandate, identifying the problem, exploring for knowledge, developing resources and reviewing the proposals, administering the project, and transferring technology or facilitating spin-off.[6]

**Obtaining a Mandate.** Receiving written authorization from top management before beginning the program is an important first step. This formal legitimization process will help ensure cooperation from all levels of management. In addition, to provide the structural and creative integration that is necessary for successful program management, a small group (oversight committee) representing most segments of the organization should be formed to oversee the program. This group may or may not directly participate in the actual planning, but its presence provides an information link with the rest of the organization that can facilitate cooperation. A program manager should be named to chair this group. The program manager is responsible for maintaining program legitimacy, securing resources, and planning and coordinating. Delbecq and Van de Ven suggest certain requirements for the program manager: a person who is considered an "elder statesman" in the organization, has an extensive network of informal contacts, is nondogmatic, and tolerates ambiguity.[7] The program manager and program committee then monitor, evaluate and approve all phases of the operation.

**Identifying the Problem.** The next step is to seek the help of all interested parties who have some knowledge of the situation. Generally, the best procedure is to bring them all together to define the problem situation as clearly as possible. Formal research procedures, such as those discussed in Chapter 6, should be used to provide input to the process in addition to less formal sources of information. As an initial step, the group should identify the overall objectives of the project and specify the relationship of these to the organization's mission. This stage of planning should focus on problem definitions; solutions should not be discussed at this point. The product of this step should be a formal report submitted to the oversight committee.

**Exploring for Knowledge.** Once the problem is adequately defined, the program manager assembles a group of specialists to analyze it. The nature of these experts depends upon the problem being considered. Experts in media selection, financial relations, employee relations, or institutional advertising might typically be called upon for most public relations campaigns. When the organization is too small to have such specialists on the staff however, the practitioner must do these jobs alone or contract with outside consultants. When specialists are available they should dissect the problem and prepare a formal proposal for the oversight committee. The report should list the major divisions of the problem, alternative strategies for dealing with them, and a recommended plan for solving the problem. The expert group should provide at least two possible courses of action to give the reviewers at the next stage of the process a legitimate choice.

**Developing Resources and Reviewing Proposals.** Once alternatives have been generated it becomes necessary to secure cooperation from those outside the program group who can implement the plan. The written proposals for campaign alternatives must be distributed to key decision-makers and resource controllers in the organization for their selection and modification. These people, who must decide whether the campaign is feasible and how it will be funded, should be provided with real alternatives so that they know their input is genuinely sought. Other powerful individuals, both inside and outside the organization, who have the ability to veto or sabotage the campaign should be included at this point. Based upon recommendations from all these sources, a formal proposal should be prepared and presented to the oversight committee.

**Administering the Program.** A program administrator, usually not the program manager, will be assigned to direct the campaign once the proposal is reviewed and accepted by the oversight committee. The administrator will appoint a staff group to help him or her implement the program. The role of a public relations manager named to administer a campaign should be significantly more than that of writer or editor. Communication tasks should be delegated to the campaign staff. The administrator's role is one of consensus-building among various groups involved in planning and overseeing the campaign.

**Pilot-Testing the Program.** Often proposals that call for major changes in the way an organization operates need to be implemented gradually or tested previously. For example, a public relations campaign that represented a major increase in the funding or scope of public relations activities for an organization could first be pilot-tested on a small portion of the public. After the results of the pilot program were available, the oversight committee could decide either to stop the program or to expand it to other problem areas.

Program management is a method for planning public relations campaigns that can secure widespread assistance from other areas of the organization. This planning system maximizes the quantity and quality of inputs available to planners, and secures cooperation from everyone who can effect its implementation. Although time-consuming, its potential for success seems to outweigh the time required. Figure 7-2 illustrates the program-management planning process.

**Budgets**     Budgets are perhaps the most common type of single-use plans in any organization. Generally they are short-range plans designed to project ahead only through the coming year. The budgeting process normally occurs anywhere from three to six months in advance of the period being planned. Therefore, there is roughly an 18-month span between the initiation of planning and the close of the budget year for which planning is being done.

Budgets are also important messages in an organization concerning its priorities. Regardless of what the goals may be and how the organization chart is drawn, an organization's budget reveals its true objectives. The way in which an organization allocates its resources is a statement about its *operational goals and objectives* as opposed to the officially published *formal goals and objectives*. If an organization has not been realistic enough in its formal planning procedure, the budget will reflect a set of priorities different from those published. The extent of an organization's real commitment to improved community relations, for example, can be assessed by whether or not it is willing to allocate adequate funding for an effective program.

**Figure 7-2**
Stages in Program
Management

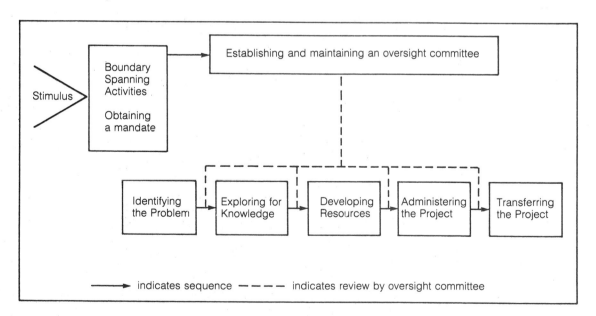

Mark P. McElreath, "Planning Programs for Exceptional Events," *Public Relations Review,* Fall, 1979, p. 41. Reprinted by permission.

Because the budget represents the lifeblood of each subunit of an organization, there is inevitably competition for limited resources. One of the public relations manager's most important jobs, therefore, is to make certain that the public relations function gets its fair share of the budget. This means that the practitioner must be able to understand balance sheets as well as galley proofs. In most organizations the budgeting process is decentralized. Budgets are initially planned by those who must implement them; thus, supervisors submit their budget proposals to their department heads, who prepare a department budget to submit to their supervisors for approval. This process continues in an upward flow until the controller or budget director for the organization assembles all the budgets into one integrated package and submits it to the president or the budget committee. Finally, the master budget goes to the board of directors for approval. At each step of this process there is negotiation and alteration.

**Types of Budgets**   Organizations usually divide this planning process into two parts: operating budgets and financial budgets. *Operating budgets* forecast the goods and services the organization expects to consume both in terms of physical quantities (e.g. reams of paper) and costs. *Financial budgets* give detailed estimates of how much money an organization expects to spend in the budget period and where the funds will come from (i.e. cash or financing). Figure 7-3 illustrates the components of these types of budgets. Although public relations managers are typically responsible only for preparing their own operating budget, an understanding of the entire process will make them more effective in defending their requests.

Organizations are typically divided into four responsibility centers for purposes of budgetary control:[8]

1. *Revenue Centers.* Organizational subunits in which outputs are measured in monetary terms, such as sales, but are not compared to costs of input because they have little influence over factors such as product cost and design.
2. *Expense Centers.* Budgets reflect only expenses for these subunits because only inputs (expenses) can be measured in monetary terms. These subunits (such as PR departments) do not directly generate any revenues for the organization.
3. *Profit Centers.* Any organizational subunit that is charged with earning a profit will have its performance measured as the numerical difference between outputs (revenues) and inputs (expenditures).
4. *Investment Centers.* In addition to measuring monetarily the inputs and outputs of these subunits, depreciation and costs of capital investments are subtracted before profit is determined.

**Public Relations Budgets.** Public relations units are generally considered as *expense centers* for budgetary purposes because their budgets reflect only expenditures. There are two types of expense centers: engineered and discretionary. Engineered costs budgets are most often used for manufacturing operations. Public relations and many other administrative staff functions use

**Figure 7-3**
Budget Components

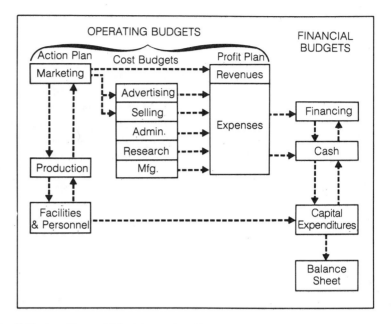

Gordon Shillinglaw, *Managerial Cost Accounting*, 4th ed. Homewood, Ill: Richard D. Irwin, Inc., 1977, p. 137. Reprinted by permission.

discretionary cost budgets. Because output cannot be accurately measured this type of budget is concerned only with inputs. Comparisons are made periodically during the budget period between actual and budgeted expenses. Discretionary cost budgets cannot be used to assess efficiency, however, because of the difficulty involved in setting performance standards for these functions. This fact makes the public relations manager's task more difficult when a budget request must be justified because normal control procedures cannot be used to evaluate performance. In Chapter 9 we will discuss some alternative comparisons to help justify public relations expenses to top management.

Public relations budgets are typically concerned with two basic expenses: administrative costs such as salaries, benefits, and overhead, and program costs which include research, publications, special events, films and other program-related activities.[9] Budgets are usually justified by one or more of the following factors:[10]

1. *Total funds available.* Public relations is allocated a percentage of available revenue.
2. *Competitive necessity.* Sometimes public relations receives a budget allocation designed to match or equal the public relations budget of a competing organization.

3. *Task to be accomplished.* Public relations under this method would share in an overall budget allotted for the accomplishment of a particular objective. Advertising and marketing promotion, for example, might also share in these funds.

4. *Profit or surplus over expense.* This method uses a fluctuating budget that can increase or decrease depending on the amount of profit or surplus generated.

**Zero-Based and PPBS Budgeting.** Two relatively new approaches to the process of budgeting are zero-based budgeting and the Planning-Programming-Budgeting System. Neither of these systems is widely used in private sector organizations, but they are both becoming common in all types of governmental organizations. In the traditional budgeting process the level of expenditures from the previous year is frequently assumed to have been appropriate and is therefore used as a base from which to build the budget for the following year. In such a system management must justify any increases. In zero-based budgeting, however, an organization is forced to take a fresh look at its activities each year, and each manager must justify the entire budget request without using the previous year as a base.[11]

The Planning-Programming-Budgeting System was once widely used in the federal government. This system is designed to identify duplication of programs, estimate the potential impact of various government programs, and connect those programs more closely with the budget. While this system has diminished in the federal government it is still used in many types of government and educational institutions.[12]

**Strategies for Fighting Organizational Budget Wars.** As we stated earlier, one of the public relations manager's most important responsibilities is to secure an appropriate share of the organization's resources. The best writers, designers, and media-relations experts cannot be effective if they are not provided with the necessary resources to do their jobs. In addition public relations, like all staff functions, must continually fight to maintain a position of influence within the organizational stucture. The skill of the public relations staff in preparing budgetary proposals and getting them funded is often an important measure of their influence throughout the organization.

While there is no substitute for a basic knowledge of financial planning and accounting procedures in understanding the budgeting process, there are other factors to consider as well. Competition among subunits for budgeting funds involves certain vital aspects of organizational politics. One of the most important things to remember is that public relations must constantly "sell" the value of its services to the organization. Unfortunately, too many public relations departments fail to understand the needs of their own internal publics and do not communicate with them as they should. Public relations practitioners in an organizational environment must maintain a professional image as members of the "management team."

It is important to identify the people in your organization who have both formal and informal power to influence budget allocations and to establish a regular program of communication with them. They should be constantly reminded of the effective and professional way in which the public relations function is being carried out. Some ways to demonstrate and communicate effectiveness are discussed in Chapter 9. If these individuals are ignored until just before the budget request is submitted, they cannot be expected to understand fully the needs of the public relations unit.

Some of the factors that must be considered when preparing a budget request are: continuing programs, new programs, and contingencies. Some programs must be carried over from the previous budget period for completion, and the carry-over must be justified. Was it expected from the start and included in the original plans? If so, this must be made explicit to avoid criticism for not finishing the job with the previous budget. If this was an unforeseen circumstance, however, the factors that make it necessary to continue the program beyond its original completion date must be explained. Of course, many activities are by nature continuous but they should not be taken for granted. Those who make budgetary decisions must be reminded on a regular basis, and especially at budget time, about the value of these activities.

Requests for new programs must be well-documented, particularly in slow economic periods. The need for each new program must be specified in terms that relate to the most basic functions of the organization. Projections concerning the potential effects of a program should be secured from other departments, as well as from the public relations staff. Unexpected contingencies must also be included in the budget request. Some organizations have a standard percentage that is acceptable for contingency funds, others do not permit such items in a budget. If an organization does not permit the direct budgeting of contingency funds, these are generally included as part of the other budget items from which funds can be diverted if necessary. Many organizations also build an inflation factor into their budgets. Economic forecasts are generally used to establish a percentage figure that will minimize budget erosion due to inflation.

Budget padding is a common practice in many organizations. This is more of a political than financial activity, but it can severely penalize a manager who does not understand how the "game" is played. The padding process normally occurs when the people who propose budget requests know that top management will routinely cut every budget by a certain percentage. Those who prepare budget requests then increase their budgets such that they can be cut and still contain enough money to accomplish their objectives. Such political maneuverings are generally dysfunctional and should be discouraged by top management. Managers who are not aware of such a situation, however, may find that they are left without sufficient resources to accomplish their assigned function.

**STANDING PLANS**   Within all organizations certain *programmable decisions* exist that call for a standardized, consistent response. Standing plans are made to provide routine responses to recurring situations. Once they are set, standing plans allow managers to make more efficient use of their planning time because new plans do not need to be formulated for every occurence of similar situations. Before going further in our discussion let us provide one note of caution:

overuse of standing plans may limit an organization's responsiveness to its environment, a critical issue for public relations. Nevertheless, standing plans do have a place in the public relations function of an organization. We shall discuss three types of standing plans: policies, procedures, and rules.

**Policies**   Policies are generally established by an organization's top management as guidelines for decision making. The purpose of those who make policy is usually to form some boundaries around decision-making activities that will serve to direct decisions in ways consistent with organizational objectives. Sometimes policies originate informally at lower organizational levels as a pattern of decision making occurs over a long period of time. In such cases, top management merely formalizes what is already happening. In other situations policy may be established either as a result of recommendations from lower-level managers or directly as a result of top management's observation of some conflict or confusion that has occurred. Other policies are formulated to improve effectiveness or to impose the values of top management. Increasingly, outside organizations, such as governmental agencies, are setting policies or at least influencing them. Health and safety policies in most large organizations have been changed considerably in recent years as a direct result of actions by government agencies.

Public relations departments, like all other subunits of an organization, must plan their daily operations to avoid conflict with policy. More importantly, public relations practitioners should be included in the strata of policy makers in any organization to ensure sensitivity to the interests of its publics. For example, policies that direct all contact with the press through the public relations department for approval and advice should be reviewed by the public relations staff.

**Procedures**   Detailed guidelines for implementing policy decisions are called standard procedures. Standard procedures or standard operating procedures provide a set of detailed instructions for performing a sequence of actions that occur regularly. Most public relations departments will have standard procedures for news releases, internal publications, site tours, media interviews, and many other activities that are carried on from year to year. There is one area however, where every organization needs a standard procedure for unusual occurrences—emergencies.

**Emergency Planning.**  Emergencies, although infrequent, should be handled through set procedures because of the need to respond quickly and effectively. When a disaster happens, it is too late to begin a deliberate planning process that will consider every alternative before responding. Nevertheless, coordinated, deliberate, and effective response is vitally important. When an emergency situation exists time becomes the key element in communication; plans must be made in advance so that reaction can be immediate. (See the following table of contents for a disaster response plan.) Figure 7-4 shows how St. Luke's Episopal Hospital in Houston, Texas, implemented their Disaster Response Plan in a simulated disaster.

**Figure 7-4**
Simulated Disaster at
St. Luke's Episcopal
Hospital, Houston,
Texas

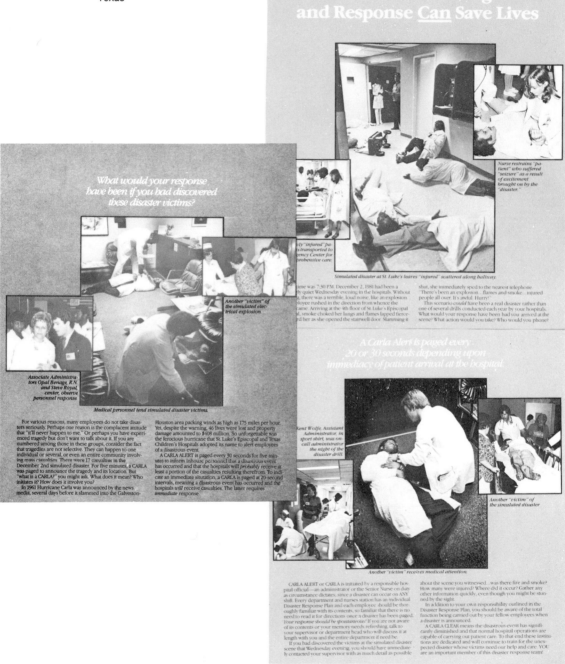

**Table of Contents for a Disaster Response Plan**

Reprinted by permission of St. Luke's Episcopal, Texas Children's Hospital, Texas Heart Institute.

There are four basic areas of emergency planning that should be specifically and carefully designed in advance:[13]

*Notification*—Specific plans should be made concerning who should be notified and in what order. Generally this is handled on a "need to know" basis. For example, an accident within a particular department will generally be reported, as soon as it occurs, directly to the department head and then to specified individuals in management including the appropriate public relations manager.

*Spokesperson*—The best strategy to avoid conflicting reports and the appearance of an attempt to conceal facts is to have all inquiries, particularly those from the press, directed to one person or task force designated to handle the problem. Generally this function is handled within the public relations department, although it may be necessary to arrange for statements from others within the organization.

*Handling News Media*—First, notify all media representatives that may be interested. An up-to-date list of these people should be kept in the emergency-procedures file at all times. Immediately issue all the facts available to press representatives who request information. Never attempt to manipulate the facts, delay, or conceal information. Anything less than full disclosure at such times runs the risk of being interpreted as a "cover-up." The following account of the mishandling of a disaster situation by NASA helps illustrate this point.

---

**Mini Case 7-1
The Need for
Emergency Planning**

There were no reporters or correspondents from any media on hand at Cape Kennedy when the fire broke out . . . The question of informing the public . . . was thus left entirely to the institutional machinations of NASA. The agency reacted predictably. It not only shut down all lines of communication, but, by either accident or design, issued statements that proved to be erroneous.

Although NASA knew within five minutes after the accident that all three astronauts were dead, the information was not released until two hours later. It was nearly midnight before UPI and AP received a NASA picture of two of the astronauts entering the capsule for the last time . . .

NASA claimed that the withholding of facts and its issuance of misleading and wrong statements resulted from the lack of a plan for handling information in emergencies. As hard to believe as this may be, coming as it does from an agency with a public information staff of 300, there is undoubtedly some validity to the claim.

NASA's information office has since maintained that an emergency plan was in effect and followed at the time of the Apollo 204 fire. NASA states that it has contingency plans for each mission.[14]

Remember that reporters want to know all the information as soon as it happens. If the public relations staff can facilitate this process, the organization will benefit from objective coverage. If the organization's representatives appear to be holding back information, however, the press will react with suspicion. Help reporters get the kind of information they want within the limits of legal liabilities. Provide them with human interest material about the people involved and as much information as possible about the causes. While it is important to work closely with the organization's legal counsel in such situations, remember that legal staff personnel are not sensitive to the issues of public and media relations. They may react too conservatively and cause unnecessary problems if allowed to control the situation. Always be sure that public relations has a direct line to top management in emergency situations.

*Notification of Families.* If the emergency has resulted in injury or death, families must be informed before any names of the dead or injured are released to the news media. Care should be taken to handle such notifications with tact and concern for the persons involved. Because of legal questions regarding liability, however, care should be taken in what is said to the families of those involved. Any acceptance of responsibility or indication of fault should be cleared through the legal department.

**Rules**  While policies and standard procedures serve as guidelines for decision making, rules substitute for decisions. They are statements which specify the action to be taken in a particular situation. No latitude for application is provided other than the decision either to follow or not follow the rule. Rules may be necessary when certain crucial steps must be taken. For example, it is often wise to have a rule requiring that signed releases for photographs and other personal information be obtained before these are used.

---

**CASE STUDY:
LIONS CLUB BOOK
SALE**

By Artemio R. Guillermo
Assistant Professor of Speech,
University of Northern Iowa, Cedar
Falls, Iowa

---

Each spring the Waterloo, Iowa, Lions Club holds a used-book sale. The books, which are sold for as little as 10 cents, are donations from the public. Proceeds go to various sightsaving projects including the cornea eye bank in Iowa City.

Since the Lions started the book sales, there has been only limited participation by its members. $3,000 has been the most ever raised in one year. Still, the 1981 goal was set at $4,000. While the goals were raised, no changes were planned for promotion of the event. The Lions would use the same public-service announcements, posters, and press releases that had not done the job before.

Fortunately, however, a group of senior public relations students decided to help the Lions. After analyzing the promotional efforts in the past year and determining target audiences, the team created a public relations plan using the communication tools used before and adding advertising and staged events. The target area was expanded to include Waterloo, Cedar Falls, and the surrounding communities within a fifty-mile radius. The club provided $150 to the team for publicity expenses.

All promotional efforts centered on the slogan "Buy a Book and Help Someone See!" Simple television announcements using two-color slides were placed during news breaks. Weekly media releases were issued to newspapers and radio stations for a month before the sale. Two-color posters were placed in strategic places in shopping malls, dining centers at the university, and restaurants and other local businesses. Two students donned lion costumes and paraded in the shopping mall during the book sale week.

Local media supported the promotional effort by donating space and time. Expenses, including classified ads in the student newspaper, display ads in the local papers, rental of the lion costumes, and printing of posters, were carefully budgeted.

The five-day book sale was held in Waterloo's biggest shopping mall after saturating target audiences for four weeks. The receipts were counted. The Lions grossed $5,137—twenty-eight percent above their ambitious goal.

**Questions**   1. What made the difference between this year's book sale and those that preceded it?

2. How was public relations planning used to promote the sale?

3. Plan a similar campaign for a not-for-profit group.

4. What was missing from the public relations campaign described in this case?

---

**NOTES**   [1] James A. F. Stoner, *Management* (Englewood Cliffs, New Jersey: Prentice-Hall, 1978), pp. 91–139.

[2] For example, a more extensive discussion of the components of goals can be found in Charles H. Granger, "The Hierarchy of Objectives," *Harvard Business Review* (May–June 1964): 63–74. Here Granger uses the term *objectives* to describe what we call goals.

[3] Peter F. Drucker, *The Practice of Management* (New York: Harper & Row, 1954.

[4] Stoner, *Management,* p. 101.

[5] Mark P. McElreath, "Planning Programs for Exceptional Events," *Public Relations Review* (Fall 1979); 34–46.

[6] André L. Delbecq and Andrew Van de Ven, *Organizing for Program Planning Development* (Madison, Wisconsin: Center for the Study of Program Administration Reprint Series).

[7] Ibid.

[8] Stoner, *Management,* pp. 594–596.

[9] Raymond Simon, *Public Relations: Concepts and Practice* (Columbus, Ohio: Grid, Inc., 1976), p. 95.

[10] Scott M. Cutlip and Allen H. Center, *Effective Public Relations* (Englewood Cliffs, N.J.: Prentice-Hall, 1978), p. 175.

[11] Peter A. Pyhrr, "Zero-Based Budgeting," *Harvard Business Review* (November-December 1970): 111–121.

[12] Allen Schick, "A Death in the Bureaucracy: The Demise of Federal PPBS," *Public Administration Review* 32 (March-April 1973): 146–156.

[13] Lawrence W. Nolte, *Fundamentals of Public Relations* (New York: Pergamon Press, 1974), pp. 317–318.

[14] James Skardon, "The Apollo Story: What the Watchdogs Missed," *Columbia Journalism Review* 6 (Fall 1967): 13–14. Reprinted by permission.

# THE FUNDAMENTALS OF PLANNING

Public relations efforts often fail because of communication breakdowns, occuring not between the organization and its publics, but between public relations practitioners and other managers within the organization. The cause of these breakdowns can frequently be traced to an imperfect alignment between the public relations planning process and the planning done in the rest of the organization. These misunderstandings can usually be prevented if public relations practitioners analyze their organization's management as carefully as they do any other audience. Planning documents are messages prepared to communicate the needs and potential contributions of the public relations unit to other segments of the organization. Therefore, when we plan we must learn to do so using the terms and methods common to organizational management. In this section we will discuss a four-step process that is characteristic of managerial planning. An understanding of this process, along with the specifics of planning discussed here, should help public relations practitioners to adapt their planning messages to other managers. The elements of the process are: 1) establishing goals, 2) determining the present situation, 3) determining aids and barriers to goals, and 4) forecasting.

**ESTABLISHING GOALS**

Agreeing upon a goal or set of goals must be the first step in deciding what the public relations subunit wants or needs. Frequently, when a list of possible goals is generated, it is discovered that two or more of them are mutually exclusive. When possible goals conflict, each must be evaluated to determine the long and short-range effects of acceptance or rejection. Resources often dictate the selection of goals. An organization may not have or be willing to devote the time, personnel, and capital necessary to accomplish some goals. Goals that are selected for the public relations function, however, must always relate to the broader statements of organizational purpose and mission. When seeking approval for public relations goals, a manager will be more successful if he or she is able to relate them to the goals and objectives of the entire organization.

**DETERMINING THE PRESENT SITUATION**

In reality, it is impossible to separate this step from the first because they occur almost simultaneously. As a goal is considered, data about the current state of the organization's environment must be collected and used to evaluate the likelihood that the goal can be reached. The need for information provided by the kind of fact-finding research discussed in Chapter 6 is crucial at this point. It is useless to set unrealistic goals or goals that have already been accomplished. Even after the goal has been firmly set,

# PRACTICING
# PUBLIC
# RELATIONS

data about the current situation need to be monitored. If the situation changes, it may be necessary to alter the goal or goals. Goals must be set with full knowledge of the current situation, the available resources, and what limitations must be placed on them.

**DETERMINING AIDS AND BARRIERS TO GOALS**

After reasonable goals have been determined, based on an analysis of the current situation, a more careful investigation of the environment must take place to identify aids and barriers. The resources of an organization in terms of people, money, and equipment are the most common assets to goal achievement, but the lack of proper funding or the absence of crucial individuals or equipment can be a hindrance. The structure of the organization itself can also be a barrier to certain goals. For example, a goal of increasing the sense of unity between labor and management could be severely hindered by an organizational design that prohibits all communication except that which flows through formal channels. Many barriers will be found outside the organization from such sources as government, consumer groups, competitors, and special interest groups.

**FORECASTING**

Planning must always involve the future. Predicting the aids and barriers that will exist in the future is a much more difficult job than evaluating the existing situation, yet predictions must be made to determine the effects of future conditions on the programs that are being planned. Such variables as unemployment, economic situations, and inflation can reasonably be predicted a year or more in advance through the use of quantitative techniques. Econometric models and other statistical tools are widely used in most large organizations to predict future events. Public-opinion surveys are used to forecast reaction to initiatives or actions contemplated by politicians, government officials, and managers. Public relations management must become familiar with these methods and use them to evaluate future effects on publics (see Chapter 6).

Predictions should also be made concerning the effects of planned public relations activities on various publics and the corresponding effects they will have on the programs that are being planned. Frequently these judgments must be made by qualitative rather than quantitative means. Juries of executive opinion, sales force composites and customer expectations are some of the methods frequently employed.

Other forecasting methods may be employed as well. *The Delphi Model* is a method developed by the Rand Corporation as a systematic procedure for arriving at a consensus among a group of experts. The panel of experts is normally separated by great geographical distances and never meets to interact about the topic. A series of detailed questionnaires is mailed to each panelist. Their responses are used to construct subsequent sets of questionnaires that are sent to the same panelists. The process continues until a consensus is apparent.

*Brainstorming* is a technique of group discussion used to generate large numbers of creative alternatives on new ideas. This technique has been used for some time by advertising agencies, public relations firms, and others who needed to generate creative ideas. The basic rule of brainstorming is that no one is permitted to interject negative feedback or criticism into the discussion. As the group proceeds to generate ideas they are all carefully recorded to be critiqued later. No idea is considered too absurd or simple to be included because it may produce the spark necessary for a truly creative idea. Brainstorming can be effective with a group that is comfortable functioning in this type of freewheeling atmosphere.

*Scenario Construction* has been used by "think tanks" like the Rand Corporation to create very long-range forecasts. A logical, hypothetical description of future events (scenario) is constructed to explore the dynamics of various alternatives. For example, if a large auto company wanted to choose one of several manufacturing plants to close, a scenario could be constructed in each case to detail possible effects on the environment, economic future of the community, availability of other jobs for workers, and many other results, both positive and negative.

**DEVELOPING A PLAN FOR REACHING THE GOAL**

Once the groundwork of determining aids and barriers is completed, the planner is ready to begin generating a list of possible alternatives. If the first three steps have been completed successfully, the listing of alternative courses of action should be relatively automatic. After as many feasible alternatives as possible have been generated, the process of evaluating them should begin. This should be a comparative process that balances the costs and benefits of each alternative.

Professor Walter W. Siefert of Ohio State University recommends the management-by-objectives approach to planning that is detailed in Exhibit 7-1. It must be remembered that the public relations plan is itself a message that must be communicated to management in other segments of the organization. Its success depends not only on how well the planning process has been executed, but also on how it is transmitted to decision makers who must understand and approve public relations plans.

**OPTIMIZING/ SATISFICING**

Most managers would agree that the best alternative available to the organization should be selected (*optimizing*). In actual practice, however, many limitations are placed on the planning/decision-making process:

1. The manager may lack important information when making the decision.

# PRACTICING
# PUBLIC
# RELATIONS

**Exhibit 7-1**
"PR" by Objectives

PR often fails because managers do not understand what PR people are saying and doing. This can be prevented if we talk in *management's* terms rather than trying to educate them in *ours*.

"Management by Objectives" is widely practiced in the business world today. Many perceptive PR people "cast" their programs in this form.

## MBO

### The Advantages

1. Business people think in terms of *business problems and objectives*.
2. Raises the *importance of PR* in the corporate structure.
3. Presents a *structure* for implementing effective communications programs.
4. Helps keep the PR practitioner on *target* in solving PR problems.
5. Contributes to the *PR body of knowledge*.

### The Process

1. *Get a fix on the business problem:*
   Analyze the business problem using all available research techniques. Then develop a clear, concise statement of what the problem is.

2. *Translate the business problem into PR objectives:*
   This is the most difficult part of the process. The objectives should be stated in measurable terms.

3. *Determine the audience* (s):
   Identify who your message will be directed to. There may be several audiences.
   Examples: print and broadcast media, company employees, customers, government officials.

4. *Determine program elements:*
   Exactly what vehicles will be used to effect the program.
   Examples: T.V. news clips, news releases, institutional ads, speeches, and publicity events.

5. *Determine budget:*
   The ideal situation is to *fit the budget to the need* using "objective and task" approach.

6. *Evaluate the program:*
   Utilize appropriate measuring instruments and techniques.

Used with permission of Walter W. Seifert, School of Journalism, The Ohio State University, Columbus, Ohio.

2. There is pressure on the manager to act quickly and with apparent decisiveness.
3. The manager may have overlooked more attractive alternatives in the early stages of the process.

Another term, *satisficing*, has been used to describe the selection of a solution that will be minimally acceptable due to one or more of the reasons above. Thus, the decision would not be the best one available, rather it would merely be acceptable.

Planning is an important process in public relations programming that must be approached with the same rigor as research. Adequate planning will produce effective and efficient results and enhance the professional reputation of public relations practitioners within their organization. To be effective planners, public relations professionals must practice the skills of other managers and take their rightful place as organizational executives.

# CHAPTER 8  BUILDING MESSAGES

**PREVIEW**  Publicity and advertising are two primary tools public
relations practitioners can use to create a public image
favorable to their organization or client.

Practitioners must have a good working relationship with
media representatives and an understanding of the needs
and restrictions of various media to plan an effective publicity
campaign.

Publicity has the advantage of reaching members of an
organization's publics that might be cautious about advocacy
advertising; however, it is a relatively uncontrolled message.

Advocacy advertising is used to "sell" the organization's
image rather than a product or service.

Large organizations have increased their use of advocacy
advertising because it allows them to reach large audiences
with a controlled message.

The third step in the process of public relations, communication, is often mistaken for the entire practice. Because, as we discussed in Chapter 7, public relations practitioners are action-oriented managers, they are frequently tempted to begin the process of communication without adequate research and planning. Experienced practitioners, however, know the value of discovering the facts and planning strategy before action is taken. Once research and planning have taken place, however, communication must quickly follow.

**BUILDING PUBLIC IMAGES**   An organization's public image consists of the essential qualities attributed to it by its publics. A public image is not the product of some phenomenon of mob psychology that causes everyone to think with one mind about the organization. Instead, a public image results when a fairly large number of people develop similar meanings for an organization. This process of developing similar meanings is explained by Kenneth Boulding as follows:

> **A public image is a product of a universe of discourse, that is, a process of sharing messages and experiences. The shared messages which build up the public image come both from nature and from other people. A group of people talking around a table do not receive the same messages. Indeed, each perceives the situation from his own position. Nevertheless, the image of the situation which is built up in each of the individuals is highly similar.**[1]

The task of public relations is to create a "universe of discourse" that is beneficial to the organization. An organization communicates its public image through a variety of messages, both internal and external. Publicity (uncontrolled media) and advertising (controlled media) are the two primary means employed to communicate these messages. The nature of controlled and uncontrolled media will be discussed later in this chapter; for now we will stress the point that practitioners do not control the final publication of a publicity release as completely as they do a message for which they purchase time or space.

**PUBLICITY**   Publicity is a broad term that refers to the publication of news about an organization or person for which time or space was not purchased. The appeal of publicity is credibility. Because publicity appears in the news media in the form of a story rather than an advertisement, it receives what amounts to a third-party endorsement from the editor. Since the editor has judged the publicity material to be newsworthy, the public is not likely to perceive it as an advertisement. Publicity may, therefore, be able to reach members of an organization's publics who would be suspicious of advocacy advertising.

Publicity can be divided into two categories: *spontaneous* and *planned.*[2] A major accident, fire, explosion, a strike, or any other unplanned event creates spontaneous publicity. When such an event occurs, news media will be eager to find out the causes, circumstances, and who is involved. While spontaneous publicity is not necessarily negative, it should be handled through standing plans such as those for emergencies discussed in Chapter 7.

Planned publicity, on the other hand, does not originate from an emergency situation. Time is available to plan the event and how it will be communicated to the news media. If a layoff, plant expansion, change in top personnel, new product, or some other potentially newsworthy event is contemplated, the method of communicating the information is a major concern. Depending on how an event is perceived by an organization's publics, it can generate good or bad publicity. The method by which the event is communicated can determine its impact. Thorough preparations for such an event may include plans for news releases, press kits, news conferences, photographs, interviews, and other methods of communication.

**Preparation of Publicity Releases**

The publicity, news, or press release is the heart of any publicity effort. Publicity releases take many forms, depending upon the audience and medium for which they are intended, but some general rules apply in most instances. A publicity release should always be prepared to conform to accepted journalistic style. The opening paragraph (lead) should generally be planned as a complete account that can stand by itself. If the lead answers the five basic questions of who, what, when, why, and where, an editor with a very limited amount of space or time can still use the story.

Some stories can lose their impact, however, if too many facts are forced into the lead. In such cases the writer should select only one or two major facts that will attract the reader's (and editor's) interest for inclusion into a story. If the person being written about is not prominent, the writer may choose not to mention his or her name in the opening; this technique is known as a "blind" lead. More specifics about how to write a news story are covered in the *Practicing Public Relations* section of Chapter 10 where we discuss the publication and writing of internal newsletters and magazines. Exhibit 8-1 contains some helpful information Professor Walter W. Seifert of Ohio State University gives to his public relations students. Once the essential facts have been organized into an opening paragraph, details and elaboration should follow in a descending order of importance to allow editors to cut the story to fit the space or time they have available.

Attention to a few general guidelines will result in more effective publicity releases:

1. Keep releases direct and factual. Supplemental information can be provided on a separate "fact sheet" included with the release.
2. The information included should be appropriate to the medium to which it is sent. Do not bother editors with material you know they cannot use.

**Exhibit 8-1** | TO: | Jewel Club, PRSSA, PR Students.
**Writing Publicity** | FROM: | Walt Seifert
**Releases** | RE: | Writing Rules

Most old hands in journalism follow certain rules. Here are some basics I like. (With a request that you add yours):

1. Write to express, not to impress or depress.
2. Prefer short words, sentences, paragraphs.
3. Don't jam several ideas into one sentence. (Feed bite-size chunks.)
4. Don't start sentences with modifying material. Put the subject first—in most cases.
5. Prefer active to passive verbs.
6. Avoid "first and foremost" as you shun "consensus of opinion."
7. Keep it simple. Don't say optimum for best.
8. Make pronouns agree with antecedents. Never say "England expects every man to do THEIR duty."
9. Edit your own copy tightly. Hack out superfluous words.
10. Go to bed now and then with a good dictionary. Read it kivver to kivver at least once yearly.
11. Don't be ashamed to have a keen colleague check your copy.
12. Never lie; not that you'll get warts, but because you'll get caught.
13. Write to the *heart* and you reach all. Write to the *head* and you reach a few. Some people *think;* all *feel.*
14. Use headlines that lure readers into stories.
15. (In letters to the editor)—Sell one idea only. If you can't say it in 100 words you won't in 500.
16. Avoid polysyllabic jawbreakers. (Study the 23rd Psalm!)
17. The only persons entitled to say "we" are pregnant women & twins.
18. Shun awkward metaphors like "The company laid off 200 workers for retooling." Prefer picture words like "The steak *sizzled.*"

*What NOT to do:* A young lawyer, describing a man whose wife is suing him for divorce, said: "The defendant is known as an individual who partakes in intoxicating beverages, cultivates the company of others on the distaff side, and abstains from endeavor to secure gainful employment."
*He meant:* "Smith drinks, chases women and won't work."

*How to write for broadcast media:*
   In general, follow the above instruction for releases with these particulars:
—write all copy for the voice rather than the eye, i.e., how it sounds, not how it reads
   • less formal than printed copy
   • don't use full words, use contractions
     Example: Use "don't" instead of "do not"
   • follow normal conversation guidelines for sentence structure, vocabulary, etc.

- use simple, descriptive words that form pictures, giving dimension and color
- avoid tongue-twisting phrases or complicated sentences
- keep verbs in the present tense

For TV scripts synchronize copy with slides, demonstrations or other visuals
—slides/pictures, etc., should flow smoothly at an interesting pace
—demonstrations should be lively to keep the viewer's attention

Type all copy *triple spaced* on 8½″ × 11″ paper, using one side only:
—begin message one-third way down first page
—leave ample margins
—for radio, never submit material on onion skin paper
—supply station with two copies of material to be read on air
—give your full name, affiliation and address in the upper right hand corner
—specify exact dates in the upper right hand corner

Write: "For Use Monday, July 8 through Friday, July 12," or, if timing is not crucial write, "For Immediate Release"
—time the script and count the number of words. Position these prominently on the first page. Radio timing is about 10 seconds for 25 words. TV runs slightly slower.
—write out all abbreviations, titles, names
—spell difficult names/words phonetically
—indicate additional pages and end of the script as with print media releases

*Localizing material*

Material that is "localized" is more attractive to the media serving a particular geographic area. Always make certain national material contains the name of the local contact person, as reporters may not have the time or finances to contact the national public relations chairperson.

*Editing your work is important*

Before producing or mailing any material:
—correct grammar, punctuation, spelling
—check facts such as titles, dates, figures
—have someone else read to check for typing errors
—rewrite awkward sentences
—re-read to be sure thoughts and facts follow logically

*Tell these things in your "lead"*

—WHO . . . . . . . . . said or did something
—WHAT . . . . . . . . was said or happened
—WHEN . . . . . . . it was said or happened
—WHERE . . . . . . it was said or happened
—WHY . . . . . . . . . it was said or happened
EXAMPLE:   Ohio State University (who) will open new administrative offices (what) at 100 Oval Drive (where) Saturday, Oct. 1 (when) to provide better facilities (why).

*Support all facts and figures for credibility*

*Follow the media's writing style*
—study the media to learn the style; read issues, listen to programming
—request a copy of the stylebook and follow
—in general:
  • use commas where it will make your message clearer
  • a sentence that needs a semi-colon should be broken into two sentences
  • use a colon to call attention to something
  • use questions and question marks sparingly
  • don't overuse exclamation points
  • make sure to use quotes around verbatim statements
  • avoid parentheses as they complicate reading
  • never underline. If a fact is that important, repeat it again in another way (quote, paraphrase, etc.).

*Type all copy double space on 8½" × 11" paper, using one side only*
—set typewriter for 62 characters to a line
—give your full name, affiliation and address in the upper left hand corner
—put the release date (For Immediate Release or For (date) Release) in upper right hand corner
—begin your story one-third way down the first page
—if release is longer than one page, write "more" at the bottom of each page
—indicate the end of the release by typing ### signs centered below the last line of copy
—avoid too many "plugs" (ads belong in paid space.)

*How to write a caption*
Provide a capsule summary of the action taking place in the picture
Should contain all the essential information from the story's lead
Identify people in photograph from left to right
Should contain enough information to stand alone without a story if that is the editor's need
Type on the lower portion of 8½" × 11" paper
—double space
—identify release date

Used with permission of Walter W. Seifert, School of Journalism, The Ohio State University, Columbus, Ohio.

3. The contact person's name, agency or organization name, address and telephone number should be given in case the editor has any questions. Normally this information is placed at the top of the releases as a heading.
4. A release line should also be included at the top of the page indicating the date for release. If the release is distributed in advance the release line should read: "Hold for release .  . ."

5. The standard format for most publicity releases calls for the use of 8½″ by 11″ paper, double-spaced copy, wide margins, and copy typed on only one side of the page.

6. Releases which run more than one page in length should carry a page number at the center top of each page beginning with the second. Also, each page should end with a complete sentence in case the pages are separated. To indicate that the material is continued on another page "MORE" is generally typed in the center at the bottom of the page. Usually -30- is typed in the center at the bottom of the last page of a release to indicate the end of the copy.

7. When photographs are included with a release, they should always contain the caption line glued to the bottom border with rubber cement. The name, address, and telephone number of the contact should appear on the back of the photograph.

Exhibit 8-2 shows a sample publicity release that illustrates the guidelines stated here. Always check each publicity release carefully for accuracy. Errors in facts or omission of important details can be embarrassing both to the public relations manager and to the organization. Some common errors are described in the following excerpt: [3]

One of our volunteer reporters scooped up at random an armful of press kits at the recent National Boat Show in New York's Coliseum, scanned them with the professional eye of a seasoned public relations executive, then sent them along to us with some interesting—if discouraging—observations.

After checking his comments against material in the kits and adding a few findings of our own to the list, we came to the conclusion that some product publicists in the marine field are careless, some are lazy, and some simply don't know how to put together a proper news release. For example:

1. Three-quarters of the releases were undated.

2. At least half either lacked any follow-up press contact information (gave only name and address of manufacturer) or the information was incomplete (no telephone number, or PR firm name but no individual to ask for).

3. Some picture captions were stapled to photographs, while others were so flimsily attached they came apart when handled.

4. One company's release was single spaced flush left, contained quotes without attribution, and misspelled "Coliseum."

5. The lead in another company's nine-page release was exactly the same this year as last except that the date had been changed. The president's statement about the new product line also was precisely the same in both years; and the balance of the nine pages closely followed the previous pattern—word for word in some short paragraphs.

6. In one almost unbelievable case, a PR firm handling the publicity for three marine equipment companies (two are competitors, incidentally) not only single spaced all the releases but left practically no margins

**Exhibit 8-2**
Sample Publicity
Release

# NASA News

National Aeronautics and
Space Administration

Washington, D.C. 20546
AC 202 755-8370

David Garrett                                          For Release
Headquarters, Washington D.C.
(Phone:  202/755-3090                                  IMMEDIATE

RELEASE NO:  82-87

SPACE SHUTTLE LAUNCH SET FOR FOURTH FLIGHT

The fourth and final development flight of the
Space Shuttle is scheduled for launch from the Kennedy
Space Center, Fla., on June 27, 1982 at 11:00 a.m. EDT.

Columbia's fourth mission is scheduled for seven days
and will complete the shakedown of the Shuttle orbiter
and booster systems as the nation's Space Transportation
System becomes operational with flight five.  Among top
priorities listed for STS-4 are the continued studies
of the effects of long-term thermal extremes on the orbiter
subsystems and a survey of the orbiter induced contamination
on the payload bay.

The flight crew for STS-4 is commander Ken Mattingly
and pilot Henry Hartsfield.

The Columbia is scheduled to land on the dry lake bed
at Edwards Air Force Base, Calif., on July 4, 1982.

- end -

Courtesy of the National Aeronautics and Space Administration and then framed the stories with a heavy rule. Included in the kit were several unidentified photographs. Compounding the agony: Every release had a return card attached so the editor could report when and how he planned to use the story.

**News Releases.** The most common type of publicity release is the news release. Any occurrence within the organization that may have local, regional, or national news value is an opportunity for publicity. Sometimes this news is not favorable to the organization. Even in these cases, however, a release is necessary. The news will always get out when something goes wrong. The role of the public relations practitioner is to be certain that the full story is told and that corrective actions are reported.

**Business Features.** An important form of publicity, and one highly prized by many organizations, is the feature article carried by the business, trade, or technical publications. Specialized periodicals that address a narrowly-defined audience have increased dramatically in recent years, and these allow public relations practitioners to focus on a particular audience for maximum effectiveness. Some analysis of feature articles will provide an insight into the type and style of story editors prefer. Such publications tend to publish articles that define problems common to a particular industry and describe an organization's attempts to deal with it. Unique uses of existing products, or products developed to meet old problems, are also frequent subjects. Public relations professionals often employ the services of freelance writers who specialize in the particular field of the target publication to help ensure acceptance. Most organizations have numerous further outlets for this type of publicity, including in-house technical reports, speeches discussing new technology or products, and papers prepared for professional societies.

---

**Steps to Clear a Publicity Release**

News releases and other publicity material are designed to create positive perceptions of your organization or client in the minds of target publics. Even the most experienced practitioner, however, cannot foresee all the potential consequences of any message. Thus, it is important to plan a system of checks for any message before it is released from your office. The following are some suggestions:

1. Preparation Stage
   Preliminary approval of your first draft should be secured from the person(s) involved or in charge.
   A later draft should be sent to the top officer of the organization who is responsible for public relations activities.
   After any further revisions, the next draft should go to the legal department for review.
   In some cases, other managerial personnel should receive draft copies with an opportunity to comment

before publication. This decision must be made
based upon responsibilities and sensitivities
in the organization.

2. Distribution of Final Copy of Release
   An internal distribution list should be prepared for each
      release to target important internal publics.
   All personnel mentioned by name in a release;
   Editors of local and national internal publications;
   Everyone involved in the draft-approval stage;
   Public relations and advertising firms associated with
      the organization; and
   All target media representatives should receive copies.

---

**Consumer Service Features.** Many newspapers and magazines, as well as some
television stations, publish or broadcast material designed to assist consumers. Information about almost any consumer product or service can
become a vehicle for both product and institutional publicity. Stories that
provide consumer-oriented information concerning food, travel, fashion, child
care, books, home management, and numerous other topics are in demand
by many publications. Frequently the recipes, food photographs, travel stories, and fashion news contained in special newspaper sections are provided
by public relations practitioners representing various manufacturers and industry associations.

**Financial Features.** Most newspapers and television stations and some magazines and radio stations carry financial news and feature articles, and there
is a growing number of publications that specialize in financial news. Publicity
in such publications can be especially effective tools for shareholder relations
(see Chapter 17) because current and potential investors assign more credibility to information when an independent editor selects it for publication.
Potential sources of financial publicity include: dividend announcements,
mergers, profit reports, expansions, new product lines, major orders, changes
in top personnel, research breakthroughs and many other events that might
be of interest to the financial community in general.

**Product Features.** Product publicity can frequently be newsworthy enough to
be selected for use by news editors. Longer, more detailed stories and less
newsworthy stories about products should be directed to periodicals, newspaper sections, and television and radio programs specializing in consumer
product information. Editors and others who use this type of material are
interested in information concerning the features, composition, performance,
and application of products that will help consumers with their purchasing
decisions. This type of publicity can build goodwill, develop customer loyalty,
and create product awareness for manufacturers, distributors, and retailers
of the product. In addition to exploiting unique product features, the public

relations practitioner can create newsworthy events to dramatize and illustrate product performance for media representatives.

**Pictorial Features.** The increasing popularity of photojournalism has made most newspapers and magazines receptive to newsworthy or unusual photographs that can communicate a message by themselves. Such photographs are often used with only a caption line and no accompanying story. Because these high-quality, unique photographs are difficult for assignment editors to plan, they provide an excellent opportunity for publicity. A public relations manager should always be alert for photographs that might be good enough for this purpose. Many organizations employ staff photographers, and their work should be constantly examined for exceptionally good or unusual shots. Photographs taken for in-house publications, annual reports, or even advertising may present opportunities for publicity. Special events should always be planned to provide good publicity photographs. Frequently newspaper and television editors will assign photographers to special events if they know in advance that there will be a good possibility of getting an unusual or newsworthy photograph.

Publicity photographs should normally be printed on 7 × 9 or 8 × 10 paper, depending on the editor's preference. Print media prefer high-gloss photographs with a caption line attached, while television stations prefer slides instead of prints, but specifications should be determined in advance. Photographs for television should always be in color. Color photographs are sometimes used by newspapers and magazines, but black-and-white photos are standard.

---

**Tips for Getting Good Photographs**

Whether or not you have to actually take the photographs that will accompany your releases, there are some things a practitioner can do to make them more effective:

1. Avoid busy, cluttered backgrounds that may detract from your subject.
2. Don't photograph subjects head on. Photographs taken from a slight side angle are more natural.
3. Candid shots of subjects are better than posed "mug shots."
4. Too much space around a subject can be distracting. Try to keep your photographs tightly framed.
5. Photograph groups in a natural cluster, never in a stiff row.
6. Avoid the temptation to photograph too many people in a group.
7. Generally, faces should be at least as large as the nail of your little finger.
8. Ask for proof sheets from the processor before selecting negatives for printing.
9. Make sure the people in your photographs receive prints.

10. Always obtain a release even for internal publications
and file photos. A release should contain the following:
Subject's name
Signature of person (parent or guardian for minors).
Statement granting permission for all photographs
taken.
Date, time and place photographs were taken.
Statement that they may be used for either publicity or
advertising.
Name of the organization.

---

**Press Kits—Packaging Publicity Releases.** Packaging can frequently increase the probability that information from a publicity release will actually be used by an editor. Press kits are simply a collection of publicity releases enclosed in a cover or some other packaging device. Although attractive packaging can be helpful in attracting the attention of a busy editor whose desk is covered with competing releases, design is not the primary consideration in compiling a press kit. News releases, photographs, fact sheets, background information, and features should be packaged in an organized and readable form to enable the editor to select the information he or she wishes to use. The strategy behind any press kit should be based on the realization that most major media will not use a release verbatim. Instead editors will select information to be rewritten into a story unique to their publication. A press kit should be designed to help editors select the information they need.

Jane Paley, a vice-president of Manning, Selvage and Lee Public Relations, lists the following standard components of a press kit:

A *lead story*—the strongest news piece you have. Keep it short; one page is terrific; don't exceed two.

*Backgrounders*—these may run five to seven pages and should offer depth, detail and well-documented facts and figures.

*Photographs, diagrams, graphs*—should be 8″ × 10″ black and white glossies designed to reproduce clearly. Each should be captioned to identify and clarify subjects. Photos of products, personalities and action shots are all acceptable.[4]

The basic rules for preparing any releases apply to the press kit. Always check your facts, avoid being overly commercial, never lie or deliberately misrepresent, and use only credible sources for value judgments and quotations. While photographs and artwork help to attract an editor's attention, they must be appropriate to the subject of the release. Folders, binders, and other packaging devices must be functional for the editor as well as unique and attractive. The following mini-case provides an example of a creatively designed press kit that was strategically planned for maximum effectiveness (*Figure 8-1*).

**Mini-Case 8-1**
**Quality Kit**
**Produced for**
**Johnson Wax U.S.**
**Consumer Products**

The objectives of producing this kit were 1) to communicate the scope and diversity of the company's product lines, 2) to emphasize the quality of the products, 3) to offer consumers a host of free resources available through the consumer services division 4) and finally, to apprise the consumer of the economic benefits of buying quality products and using them correctly.

The phrase "Quality is $ In The Bag" was developed as an umbrella or overall theme for the kit, which was housed in a brown paper shopping bag that included product samples, consumer literature and the kit, whose graphic elements complemented the grocery bag theme.

In fact, the kit's hard-bound laminated folder contained vertically bound shopping bags complete with serrated edges. On each bag was printed a calendar month with ample space for appointments and deadlines. And each bag held releases with consumer information geared to surviving in tight money times.

Each kit also contained a response card for feed-back which was incorporated into follow-up mailings. Each month, a new release and product sample followed, as a reminder of the initial mailing, and more significantly, as a means of continually expanding editorial awareness of Johnson Wax products and services.

From Jane Paley, "The Press Kit: Staple of the Public Relations Cupboard,"
*Sky,* Delta Airlines, June, 1980, p. 36. Reprinted by permission.

Press kits do not need to be as elaborate and costly as the example in mini-case 8-1 to be effective. Releases can be packaged in simple but well-designed one- or two-color folders, as long as they are adaptable to a variety of media needs. The basic role of a press kit is to provide information to editors that would otherwise take many hours to research. Press kits can provide a service for the media by saving research time and identifying important information for consumers and others. The organization, of course, stands to gain favorable publicity.

**Timing Publicity Releases.** The planning process for any public relations campaign should include some consideration of when to issue publicity releases to achieve maximum impact. Many considerations affect the timing: information should not be released too far in advance of an event because it may become lost on an editor's desk or, if published, it will be forgotten before the event occurs. Release too close to an event, on the other hand, can be a problem if editors do not have enough notice to plan for the material. Time of day can be an important factor in the delivery of a release. It is always wise policy to check with editors about deadlines. These will differ depending upon the medium. Some newspapers and broadcast media have days that are usually lighter than others and these provide good opportunities to get a release used.

**Tips for Setting Up a Newsroom**

Getting media representatives to cover an event is only the start. The quality, quantity, and favorableness of their coverage as well as whether or not they will come back the next time you invite them may depend upon the facilities you provide for their use. The following tips will help you get started.

1.  Information must be accessible. All fact sheets, releases, photos and people to be interviewed must be readily available.
2.  The staff must be qualified and experienced. The impressions media representatives gain of the organization and the event are influenced by the competence of those who are assigned to help them.
3.  A convenient, yet insulated location is important. The newsroom, interview rooms, and other media facilities should have easy access to the events, but be separated enough to prevent interference.

**Figure 8-1**
Quality Kit Produced for Johnson Wax U.S. Consumer Products by Manning, Selvage and Lee Public Relations

Photo by Rex L. Nutt

4. Both print and broadcast facilities should be provided. For example, three separate interview rooms should be set up: television, radio, and print.

5. Newsrooms must be well supplied:

   Telephone lines and any special hook-ups needed for broadcasts.

   Copy machines.

   Individual stations (desks, tables, cubicles) for reporters.

   Adequate lighting and electrical outlets.

   Typewriters and supplies.

   Sometimes Telex transmitters and newswire receivers.

6. It is accepted custom to provide refreshments for the newsroom. These can range from meals and cocktails to coffee and donuts. The event and the length of time media representatives must stay in the newsroom should be considered in determining what is appropriate. The objective is to encourage representatives to stay close to the action.

---

**Tips for News Conferences and Interviews**

Generally, media representatives feel news conferences are overused. Therefore, unless your event is extremely newsworthy and simply could not be handled through releases, or unless you have someone newsworthy to interview, don't call a news conference. For those rare occasions when they are appropriate, however, the following guidelines may help.

1. Plan the event carefully.

   Invite all representatives of all media that may have an interest far enough in advance for editors to plan to send reporters and photographers.

   Select an appropriate site close to the event being covered and convenient for major media (hotel, press club, airport, board room—never a public relations office). Check for enough electrical outlets and telephones.

   Time the conference to accommodate major media deadlines.

   Make certain you prepare enough handout material for everyone.

   Prepare any visuals that may be used so that they will photograph well from any place in the room.

   Prepare a poster of the organization's logo or name to go over the one on the speaker's stand if you use a rented facility.

Plan to phone major media the morning or afternoon
before the conference as a reminder.
Simple refreshments are generally a nice touch.
2. Prepare executives and others to be interviewed.
Make certain they understand the topics that will be
discussed.
Help them anticipate and prepare for difficult or touchy
questions.
Advise them to be completely honest. If they don't
know an answer they should say so and offer to find
out. If the answer to the question is considered
proprietary information they should say that it is not
for public disclosure.
Cultivate a pleasant, cooperative attitude among those
who will be interviewed. If they are afraid of or
resent the media it will show.
Advise them to avoid off-the-record comments.
3. Public relations practitioners are the directors and
stage managers of such a production, never the
stars.
Keep the meeting moving and interesting, but don't
take over the jobs of the media.
Try to keep relationships cordial and professional even
in the heat of questioning.
Never take obvious control of the meeting unless
things get out of hand.

---

**ADVERTISING**  Any media time or space that is purchased is advertising. Advertising is an important tool of public relations practitioners, even though most organizations have a separate department or unit for advertising. Because the advertising most companies engage in is predominantly concerned with selling its products or services, the function of advertising is most frequently associated with marketing, but there are forms of advertising that do not attempt to sell products or services directly. Advertising has become a popular public relations tool because it allows the sponsoring organization to control the content and timing of its message.

**Advocacy Advertising**  Also called public service advertising, public relations advertising, identity advertising, and institutional advertising, this form of public relations message is gaining popularity with very large organizations. Many organizations feel the need to sell their ideas as well as their products. The content of advocacy advertising is usually referred to as a *position statement* (Figure 8.2). Oil companies, public utilities, and other organizations involved in the energy business have made frequent use of position statements to help clarify their role in the energy crisis. Such statements give the organization the opportunity to explain to its publics price increases, increased profits, and the allocation of revenue. Frequently organizations buy advertising space or time to support an idea related only indirectly to their business. Several large corporations have purchased time and space for position statements supporting the ideals of democracy and the free-enterprise system. Phillips Petroleum Company purchased time on radio and television as well as space in national publications to explain its view of free-enterprise economics in the aftermath of widely-publicized profit increases in the oil industry during 1979–80. Figure 8-2 provides an example of another approach to this same problem. The appeal of this type of message to an organization is the ability to control its content and be certain that a negative connotation is not built into the message.

**Sustaining Or Image Advertising.** These are messages that are more subtle in content. Oil and chemical companies during periods of heavy attack from environmental organizations frequently respond with advertisements that show their factories in harmony with nature. Public utilities, because they are monopolies frequently attempt to create images of responsiveness to public needs through this form of advertising. The "We may be the only phone company in town but we try not to act like it" campaign by Southwestern Bell is an example of image advertising.

**Figure 8-2**
Mobil Oil Corporation
Advertisement

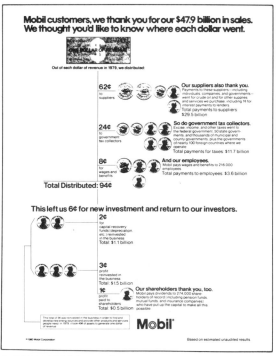

© 1980 Mobil Oil Corporation

Advocacy advertising differs from product or service advertising because it sells a corporate image rather than a product or service. In recent years the content of this type of message has tended more toward advocacy of social, political, and economic concepts. Many organizations feel that negative images of business in general are due to incorrect or insufficient information regarding certain aspects of American life. Through institutional advertising various organizations have identified themselves with positive social values while advocating such things as free enterprise, prevention of child abuse, and energy conservation.

The increasing use of advocacy advertising by organizations has brought them into conflict with the media. In January of 1980, for example, Mobil Oil Corporation attempted to buy time on all three major television networks to air an institutional advertisement that compared its 1979 profits to those of the networks. This followed extensive news coverage of tremendous increases in Mobil's 1979 profits and of the acquisition by Mobil of the Ward's retailing chain. News stories had questioned the size of the profits and their use to purchase a non-energy-related business during a period of rising energy costs and shortages. Mobil responded with an aggressive media campaign stressing that it did not use energy profits to buy Wards, and that the return on its investment was actually less than that of many other corporations, including the networks. Ads were placed in several major newspapers, but all three networks refused to sell Mobil time for the campaign. This refusal brought charges of censorship from Mobil and placed them in a position of direct conflict with the networks.

Although direct conflict with the media is an unusual and potentially dangerous situation, more and more large organizations are taking aggressive action to defend and control their image through the use of advocacy advertising. These organizations appear less inclined to rely on press releases and planned news events, which allow reporters and editors freedom to use what they wish in a story. Advocacy advertising campaigns have a growing number of uses: community relations, employee relations, recruitment, statements of policy, company positions in proxy fights, accomplishments, positions on pending legislation, and many other matters of public concern.

**Consumer Publications**

The rapid rise of consumer-interest groups and legislation has made organizations more aware of the need to project a positive image to this vast public. In addition to some of the institutional advertising already mentioned, many organizations publish booklets and other material designed to inform consumers about a variety of issues relevant to their needs. J. C. Penney has published a *Buying Guide* that provides information about topics such as guarantees, label information, fabric care, and other tips for consumers. Shell Oil Company has published a series of booklets to help consumers use energy more efficiently. Figure 8-3 provides an example of this type of message. Such publications not only provide useful consumer information, but also convey a responsible and concerned image to this important public. These and other messages about consumer affairs are discussed in more detail in Chapter 20.

**Figure 8-3**
Sample Consumer
Publication

Courtesy Shell Oil Company. Reprinted by permission.

**Public Service**
**Announcements and**
**House Ads**

These are two forms of advertising that frequently cause confusion between publicity and advertising. Public service announcements (PSAs) are often classified as publicity because the client does not pay for the time or space, but they resemble advertising more than publicity in their format and content. PSAs are generally treated like advertising by the media that use them. Although the client, usually a non-profit or charitable organization, does not pay for the advertising space or time, the medium does. Most print or broadcast media send credit slips to the client indicating the value of the time donated.

House ads may be either product or institutional advertising. The confusion over these arises from their format, which is designed to appear as much like an article as possible. Frequently the only markings that distinguish a house ad from any other article in the publication will be the word "advertising" at the top or bottom of the page. Some publications refuse to run house ads because they feel the advertiser is attempting to deceive the reader. Except for the fact that space must be purchased, house ads are prepared much like any news release.

**MEDIA SELECTION**

Various media and their audiences will be discussed in detail in Section III, but it is appropriate at this point to outline strategy for media selection. Although it is necessary to construct messages carefully so that they communicate the desired meaning to an audience, it is equally important to choose the proper medium to carry the message to the intended public. There are three basic considerations for media selection: the *audiences,* the *timing,* and the *budget available.*

*Audiences* must be the first consideration in any public relations effort (see Chapter 6). It is necessary to identify the publics you are trying to reach and determine what will interest them. The preparation of a publicity release is different from the preparation of an institutional adveritising message, because the former depends upon a third party to deliver the message. This is the basic difference between controlled and uncontrolled media. *Controlled media,* such as internal publications, direct mail, posters (Chapter 10) and advertising, allow the public relations practitioner to dictate what is published and how it is delivered to the primary audience. *Uncontrolled media,* for which someone else makes decisions about content, include newspapers, television, and radio.

Uncontrolled media present a special problem to the public relations practitioner because publicity releases must be planned for two audiences. The primary audience, or the public for whom the message is intended, is the most important, but the editor or media representative who selects or rejects the release for publication or broadcast is the first hurdle. Thus, although the release is designed to communicate a particular message to the primary audience, it must first attract the attention of an editor.

Having determined the target audience, it is next necessary to know which media are likely to be interested in given types of information. By researching available media carefully, a public relations practitioner can become familiar with the type of stories they use and the audiences they attract. Then select the media for each release and package the information in a way that will attract the editor's attention. Avoid mass mailings of publicity releases. They are too general to be useful. The best approach is to use the same information to prepare several different releases to interest the different types of media. One way to get more attention for a news release is to dateline it from regional offices of the organization near the media to which it is sent. A release for a large organization could be issued with datelines for each part of the country in which it operates. Chapter 12 discusses various strategies for media relations in greater detail.

The *timing* necessary to reach an audience is another important factor in media selection. Once the appropriate media have been selected, the time required to reach the primary audience may become critical. Some publications have backlogs of material and may not be able to get a story out in time. Therefore, the question of when the primary audience receives the message may be just as important as whether or not they receive it at all.

*Budgets* are always limited and frequently they limit media selection. Usually the first decision that must be made is whether or not the message needs to be delivered by more than one medium. If a media mix is desirable, it may be necessary to include cost as an important consideration in the decision of which media to include. Remember that while the costs of controlled media like advertising are obvious, costs associated with uncontrolled media must also be counted.

Table 8-1 contrasts advantages and disadvantages of several different media. Consideration of these points with regard to audiences, time, and budget will help public relations practitioners select the media most appropriate to their message.

**MESSAGES AND PROCESS**

We began our discussion of public relations messages by saying that the job of public relations was to create a positive "universe of discourse" about the organization. It is this universe of discourse that creates the mental pictures publics develop about organizations. These public images are, as Kenneth Boulding explained, different for each individual, yet highly similar. They are the collective impressions various publics use to judge the value and effectiveness of organizations in society. The public relations practitioner's first task is to assess these images accurately and then to plan and execute communication programs based upon that information. The final step in the process of public relations, measuring the effects of these messages, will be discussed in the next chapter.

**Table 8-1**
Principal Media:
Advantages and
Disadvantages

| | Advantages | Disadvantages |
|---|---|---|
| **Television** | 1. Combines sight, sound, and motion attributes<br>2. Permits physical demonstration of product<br>3. Believability due to immediacy of message<br>4. High impact of message<br>5. Huge audiences<br>6. Good product identification<br>7. Popular medium | 1. Message limited by restricted time segments<br>2. No possibility for consumer referral to message<br>3. Availabilities sometimes difficult to arrange<br>4. High time costs<br>5. Waste coverage<br>6. High production costs<br>7. Poor color transmission |
| **Magazines** | 1. Selectivity of audience<br>2. Reaches more affluent consumers<br><br>3. Offers prestige to an advertiser<br>4. Pass-along readership<br>5. Good color reproduction | 1. Often duplicate circulation<br>2. Usually cannot dominate in a local market<br>3. Long closing dates<br>4. No immediacy of message<br>5. Sometimes high production costs |
| **Radio** | 1. Selectivity of geographical markets<br><br>2. Good saturation of local markets<br><br>3. Ease of changing advertising copy<br>4. Relatively low cost | 1. Message limited by restricted time segments<br>2. No possibility for consumer referral to message<br>3. No visual appeal<br>4. Waste coverage |

**Newspapers**

1. Selectivity of geographical markets
2. Ease of changing advertising copy
3. Reaches all income groups
4. Ease of scheduling advertisements
5. Relatively low cost

6. Good medium for manufacturer/dealer advertising

1. High cost for national coverage
2. Shortness of message life
3. Waste circulation
4. Differences of sizes and formats
5. Rate differentials between local and national advertisements
6. Poor color reproduction

**Direct Mail**

1. Extremely selective
2. Message can be very personalized
3. Little competition with other advertisements
4. Easy to measure effect of advertisements
5. Provides easy means for consumer action

1. Often has poor image
2. Can be quite expensive
3. Many restrictive postal regulations

4. Problems in maintaining mailing lists

**Outdoor Posters (on stationary panels)**

1. Selectivity of geographical markets
2. High repetitive value
3. Large physical size
4. Relatively low cost
5. Good color reproduction

1. Often has poor image
2. Message must be short
3. Waste circulation
4. National coverage is expensive
5. Few creative specialists

**Point-of-Purchase Displays**

1. Presents message at point of sale
2. Great flexibility for creativity
3. Ability to demonstrate product in use
4. Good color reproduction
5. Repetitive value

1. Dealer apathy in installation
2. Long production period
3. High unit cost
4. Shipping problems
5. Space problem

**Transit Posters (on moving vehicles)**

1. Selectivity of geographical markets

2. Captive audience
3. Very low cost
4. Good color reproduction
5. High repetitive value

1. Limited to a certain class of consumers
2. Waste circulation
3. Surroundings are disreputable
4. Few creative specialists

**Movie Trailers**

1. Selectivity of geographical markets
2. Captive audience
3. Large physical size
4. Good medium for manufacturer/dealer advertising

1. Cannot be employed in all theaters
2. Waste circulation
3. High production costs
4. No possibility for consumer referral to message

**Advertising Specialties**

1. Unique presentation
2. High repetitive value
3. Has a "gift" quality
4. Relatively long life

1. Subject to fads
2. Message must be short
3. May have relatively high unit cost
4. Effectiveness difficult to measure

**Pamphlets and Booklets**

1. Offer detailed message at point of sale
2. Supplement a personal sales presentation
3. Offer to potential buyers a good referral means
4. Good color reproduction

1. Dealers often fail to use
2. May have a relatively high unit cost

3. Few creative specialists

4. Effectiveness difficult to measure

Reprinted with permission from *Advertising Campaigns: Formulation and Tactics* by Leon Quera, Grid Publishing, Inc., Columbus, Ohio, 1973, pp. 71–74.

CASE STUDY:  **By Carolyn Cline**
ROCKEFELLER'S  **Assistant Professor of**
PASSING  **Communication, The University of**
**Alabama, University, Alabama**

On January 26, 1979, former Vice President Nelson Rockefeller died of a heart attack in New York City. Details were released to the media by Hugh Morrow, a longtime family spokesman, who told reporters that the former vice president had been in excellent health. His last day had been busy—after a family dinner, Rockefeller "returned to his office in Rockefeller Center. He was working on his book about his modern art collection. He was stricken and died, apparently instantly," about 11:15 p.m. "He was having a wonderful time with the whole art enterprise. He was 'having a ball,' as he put it."

Editorials the next day praised Rockefeller for his involvement with the art collection and his dedication to duty, as evidenced from his death late at night in his office. The *New York Daily News* wrote that "it was typical of Nelson Aldrich Rockefeller's life that death, when it came on Friday night, found him hard at work. Idleness was one luxury of the rich that Rockefeller steadfastly disdained."

Reporters gradually discovered, however, that all of the material released by Morrow was false.

Rockefeller was, in fact, at his townhouse, in the company of a female aide, Megan Marshak. Medical assistance was not summoned until 61 minutes after Rockefeller's attack, and then not by Marshak, but by a friend of hers.

The New York press coverage of the new information was sensational. The *Post* said that Marshak was paid $60,000 a year for her work on the art project, and that Rockefeller helped pay for her apartment. The *Times* reported that the aide was wearing "a long black evening gown" that night. The *Daily News* interviewed sources who said that Rockefeller always sent Marshak flowers before his visits, and that there was food and wine on the table when paramedics finally arrived at the townhouse.

In the subsequent days, the New York and national media investigated every aspect of the Rockefeller-Marshak relationship and, in the opinion of some critics, turned the event into a media circus.

**Questions**  1. Was Morrow justified in his first statement? If not, what should he have said?

2. How does the public's right to know conflict with the right to privacy? Did Rockefeller's widow or children have a right to request that the story be downplayed?

3. Immediately after the first disclosures appeared in the paper, you have been called in as a media consultant to help the Rockefeller family deal with the situation. What would you suggest?

The material for this case is taken from Stanford Levinson, "An Exemplary Death," *The Columbia Journalism Review*, May/June 1979, pp. 31–33.

**NOTES**    [1] Kenneth Boulding, *The Image* (Ann Arbor, Michigan: University of Michigan, 1956).

[2] F. H. Moore and B. R. Canfield, *Public Relations: Principles, Cases, and Problems* (Homewood, Illinois: Richard D. Irwin, Inc. 1977), p. 140.

[3] *PR Reporter*, February 12, 1973, p. 1.

[4] Jane Paley, "The Press Kit: Staple of the Public Relations Cupboard," *Sky* [Delta Airlines publication], June 1980, pp. 34–36.

PRACTICING
PUBLIC
RELATIONS

# THE AUDIOVISUAL BOOM

Publicity releases and advocacy advertising are primary tools used by public relations practitioners, but they are certainly not the only ones necessary to a successful effort. In addition to face-to-face interpersonal communication, practitioners often find themselves involved with a wide variety of audiovisual messages. The following is a brief look at the vast array of audiovisual media that may be useful in the practice of public relations, especially for internal publics in organizations.

Audiovisual technology is widely used in American organizations. Audiovisual communication in its broadest sense refers to communication media that engage both sight and hearing. In the strict sense, audiovisual communication has been around since the first cave artist explained his or her work to other prehistoric humans. Flip charts and chalk boards are forms of audiovisual communication, since they are used to illustrate a spoken explanation, but these have come to seem unsophisticated. Audiovisual communication today usually refers to electronic media. Some time ago, organizations realized that face-to-face communication with everyone was no longer possible, and public address and telephone/intercom systems were installed. Soon motion pictures and slide/filmstrips were used to add visual effect to messages within organizations. More recently, closed-circuit television and videotape have combined the advantages of almost all audiovisual media into what is becoming a flexible and cost-effective method of communication within organizations.

The applications of electronic audiovisual communication in America have increased dramatically in recent years. It is estimated that the use of such media in business and industry is expanding forty percent each year. Moreover, the state of the art in the last five years has reduced initial investment cost. Many smaller organizations can now afford to join the audiovisual age.

This does not mean that audiovisual communication is necessarily superior to all other forms. Electronic audiovisual communication will continue to grow, creating new communication channels and expanding old ones. But to be effective, electronic media still must depend upon the communicator and his or her message. No medium alone creates good communication. It only facilitates it. The skills of preparing and delivering oral and written messages discussed elsewhere in this book will never be replaced by hardware. Electronic media are supplementary to interpersonal communication, not a replacement for direct person-to-person contact. Such media must be fitted into an organization's total communication plan.

**PLANNING A-V
MESSAGES**

**Message Content and
Objectives**

Before a medium is selected, the message should be outlined with care. A communicator should decide what needs to be said before deciding how it will be delivered. Audiovisual media must be selected to fit both message and audience. The following questions can help the practitioner identify important aspects in planning audio visual messages.

For whom is the message intended?
What do I want those who hear and see the message to
   do?
What are the goals and interests of the audience?
What does the audience know about me or those I
   represent?
What experience has the audience had with the topic?
How is the audience likely to feel about me or those I
   represent?
What kind of circumstances will surround the
   presentation?

Once these questions have been answered, the next step is to organize the content of the message. There should be a workable order of presentation to accomplish the desired ends. A complete script is not as useful at this point as an outline of ideas. These basic ideas, or major points, then become the body around which an introduction and conclusion can be planned. Be sure to let the audience know what you want them to do, whether this is merely remembering the content of the presentation or taking a specific action.

**Audience
Characteristics and
Setting**

The message must meet the needs and interests of the audiences that will be exposed to it. The language used should reflect the audience's education and level of knowledge about the subject. A message for aerospace engineers may be too technical for the workers who assemble a spacecraft. The message should relate to the vocabulary and experiences of the workers. Naturally, a different message need not always be prepared; many groups have enough common experiences to permit the use of a single audiovisual presentation addressing areas of common need and interest. Careful planning will help to identify these cluster groups, as well as audiences who need separate messages.

**Media Selection and
Mix**

Once the purpose, objectives, audience, and content have been decided, you are ready to choose a medium or combination of media. The newest, most expensive, or most technically impressive medium is not always the best. A medium can overpower or distort a message. Similarly, audiovisual

# PRACTICING PUBLIC RELATIONS

media alone cannot inform employees about their benefit plan. Other media must be used as well—face-to-face interviews, booklets, group meetings, articles in the company publication. In the overall communication effort, audiovisual media are only one part of the mix. They must complement the other media (Exhibit 8-3).

Some factors to consider when selecting audiovisual media are:

Size of audience—Some media are more appropriate for small groups and rooms. Others are better in large areas.

Composition of audience—Executives? Clerical? Blue-collar? Union? Nonunion? Educational level? Technical knowledge?

Interest of audience—Why are they likely to be there? Forced or voluntary? The presentation may need to be extra impressive and shorter if the audience is forced to attend.

Location of audience—If audiences will be in various locations the presentation will have to use a medium that is portable and easily adapted to different settings.

Equipment—Are the production as well as presentation facilities adequate? Is the cost reasonable in relation to what can be accomplished?

Wear-out potential—If a message is expensive to produce, this cost can be offset if the message can be reused.

## AUDIOVISUAL MEDIA: ADVANTAGES AND DISADVANTAGES

### Overhead Projectors

Overhead projectors are a good support system for an oral presentation. Of the two types, transparency projectors are the most popular. They can be used in a fully-lit room. The transparency can be easily made from typed material or photographs; an office copy machine will do the job. Opaque projectors are not as common, and must be used in a dark room, but they have the advantage of not needing a transparency. They project an image from any copy or photograph directly onto a screen.

### Slide Presentations

Although more expensive than overhead transparencies, 35mm slides are still relatively inexpensive, and slides can be made with relatively inexpensive equipment. Projection equipment is readily available, compact, and portable. The size of the image can be adjusted to that of the room. A darkened room is necessary, except when rear projection is used. Slides can be effective when used silently or with an accompanying audio message. More elaborate syncronized audio tape recorders and projector dissolve units can almost achieve the effect of sound motion pictures or video tape.

**Exhibit 8-3**
A Guide to Making
Audiovisual Equipment
Decisions
(*Figures are based on
information and
experience of users*)

| Equipment | Reasons for using equipment | Equipment cost (and weight) | Presentation materials costs | Audience size | Image area size | Lead Times Needed Preparing scripts | Producing materials | Equipment rehearsal & first set-up time |
|---|---|---|---|---|---|---|---|---|
| Flip Chart | Short lead time; little investment warranted | $63 (15 lbs.) | Per word cost: $25–$40 for 1–5 words per page; $75–$90 for charts, cartoons, etc. | 10 or under | 27″ to 34″ maximum | From hours to days | Up to 18 pages per day per worker | Minimal, but needed |
| Chalk Board | Informal in-house communications in board rooms & offices | $15–$150 | None | Approx. 20 | 18″ × 24″ to 48″ × 96″ | None | None | None |
| Velcro Boards, Felt Boards, etc. | Informal but professional presentation to valued audience | $70–$100 (21 to 33 lbs. for portables) | $1.50 per letter | Up to 24 | 48″ × 36″ to 72″ × 48″ | From several days to weeks | Usually several days | 3 to 4 hours or more |
| Overhead Projector (3M) | Complex materials requiring extensive discussion | $300–$500 (15 to 21 lbs. for portables) | $4–$7 made in-house; $25–$85 professional | 48 maximum | 60″ × 60″ | Hours to days | Up to several days | Allow a few hours |
| Slides (1 Projector Presentation) (Kodak) | Important audience & message; professional tone wanted | $110–$875 for random access (10 to 15 lbs.) | Type only: $5–$50 Art: $15–$75+ | Usually ltd. only to room size | 6′ or more | Plan on 2 or more weeks | Ideally, several weeks from story-board to finished art | Several hours or longer for script presented live, less with programmed tape |
| Filmstrip with Sound, Pulse Advance (Singer) | Mechanically somewhat easier than slide & sound | $360 + (20 lbs. +) | Same as slides | Same as slides | Same as slides | Same as slides | Same as slides; (Note: frame ratio is different from slides) | Same as slides |
| 16mm Sound Movies (Kodak) | Highly important audience; greatest impact; long life; simple, universal display | $735–$1775 (35 to 40 lbs.) | $1500–$6000 per minute of finished film | Usually ltd. only to room size | 6′ or more | Several weeks | 1 to 5 min. of useable footage per day's shooting | One hour or so |
| Videotape 1. Seen on monitor from pre-recorded videocassette (Sony) | 1 & 2: Important audience; credibility; cheaper, quicker production than film; quality not as critical as film | 1. $1350 (50 lbs.) | 1 & 2: Very roughly, half the cost of film and less | 1. 1 person per 1″ of monitor size; e.g. 25 for 25″ mon. | 1. up to 25′ | 1 & 2: days to weeks | 1 & 2: 3 to 5 days to duplicate videocassettes | 1 & 2: several hours |
| 2. Seen projected on screen (Sony) | | 2. $3000 (up to 200 lbs.) | | 2. 36 or so | 2. 40″ × 30″ | | | |

Other speciality systems which may be of interest are: 3M's sound-on slide; multimedia using multiple slide projectors or slides with movies; Super 8 sound movies; sound tape presentations or sound with auxiliary materials; opaque projectors which are best for small conference situations.

*Note:* Overtime for professional assistance, studio or lab time can add 50% to 100% to production costs.

Reprinted with permission: May, 1979 issue of *Public Relations Journal,* © May, 1979.

# PRACTICING
# PUBLIC
# RELATIONS

**Motion Pictures**   Motion pictures can be combined with sound-on-film, color, and animation, and shown on large screens. Films can be shipped anywhere and shown by a person with only a basic knowledge of projectors. Each time the message is presented it has the same content. Little is left to speakers or operators.

**Television and Videotape Recordings**   The use of closed-circuit television and videotape recordings began principally in plant security and employee training. Today it is the fastest growing audiovisual medium for intra-organizational communication. More than a thousand private-sector organizations use some form of television to communicate with their employees. At least eighty percent of these produce some or all of their own programming. The programs produced in-house are growing about twenty percent per year. A conservative estimate puts corporate spending on in-house closed-circuit television in the United States at more than $1.6 billion. Most Fortune-100 organizations have more than $1 million already invested in videotape and closed-circuit systems.

Because of increased use and recent technological advancements, organizations will have to learn to deal with this powerful medium. As television moves away from specialized applications such as training and security, practitioners must know its potential and its limitations. Television, like any medium, is just a carrier of a message. We know that an expensive printing press cannot help a publication that is poorly written. A fancy typewriter cannot make a vague letter easier to read. Public relations must give direction if an in-house TV system is to be effective. Practitioners must learn which messages are appropriate for this medium, just as they understand when to send a press release and when to call a news conference.

From the viewer's standpoint, corporate television systems are readily acceptable. Employees readily adapt to watching television on breaks or lunch hours. Younger employees have grown up with television as their main source of news and entertainment. Television is usually not regarded as an interruption or irritant, as printed material sometimes is. Television requires minimum effort by the viewer and is unlikely to be resisted or ignored.

Videotape is reusable and can be edited easily and recorded quickly. It is fast becoming a relatively inexpensive technique for producing the kind of in-house messages that were once bought from film distributors. Now an organization can produce a safety program to meet its own needs rather than buying a film about safety in general. If a videotaped message is produced to tell employees about an organization's benefit plan, it can be updated when changes occur, an advantage film cannot match. With videotape organizations can now prepare messages on subjects that change often. Even the drawback of the small screen has been overcome; there are now video projection systems big enough for tens of thousands of people to view simultaneously.

The uses for television and videotape messages seem endless. As organizations and managers recognize the potential of the medium they discover new ways to use it. CNA Insurance Co. produces regular programs on videotape for all employees. These "Services News and Commentary" tapes are sent to all CNA offices to inform personnel about developments and policies. Shell Oil has a ninety-minute videotaped presentation describing its benefit package. Despite the length of the program, Shell has found that employee response is better than ever before. Barnes Hospital in St. Louis, Missouri, like many other hospitals, has a series of patient-education programs that are shown on the hospital's closed-circuit TV network. The network reaches waiting rooms as well as patient rooms. Monday through Friday at regular times, patients and visitors can see programs on anatomy and physiology, pregnancy, nutrition, contraceptives, and the "Patients' Bill of Rights."

**Mini-Case 8-2
GT/F: A Success
Story in Corporate
Television**

General Telephone Company of Florida and the International Brotherhood of Electrical Workers were engaged in contract negotiations when President Richard Nixon announced a wage-and-price freeze. Confusion and rumors were abundant. Employees and management needed to know at once what effect the freeze would have. Before rumors could increase, a videotape was made of labor and management officials describing their views of the situation. Within hours, the company was broadcasting the tape to all employees over its microwave television network. This single message filled the need for an immediate response in a volatile situation; employees' apprehensions were relieved, and the contract negotiations were routinely completed within a few weeks.

Three years later, when GT/F was reorganized, President George Gage announced the move in a live two-way television meeting. All employees saw and heard the explanation simultaneously, and could ask questions. No group of employees got the message before another, and rumors were held to a minimum.

General Telephone Company of Florida uses continuous programming on its microwave network. One of the most popular programs is a weekly ten-minute news show. Much like a company newspaper, it aims at both hourly and salaried employees. The program presents a balance of spot

# PRACTICING
# PUBLIC
# RELATIONS

news and feature stories. Features focusing on the jobs of various people in the company have been popular. The television programs present highlights, while company publications give complete details.

Longer programs explore issues in depth at monthly intervals. These semi-documentaries run twenty minutes and typically deal with subjects such as corporate policy, legislation, or new products and reviews. Other programs are produced as needed.

All major lounges and break areas at GT/F are equipped with one or more television sets fed by cable or microwave. In remote locations the same programming is available on video-cassette playback units. Between major programs, the TV screens are filled with useful announcements and other information for employees. This video-bulletin board keeps employee attention high. Major programs thus have ready audiences when aired.

---

The GT/F example is becoming common practice today. Corporate television grows rapidly and steadily. More and more companies are finding closed-circuit television to be fast, flexible, and cost-effective. Today's managers find it necessary to adapt their communication skills and habits to include this new message carrier.

**Multi-Media Presentations**  By combining two or more of the media mentioned above, it is possible to achieve even greater impact. Such a presentation will usually use two or more visual media with recorded sound. Slides, motion pictures, and recorded sound can be put together into a single message to step up the amount of information sent and to use the sensory capacities of the audience. Elaborate productions can be constructed using several screens and electronic mixers and phasing units. These give the audience an impression of one continuous message.

A few years ago, an executive of a leading tire manufacture was scheduled to deliver an address to an industry convention. He was to appear late on the last day. His talk concerned a breakthrough in tire manufacturing, and his organization felt it should be forcefully presented. To overcome his unfavorable time slot on the program, the staff decided to do something different. A multi-media program was prepared, using stereo sound, slides, motion picture film and three large screens. The complete history of the industry, from the invention of the wheel to the moment of the new discovery, was presented in a colorful and dynamic five-minute presentation. The audience's attention was quickly directed to the speaker and his subject, and the speech was well received, easily overcoming its difficult place on the program.

Multi-media presentations are not always so elaborate, but they are often more effective than single-medium messages for showing comparative information. Combined images can create a wide-screen effect, or several images can be presented simultaneously to offer "bits" of information that are easier to absorb.

**Telephone Messages**   Telephone centers that give prerecorded information are increasingly used in organizations. Such recordings have long been used for time and weather service. In recent years their effectiveness in combatting rumors and misinformation in an organization has become clear. The effectiveness of telephone message centers is due to the speed and ease with which a message can be put into service. Within minutes, management can have a recorded message ready for anyone who dials a selected telephone number. Employees can confirm rumors or check for new information by dialing and listening. An employee who might be unwilling to ask a manager about a rumor can get information without embarrassment. Proof of the success of these telephone message systems can be found in their heavy use during periods of crisis and uncertainty. Recorded messages offer a human voice with authoritative information. This means high credibility and frequent usage when most needed.

It is awfully easy to get carried away by sophisticated technical gadgetry. Huge sums of money are wasted by corporations on complicated but ineffective communication. Climate, policy, and planning come first. Media are, after all, the means and not the ends of the public relations effort.

# CHAPTER 9 EVALUATING PUBLIC RELATIONS EFFECTIVENESS

**PREVIEW**  Evaluation of a public relations program is an essential step, permitting the practitioner to assess the effectiveness of the effort, demonstrate that effectivenesss to management, and plan for future efforts.

The question of "worth" or "value" of public relations effort is more important than volume in evaluating its effectiveness.

Public relations effectiveness needs to be measured through an open-system model that takes into account environmental factors as well as pretest/posttest results.

Open-system evaluation models include effectiveness measures for such factors as administrative processes, employee publications, media relations, and advertising.

For the sake of illustration and emphasis we have separated this chapter from the discussion of research in Chapter 6. If you refer back to our model of the Process of Public Relations in Figure 6-1 you will notice two components of the research function: fact finding and evaluation. We have arbitrarily broken the process of public relations down into four related functions: fact finding, planning, communication, and evaluation. In reality however, fact finding and evaluation are simply different applications of the research function of public relations. For this reason, much of what we have to say about evaluating the effects of a public relations program will relate directly back to the research methods mentioned in Chapter 6.

While we might at first glance assume that evaluation is the final stage of the public relations process, in actual practice evaluation is frequently the beginning of a new public relations effort. As we saw in Figure 6-1, the research function overlaps both the planning and communications functions to form an interdependent process that once set in motion has no beginning or end. Research should be a continuing function in the public relations process, constantly evaluating the process and its environment and providing new information to sustain it. Learning about the failures and successes of a public relations campaign provides information that can be used to plan more precisely for the next effort. Therefore, evaluation research can be valuable for its ability to contribute to a new campaign as well as its ability to assess an existing one.

Another important reason that evaluation research has become a necessity for effective public relations programs is that it enhances organizational support. Public relations professionals must assume the same responsibility for effectiveness that their management colleagues have. Organizational resources are always limited and competition for them is keen. Those who manage the public relations function of an organization must be able to demonstrate their effectiveness in ways that can be measured against other competing functions, as Robert Marker, manager of press services for Armstrong Cork, reveals in the following Mini-Case.

---

**Mini-Case 9-1
The Importance of
Fact Finding**

I remember an occasion, some years ago, that started me thinking about the need for some kind of measurement device and internal reporting system to help explain the public relations function.

I was asked by a marketing executive at Armstrong to come to his office and inform him, as succinctly as possible, just

what it was he was getting for what he was spending on
public relations. It really didn't bother me at the time,
because we had had these inquiries before, and I was pretty
sure I could handle it. I came prepared with a considerable
volume of newspaper clippings, magazine features and case
histories that we had produced in support of his product line
that year.

I laid all this out in front of him . . . after an appropriate
interval, I pointed out that all this publicity—if strung end to
end—would reach from his office located in the west wing of
the building, clear across the center wing to the east wing,
down the stairs, and out into the main lobby—and there'd still
be enough left over to paper 1½ walls of his office.

(That was a favored "measurement" device back in those
days. We used to have our secretaries total the column
inches, and then convert it all into linear feet of hallway
space. . .) . . . and then it came, the question no one
had ever asked before: "But what's all this *worth* to us?"

I stammered for a moment and said something to the effect
that I thought the material spoke for itself. After all, this was
highly coveted editorial space we were talking about . . . I
said it would be difficult to attach a specific value to it.

He smiled. "My boy," he said, "I have to attach a value to
everything in this operation . . . why don't you go back
and write me a memo outlining clearly what this function
does for us, and then we'll talk about your budget for next
year."[1]

---

Too many public relations programs have been eliminated or severely cut
back because "no value" could be attached to them. The harsh realities of
corporate existence make it necessary for public relations practitioners to
demonstrate the worth of what they do. Particularly in difficult economic
situations, every aspect of organizational activity is measured by its relative
benefit to the firm. Public relations departments that cannot demonstrate
their value to the organization will not be in a position to influence the
policy decisions that affect their own fate.

**MEASUREMENT STRATEGIES**  The concept of measurement itself is nothing new to the practice of public
relations. The problem, as Robert Marker discovered, is that the rest of the
business world has been using different standards. Marker's measurement
system was quantifiable (linear feet of hallway) and it accurately reflected
the effort that had been expended. When faced with the devastating question
of "worth," however, the measurement strategy could not provide any data.
Because the nature of public relations is intangible, assigning a value to its
activities is particularly difficult. Often this problem has led practitioners
into the use of erroneous measures or to measures incorrectly applied.

**Sources of Measurement Error**   Some common mistakes in the measurement of public relations effectiveness are:

1. *Confusion of volume and results.* As Marker learned, a large stack, or even a long chain, of press clippings may be proof of effort. But results in terms of the effect of those clippings on the publics for which they were intended cannot be measured by volume. Even audience measurement devices designed to count the number of people exposed to a message do not show whether or not those exposed actually paid any attention or, if they did, what effect the message may have had on them. Too often the working assumption has been that if one press release is effective then three will be three times as effective.

2. *Estimate is not measurement.* Reliance upon experience and intuition to gauge the effectiveness of public relations efforts is no longer acceptable as objective measurement. The one thing experts know is that appearances, even to the trained eye, can be deceiving. Guesswork has no place in a measurement system. It can be appealing and comfortable because it is so easy to accomplish and is flattering to the "expert." However, when it comes to budget requests, managers like the one Marker encountered demand hard facts.

3. *Samples must be representative.* The problem of the convenience sample is a frequent source of error. Many wrong decisions have been made about the future of a public relations campaign based on a few favorable comments that were either volunteered or collected unsystematically. The danger here is that only those who have positive (or negative) comments may volunteer them. Even when you actively seek comments some people may tell you what they think you want to hear, or you may unconsciously bias your selection. Samples must be selected scientifically and systematically to avoid this type of error.

4. *Effort is not knowledge.* One of the most common public relations objectives is increased public knowledge regarding the subject of the campaign. Sometimes practitioners assume that there exists a direct relationship between the amount of effort they expend in communicating a message and the amount of knowledge a public acquires. This erroneous assumption leads us into a problem that is similar to the volume error we discussed earlier. The study of human learning suggests that after a certain level of knowledge is reached the rate of learning slows in most people. Therefore, in spite of any communicator's best efforts, all publics will reach a level of knowledge at which the learning rate will slow.

5. *Knowledge is not favorable attitude.* Communication is often assumed to be successful if it can be demonstrated that the public has knowledge of the subject of the message. Even when pre- and post-test results indicate an increase in knowledge attributable to the communication effort, it cannot be assumed that this has resulted in more favorable attitudes. A high degree of name recall or awareness is not necessarily an indication that the public relations effort has been effective. Familiarity does not necessarily lead to positive opinion.

6. *Attitude is not behavior.* While positive public opinion may be a legitimate goal of public relations, it is incorrect to assume that favorable

attitudes will result in desired behavior. When a particular public has favorable attitudes toward a client or organization it may be assumed that they will not consciously oppose that person or group. However, this does not mean that they will actively support the goals of the public relations campaign. Our discussion of latent, aware, and active publics in Chapter 6 emphasized this point. Practitioners must be aware of the need to predict behavior, or at least potential behavior, in the measurement of public opinion.

**CLOSED-SYSTEM EVALUATION**

Mark P. McElreath describes two models of public relations evaluation research into which most measurement efforts can be categorized: open and closed evaluation systems.[2] A closed-system evaluation effort limits its scope to the messages and events planned for the public relations campaign and their effects on the intended publics. This is the model of public relations evaluation most frequently employed. The intent of this system of evaluation is to test the messages and media planned for a public relations campaign before they are presented to the intended publics. This pretest strategy is designed to uncover miscalculations in the planning stage that may have gone unnoticed to that point. The posttest evaluation is conducted after the campaign has been underway long enough to produce the desired results. Posttesting provides data that can be compared to pretest results and campaign objectives to evaluate the effectiveness of the effort. These results also provide input to the planning stage of the next campaign.

**Pretest/Posttest Design**

Factors normally considered in the standard pre- and posttest evaluation design are:

1. *Production.* An accounting of every public relations tool used in the campaign (press releases, press kits, booklets, films, letters, etc.) The amount of material actually produced and the total cost of production yield important cost-effectiveness information. The amounts of time and budget devoted to each segment of a public relations effort can be reassessed with this type of data.

2. *Distribution.* The channels through which the messages of the campaign were distributed. Clippings collected by professional services are often used to measure how many stories were actually printed. The number of radio and television stations that picked up the story can be important data. These kinds of data are perhaps most frequently used to evaluate public relations campaigns. It should be noted that while they provide a reasonable measure of the efficiency of the campaign, distribution data do not really address the issue of effectiveness.

3. *Interest.* Reader-interest surveys are conducted to determine what people read in various types of publications. A representative sample of the total potential reading audience is surveyed to obtain a quantative measure of which items attract more interest. These are relatively good measures of what readers actually consume, but they do not measure comprehension or the effect of the message on the reader. Television and radio

use similar survey methods to determine what shows people watch and when they listen to their radio.

4. *Reach*. Reader-interest surveys not only provide information concerning whether or not a story was read, but also describe the people who read it. This information can be valuable because messages frequently reach publics other than those for whom they are intended. The efficiency of a message is the extent to which it actually reaches the intended audience. Some reasonably accurate measure of which audiences are being reached by which messages is imperative to any evaluation effort. Television and radio ratings services provide information concerning the characteristics of audiences at various times of the day.

5. *Understanding*. While it is important to determine whether the target audience is being reached by the correct message, it is equally important to know whether or not they can understand it. A public relations campaign cannot be considered successful in any regard if the public does not get the point. Frequently readability tests are applied to printed messages to measure their reading ease. Generally such measures are a function of sentence length and number of syllables in the words. While much criticism has been directed at these, they remain standard instruments for pretest evaluation. The Flesch Formula produces both a Reading Ease Score and a Human Interest Score,[3] while the Gunning method measures reading ease only and is one of the simplest test[4] to use. Sentence length and the number of infrequently used words are the major factors of the Dale-Chall Formula. A technique designed to measure readability and comprehension of both auditory and visual messages is the Cloze Procedure.[5]

   Other methods of measuring understanding of the target public include recall and comprehension tests. Recall tests or surveys are frequently used with radio and television messages to determine what portion of an audience recalls seeing or hearing the message and how much they remember about the message's content. Often when a public is relatively confined or can be easily sampled, written comprehension tests can be used to measure understanding. Comprehension tests are frequently used with employee publics that are likely to have an interest in taking the tests.

6. *Attitudes*. Creating and maintaining positive attitudes or changing negative ones is a central purpose of all public relations activity. Therefore measuring attitudes or preferably attitude change is a highly prized form of evaluation. Frequently a pretest/posttest attitude measurement is conducted to determine the amount of change in the attitudes of target publics that can be attributed to the public relations campaign.

   Measuring attitudes is a sophisticated behavioral-science technique that presents many opportunities for error. Few practitioners attempt major attitudinal studies without the help of professionals who specialize in this type of measurement. Several of the research techniques discussed in Chapter 6 use some form of attitudinal measurement. Professional research organizations frequently provide attitudinal data for public relations evaluation. Many factors ranging from the need for a scientifically selected sample to the construction of a questionnaire that will not bias results make attitude measurement a difficult task for most practitioners.

While closed-system evaluation is the most widely used model for public relations evaluation, it has two major drawbacks. First, as we have already discussed, the fact that a message was transmitted to the intended audience in a form that they could easily understand and that it produced favorable attitudes concerning the client or organization involved does not mean the campaign goals have been reached. The likelihood that desired results will occur, especially physical behavior, is influenced by a number of factors outside of the elements of the campaign. If a public relations effort fails to achieve its goals it may not mean that the elements or the plan of the effort were faulty. A number of environmental factors such as economic, political, and social changes can occur to nullify what might otherwise be positive results.

Oil companies caught in the grasp of an oil embargo that caused rapidly rising prices, shortages, and long lines at the pumps experienced losses in favorable public opinion in spite of massive public relations campaigns during the early 1970s. The effectiveness of their messages was being eroded by events outside of the control of a public relations campaign. Therefore, these events had to be considered in order to evaluate the effectiveness of their public relations efforts. While losses rather than gains were experienced in positive public opinion the campaigns may have still been effective. Without effective public relations efforts in place when unexpected events occurred, the losses in favorable public opinion could have been even more devastating. Open-system evaluation models attempt to incorporate factors outside the control of a public relations campaign in the evaluation of its effectiveness.

## OPEN-SYSTEM EVALUATION

The open-system approach to evaluation attempts to include a number of factors that are not part of the closed-system model.

The open model emphasizes the extent to which the public relations function is encompassed by numerous other aspects of an organization and its environment. Factors such as unintended audiences, the administration of the organization, and the effectiveness of the organization itself are also included.

In Chapter 6 we discussed the growing use of environmental monitoring and social audits as methods of gathering information for public relations planning. These same techniques provide valuable data for the evaluation of effectiveness in public relations campaigns. The effects that public relations efforts have on various environmental factors can be one useful measure of results. Environmental data can also be used to help explain the effects of a campaign. Because most of these factors are outside of the organization's control they can operate as confounding variables in a closed-system evaluation. Economic conditions, for example, can have a significant effect on the attitudes of consumers about an organization. Thus what might appear to be little or no positive results from a public relations effort might really be significant when the negative effects of certain economic conditions are considered.

Internal climate data are also useful for the evaluation of public relations campaigns. Public relations messages should be expected to have as much effect on the managers and employees of an organization as they do on other publics. In Chapter 6 we suggested that organizations research their internal climate for public relations planning information, and this is also true for evaluation. Public relations practitioners should look inside as well as outside of their organizations to measure the effects of their efforts. Just as with environmental factors, the internal climate of an organization can help explain the effects of a public relations effort. Union activities, management perceptions, and changes in company policy can all effect the results of a public relations campaign.

Many of the factors included in the open system evaluation model are difficult to measure accurately. Nevertheless, recognition of these factors is itself an important step forward in the evaluation of public relations efforts. The value of the open-system method of evaluation is that it considers public relations in the broader spectrum of overall organizational effectiveness.

## AN EXAMPLE OF OPEN-SYSTEM EVALUATION

James F. Tirone, public relations director for the American Telephone and Telegraph Company, maintains that public relations is a managerial as well as creative effort.[6] Tirone believes that public relations should meet the same tests of performance as other management functions. This belief is reflected in the Bell System's program to develop measurement techniques for public relations programs that can be uniformly applied in a wide variety of situations. Although the practicalities of application place some limits on measurement, the following examples from the Bell System program represent an attempt to implement an open-system evaluation model in six campaigns.

### Administrative Processes

To measure the effectiveness of public relations administrative processes, Tirone used information already available from standard organizational sources to make some unique comparisons. Figure 9-1 shows the correlation between the size of the public relations budget of each of the companies used in the study and their revenues. The graph shows a clear positive correlation (0.91) between the size of public relations budgets and sales income. Figure 9-2 demonstrates an even greater correlation (0.913) between the number of telephones in service and the size of public relations budgets. By relating public relations budgets to these standards measurements in the industry, Tirone was able to show a "return" of public relations expenditures.

Figures 9-3 and 9-4 extend this analysis by comparing the increases in public relations budgets with the increases in revenues over a five-year period. Figure 9-3 illustrates that the percentage growth in public relations expenditures had not exceeded the percentage growth in revenues. Taking this comparison still futher, Tirone demonstrates that when compared to the increase in the consumer price index (one way to measure inflation) the general public relations budgets had fallen significantly behind while the advertising budget had stayed even.

**Figure 9-1**
Revenue and PR
Expense, 1976

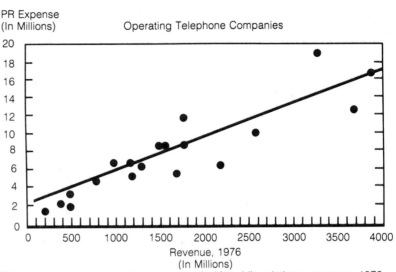

Telephone company revenues compared with public relations expenses, 1976.

James F. Tirone, "Measuring The Bell System's Public Relations," *Public Relations Review*, 3, Winter, 1977, p. 25. Reprinted by permission.

**Figure 9-2**
Telephones in Service
and PR Expense, 1976

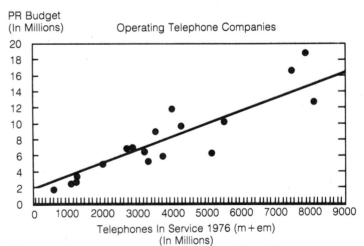

Numbers of telephones in service compared with public relations expenses.

James F. Tirone, "Measuring The Bell System's Public Relations," *Public Relations Review*, 3, Winter, 1977, p. 25. Reprinted by permission.

**Employee Publication**   The success of employee publications in the Bell System was measured against corporate objectives for these publications: ". . . reach all employees, create awareness, establish a reputation for reliability, be written so the material can be understood, and be readable at an educational level appropriate to the audience."[7] These objectives were translated into the

**Figure 9-3**
Increases in Revenue
and Public Relations
Budgets

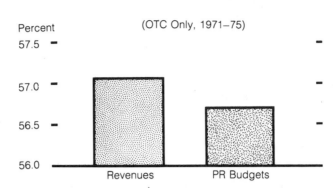

A Comparison of the Growth of Bell Telephone Company Revenues with the Growth of
Public Relations Budgets from 1971 to 1975.

James F. Tirone, "Measuring The Bell System's Public Relations," *Public Relations Review*, 3, Winter,
1977, pp. 26–27. Reprinted by permission.

**Figure 9-4**
Percent Increases in
OTC PR Accounts and
CPI, 1971–1975

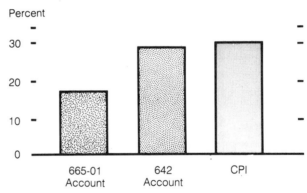

Comparison of the Increase in Total Bell Telephone Company Public Relations (665-01)
and advertising (642) Expenses with Growth of the Consumer Price Index.

James F. Tirone, "Measuring The Bell System's Public Relations," *Public Relations Review*, 3, Winter,
1977, pp. 26–27. Reprinted by permission.

following measurement criteria: ". . . . how effectively the publication was
distributed within forty-eight hours, an average estimate of reader awareness
of stories, a reliability index, understanding, and readability (as measured
on the Gunning scale)." Table 9-1 reports the ability of a sample of employees
to recall (without any help) certain stories which appeared in the company's
weekly newspaper. Table 9-2 reports measures of all the components of
publication efficiency as operationally defined:

*Distribution*—percentage of issues delivered in forty-eight
   hour period.
*Awareness*—average of recall data.

*Reliability*—average response to three questions: whether the newspaper is very understandable, excellent at presenting both sides, and an excellent source.

*Understanding*—percentage of those recalling the corporate-policy seminar story who understood its message.

*Readability*—the Gunning score for the corporate-policy seminar story which is roughly equal to the number of years of education required for comprehension.

**Table 9-1**
Top Recall by Employees of Company Newspaper Articles (Three Issues of the Publication)

| Subject Matter | Unaided Recall |
|---|---|
| Employment Office Hiring (1) | 56% |
| Defending The Company (3) | 42% |
| Pioneer Circus (1) | 40% |
| Marketing/Competition (3) | 36% |
| Corporate Planning Seminar (3-Week Average) | 6% |
| Averaged Recall | 36% |

James F. Tirone, "Measuring the Bell System's Public Relations," *Public Relation Review* 3 (Winter 1977): 29. Reprinted by permission.

**Table 9-2**
Employee Publication Scoring

| Component | Score |
|---|---|
| Distribution | 67% |
| Awareness | 36% |
| Reliability (average) | 34% |
|    Very Understandable | 61% |
|    Both Sides/Excellent | 12% |
|    Source/Excellent | 30% |
| Understanding (CPS Only) | 40% |
| Readability (CPS Only) | 16.5 (Years) |

James F. Tirone, "Measuring the Bell System's Public Relations," *Public Relations Review* 3 (Winter 1977): 30. Reprinted by permission.

**Table 9-3**
Newspaper Stories by Region (Total: 3,848)

| | Favorable | Unfavorable | Neutral | Totals |
|---|---|---|---|---|
| Northeast | 14% | 5% | 5% | 24% |
| South | 18% | 5% | 8% | 31% |
| North Central | 18% | 3% | 10% | 31% |
| West | 9% | 2% | 3% | 14% |
| | 59% | 15% | 25% | 100% |

James F. Tirone, "Measuring the Bell System's Public Relations," *Public Relations Reveiw* 3 (Winter 1977): 34. Reprinted by permission.

**Table 9-4**
Treatment by Media
Services

| | Favorable | Unfavorable | Neutral | Total |
|---|---|---|---|---|
| AP | 61% | 18% | 21% | 100% |
| UPI | 19% | 33% | 48% | 100% |
| Syndicates | 43% | 22% | 35% | 100% |

James F. Tirone, "Measuring the Bell System's Public Relations," *Public Relations Review* 3 (Winter 1977): 34. Reprinted by permission.

**Media Relations**   Measuring the effectiveness of an organization's relationships with media representatives is a difficult task. Tirone reports three aspects of these relationships that can be measured to some degree: "... the media's views of those relationships, the consequences which follow from news release output, and the activity of our (Bell System) media representative."[9] To accomplish these measurement objectives Tirone proposed a nationwide survey of news media representatives to estimate their rating of the quality and quantity of Bell System releases and an analysis of the media to determine what is actually being said about Bell.

To begin the second phase of the process, Bell hired P R Data Systems, Inc. to code and computerize information collected from clippings and reports from electronic media. Figure 9-5 summarizes the percentage of favorable, unfavorable, and neutral news articles about Bell companies in the media surveyed. Figure 9-6 sorts the news items into ten categories relevant for Bell operations and provides favorable, unfavorable, and neutral data for each category. Figure 9-7 reports the number of rebuttals by Bell representatives that were printed in the 503 unfavorable stories included in the sample. Tirone explains that Bell news people are expected to maintain effective relationships with news media representatives that will encourage a reporter

**Figure 9-5**
Total News Stories By
Tendency

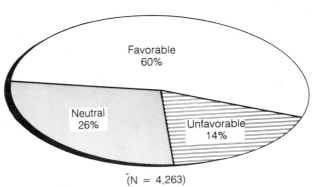

(N = 4,263)

Central tendency of all news items during one-month period

James F. Tirone, "Measuring The Bell System's Public Relations," *Public Relations Review*, 3, Winter, 1977, p. 32. Reprinted by permission.

or editor to call for a reaction from the company before printing an unfavorable story. Figure 9-7 shows that forty-five percent of the unfavorable stories had rebuttal statements from Bell representatives included. Over a long period this type of data could help measure both access to Bell spokespersons and the quality of their relationships with media representatives. Tables 9-3 and 9-4 report the percentage of favorable, unfavorable, and neutral stories by region of the country and by media service respectively. From these data certain discrepancies can be discovered which are useful in pinpointing problem areas and in planning future efforts.

Frequently evaluation is assumed to be the final step in the process of public relations; however, it is really best described as a new beginning. Measuring the effectiveness of a public relations effort frequently provides new direction and emphasis for an ongoing program. Even when the project that is being evaluated does not continue, the lessons learned concerning

**Figure 9-6**
Stories By Tendency

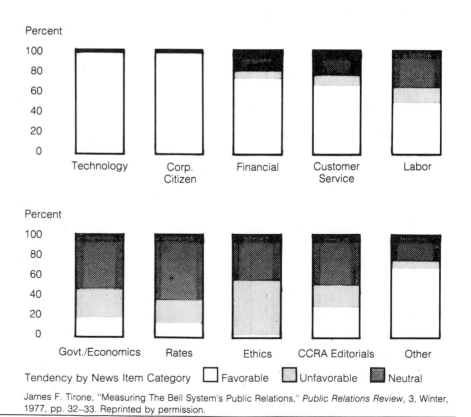

Tendency by News Item Category    ☐ Favorable   ▨ Unfavorable   ▪ Neutral

James F. Tirone, "Measuring The Bell System's Public Relations," *Public Relations Review*, 3, Winter, 1977, pp. 32–33. Reprinted by permission.

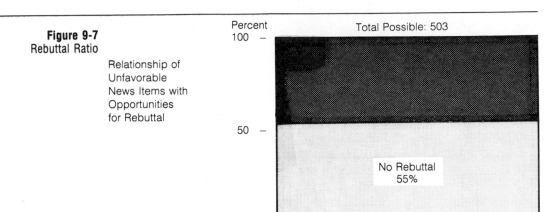

**Figure 9-7**
Rebuttal Ratio

Relationship of
Unfavorable
News Items with
Opportunities
for Rebuttal

Percent

Total Possible: 503

No Rebuttal
55%

James F. Tirone, "Measuring The Bell System's Public Relations," *Public Relations Review,* 3, Winter, 1977, p. 33. Reprinted by permission.

its effectiveness will be useful in numerous future activities. Knowledge gained through careful evaluation is an important payoff to any public relations effort. Evaluation of projects that are obvious failures can help prevent future mistakes; careful measurement of successful efforts will help make it possible to reproduce successful elements in future programs.

Public relations can no longer afford to ignore the question "But what's it all *worth* to us?" Practitioners must be ready to respond with appropriate methods, solid data, and accurate predictions.

## CASE STUDY: AMERICAN RED CROSS CENTENNIAL CELEBRATION

**By Artemio R. Guillermo**
**Assistant Professor of Speech,**
**University of Northern Iowa,**
**Cedar Falls, Iowa**

Anniversary celebrations can be major public relations events in the life of an organization. Celebrations are especially significant when they mark centennial observances that not only generate mass media coverage but also produce activities highlighting the image of the institution.

Although the planning of most celebrations follows the four-step process of public relations, evaluation is often neglected during the enthusiasm of planning. After activities and programs have been executed, how can planners know whether the celebration was a success? How can they know to what extent their celebration affected their target audience's attitudes toward the organization? What information can the planners get that could be used to evaluate the results of the celebration?

These questions were posed to a public relations student team that undertook to help the Hawkeye Chapter of the American Red Cross celebrate its centennial. When the team volunteered its assitance, the program and activities had already been planned. The overall objective was to project the humanitarian services of the American Red Cross and encourage volunteer participation.

The plan called for a week-long celebration. There were twenty events and activities, including a hot air balloon, a mock disaster, a historical display, a speaker's bureau, an open house, an annual meeting and banquet, a centennial blood donor day, a birthday party, and the like.

Printed communications, including a sixteen-page historical booklet and a six-page newsletter, were sent to local institutions and community leaders. The local papers gave the celebration full-page, pictorial coverage with the headline "Happy Birthday." Billboards, media releases, and public service announcements on radio and television were also used to publicize the event.

Although an evaluation was planned by the Red Cross centennial committee, they did not quite know how to proceed. When the students became involved, they decided that their first task was to develop an evaluation instrument.

After consulting with several professors, they devised a form on which to note the following items:

Project name:
Description:
  Time—
  Place—
  Has project been done before?
  If so, describe:
Intended Publics
  Primary—
  Secondary—
Goals and Objectives
  Strategies—
Cost:
Possible Public Relations Problems
Method of Evaluation
Results:
Conclusion:

When the centennial celebration started, the public relations team monitored the activities. Twelve out of twenty projects/activities were evaluated.

When all the evaluations were compiled, the students had some interesting findings. One of the hottest items in the celebration as a crowd-drawer was the hot air balloon. An evaluator stated: "Such an event draws attention (biggest advantage), location was good . . ."

On the other hand a leaflet enclosed with monthly bank statements, describing the centennial activities received a low evaluation. Evaluator's comment on the possible public relations effect was: "Confusion by general public as to purpose of stuffer." And the conclusion was that it had low visible response from customers.

All of these evaluations were placed on file with the Hawkeye Chapter of the American Red Cross for future reference and as a record of its 100th anniversary celebration.

**Questions**  1. What is the value of an evaluation of this kind of program?

2. How would you improve the evaluation instrument used in this project?

3. What other forms of evaluation might be appropriate in this situation?

---

**NOTES**  [1] Robert K. Marker, "The Armstrong/PR Data Management System," *Public Relations Review* 3 (Winter 1977): 51–52.

[2] Mark P. McElreath, "Public Relations Evaluative Research: Summary Statement," *Public Relations Review* 3 (Winter 1977): 133.

[3] Rudolph Flesch, *How to Test Readability* (New York: Harper and Row, 1951).

[4] Robert Gunning, *The Technique of Clear Writing,* rev. ed. (New York: McGraw-Hill, 1968).

[5] Edgar Dale and Jeanne Chall, "A Formula for Predicting Readability," *Educational Research Bulletin* 27 (January-February 1948).

[6] Wilson Taylor, "Cloze Procedure: A New Tool for Measuring Readability," *Journalism Quarterly* 3 (Fall 1953) 415–33; "Recent Developments in the Use of 'Cloze Procedure,' " *Journalism Quarterly* 33 (Winter 1956).

[7] James F. Tirone, "Measuring The Bell System's Public Relations," *Public Relations Review* 3 (Winter 1977): 21–38.

[8] Ibid., p. 31.

[9] Ibid., p. 31.

PRACTICING
PUBLIC
RELATIONS

# IMPACT ANALYSIS

Measurement of the impact or results of a public relations effort is always difficult and never totally objective. As we have discussed in this chapter, however, the more public relations practitioners can quantitatively measure the effects of their work, the better they will be able to plan future efforts and demonstrate their value to organizational decision makers. The examples from AT&T already discussed provide a good perspective on what can be quantified in large organizations to evaluate public relations results. In this section, we offer four dimensions of measurement that can be applied to assess the impact of any public relations campaign regardless of its size: *audience coverage, audience response, campaign impact,* and *environmental mediation.*

**AUDIENCE COVERAGE**  Perhaps the first thing that must be documented in any evaluation of public relations efforts is whether or not the intended audiences were reached. Additional questions that should be answered in this initial phase of analysis are: to what extent was each target audience exposed to the various messages? and which unintended audiences also received your messages?

Two basic measures are used to help answer these questions. First, accurate records must be kept of what releases were prepared and where they were sent. Next, some method of keeping track of which releases are used by whom must be employed. While the first measure is the easiest to calculate, it is worthless without the second for comparison. The generation of massive numbers of publicity releases has no value unless some of them actually reach their intended audiences. Therefore, some method must be devised to accurately measure the use of releases and the coverage of events.

Essentially, this can be accomplished by the practitioner and/or other staff members keeping a careful check on target media and maintaining clipping files. This, of course, is easier for print than for broadcast media. However, some radio and television stations give periodic reports to public relations practitioners if requested. In addition, clipping services are available that will monitor both print and broadcast media and provide regular reports for a fee. Such a service must be selected carefully, based upon the recommendations of other users concerning their accuracy.

The measurement of audience coverage must involve more than just the ratio of releases sent to releases used. The practitioner must also be able to specify what audiences (both intended and unintended) were reached by which media. This type of data is available from readership and audience rating information that can be obtained from the media advertising sales departments. These audience profiles for each publication or broadcast station can be calculated with the amount of coverage given to yield a complete measure of audience coverage. Such data can be reported in terms of total column inches and airtime per audience for each release or event (*see Table 9-5*). For more of a "bottom-line" effect, many practitioners like to translate media time and space into its dollar value according to prevailing advertising rates.

**AUDIENCE RESPONSE**  Once it has been determined that a message has reached its intended audience, the practitioner must then evaluate the quality of that audience's response. Frequently this type of information can be obtained from various forms of message pretesting such as those we discussed in this chapter and in Chapter 6. Samples of each target audience can be exposed to various messages before they are released to predict whether: the message causes a favorable or unfavorable reaction; the message attracts the attention and arouses the interest of the audience; the audience understands the message. Through the application of good sampling techniques and questionnaire design (Chapter 6), accurate predictions can be made and problems can

**Table 9-5**
Some Available
Measures of Audience
Coverage

| Column Inches of Space / Air Time in Seconds | Audience Type I | Audience Type II | Audience Type III | Audience Type IV | Magazine A | Newspaper B | Radio Station C | Television Station D | Wire Service |
|---|---|---|---|---|---|---|---|---|---|
| Release 1 (column inches) | 271 | 450 | 175 | 206 | 250 | 375 | | | 400 |
| Release 1 (air time) | 600 | 1320 | 480 | 540 | | | 1250 | 300 | |
| Release 2 | | | | | | | | | |
| Event 1 | | | | | | | | | |
| Release 3 | | | | | | | | | |
| Event 2 | | | | | | | | | |

# PRACTICING PUBLIC RELATIONS

be corrected before the messages are released. Some messages, however, such as news coverage of an event or feature and news stories written from releases, cannot be measured in advance because they are not controlled by the practitioner. Thus, it is necessary to measure the response of audience samples after messages have been released using the survey techniques discussed in Chapter 6. Frequently, audience response can be predicted by tracking media treatment of stories in terms of favorable, neutral, and unfavorable tendencies, as in Figures 9-5, 9-6, and 9-7, and Tables 9-3 and 9-4.

Messages can also be pretested through the use of readability tests. The basic premise of these tests is that written copy will be ineffective if it is too difficult to read. Most of the methods for measuring readability generate an index score that can be translated to an educational level that would be required to understand the material. For example, magazines such as *Time* and *Reader's Digest* are written at an eleventh- or twelfth-grade level. This indicates that the readership of these publications consists primarily of persons with a high school or more advanced education. There has been a great deal of controversy over which formulas are the most accurate and concerning what factors are necessary to compute readability. Whether or not a score of 9 on a particular index actually means that someone with a ninth grade education could easily read the material is not the only consideration for public relations writing. Readability tests can be used to tailor writing styles for target publications. The index score of a release can be compared to the score of the publication for which it is intended to determine whether or not they are compatible. One of the easiest of these formulas to use is the Gunning Fog Index detailed in Table 9-6.

It should be remembered that the simplest writing is not always the best message. It is possible to lose meaning through oversimplification as well

---

**Table 9-6**
Computing the Gunning Fog Index

To check the reading ease of any passage of writing compute:

1. The number of words in the copy.
2. The number of complete thoughts in the copy.
3. The average sentence length.
   [number of words ÷ number of complete thoughts]
4. The percentage of difficult words.
   (words having three or more syllables except: proper names, combinations of short easy words, and verb forms made three syllables by adding -ed or -es)
   [number of difficult words ÷ total number of words]
5. Average sentence length + percentage of difficult words.
6. The figure derived in Step 5 is multiplied by .4 to get the Fog Index Score, the grade level at which the copy is easily read.

as complexity. Abstract or complex concepts cannot be adequately expressed in simple, short sentences using one- and two-syllable words. The important point is to match your copy to the publication and audience for which it is intended. This textbook, for example, was written for college students who are studying public relations, not casual readers. Frequently editors of internal publications in highly technical organizations have to avoid talking down to their readers as much as they have to avoid "fog."

**CAMPAIGN IMPACT**    In addition to the response of the audience to individual messages, the practitioner must be concerned with the impact of the entire campaign as a whole. In this case, the whole is not equal to the sum of its parts. If a campaign is correctly researched and planned, its elements will interact with each other to produce an effect that is much greater than the sum of the response to the individual messages. If the mix is not right, however, the elements of a campaign, no matter how individually excellent, can combine to fall far short of the goal.

Therefore, it is important to measure the cumulative impact of a public relations campaign, keeping in mind the goals developed in the planning phase. This can be done only after the campaign has been in progress long enough to achieve some results. These effects are generally attitudinal, although they can also be behavioral. If one of the goals for the campaign was to maintain or increase favorable attitudes toward an organization among members of certain publics, the methods described in Chapter 6 can be used to gauge achievement of this goal. Usually this calls for both pre- and posttests, or for a series of surveys to track attitude trends. In addition, certain actions on the part of members of a public can be measured, such as complaints, inquiries about services, and requests for reprints.

**ENVIRONMENTAL
MEDIATION**    Practitioners must realize that the public relations campaign is not the only influence on the attitudes and behaviors of their publics. As we have discussed earlier in this chapter, public relations campaigns exist in an environment of social processes that can have as much or more effect on the goals of a public relations effort as the prepared messages. Therefore, the results measured in the campaign impact analysis must be interpreted in light of various other forces in operation at the time. Failure to reach a goal may not be failure at all when unforeseen negative conditions arise. Likewise, a striking success may not all be attributable to a campaign when positive environmental forces are acknowledged. Therefore, techniques such as environmental monitoring and others discussed in Chapter 6 should be used to evaluate the results of a campaign.

One method that can be used to check for environmental influences, even when the practitioner has a small budget and staff, is focus group interviewing. Focus groups are small groups randomly selected from a

# PRACTICING
# PUBLIC
# RELATIONS

public who are invited to meet together to discuss the campaign. When the group meets, it should be presented with the elements of the campaign and then directed through a discussion of its effects and their causes. A skillful interviewer will direct the group's discussion to keep it on the subject without disturbing the free flow of ideas or candor. Focus groups should be asked to discuss their reactions to the elements of the campaign and to assess its overall effect. They can also help to interpret data obtained in the campaign impact stage in relation to historical, social, and political events that may have had an effect.

These four stages of measurement can help a public relations practitioner gain a more complete assessment of the results of a campaign and plan future efforts more effectively. In addition, they provide the kind of real-world data managers in other areas of an organization use to support their activities.

# SECTION III PUBLIC RELATIONS: THE PUBLICS

A public is a group of people with certain common characteristics. A public can be very large—college students, Republicans, blue-collar workers, even the entire population of the United States. A public can also be quite small—the city council, the budget committee, newspaper editors and television news directors in a middle-sized city, sometimes a single person.

Different organizations have different publics. Big businesses have publics different from those of small businesses. The publics for the steel industry are different from those of the computer industry or agriculture. Not-for-profit organizations have publics different from profit-seeking organizations. Different levels of government organizations deal with different publics.

There are three kinds of publics, however, that all organizations which use public relations on a continuous basis must address themselves to: the organization's employees; the people of the community or communities in which the organization operates; and the mass media. Discussions of how to work with these three crucial publics constitute Section III.

**PREVIEW**  When organizations achieve effective employee communication, the results may include: more satisfied and productive employees; improved achievement of organization goals; and improved customer, community, investor, and public relations.

Effective employee communication depends on the establishment of a positive organizational climate. Feelings of trust, confidence, openness, candor, supportiveness, security, satisfaction, involvement, and high expectations characterize ideal organizational climates.

Public relations should seek to help employees become well-informed about their organization and help them express their views to management.

Michael H. Mescon, a management professor and consultant, tells the story of an experience aboard a Delta Airlines jet:

**I was just settling into my seat when I casually remarked to the fellow sitting next me about the skyrocketing cost of airline tickets. The fellow didn't take my remark very casually.**

"Do you know why that ticket costs what it does?" he asked.

"No," I said, "And I don't really care."

"Well you ought to care," he said. "Because what that ticket pays for is your safety, comfort and convenience."

Well, by now I knew I was in for it. The guy told me what the carpet on the floor cost and why that particular kind of carpet had to be used. He explained the construction of the seat I was sitting in. He talked about support personnel on the ground for every plane in the air and, of course, he dealt with the costs of jet fuel. Finally, I stopped him.

"I know the president and several of Delta's vice presidents," I said. "You must be one of the vice presidents I don't know."

"No," the fellow said, "I work in the upholstery shop."

**"Well, how do you know so much about Delta's operations?"**

**"The company keeps us informed."**

When organizations commit themselves to effective communication with their employees, a number of important benefits can result. Well-informed employees are usually satisfied employees. They are better, more productive workers who get more out of their work and do a better job for the company. Where communication lines are open, organizational goals are more easily achieved. Moreover, as the above example shows, well-informed employees interact with the public and can have significant positive effects on relations with customers, the community, investors, and the general public.

Achieving effective employee communication is no simple task. To understand the process by which it is accomplished, and the role of public relations in that process, we propose to discuss in some detail the concept of organizational climate.

**ORGANIZATIONAL CLIMATE** Over fifty years of research in the field of organizational behavior demonstrates that the most powerful forces in the workplace are psychological. An aspect of the collective psychological forces at work in an organization is called organizational climate. Several definitions of this concept exist. Here are two of the most widely accepted.

Organizational climate is a relatively enduring quality of the internal environment of an organization that (a) is experienced by its members, (b) influences their behavior, and (c) can be described in terms of the values or . . . characteristics of the organization.[1]

We might define (organizational) climate as a set of attributes specific to a particular organization that may be induced from the way that organizations deal with their members and their environments.[2]

In effect, organizational climate consists of the subjective perceptions held by employees of such organizational realities as policy, structure, leadership, standards, and rules. Various researchers have noted important connections between climate and motivation,[3] and between climate, creative ability and performance.[4]

Ideal organizational climates are characterized by such feelings as trust, confidence, openness, candor, supportiveness, security, satisfaction, involvement, and high expectations. To a large extent, successful employee relations in general, and effective employee communication in particular, depend on the existence of positive organizational climates.

William Whyte makes this point very clearly:

**Only with trust can there be any real communication. Until that trust is achieved the techniques and gadgetry of communications are so much effort. Before employees will accept management's fact, they must have overall confidence in its motives and sincerity.[5]**

Public relations researcher Jim Grunig makes a similar point specifically related to company media:

**How much employees use company media and how they evaluate them is more a function of what they think of the company and their role in it than it is of anything the communications professionals do.[6]**

All of this suggests that the crucial prerequisite for effective employee relations and communication is the creation of a positive organizational climate based on feelings of trust, confidence and openness. How this can be accomplished and public relations' role in its accomplishment is our next focus of discussion.

**PUBLIC RELATIONS AND ORGANIZA- TIONAL CLIMATE**

The primary responsibility for organizational climate belongs to line management, from the chief executive officer to supervisors. The public relations staff can make significant contributions to a positive organizational climate in terms of their inputs to organizational decisions, their roles as internal communication consultants, and, perhaps most importantly, by helping to establish organizational communication policy based on a goal-oriented approach.

In terms of decision input and internal consultation, public relations managers must constantly remind line managers that nothing an organization says to its employees can communicate more effectively than what it does to or for them. Moreover, to ensure an understanding of the organization's philosophy, policies, and actions, the public relations staff must consistently stress the need for effective two-way communication. Employees must be well-informed, and they must have the means of expressing their views to management about organizational affairs (more on this later).

**Organizational Communication Policy**

According to communication expert Norman Sigband, top management generally recognizes the need for and sincerely desires two-way communication.[7] The bottleneck in corporate communication is usually found in the middle of the corporate hierarchy. Although they may want to communicate, middle- and lower-level managers often find it difficult because they have no parameters, no boundaries, and no policies to guide them.

Public relations managers can greatly facilitate the creation of positive organizational climates if they can convince top management that communication, like finance, personnel, marketing, promotion, and almost every other area of organizational activity, should have established policies.

Communication policies must be goal-oriented rather than event-oriented. In other words, rather than addressing specific issues or topics about which managers and employees communicate, policies should focus on the process and objectives of communication. They should focus on gaining employee understanding of, inputs to, and identification with organizational objectives and problems.

Successful communication policies must be based on management's desire to:

1. Keep employees informed of organizational goals, objectives, and plans.
2. Inform employees of organizational activities, problems, and accomplishments.
3. Encourage employees to provide inputs, information, and feedback to management based on their experience, insights, feelings, creativity and reason.
4. Level with employees about negative, sensitive, or controversial issues.
5. Encourage frequent, honest, job-related, two-way communication among managers and their subordinates.
6. Communicate important events and decisions as quickly as possible to all employees.
7. Establish a climate where innovation and creativity are encouraged.
8. Have every manager and supervisor discuss with each of his subordinates the latter's progress and position in the firm.

When such guidelines are accepted and practiced by all levels of management as corporate communication policy, the organization's climate will improve.

**THE IMPORTANCE OF EMPLOYEE COMMUNICATION**

Having established that climate and policy are the bases of effective employee communication, we can explore its importance and the means by which it is achieved.

**CEO Perspectives**

"Employee communication, the Johnny-come-lately of the public relations/communication business continues to inch its way into corporate executive thinking," according to the report of a recent survey of corporate chief executive officers by the International Association of Business Communications.[8] It continued, "In terms of corporate priorities, the vast majority of CEOs rated employee communication in the 'extremely important,' 'very important' or 'tops' categories."

The survey report included a variety of statements by CEOs about employee communication. Here is a sampling of their responses:

"**The success or failure of everything from new products to advertising campaigns to reaching our goals for the fiscal year are affected by how well our employees understand what we are trying to accomplish and how we accomplish it.**"

"**There is a direct correlation between employee communication and profitability.**"

"**I find that making good profits really goes hand in hand with having good communication.**"

"**The best (business) plan is meaningless unless everyone is aware of it and pulling together to achieve its objectives. Good communications are the lifeblood of any enterprise, large or small. Communications are essential to keep our entire organization functioning at maximum levels and to make the most of our greatest management resource—our people.**"

"**Employees can't be happy in their work or with their company unless they're well informed.**"

"**If employees understand what you're trying to do and get involved in the process feeling like they're really a part of it, then the job gets done much more easily, and there are fewer grievances and fewer problems.**"

Not surprisingly, public relations managers share the concern expressed in these quotations. A 1976 survey of the public relations departments of the *Fortune* Top 50 companies demonstrated an overwhelming consensus that employee communication is an area of expanding interest.[9] Another indication of the trend is found in the membership of the International Association of Business Communicators, a professional organization consisting largely of employee communication specialists. In one recent year its membership increased from 5,000 to about 7,000 or forty percent, while the membership of the Public Relations Society of America stood still. Employee communication is the faster-growing component of public relations practice.

**Traditional Public Relations Views of Employee Communications**

Rather than recognizing the comprehensive nature of employee communications, public relations traditionally has viewed employees as just one of many publics. In some ways, employees are still viewed as a "public," but a very special one. Public relations has recognized that employees are a medium through which other publics gain information and establish attitudes toward organizations.

Good relations with a community where an organization's facilities are located, or the general public, originates with good employee communications. Neighbors, family, friends, and associates of employees are themselves potential customers, employees, and decision makers on issues crucial to the organization. A Gallup poll revealed that each employee influences an average of fifty people in the community.

These facts are known to chief executive officers. In the IABC survey one CEO stated: "We just had a survey commissioned on customer opinion. It found that where the customer knew a company employee, his attitudes toward the company were more favorable." [10]

**EMPLOYEE COMMUNICATION PROGRAMS**

Employee communication programs use all media and means of conveying information. Supervisors, working primarily through interpersonal and small-group communication, are the most critical communications link. Public relations objectives in employee communication seek to improve support, and reinforce this link. Supervisory communication is supported with small and large meetings, letters, periodicals, bulletin boards, exhibits, annual reports, advertising, handbooks and manuals, envelope stuffers, reading racks, public address systems, telephone hotlines, surveys, suggestion systems, films, close-circuit television and other means, all used in total employee communication efforts.

In the 1970s, several forces combined to reshape organizational communication policies and practices. Employees have demanded more challenging jobs and greater work flexibility. Consumer groups have demanded greater input and more product information. New government regulations have had a variety of impacts. As a result, more organizations are concerned about their public response. They are more receptive to incoming communication from their publics, more concerned about openness and truthfulness, and increasingly prepared to communicate with their policies.

Internally, organizations have put greater emphasis on keeping employees informed on the organization's positions on political issues, future organizational plans, and the economics of the organization. Moreover, James Lahiff and John Hatfield found that organizations have become active in soliciting ideas from employees, listening to employee suggestions, and creating an atmosphere in which employees feel free to speak their minds. [11]

All of this suggests that the specific jobs of public relations managers in the 1980s in relation to employee communications include:

Promoting awareness and understanding of organizational
   goals;
Interpreting management and personnel policies;

Fulfilling employees' informational needs;
Providing means for and stimulating two-way
    communication.
Encouraging favorable employee attitudes and increased
    productivity;
Making all employees ambassadors from the organization
    to the general public

We will discuss how various organizational media are used to meet these goals in the "Practicing Public Relations" section following this chapter.

**What Communication Programs Can Accomplish**    When communication programs work they can be tremendously cost effective. Sweetheart Plastics, for example, invested $7,000 in a communication program to increase productivity. The company realized a savings of $250,000 the first year and expects a ten-year saving of $2.5 million. Mini-case 10-1 cites another such example.

---

**Mini-Case 10-1 Communication Aids Productivity at Westinghouse**    The Westinghouse major appliance division plant in Mansfield, Ohio, had an old physical facility and some old ideas about management. As a result, it suffered low productivity, rampant absenteeism, high unit costs, and sometimes hostile labor relations. Moreover, in a town where Westinghouse was the largest employer, press relations were indifferent at best.

The plant had been losing money for years, and had the highest production cost per finished unit in the fiercely competitive appliance market.

According to Tom Christensen, communication and training manager, "It was a 'produce-or-perish' situation." To deal with the situation, Westinghouse developed a program designed to accomplish five goals: increase salable hours; reduce defective product costs; reduce accident costs; increase cost improvement savings; improve teamwork. Communication was the primary means by which these goals were achieved.

Communication efforts included:

Sixty hours of supervisor training in which information was shared on the nature of the plant's problems and how they might make positive contributions.
Face-to-face meetings (for the first time) between the plant's general manager and all employees. The manager explained the problems, goals and how the employee could help.

A beefed-up suggestion system to promote upward communication. In its first year, the system netted sixty-seven percent more cost-saving ideas and fifty-eight percent greater savings than experienced in previous years.

Company media were used to supplement and reinforce the program. The plant's publication, *The Conveyor* featured articles in every issue on some phase of the program. Posters were developed for bulletin boards. Brochures supported the suggestion system. Visual displays were produced. Plant communication media reached employees at work and at home.

Labor relations were improved through frank interaction between management and union officials. Union stewards were offered special training classes.

Plant problems were also discussed frankly with local media. The media responded with improved coverage and, in effect, reinforced management's message with headlines like "Future Of Westinghouse In Workers' Hands."

The results of the program included:

Productivity gains ranging from ten to seventeen percent.
$100,000 annual savings in incentive plan subsidies.
Unjustified absences down twenty percent.

Christensen concluded: "Now, if the economy would just pick up so that we could sell some of those appliances we're producing . . ."

---

## Why Communication Programs Fail

When emloyee communication programs are ineffective, the costs are immeasurable. Inefficiency, waste, higher costs, low morale, absenteeism, strikes, turnover, and accidents are just some of the ways that poor employee communication can have adverse effects on sales, profits, productivity, public image, and the individual employees themselves.

Some reasons for ineffective communication have already been indicated: unclear corporate images, negative organizational climates, lack of employee communication policies, lack of mutual trust and respect between employees and management.

One of the most common reasons for failure is that employee communication too often attempts to "sell" management's line to employees. The stimulation of upward flows of information based on employee inputs is neglected. One of the CEOs participating in the IABC survey emphasized this point:

**If we are making an attempt to communicate with our employees specifically to sell them something, our effort is going to fail. If we are attempting**

to communicate, to tell them something and invite feedback, then our effort will be successful, even if we make mistakes.    .    .[12]

Richard Nemec offers a more unsettling explanation for the failure of employee communication. In effect, he returns us to the consideration of organizational climate: "If you had to condense modern corporate communication problems into one word," he maintains, "it would be 'fear.' Fear of reprisal .    .    . fear of being innovate .    .    . fear of honesty."[13]

## PUBLIC RELATIONS AND EMPLOYEE COMMUNICATION WITH A UNIONIZED WORKFORCE

An understanding of the evolution and role of organized labor in the United States is essential to the understanding of the American economic and business system. Crucial matters of inflation, productivity, the quality of life on and off the job, and international trade are strongly influenced by the collective bargains struck by businesses and unions. Union activities in the political arena—sometimes in conjunction with business and sometimes in opposition to business—are a powerful influence on the government's role in the economy.

Unions are active in many kinds of organizations. The crushing of the air traffic controllers union by the Federal Aviation Administration in 1981 showed that bad management/union relations can be as costly in the public sector as in the private sector of the economy. Teachers, nurses, municipal employees, police and fire personnel, and other employees of not-for-profit or government organizations are increasingly unionized. Indeed, these are the fastest areas of union growth. Virtually no organization is immune from the costs of poor labor relations, as the AFL-CIO learned when its own clerical employees went on strike.

Unionization of an organization's workforce places employee communication and public relations in a slightly different light. Basic practices of effective employee communication hold, however, whether or not an organization is unionized.

Many organizations attempt to utilize effective employee communications to ward off union efforts to organize their labor force. The threat of unionization, in effect, scares management into instituting the effective communication policies and programs that should have existed in the first place. It is unfortunate that the timing and motivation of efforts to establish the proper communication climate and facilitate upward communication sometimes have caused these important activities to be perceived as anti-union techniques. As personnel specialist Don Crane states: "Progressive organizations, whether unionized or not, encourage employees to express their complaints, questions, or job problems; insist they be given a fair hearing, and give them a timely answer."[14]

## Why Workers Join Unions

Conventional wisdom has it that unions exist because of management failures. Other variables—like the size of organizations—play a role, of course, but in many cases the conventional wisdom is true.

Workers join unions to gain power so that they can better pursue their needs and goals. Better pay, shorter hours, and improved working conditions are common reasons for unionizing. But other factors, including the opportunity to be heard and the need to be recognized and respected motivate workers to form and join unions. Good management provides for worker's physiological and social needs and thus can alleviate pressures toward unionization.

**Why Management Resists Unions**

Unions are not inherently evil things as some might have you believe. Some corporate managements even prefer to deal with unions when they offer consistency, predictability, control, and a pool of qualified workers. However, initial efforts at union organization are almost always resisted. When management is used to making decisions by itself, it finds it difficult to make decisions with others. When unionization occurs, managements' discretion is limited and freedom constrained. What were once unilateral decisions become shared.

Management has considerable, but not unrestrained freedom in relation to its efforts to resist unionization. Charles Coleman explains:

**Management's right to communicate its position is protected as long as the communication is not coercive. Outright threats or promises of benefit are prohibited. The law does not permit management to threaten a plant closing upon unionization, or to offer a special wage increase during a representation campaign.**

**Management may question the union's statements, explain to workers the nature of the benefits they already have, call to their attention the strike record of the union or its record in securing terms less favorable than those already enjoyed by the employees, or offer comparisons with other organizations. Written communication may be sent to employees' homes, posted on bulletin boards, or placed in company newspapers.[15]**

**Collective Bargaining**

When union representation has been established, management is required to bargain with its agents in good faith. All matters relating to a previously established set of issues are resolved through a process known as collective bargaining. Harold Davey defines collective bargaining this way:

**A continuing institutional relationship between an employer . . . and a labor organization . . . concerned with the negotiation, administration, interpretation, and enforcement of written agreements covering joint understandings as to wages or salaries, rates of pay, hours of work and other conditions of employment.[16]**

Davey's term "continuing institutional relationship" is an important one for the general public has a poor understanding of collective bargaining, associating the process with strikes, labor unrest, or protracted negotiations. In fact, these are exceptional circumstances. In ninety-eight percent of negotiations, contracts are agreed upon without resorting to strikes or lockouts.

Contract negotiations and strikes often draw intense public scrutiny. At such times the public relations function becomes very important, and public relations practitioners really earn their pay. Nevertheless, as Harold Marquis points out, "One area in which large corporations and industry groups have been singularly ineffective is their public relations during labor controversies."[17] Part of the problem in effective public relations under these circumstances is the sensitive nature of the negotiations under way. Management and labor usually agree that public disclosure of the negotiating process would result in increased posturing, disruption, and intransigence. Abe Raskin, who covered labor relations for several decades for *The New York Times*, puts it another way:

**Outside the realm of diplomatic negotiations between the great powers no field compares with collective bargaining in reluctance of the parties to let the public know what is really going on. The settled conviction of labor and management is that the only time the rest of the world is entitled to any useful information is when an agreement has been reached. Until then the statements issued by both sides are self-serving flapdoodle intended to mislead much more than to illuminate.[18]**

As a journalist Raskin favors opening the bargaining to the media and the public, a view that gets little support from labor or management. During negotiations, then, public relations is left with the thankless task of disclosing nothing of the proceedings while at the same time avoiding alienating journalists like Raskin who operate on a primary assumption of the public's right to know.

When negotiations are successfully concluded, the public relations spokesperson should tell the story of that success and explain the terms of the contract to the public. The terms of the contract and their impact on the local or national economy are matters of critical public interest and importance. Even when there has been a strike, and the main story seems to be the ending of conflict, information concerning these factors should be spelled out clearly in organizational and mass media.

**Strikes** Although strikes are rare, their effects can last for years. Moreover, as we mentioned above, public sentiment can have significant influence on the ultimate outcome of lengthy job actions.

The impact of public opinion was clearly demonstrated in one case in which the local community had become antagonistic toward a union because a prolonged strike was adversely affecting the local economy. Community leaders were attempting to pressure the union into a settlement. As the pressure increased, a union spokesman approached the company's representative and proposed arbitration of the unresolved issues. The company resisted, but the union spokesman offered to permit a three-member arbitration panel consisting solely of businessmen to rule on the issue. All three of the proposed arbitrators were customers of the company. The union representative was betting that the company would never place its clients in the difficult position of judging one of their suppliers. He bet right. The next day's newspaper carried the headline: "Company Refuses Union Proposal To Have Businessmen Settle Strike." The resulting shift in public sentiment forced the company to concede.

Unions frequently have the public relations edge in strike situations. Abe Raskin observes:

**Unions locked in battles with corporations win more often than they lose in the propaganda exchange . . . unions have become adept at getting their story across whenever anyone is interested enough to listen.**

**Union leaders are almost invariably more accessible than their industrial counterparts. . . . The other great union asset in a strike is its members and their families. When a strike turns into a siege it is standard practice for newspapers to carry sob stories detailing the hardships the strikers are suffering and proclaiming their determination to stay out until the flint-hearted bosses meet demands of elementary justice. . . . The human factor—little people fighting a faceless profit machine—is a plus for the union which the company's image-makers can't match.[19]**

Successful organizational public relations in strike situations consists of humanizing the organization's position while clarifying the strike's impact on the local economy. Management's intrepid efforts to maintain operations, the strike's impact on local merchants, and the inflationary impacts of the worker's demands are angles that can build sympathy for organizational positions. In recent years, management's public position has been improved by what often appears as union greed. When the worker is already making $15 per hour or more, much of the public responds with envy rather than sympathy.

**COMMUNICATING EMPLOYEE BENEFITS**
A major area of misunderstanding in most organizations is the employee benefit program. Managers claim employees "just don't appreciate what they have." Perhaps this lack of "appreciation" often is the result of poor communication on the part of management, as the following episode illustrates.

Workers at a corporation had just voted for union representation, and one of the strongest appeals the union offered was its benefits package. Management could not understand why employees had been attracted to this. "Those benefits offer no substantial improvements over the package we already had," complained one executive. Upon closer examination, however, it was discovered that the company had never prepared publications to explain its package. Employee meetings to discuss benefits were irregular, almost non-existent. No employee handbook or guide had been published. There was no orientation program for new employees. There is little doubt that when the employees cast their ballots for the union, they were not voting for better benefits, but for a plan that had been explained.

Another company, which had a really outstanding benefit program, was alarmed by inaccurate rumors about the package. Consultants called in to investigate found that the company's communication program consisted of a confusing booklet on group insurance and a dull monthly newsletter. The newsletter never discussed or rebutted the rumors circulated through the grapevine. The communication void in that company was a breeding ground for misunderstanding, mistrust, and dissatisfaction.

U. S. Chamber of Commerce figures show that from 1957 to 1977 the cost of benefits in American companies rose seventy-eight percent. In 1975, fringe benefits payments in organizations throughout this country amounted to 35.4 percent of total payroll. That was more than $3.00 per hour, or almost $4,000 per employee in that year. Richard Huseman and John Hatfield comment:

**What is paradoxical about these expenditures is that organizations seem to be accruing few advantages from them. Benefit programs possess a diversity of goals, ranging from attracting and holding good employees to simply keeping the union out; however, there is little evidence to indicate that any of these goals are being met, through either the mere existence of benefit programs or increases in indirect compensation.[20]**

The authors attribute this failure, at least in part, to the employees' lack of knowledge and understanding of their own benefits program.

Helping employees to understand their benefits has always been an important area for public relations work. But it is increasingly difficult to expect employees to react with gratitude and appreciation to a standard benefit package. Traditionally established on the single-breadwinner models, benefit programs are hard-pressed to respond to changing sex roles; new realities of divorce, marriage, and non-marriage; flexible retirement age; career interruptions; childless and smaller families; and multi-income families. Jerry Rosenbloom, professor of insurance at the University of Pennsylvania, observed in *Business Week* that more sophisticated employees realize that many benefits received at present "run exactly counter to people's needs."[21]

The role of corporate communicators in dealing with employee benefits can be of vital significance. The public relations practitioner working in this area need not be limited to disseminating information about existing programs, but more importantly, can serve as a conduit for the expression of employees' needs and desires, and play a significant role in the determination and evaluation of benefit programs.

Figure 10-1 is a Huseman/Hatfield model of the benefit communication process, demonstrating the various points at which corporate communicators can become usefully involved.

With changing employee needs, government regulatory requirements, and the tremendous corporate resources devoted to employee benefits, this promises to be an issue of great importance to organizational communicators throughout the 1980s.

Employee communication is a large, and complex aspect of public relations practice. Many different topics and issues confront practitioners working in this area. Not surprisingly, it is the fastest-growing segment of the public relations field both in terms of numbers and perceived importance. In this chapter we have discussed the importance of keeping employees informed, creating the proper organizational climate to facilitate proper communication, establishing communication policy, and building employee communication programs. We have also considered the special issues of employee communication with a unionized workforce and communication of employee benefits.

**Figure 10-1**
**A Model of Benefit Communication**

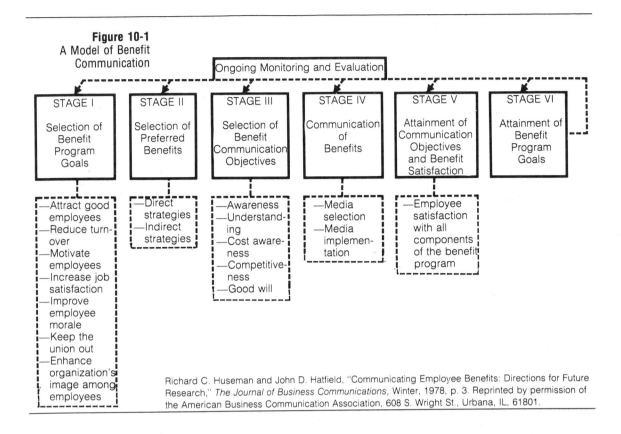

Richard C. Huseman and John D. Hatfield, "Communicating Employee Benefits: Directions for Future Research," *The Journal of Business Communications*, Winter, 1978, p. 3. Reprinted by permission of the American Business Communication Association, 608 S. Wright St., Urbana, IL, 61801.

In our "Practicing Public Relations" section coming up next, we continue to focus on employee communication, dealing specifically with the media most commonly used to transmit messages to employees.

**CASE STUDY:
THE FAST-FOOD
TURNOVER**

**By Betsy P. Graham**
**Associate Professor of Journalism,**
**Georgia State University, Atlanta,**
**Georgia**

A particular fast food chain is generally admired as one of the most efficiently run corporate empires in the world. But even an emperor has problems if the trainees in his troops don't stay in boot camp long enough to hone their skills. Too often the teen-aged employees of the company sign up for a stint with the spatula, and then—quicker than you flip a hamburger patty—leave.

Because it takes time and money to recruit and train a constant stream of new troops, the corporation would like to remedy this state of affairs.

Consequently, since you're on the public relations team at headquarters, you are called in to discuss the problem. Top management is thinking of launching a new in-house publication or newsletter to sell teen-aged employees on staying with this company—perhaps even on making a career of cooking french fries and hamburgers. They want your suggestions on what this new publication should look like and what its contents should be.

How should you respond?

**Questions**

1. What questions should you ask before making any recommendations at all?

2. What kinds of results can you encourage management to expect from a newsletter? From a magazine?

3. What additional measures should you encourage management to take to supplement your plans for better communications between management and teen-aged employees?

4. What kind of publication would you plan that would be attractive enough for teenagers to want to read and at the same time keep management happy? Discuss content and design.

---

**CASE STUDY:
THE BEER BARREL
LAYOFF**

**By Robert Taylor
Professor of Journalism and Mass
Communications, The University of
Wisconsin-Madison, Madison,
Wisconsin**

---

The Madison Cooperage Co., founded in 1861, one of the town's oldest firms, is the current employer of 1,200 people who "make the best kegs in the world," according to its nationally advertised slogan.

Having weathered the change from wooden to aluminum beer kegs, the firm now has come upon hard times because of the swing from wood to steel and plastic in vats and kegs for wine making.

Company president Harry R. Jones makes the difficult decision to eliminate the second shift and lay off 500 people at the end of this month.

Harold Storm, president of Amalgamated Coopers Union Local 5, after pledging his secrecy, has been informed and has given the company president this statement and permission to release it if the company so desires:

This is tough on our workers but I've been assured by President Jones that every effort has been made to avoid it, and every effort is being made to abide by the seniority specified in our contract, that the severance pay provided in the contract will be paid in a lump sum to each employes, and that hire-backs will be made strictly in seniority fashion and that workers hired back won't have to refund severance payments but will begin accumulating severance pay time when hired. This last is not in the contract and indicates, I think that the company's heart's in the right place.

While talking the situation over with Storm, Jones makes the following points:

Madison Cooperage is a good and responsible employer and corporate citizen of Madison and, as a unique sort of business these days, has attracted a lot of national attention.

We love our workers. They're mostly good and devoted and some of them have been with us for fifty years. My grandfather, Oscar Jones, who started this company, hired some of their fathers—old world artisans.

It's hell that this is coming at this time of year.

Although we hate to lose some of our older workers, we are going to reduce our retirement age from 65 to 60, for those who want to leave, and provide those 60 and over the same retirement pay that they would get if they were 65 on the day they leave.

Those on the second shift who have more seniority than those on the first will be able to bump (take the jobs of) people of lesser seniority on the first shift. Thus, some of those we have to let go may come from the first shift—though that's mostly made up of people of higher seniority.

We are providing full severance pay—one week at present pay for every year served, to all those who are let go, except the ones who take early retirement.

My guess is that of the 500 jobs we have to cut, about fifty may be made up by either regular retirement or early retirement. Ten of the 500 jobs are supervisory—night foremen, but some of them also may take the early retirement.

I will be in my office during all of next week, and those who receive notices are welcome to make appointments to see me, if they have some question about the layoff. They should remember, however, that we must do this strictly by seniority since that is what their union contract demands.

This will be the first time since President Roosevelt brought back beer that we won't have a night shift at the plant—our first big layoff, though we have been dropping in employment since our high of 2,000 in 1945 when the aluminum keg came into the beer business. We have tried to diversify some in our plant—butter vats, flower pots, and things like that—but they make up only ten percent of our business today. We still have about five percent in beer, cider, and vinegar kegs, but eighty-five percent of our business is with the wineries—and that's been declining now for ten years.

Madison Cooperage has a once-a-month employee newsletter distributed to employees which has traditionally contained an abundance of bowling scores and birth announcements.

**Questions**  1. What is the best strategy for informing employees about the layoff?

2. What information should be provided to employees and the public?

3. Within the ranks of current employees are there different audiences that must be communicated with? What is the basic message that should be communicated to each group?

4. What ongoing communication efforts would you recommend implementing for remaining employees?

---

**NOTES**   [1] R. Tagiuri and G. H. Litwin (eds.). *Organizational Climate: Explorations of a Concept* (Boston: Harvard University Press, 1968), p. 27.

[2] J. Campbell, M. D. Dunnette, E. E. Lawler, and K. E. Weick. *Managerial Behavior, Performance and Effectiveness* (New York: McGraw-Hill, 1970), p. 390.

[3] D. R. Hampton, C. E. Summer and R. A. Webber, *Organizational Behavior and the Practice of Management*, 2nd ed. (Glenview, Ill.: Scott, Foresman, 1973), p. 520.

[4] L. G. Hrebiniak, *Complex Organizations* (St. Paul: West Publishing, 1978), p. 273.

[5] William Whyte, "Is Anybody Listening?" *Fortune Magazine* (June 1951): 41.

[6] James E. Grunig, "Some Consistent Types of Employee Publics," *Public Relations Review* (Winter 1975): 35.

[7] This discussion is based on Norman B. Sigband, "What's Happening to Employee Commitment?" *Personnel Journal* (February, 1974): 133–135.

[8] Louis C. Williams, "What 50 Presidents and Chief Executive Officers Think About Employee Communication," *Journal of Organizational Communication* (Fall 1978).

[9] Paul Keckley, "The Increasing Importance of Employee Relations," *Public Relations Review* (Fall 1977): 70–76.

[10] Williams, "What 50 Presidents Think."

[11] James M. Lahiff and John D. Hatfield, "The Winds of Change and Managerial Communication Practices," *Journal of Business Communication* (Summer 1978).

[12] Williams, "What 50 Presidents Think."

[13] Richard Nemec, "Internal Communications—A Scary Science," *Public Relations Journal* (December 1973): 28.

[14] Donald P. Crane, *Personnel: The Management of Human Resources*, 2nd ed. (Belmont, CA: Wadsworth, 1979), p. 79.

[15] Charles J. Coleman, *Personnel: An Open Systems Approach* (Cambridge, Mass: Winthrop Publishers, 1979), p. 392.

[16] Quoted in Crane, *Personnel*, p. 80.

[17] Harold H. Marquis, *The Changing Corporate Image* (New York: American Management Association, 1970), p. 141.

[18] Abe H. Raskin, "Double Standard or Double-Talk?" in *Business And The Media*, C. E. Aronoff ed. (Santa Monica, CA: Goodyear, 1979), p. 252.

[19] Ibid., p. 251.

[20] Richard C. Huseman and John D. Hatfield, "Communicating Employee Benefits: Directions For Future Research," *The Journal of Business Communication* (Winter, 1978): 3.

[21] "New Benefits for New Lifestyles," *Business Week,* 11 February 1980, p. 112.

# THE MEDIA OF EMPLOYEE COMMUNICATION

In the first part of this chapter we took a general approach to employee communication. We discussed organizational climate and communication policy, the prerequisites of effective employee communication. We also discussed employee communication under special circumstances and for special purposes.

This section is devoted to the technical aspects of employee communication media—how to get your message across. Internal publications and supplementary publications are means of reaching large numbers of employees on an ongoing basis. Personnel and resources devoted to these media for employee audiences have increased markedly in the past decade. This is the fastest growing aspect of the overall public relations effort.

**WHAT ARE INTERNAL PUBLICATIONS?**

In-house publications take about as many forms as the organizations and individuals who publish them (*Figure 10-2*). Effective, professionally written publications can be mimeographed newsletters, newspapers with editorial staffs of various sizes, glossy full-color magazines, or any variation on these. Their common purposes: to give an organization the chance to tell its story the way it wishes it told. This is one reason why in-house publications have become popular; it is also the reason why so many fail to meet their objectives. When management speaks only from its own point of view, without considering the intended readers, in-house publications are only propaganda sheets. Like the other media discussed in this book, however, in-house publications can be effective tools if produced with the needs of their intended audience in mind.

There are more than 50,000 in-house publications in the United States with a combined circulation of more than 460 million. Many large organizations find it useful to have more than one publication. One automaker, because of its size and the variety of its audiences, has thirty-eight. Most such media are internal and not intended for the general public. Occasionally, however, they are distributed to influential people outside the organizations or even used a marketing tool.

**THE PURPOSE AND POTENTIAL OF INTERNAL PUBLICATIONS**

Most organizations communicate imperfectly with their employees. A corporation preparing to honor an employee for twenty-five years of service discovered that he knew shockingly little about the organization he had been a part of for a quarter of a century. The employee did not know the name of the company president, the location of headquarters, the number of plants the company had, the year the firm was founded, or the source

## PRACTICING
## PUBLIC
## RELATIONS

**Figure 10-2**
Internal Publications

of the raw material used in the manufacturing process. After twenty-five years of experience, he could name only two of his firm's 200 products.

Such examples often come up. The standard response from managers, "what we have here is a problem of communication," does no more than label the situation. Even deciding to increase communication does not guarantee a solution. Too often, print communication is suddenly increased and the problem is made worse. Communication problems cannot be solved by simply increasing the flow of printed messages. While printed media have their advantages, they cannot be regarded as an appropriate response to every problem. Printed communication must take its place as a part of an overall program including interpersonal communication, meetings, and public exposure of high corporate officials, all within the context of establishing appropriate climate and policy. In-house publications can do a lot of good work within an organization. But they can never take the place of person-to-person manager-subordinate relationships.

**COMMUNICATION FUNCTIONS OF INTERNAL PUBLICATIONS**

*Downward communication* is the most common use of in-house publications (*Figure 10-3*). The need of management to "inform" its employees is the justification behind most company publications. Internal publications are well suited for this, because they publish regularly. The house publication can report news and information in a timely and relatively inexpensive way.

Internal publications can be counter productive, however. There is a fine line between telling intended readers what management would like them to know and providing them with the information they want and need. The former is the leading cause of failure for in-house publications. The latter ensures success. If an in-house publication appears to be limited to the "management line," it loses readers. Those who do read it do not take it seriously. When this happens, the publication becomes a communication liability.

*Upward communication* is an equally important, but sometimes overlooked function of in-house publications. It can help avoid the propaganda problem just mentioned. Those responsible for in-house publications must never forget that management itself is a prospective audience. Letters to the editor, question-and-answer columns, articles written by employees, and other devices such as readership surveys give information about issues important to employees (*Figure 10-4*), and this is valuable—even vital—to management decision-making.

*Lateral communication* is a growing need in modern organizations. Hierarchial organizations are usually designed only to pass information up and down. Yet management needs some plan for communication among employees at the same level. Horizontal communication flow increases employee knowledge about the overall operations of the company, and helps to create a sense of community among the divisions of an organization.

# PRACTICING
# PUBLIC
# RELATIONS

**Figure 10-3**
Downward
Communication

# Brennan: selling the philosophy of the basics

Nine months ago Edward A. Brennan brought to his new job as territorial executive vice president, 22 years of experience in 15 assignments and the unshakeable conviction that *Sears is still Sears.*

Despite the fact that retailing has become an increasingly competitive and segmented industry, causing Sears to respond with adjustments in promotional strategy and changes in organizational structure, Brennan believes that the basic fabric of the company is intact and that its source of strength—as well as its hopes for the future—rest with the people who work there. And those people, he maintains, have always responded to the challenge of a solid program.

"People can make a difference," he never tires of reminding management. "I sense we have exceptionally strong, fine people here who want to do their jobs,

to derive satisfaction from those jobs and to take care of customers by treating them the way they themselves like to be treated. It's up to us as managers to challenge them."

With the Southern Territory encompassing some of the fastest growing markets in the nation, Brennan feels that the South has the greatest opportunity of any of the five territories to boost sales and profits. "We are fortunate because the population shift is in our direction," he said. "Unlike some other sections of the country —which at best can only gain 2-3 per cent real growth a year—we have the chance to make great progress as the markets in our area continue to expand."

But Brennan cautioned against the folly of relying solely on shifting demographics to trigger huge sales increases to generate the level

of profits Sears will need in the future to remain the world's leading retailer. He pointed to the company's overall performance in 1977 to emphasize that a double-digit sales increase alone cannot substantially increase year-end earnings.

For the South's part he advocates a rededication to the fundamentals of sound retail practices. "We have to move our expense levels into line with the rest of the company and move our margins up. When you do that you don't need a huge sales increase to improve your profits," he noted.

The vice president added that the situation in the territory need only be adjusted to show improvement; drastic change, Brennan warned, is never the answer. Instead, he espouses a business philosophy that emphasizes the basics of smart retailing, the same principles upon which the company's

**"...We have exceptionally strong, fine people here who want to do their jobs, to derive satisfaction from those jobs and to take care of customers by treating them the way they themselves like to be treated..."**

historic successes were fixed: correct merchandise assortments, including a proper mix of regular and promotional goods; good operating expense control; effective merchandise presentation, meaning well-marked, full bins in sparkling clean stores; competitive pricing, and Sears traditional customer service.

Underpinning Brennan's approach is his firm belief in good planning—and faithful execution of those plans. "You've got to live day in and day out with a plan," he said. "Decide what is possible and then run your business that way."

But corporate planning alone does not hold all the answers, said Brennan. He believes that individual employees too have the responsibility to set objectives for their jobs and then carry them out. "All of us can plan better," stress-

ed Brennan. "The outside salesperson can plan his calls better; the division manager can prepare more thoroughly for a promotion by planning effective displays and seeing that his or her salespeople receive the proper merchandise training. If we all did a better job of planning at every level, the company would perform better."

Brennan concedes that all game plans are subject to adjustment. Each season sees the introduction of new products, the discontinuation of others, shifts in strength and aggressiveness among the various headquarters merchandise departments, and of course, changes in the general economic climate. But always the territorial goal of providing maximum service to customers and ending up with a reasonable return on sales, remains the same.

"We'll have the same program next year, the year after next and

the year after that," grinned Brennan. "With good planning we can adjust for the other conditions and be able to stay on a steady course. Then if we execute well, we'll outperform everyone else."

Thinking out loud he continued, "We're always looking for magic ways to be successful. But there are no magic ways."

With understandable pride, Brennan points to the South's successful in-stock effort as a shining example of what can be accomplished in a relatively short time through planning and teamwork. "It brings tears of joy to my eyes to be No. 1 with the lowest out-of-stocks in the nation three months in a row," he admitted. "I'm thrilled with the way our people responded to get us in-stock."

Another source of satisfaction to him has been the territory's im-

provement in gross profit. At summer's end, it was apparent that the South had made substantial gains in this area. "I'm delighted with our progress in sales and profits and I believe we'll continue to improve," predicted Brennan. "It's no accident. The improvement is a direct result of what is being done in both merchandising and operating today."

Brennan assigns much of the credit for the South's performance to its division managers. "The professional division managers hold the key to the company's success," he often remarks. "I can't conceive of how Sears could operate without them. They're the real link in merchandising between the buying of the goods and the actual sale to the customers.

"In the end," he added, "they have responsibility for implementing any corporate plan."

The vice president, however, shrugs off his own role as harbinger of the mood of optimism now sweeping the South by observing, "I never talk about the past or changing things—only about what I feel is important."

What *is* important to Brennan—and in the final analysis to Sears—is that everyone, no matter what their job, perform to the best of their abilities. "The future of this company depends on how well each of us does his or her job. It demands that we all perform at a very high level," he said.

Putting it into perspective Brennan went on, "If you think of the company in terms of a single store, it's easier to see how people who do a good job in a unit contribute to that unit's success. The total is the sum of its parts. If all the employees in a store do well, then the store does well. If the store does well, the group or zone will do well. And if all 13 administrative units including the catalog organization do well, so will the territory.

"All this,"—he made an intense sweeping gesture with his hand that seemed to include his ninth floor office, the Atlanta headquarters and Sears Tower—"exists to serve one store."   —*Donna Peterman*

From *Sears South News,* Sears, Roebuck and Co. Reprinted by permission.

**Figure 10-4**
Upward Communication

### Bob Scherer's Straight Talk

# How can we know our insurance claims were figured correctly?

How can we determine if an insurance claim has been figured correctly? Why can't insurance claims be itemized (hospital, doctor, prescription, etc.) when insurance is paid? Why keep switching from one insurance company to another?
**Name withheld by request**

The group insurance area of employe benefits has among its primary goals the timely and accurate processing of medical claims. We have not been able to eliminate every error, however, and occasionally we are faced with a claim that has been processed incorrectly. Several safeguards assure that the error will be found and corrected.

When a claim has been processed, the checks are totaled to ensure they correspond to the benefits calculated for the covered expenses. This would reveal any error in addition or in typing of drafts.

Then the original work sheet and the bills are forwarded to the Provident Life and Accident Insurance Company. Provident audits the claims to verify that the benefit calculations are correct and that payments are made in accordance with the provisions of the policy. This should indicate any underpayments or overpayments.

Another safeguard is you, the employe. When a claim is processed, a check stub is sent to you. This stub lists the charges you submitted and the amount of money deducted to cover co-insurance and deductible. For further checking, you get a list of doctor and hospital fees that should correspond to dollar amounts on the stub.

The check stub includes only brief information on processing the claim. Certainly, a copy of the complete work sheet would be more helpful in reviewing the claim. A revised work sheet is being printed. Soon, the group insurance area will begin sending the completed work sheet to the employe.

With such procedures and with the emphasis employe benefits places on accuracy, we hope you never receive benefits that are incorrect. If you do, the error will be revealed and corrected before the file is closed.

Group insurance costs are high. Our management is prudent in having reputable carriers bid occasionally on the insurance programs. This ensures that Georgia Power and its employes are getting maximum benefits for their premium dollars. In 1975, we again offered our group insurance in competition, and the Provident Life and Accident Insurance Company won the contract. The only reason for changing from one insurance company to another is to get the best value at the lowest rate.

## May spouses work at the same location?

Does the company have a policy concerning a husband and wife working for the Company at the same location?
**Angie Lipscomb**
**Plant Bowen**

The policy of our Company is that when a husband and wife work in the same department or office, or if one of them works under the supervision of the other, such steps shall be taken as are deemed necessary for the good of the organization, even to the extent of the transfer, resignation, or discharge of one or the other of the employes.

## Why the long delays in processing raises?

We would like to inquire as to why the payroll department functions so unpredictably. It seems to us that this department is grossly inefficient when it comes to processing pay raises, retroactive

pay and in getting W-2 forms out to the employes. However, when an employe is docked, a mistake is made in an employe's insurance, or there is any error in favor of the Company, corrections are made almost immediately.

Can't anything be done to better organize the payroll department so they can handle all matters concerning employes with the same promptness and efficiency with which they handle the correction of errors in the Company's favor?
**Minola Road line section employes**

Every two weeks, our payroll section processes pay data and paychecks for more than 10,000 employes. This process entails a complete system update with new and changed data relevant to rates of pay and all of the various payroll deductions as well as time report information. In the processing of this volume of data, occasional errors do occur. Were it not for the dedicated effort of a fine group of payroll section employes in verifying data accuracy to the fullest possible extent, paycheck errors would be far more numerous.

Some errors, such as the incorrect reporting of hours worked, cannot be detected by payroll personnel. Nor can payroll employes control the delays that occur in the preparation and approval of pay change documents. The accurate and timely submission of these documents is the responsibility of the numerous reporting locations throughout the Company.

Payroll personnel are sometimes criticized for the time that is required to establish revised rates of pay and to pay retroactive wages to union employes. Delays that are experienced in performing these functions originate from the intricacies that are incorporated in Company/union wage settlements. Under these agreements, rate of pay increases are applied in varying amounts to different job classifications and steps.

From The Georgia Power *Citizen*. Reprinted by permission from the Georgia Power Company, Atlanta Georgia.

# PRACTICING
# PUBLIC
# RELATIONS

Moreover, lateral information can help new ideas to be born and can save duplication of effort. In-house publications should have lateral communication as a primary goal. Making available to employees information about operations outside their immediate sphere can create a broader understanding of the functions and goals of the organization as a whole (*Figure 10-5*).

**THE OBJECTIVES OF AN INTERNAL PUBLICATION**

In the broad sense, the goal of an in-house publication is the improvement of relationships between its readers and management. Setting policy and defining objectives for such a publication is a complicated undertaking. Without specific guidelines, however, it is hard for an in-house publication to be successful and even harder to measure its success.

As we have said, in-house publications must fulfill the needs of both the organization and its employees. The information in the publication must be seen by the readers as useful and meaningful. Small talk and management propaganda defeat effectiveness. Most important to the success of such a publication is the selection of content combining the common interests of management and employees. Following is a list of broad categories of topics frequently chosen in successful publications:

*Recognition of employee achievements* both on the job and in the community can encourage internal cooperation by helping management and employees become better acquainted with other members of the organization (*Figure 10-6*). This type of recognition also serves as official commendation for outstanding service and sets an example for others in the organization. Social activities can also be recognized, but these should not take precedence over job-related and community-service accomplishments. Appropriate employee recognition can promote various objectives, including:

- Strengthening positive relationships in the outside community
- Building a sense of accomplishment in individual employees
- Stimulating new ideas for company and community service.

*Employee well-being and safety* can be promoted through information on safety practices, rules, and procedures. Worker safety is always an appropriate area of concern for management and employees alike. In some organizations this involves little more than ensuring that everyone knows the location of fire exits. In others, however, the success of the operation, and indeed the operation itself, may depend on adherence to safety procedures. Internal publications are one outlet for the constant safety re-

PRACTICING
PUBLIC
RELATIONS

**Figure 10-5**
Horizontal
Communication

# The controllers

*The Gas Control Department is "Mission Control" for Transco*

*Linden sales dispatcher Jerry LaChere talks with a customer company about their gas needs.*

Remember the days when Mission Control at NASA in Houston controlled spaceships on their way to the moon?

Transco has its own version of "Mission Control" embodied in the Gas Control Department.

From their control rooms in Houston and Linden, N.J., they are responsible for moving Transco's gas from the production area to the market area.

"We like to consider ourselves the nerve center of Transco," says Department Manager Bob Withers. "Our objective is to move natural gas as safely and efficiently as possible. Consequently, we represent Transco daily with gas producers and customers, and we interface with nearly every other department in Transco."

Controlling the gas is a 24-hour-a-day business, so there are always at least two people on duty at each of the Gas Control centers located in Houston and Linden, N.J.

Customers begin calling Gas Control early in the morning, giving reports to the sales dispatchers on how much gas was delivered on the previous day and an estimate of the current day's requirements. The Houston office receives about 40 calls, while the Linden office gets between 25 and 30.

About three-fourths of Transco's 80 customers call in daily. The remaining one-fourth are smaller customers whose gas requirements are estimated by Transco.

Ronald Sampay, a Houston-based sales dispatcher, estimates that he spends between four and six hours a day on the telephone. That's enough to give anyone a sore ear!

"The hardest part of our job," says Weldon Laird, superintendent, "is trying to guess, or outguess, our customers. We have to anticipate their needs every day."

During the day, Gary Warren, the production dispatcher, monitors calls from between 150 and 200 gas producers.

"That's not an absolutely accurate figure," says Warren, "because you

don't have time to count the calls!"

By combining the calculations of the sales and production dispatchers, the department can estimate the amount of gas that will be flowing into the pipeline each day and adjust amounts to be injected into or withdrawn from storage.

Next the dispatcher on duty totals all the gas needs and subtracts the amounts that customers request be placed in storage, resulting in the "burn figure" — the gas the customers will actually use.

This information goes to one of the four senior gas controllers, Bill Roempke, Bill Landes, Mike Blackwood, or Bubba Jaenecke, all based in Houston. The controller balances the production (inflows) and sales (outflows) of gas with adjustments to storage figures. At this point he determines how much horsepower will be necessary at each compressor station to propel the given volume of gas, and then gives the orders to the stations.

Every two hours, on the odd hour, the controller calls every compressor station along the pipeline and records each station's pressures. He communicates via Transco's microwave system, which has one channel on the Gas Control telephone designated strictly for dispatch purposes.

According to Controller Jaenecke, the whole process takes only about 15 minutes. He calls the station's numbers in ascending order, and they reply with their pressure readings. Since the stations give their reports from Refugio, Texas, northward, the pressure run makes for an interesting blend of Southern drawls and Yankee brogues.

The senior gas controller in Houston determines any changes which must be made in a daily operating plan due to weather changes and other conditions, and the Linden dispatchers monitor certain operating pressures and flow information in the Pennsylvania, New Jersey, and New York areas. By constant communications with larger customer companies in that area, he

# PRACTICING PUBLIC RELATIONS

**Figure 10-6**
Employee Recognition

## Surfing Champ

Surfing champions have to be picky about where they live. Jon Motes, installation/repair technician, requested a company transfer from South Florida to Jacksonville because "the waves in Miami were too small."

"Now I keep my surf board at a friend's shop on the beach," he said. "If the waves are good at lunchtime I change into my baggies and hit the surf for an hour. I go out after work too. With daylight savings time, the best thing that ever happened to surfing, you can stay 'till about 8:30."

It's that type of dedication since age 13 that won Motes first place at the Florida State Surfing Championships last October. "You can show people how to do it, but they can't learn without a lot of practice," he said.

Motes' six-year-old son, Jason, proved himself among the younger surfing set by winning the "minihune" division in Eastern Surfing Association competition last year.

"Jason's been surfing for two and a half years now — almost as long as he's been walking," said Motes proudly. "He's scared to go out to the big swells, but he tears up the shore breakers. He's just learning now, but he'll be something else one of these days."

Motes involvement in surfing includings his directorship of the 175-member North Florida Division of the Eastern Surfing Association.

That organization is buying litter barrels for the beaches and trying to open more areas to surfers.

## Big brother

Ray Jones, a Florence, S.C., installation/repair technician, has a philosophy about child raising. "Kids who turn out bad are usually not to blame," he said. "The badness comes out of the family life — the atmosphere they live in."

As a result of his efforts to improve the atmosphere for some of the boys around Effingham, his hometown, Jones was named "Big Brother" of the year for 1977 in the five-county Pee Dee Area.

"Big Brothers is a program for boys without a father," explained Jones. "It's older boys like me spending time with younger boys — kind of directing them, showing them which way to go."

He has a personal understanding of growing up in a fatherless household. "I didn't have a daddy around either, but a friend's daddy acted sort of like my big brother. It's easy to see the value of it when you've been there yourself."

His two current little brothers, 11 and 16 years old, are often found at the Jones' home. "I try to make them feel like part of the family by doing things with them such as helping around the house or going fishing. My wife and two little girls are as much an influence as I am," Jones said.

Children come into the world as innocents, says Jones, who believes the duty of grownups is to shape that purity into productive maturity.

"You never lose anything by taking up time with kids. I can tell they appreciate it because they usually ask me 'When are you coming back?' when I take them home."

From Southern Bell *Views*, Issue 4/August 1978. Published by Southern Bell, Atlanta, Georgia. Reprinted by permission.

minders that are necessary to such organizations. There is an endless need to explain benefits, vacations, holidays, taxes, workers' compensation, affirmative action and equal employment opportunity policies. Employees can be told of community issues, and educational and training opportunities. Objectives of this type can include:

- Encouraging employee advancement
- Demonstrating the organization's concern for workers' health and safety
- Interpreting, local state, and national news as it applies to the company and the well-being of employees.

*Employees' understanding of their role in the organization* can be improved (*Figure 10-7*). The publication can stress the importance of each worker's job in meeting the goals of the company. Information about the final use of products illustrates the importance of everyone's part in the process. Internal publications should promote the idea that each employee is a salesman for the company. They should pay attention to:

- Building loyalty to the organization
- Improving cooperation and coordination
- Improving production and efficiency
- Reducing expense and waste
- Getting everyone involved in and aware of the importance of public relations.

*Clarification of management policies* must consider the point of view of management *and* employees. Employees must be accurately informed about business activities if management wants support for its programs (*Figure 10-8*). Understanding can be helped through:

- Explaining policies and rules
- Building confidence in management
- Combating rumors and misunderstandings.

An in-house publication can be effective in accomplishing these objectives *if* it meets the needs of employees, *if* it says something that employees want to think about and talk about, and *if* it is attractive and easily read.

**MANAGING
INTERNAL
PUBLICATIONS**
*Planning for Successful Communication.* Who will read the publication is a decision that will shape all others. Do not try to be all things to all people. Do not try to rival *The New York Times.* An internal publication serves the needs of the organization that sponsors it. Successful house

# PRACTICING
# PUBLIC
# RELATIONS

**Figure 10-7**
Improved Understanding
of Employee's Role

## YOU MADE IT ALL HAPPEN IN '78

**Environmental Clean-up**
We worked hard to clean up our environment. Shown here is the new 38-acre, 250-million-gallon secondary treatment system (aeration lagoon) constructed at G-P's Bellingham, Wash., Division during the year. Mill process water flows into the lagoon and is cleaned and oxygenated for release into Bellingham Bay seven days later.

**Energy Conservation**
Our energy-conscious company made news around the country during '78 as it continued to conserve and devise ways to turn wastes into energy sources. This dust cell, installed at Toledo, Ore., last year, uses a waste product —wood dust—as a fuel. By suspending flammable dust in air in the right concentration, the dust supplies a sustained source of heat. Two other dust cells are at our Eugene/Springfield Division. Creation of the dust cells earned G-P national acclaim, for the second year in a row, the latest an award from Keep America Beautiful, the public service organization that promotes involvement in environmental improvement around the country.

**Community Involvement**
We had a good year which allowed us to share with our friends and neighbors. All around the country in '78, we lent a helping hand—to people like Steven Powell (pictured with H.S. Mersereau, Southern Division senior vice president), of Augusta, Ga., who was one of 97 G-P scholarship winners. More than 1,000 high school graduates have received nearly $3 million from G-P in recent years.

**Millions of New Trees**
More than 26 million seedlings were raised in our company nurseries during '78, promising beautiful, managed, green forests on a continuing basis for future generations of Americans.

From Georgia-Pacific *Growth,* Georgia Pacific Corporation. Reprinted by permission.

**Figure 10-8**
Clarification of
Management Policies

# Voluntary employment goals work, says Graham

"Sears is the nation's second largest private employer of women
and one of the largest employers of
minorities, with almost 80,000 on
payroll," Ray Graham, the company's director of equal opportunity, said in a sworn affidavit filed in
support of recent company motions
for dismissal of EEOC charges.

"Sears has had a formal, voluntary affirmative action plan since
1968," Graham told the court. "In
1973, Sears formulated, and in
1974, implemented its Mandatory
Achievement of Goals (MAG) Plan,
which among other steps, requires
each Sears unit to hire one underrepresented member for every white
male hired until the presence of the
underpresented group in a particular job grouping equals or exceeds its presence in the local
trade/hiring area.

"For non-traditional jobs (e.g.
women in craft jobs such as automotive mechanics and men in clerical and secretarial positions), the
MAG Plan requires that one underrepresented group member be
hired for every five males (or females if the position is clerical) until
a goal of 20 per cent is reached.

"In addition, terminated minorities and women (and, where applicable, men) in underrepresented job
classfications must be replaced in
kind on a one-for-one basis before
any other assignments within that
job classification are made.

"Before they can deviate from the
MAG Plan requirements, Sears unit
managers must request advance authorization and state the reasons for
not hiring an underrepresented
group member," said Graham.

"Based on my experience in administering Sears affirmative action
plan and my knowledge of other
companies' plans, it is my opinion
and belief that Sears equal employment and affirmative action programs are unsurpassed in scope
and effectiveness in American business and industry," said Graham.

**Percentage of Female and Minority Employees in Each EEOC Job Category**
(Categories as defined by Equal Employment Opportunity Commission)

"Sears Where America Works"

| Job Categories | Female % | | Black % | | Asian/ Pacific Islander % | | American Indian/Alaskan Native % | | Hispanic % | | Employees in each job category (in thousands) | |
|---|---|---|---|---|---|---|---|---|---|---|---|---|
| Date | Feb. '66 | Jan. '79 | Feb. '66 | Jan. '79 | Feb. '66 | Jan. '79 | Feb. '66 | Jan. '79 | Feb. '66 | Jan. '79 | Feb. '66 | Jan. '79 |
| Officials and Managers | 20.0 | 37.0 | .4 | 7.3 | .2 | .5 | .1 | .3 | .7 | 2.8 | 33.4 | 51.3 |
| Professionals | 19.2 | 57.9 | .8 | 6.1 | .5 | 1.5 | .0 | .0 | .4 | 2.7 | 1.3 | 1.8 |
| Technicians | 48.1 | 51.5 | 1.1 | 11.9 | 1.5 | 1.9 | .0 | .2 | .7 | 4.4 | 1.5 | 2.0 |
| Sales Workers | 56.9 | 64.6 | 3.2 | 11.3 | .6 | .8 | .1 | .2 | 1.5 | 4.5 | 98.7 | 124.9 |
| Office & Clerical | 86.0 | 86.9 | 3.1 | 13.4 | .6 | 1.1 | .1 | .2 | 2.0 | 5.3 | 78.6 | 111.5 |
| Crafts Workers | 3.8 | 8.4 | 2.8 | 9.2 | .7 | 1.1 | .1 | .4 | 2.8 | 5.7 | 20.8 | 30.3 |
| Operatives | 12.0 | 22.4 | 13.8 | 19.9 | .8 | 1.1 | .1 | .3 | 3.5 | 6.9 | 23.4 | 11.8 |
| Laborers | 34.3 | 32.6 | 18.4 | 23.0 | .3 | .8 | .1 | .3 | 6.5 | 7.8 | 13.7 | 48.9 |
| Service Workers | 32.3 | 44.1 | 44.9 | 32.3 | .5 | 1.1 | .1 | .2 | 2.0 | 7.1 | 9.9 | 12.7 |
| All Categories | 50.7 | 57.0 | 5.9 | 13.6 | .6 | .9 | .1 | .3 | 2.1 | 5.2 | 282.8 | 395.2 |

"On Aug. 1, 1979, *Employment
Relations Report*, a weekly newsletter, published an article based upon
confidential memoranda obtained
from the EEOC. According to the
article, the memoranda were written in June 1979 by Issie Jenkins, the
EEOC's acting general counsel and
by other attorneys in the General
Counsel's office.

**'Errors And Flaws'**

"The memoranda advised the
EEOC that the case against Sears
was riddled with 'errors and flaws'
and that the evidence was too weak
to pursue litigation on the broad
scale recommended in the Commission Decision. However, it was
reported that lawsuits would be
prepared as a bargaining ploy."

In the memoranda, said Graham,
"The EEOC's then top lawyer admits
that 'Sears has been in the vanguard
of voluntary affirmative action since
1974, and with respect to minorities, possibly as early as 1969.'"

The memoranda also stated, "Although we (the EEOC attorneys) are
unable to fully evaluate the progress achieved by the MAG program, its existence may render it impossible to prove any discrimination occurring after 1973, except for
certain equal pay claims...The absence of discrimination after 1973
may affect both a court's receptiveness to our arguments regarding
pre-1974 discrimination and the issue of what relief may be appropriate for any proven violation."

Graham said, "the EEOC impli-

citly confirmed the accuracy of the
quotations from the memoranda in
a press statement issued Aug. 1,
1979, which said that the quoted
memoranda were based on a 'preliminary review of the data and
analysis in the case,' and that 'additional information and further analyses have since been obtained.'"

However, concluded Graham,
EEOC Chairman Eleanor Holmes
Norton commented on the EEOC's
decision to bring national charges
against Sears and several other
large companies in a statement
made to the Associated Press Aug.
22, 1979: "In retrospect it was
perhaps overly ambitious," said
Norton"...and the cases were
brought, as it turns out, in the most
troubled time of the Commission."

## Sears moves for dismissal of EEOC suits

Last month Sears filed motions for
dismissal of five lawsuits brought
by the Equal Employment Opportunity Commission (EEOC) against
unit in Atlanta, Chicago, Memphis,
Montgomery and New York.

The EEOC suit filed in Chicago
alleges job discrimination against
women at Sears facilities nationally.

The other four suits allege local discrimination in the hiring of minorities in those cities.

In moving for dismissal of the
suits, the company maintained that
the case is "a culmination of more
than six years of governmental
abuse and unfair treatment."

Reasons cited by Sears as

grounds for dismissal include:
• conflicts of interest, or the appearance of such, within the charging, investigative, conciliation, and
decision-making structure of the
EEOC undermine the fairness of the
proceedings and destroy the credibility of the Commission decision;
• the Commission's refusal to con-
ciliate individual issues, as required
by law — issues which are included
in the present lawsuits;
• attempts by the EEOC to deprive
Sears of property by the use or
threat of adverse publicity after the
EEOC had insisted that Sears forfeit
its right to confidentiality;
• the refusal of the EEOC to grant
Sears a hearing after facts disclosing
a violation of due process were presented to the Commission;
• disclosures on record which indicate the prosecution of Sears was
without foundation, unreasonable,
brought in bad faith, and continued
even after it clearly became so.

Sears also maintains that the
Equal Pay Act allegations should be
dismissed, because they are barred
by an earlier equal pay suit, brought
by the government against Sears
and denied by the courts. (Excerpts
from Sears brief appear on page 6.)

"The EEOC appears to have used its power and authority as a law enforcement agency...to
advance the partisan interests of private political groups," stated briefs prepared by Sears chief
counsel Charles Morgan.

### Earnings off 9.9% in 3rd quarter from '78

The company has reported
net income for the third quarter
ended Oct. 31 fell 9.9 per cent
to $212,117,000 or 67 cents per
share from last year's record of
$235,487,000 or 73 cents.

Net sales for the third quarter
were $4,523,406,000, an in-
crease of 1.6 per cent above last
year's $4,458,379,000.

The company's net income
for the nine months ended Oct.
31 was $555,753,000 or $1.74 per
share. This was 6.1 per cent below last year's net income of
$591,645,000 or $1.84 per share.
Operating income from sales
and services for the nine
months ended Oct. 31 increased 3.7 per cent.

Net sales for the nine months
were $12,409,965,000, a de-
crease of 4.7 per cent from last
year's record of $13,015, 688,000
for the same period.

Net income of the Allstate
Group of Companies was equal
to 39 cents per Sears share for
the third quarter compared
with 38 cents for the same period of 1978, and $1.07 per share
for the nine months compared
with $1.09 last year.

# PRACTICING
# PUBLIC
# RELATIONS

publications are those which identify, acknowledge, and stick to a purpose: serving their audience.

Identification of a publication's audience may not be as simple as it seems. Although the primary audience is usually limited to people inside the organization, these individuals can often be divided into several groups. A large petrochemical company has blue-collar workers who belong to one or several unions. It also hires engineers and research scientists with professional affiliations, and white-collar mid-management and clerical personnel. Each of these groups has different interests and needs different information.

When only one publication is possible, you should identify a primary audience and treat the other groups as secondary. The secondary groups can be served through special columns or stories that will interest them. Secondary audiences might also include suppliers, distributors, other company plants or divisions, competitors, and the surrounding community. Many of these external secondary audiences will read your publication even if you do not want them to. Therefore, the contents must reflect good judgment. Your audience cannot be limited. Issues of substance must be discussed if the publication is to have credibility. This is not the place to air dirty laundry, however; that will only embarrass the organization and its employees. Some large companies have begun publications that serve groups outside the organization such as the community, suppliers, and industry.

*What type of publication does your organization need?* Once the primary and secondary audiences are identified, you should decide what kind of publication will meet their needs best: a newsletter, a tabloid newspaper, a magazine, or some other format. Questions about frequency of publication and distribution should also be decided in advance, based upon the requirements of the primary audience. Most house publications are published monthly. Some appear quarterly and some weekly. The easiest, cheapest, and simplest method of distribution is to make them available around the work areas. To get wider distribution, some organizations hand them to employees, use the in-house mail, or send them to employees' homes. All of these matters are interdependent. The format (size and shape) may limit the possibilities for distribution. These considerations depend in turn on two factors: budget and audience needs.

Once a budget for the publication is established, information about the needs of the audience must be gathered. Interviews and questionnaires can tell a great deal about content, frequency, and distribution needs. To help select a format, many companies use employee panels to review sample publications from other organizations. The panel can also evaluate data obtained in interviews and questionnaires.

The result of your planning effort should be written down and kept. It can help you plan future issues and evaluate past ones.

**Starting the**  Producing an internal publication takes organization and coordination. You
**Publication**  want to be able to produce it at scheduled regular intervals. Such consisten-

cy requires budget and staff. Putting out a publication on a shoestring may be worse than doing nothing at all. A publication that cannot be properly maintained creates negative attitudes by building expectations it cannot fulfill. Therefore, organizing the details of production is important to success.

*What makes news?* What goes into an internal publication will vary from one organization to another. Still, there are things that employees will not read, and there is even more that they do not have time to read. Extraneous topics, even when educational, are not proper for a house publication. There is, however, a set of topics appropriate to your organization that will attract the interest of even the busiest executive or blue-collar worker, and these will form the backbone of your publication.

Anything that concerns what people do, feel, or think is interesting. You should select topics that grow out of the activities in the sponsoring organization. News is everywhere. Potentially, every job, group, program, and employee has news value. To identify possible stories, an editor or writer should consider the topic from the intended reader's point of view. Include items that will interest many groups within the organization. Keep the needs of your primary audience in mind first. But you can expand readership with items of interest to others as well. Look for stories that inform and entertain. No one will read everything, but almost everyone will read something. A rule of thumb for an appropriate "mix" is:

- 50% information about the organization—local and national/international
- 20% employee information—benefits, quality of working life, etc.
- 20% relevant noncompany information—competitors, community, etc.
- 10% small talk and personals

Remember, company information must satisfy the audience's needs, not just those of management. If the publication is to serve the goals of the sponsor organization, readership is essential. Topics with generally high interests are:

- New equipment or changes in existing equipment
- Remodeling or expansion
- Quality control procedures and requirements
- Safety requirements
- Achievement of quotas
- Wage rates and increases
- New jobs created
- New assignments
- Meetings

# PRACTICING
# PUBLIC
# RELATIONS

- Changes in union officers or policies
- Important visitors
- Sales and earnings
- Management policies
- President's or general manager's message

Employee news is an excellent source of feature articles or even columns (*Figure 10-9*). It has high readership because its subject is the audience. Some possible topics are:

- Promotions
- New employees
- Retirements
- Deaths
- Community involvement
- Memberships—clubs, community organizations and associations
- Volunteer service
- Educational achievements
- Awards

Relevant noncompany information consists of matters that affect the company or its employees (*Figure 10-10*). Events reported in the popular media can be followed up with the predicted effect for employees, the company and/or the industry. Relevant noncompany information usually comes from the following:

- Business, trade or association publications
- National news publications
- Daily and weekly newspapers
- Newsletters and other publications from unions, professional groups or competing organizations

The most common and severe criticism of these publications is that they are "gossip sheets." Some people erroneously believe that the way to get employees to read a publication is to get as many names and faces into print as possible. This results in an overreliance on small talk. Credibility, and eventually readership, decline. Serious content will foster credibility, and successful communication can then occur. Small talk is important if used properly, but it cannot dominate the publication. Appropriate topics in this category are:

- Hobbies
- Births and deaths

**Figure 10-9**
Employee Information
Column

### In Memoriam

Julia Branagan, mother of transmission foreman *James T. Branagan* of Linden, N.J., died December 16. Mrs. Branagan resided in Bayonne, N.J.

Lindsay E. Cary, Sr., father of *William E. Cary*, Engineering, died November 28. A native Houstonian, Cary was 87 years old.

Muriel Moore, mother of *Marjorie Maurer*, Property Accounting, died October 15.

### On the Move

**Promotions**
Marjorie A. Barron
*from senior administrative clerk to land R/W specialist, Land.*
Richard D. Bland, Jr.
*from accountant trainee to plant accountant, Property Accounting.*
John C. Boutwell, Jr.
*from assistant supervisor to supervisor, General Accounting.*
Woodrow W. Brown, Jr.
*from operator-A to chief operator, Ellicott City, Md.*
Kenneth Carter
*from maintenance man-B to maintenance man-A, Lake Charles, La.*
Joseph L. Chambers
*from maintenance man-A to repairman-A, Unionville, Va.*
Kathleen S. Conley
*from accountant trainee to general accountant, General Accounting.*
Sylvester Cooley, Jr.
*from maintenance man-B to maintenance man-A, Seminary, Miss.*

Terrance E. Crosby
*from controls specialist to area foreman, Austin, Pa.*
Gavin J. Cuccia
*from maintenance man-C to maintenance man-B, Schriever, La.*
Kathy L. Eriksen
*from senior word processing specialist to lead word processing specialist, Information Services.*
Alex Fuselier, Jr.
*from maintenance man-C to maintenance man-B, Eunice, La.*
Joe L. Gilmore
*from maintenance man-A to operator-A, Sandersville, Miss.*
Richard T. Gomez
*from garage attendant, Purchasing, to administrative clerk, Production Accounting.*
Gregg H. Hammond
*from maintenance man-B to maintenance man-A, Moore, S.C.*
Jimmie L. Harrington
*from maintenance man-B to chief operator, Cameron, La.*
Walter W. Horner
*from measurement technician-A, Masonville, N.J., to measurement engineer, West Chester, Pa.*
David S. Husband
*from maintenance man-C to maintenance man-B, Lake Charles, La.*
Clarence F. Johnston
*from maintenance man-C to maintenance man-B, Eunice, La.*
Gary W. Kana
*from maintenance man-B to maintenance man-A, El Campo, Texas.*
Sue V. Kendrick
*from senior land and R/W specialist to records supervisor, Land.*
Olen K. Kolb
*from general accounting supervisor to assistant general accounting manager, General Accounting.*
Mark B. Landry
*from maintenance man-C to maintenance man-B, Kaplan, La.*
Michael J. LeMaire
*from maintenance man-C to maintenance man-B, Kaplan, La.*
Donald W. Little
*from transmission engineer to senior transmission engineer, Lithonia, Ga.*
Charlene Marek
*from gas accountant to corporate accountant, Gas Accounting.*

Tom A. Martin
*from laborer, Seminary, Miss., to maintenance man-C, Sandersville, Miss.*
Felix L. Martinez
*from maintenance man-C to maintenance man-B, El Campo, Texas.*
Gordon E. Marttila
*from measurement engineer, West Chester, Pa., to measurement division superintendent, Linden, N.J.*
Frank J. Michelli
*from maintenance man-A to operations clerk-A, Eunice, La.*
Anyer L. Miller
*from dispatcher-B to material expeditor-B, Cameron, La.*
Jimmie T. Miller
*from maintenance man-C to maintenance man-B, Davidson, N.C.*
Jack Porter
*from operator-A to chief operator, Tilden, Texas.*
Stephen M. Price
*from maintenance man-B to maintenance man-A, Cameron, La.*
Willie L. Richardson, Jr.
*from laborer, Seminary, Miss., to maintenance man-C, Laurel, Miss.*
James R. Seymour
*from accountant trainee to production accountant, Production Accounting.*
William R. Shannon
*from maintenance man-A to operator-A, Tilden, Texas.*
George W. St. Julien
*from laborer to maintenance man-C, Kaplan, La.*
Jeffery A. Stallings
*from maintenance man-C to maintenance man-B, Refugio, Texas.*
Jesse D. Trahan
*from maintenance man-B, to chief operator, Cameron, La.*
Raphael Weizman
*from accountant trainee to gas accountant, Gas Accounting.*
Anton J. Wetter
*from area foreman to area superintendent, Austin, Pa.*

Marie Whalin
*from administrative trainee to buyer, Purchasing.*
George W. Zepp
*from maintenance man-A to operator-A, Ellicott City, Md.*

**Transfers**
David W. Freestone
*from General Accounting to Corporate Accounting.*
Tony A. Gant
*from planning analyst, Financial Planning, to contract administrator, Gas Purchases.*
James M. Hamilton, Jr.
*from Linden, N.J., to Corpus Christi, Texas, Measurement.*
Fletcher W. Hartley
*from supervising engineer, Engineering Technical Services, to staff engineer, Engineering.*
John M. Kryvanick
*from Linden, N.J., to Jackson, La., Communications.*
Harley N. McDonald
*from Engineering Technical Services to Gas Control.*
Terry D. Sparks
*from material control accountant, Property Accounting to contract administrator, Gas Purchases.*
Carol E. Tucker
*from senior credit union specialist Personnel to accountant trainee specialist, Production Accounting.*
"R" Wegner
*from Corporate Communications to Records Management.*
Catherine E. Hicks
*from Communications to Office Services.*

**New Employees**
Diane L. Adams
*Production Accounting*
Kenneth L. Adamson
*Unionville, Va.*
Peggy M. Duck
*Communications*
Johnnie Fleming, Jr.
*Cameron, La.*
Edward J. Gaspard
*Cameron, La.*
Lynette M. Hayes
*Lake Charles, La.*
Ronald L. Honefenger
*Environmental Affairs*
Harold R. Johnson
*Davidson, N.C.*

From *Hot Tap*, Transco Companies, Inc., Houston, Texas. Reprinted by permission.

# PRACTICING
# PUBLIC
# RELATIONS

**Figure 10-10**
How External Events
Affect the Organization

Space-age agriculture:
What we can expect

If you think John Deere farm equipment is sophisticated now, wait until the year 2000.

Trying to predict the future of American agriculture is just as difficult as predicting the future of American society. After all, the kind of life a farmer will be living in the year 2000 depends upon who will be buying his crops, at what prices, and for what purposes. It depends upon the energy sources available to power his tractors, dry his grain and fertilize his crops. And it depends fundamentally on the purpose and even the very definition of agriculture.

Although many people can afford to debate the question at leisure, John Deere and other farm machinery makers have no time to spare. Many tractors that will be working fields in the year 2000 will be bought in, say, 1985; these machines are in the design stage today. Agricultural engineers must have a pretty firm idea already of what is in store for us 21 years from now.

One engineer who has done a good deal of thinking—and debating—about the future of farming is Gordon Millar, vice-president of engineering for Deere & Company. Millar speaks at food conferences where he encounters critics of today's high-productivity agriculture. He defends this kind of farming so strongly that he says he has become known as the "ogre" of agribusiness.

"There is a whole set of historical facts, a whole set of reasonably quantifiable projections, which all have to fit together," says Millar. "In order to survive, people need a certain amount of food. It looks like we'll have between 6.5 and 8 billion people at the end of the century. That's about twice as many people as we have now.

"Should the food for these people come from farmers who live on six to 10 acres of land and practice low-productivity, subsistence agriculture? Or should we have high-productivity farmers who can feed 20, 30, 50 people? Is farming a way of life, a recreational activity, or is the primary purpose of farming the production of food, so that the billions of people who are not

- Marriages
- Employee sports (bowling league, softball, golf, etc.)
- Social achievements

Other topics for articles overlap the previous categories. Some are: safety training, security procedures, benefits, vacation schedules, accident and injury record, housekeeping, educational assistance programs, emergency procedures, and charity fund drives. Information about future events, especially those close at hand, makes good reading if they are of concern to the audience. Again, moderation is important. Some house publications have become little more than calendars due to requests from groups who want their activities publicized. Set and maintain strict policies about what will be published and how space will be allotted. The following criteria can help you to evaluate a topic's newsworthiness:

1. *Timeliness*—Is the topic timely enough to interest most of the readers?
2. *Scope*—Does it affect enough people directly or indirectly?
3. *Noteworthiness*—Is something or someone important or well-known involved?
4. *Human Interest*—Does it deal with things vital to the interests of the readers or those involved?

A "tickler" file is used by newspaper editors to "tickle their memory" about future news stories. The editor of an internal publication can also use this method. A futures book or file can be started with headings such as "use next issue," "if space available," and "short fillers." Updating the file gives ready material for each issue.

**Writing for Internal Publications**    Most internal publications use two types of articles: news stories and feature or human interest articles. They serve different purposes, but both are important. News stories concentrate on information about market conditions, safety, company-sponsored events, current events that affect organizational policy, and other happenings. Articles that focus on people and their lives are called feature or human interest pieces. A balance between these two types should be decided upon based on reader feedback. Both, however, must meet the criterion of general interest.

Internal publications are not daily metropolitan newspapers. People who write for them should not try to be investigative reporters. Objectivity is an important goal, but in-house publications should have a more personal tone than public newspapers or magazines. They should reflect a sense of closeness and common interest that says to the reader, "We're all in this together." One writer says a house publication "should look and read like . . . a letter from home . . . a pat on the back . . . a friendly handshake." Most importantly, the tone of in-house publications must never be condescending or frivolous.

# PRACTICING PUBLIC RELATIONS

Journalists use the inverted-pyramid style of writing. This method organizes a story so that the most important points are covered first. The inverted pyramid is equally useful for house publications. An article should begin by answering five questions: who, what, when, where, and why. The story's lead (the first one or two paragraphs) should answer these questions, starting with the one most important for that story. Each successive paragraph should contain less important details. Studies of reading habits show that most readers skim, or skip around. A strong lead gets readers' attention and directs them into the rest of the article.

The following tips for those who write or edit in-house publications can help make articles interesting and readable:

Use short, simple words.
Use short, simple sentences and paragraphs.
Write in the active, not the passive, voice.
Avoid slang and jargon.
Use adjectives and adverbs sparingly.
Be brief: one or two double-spaced typewritten pages for
    most stories.
Give the actual date of an event. Don't say "next Friday"
    or "day after tomorrow."
Be consistent when using numbers: spell out numbers
    one to nine and use numerals for 10 and above.

All copy must be carefully edited. Check spelling, delete unnecessary words, and vary the structure of sentences. A good style manual such as the one published by the Associated Press, can be very helpful. Above all, *be consistent.*

**Staff**   All editors know that a good publication requires more than sitting in an office and waiting for stories to come in. You must have a system for gathering information and preparing it for publication on time. You are more than someone who writes and rewrites stories. Editors of internal publications are managers in the best sense. Managing is generally defined as "getting things done through other people." The editor's task includes getting others to provide information and to write stories for the publication. Even when an editor has a paid staff, it will never be large enough to cover all the sources of information in the organization. Nor is a publication written entirely by the public relations staff always desirable. Readers of house organs are often more interested in articles by their coworkers, written from their own point of view. Thus there are good reasons to develop an external network to provide information and articles.

*Ways to get news.* Enlisting auxiliary writers is not difficult. Their only reward is a byline, but such recognition is a powerful inducement for many people. Others will provide information and news tips just to help out. There are several ways to organize a news gathering process:

1. *The "beat" system.* The organization can be divided into territories and a reporter assigned to cover each. This is an excellent system if there are enough people willing to be reporters. One way of recruiting correspondents is to identify the people in each area who have been there longest. Ask them whether they will help you. Then ask their supervisor if they can be a reporter for the house publication. This support is valuable motivation. When all the reporters have been selected, invite them to a "news clinic" on company time.

2. *The telephone network.* If an editor cannot recruit enough reporters, people who are willing to phone in information can be used. The editor should stay in touch with every link in this network even if there is no news. Constant contact with the editor keeps lines open. Regular conversations may turn up information that the contact did not realize was newsworthy.

3. *News request forms.* Memos or notices asking for information are seldom effective. Most people do not understand what news means. They seldom think what is happening to them is important. A news request form which asks for information about specific things such as promotions, awards, and achievements, however, produces excellent story topics.

*Editorial staff.* A house publication needs columnists, feature writers, photographers, and artists. How many of these skills can be bought depends upon the funds available. Recognition can often substitute for pay, however. A list of the names of all those who contribute to an issue is one way to recognize those who do not have bylines.

**Controlling Internal Publications**

Every publication should evaluate periodically its progress toward its objectives. Purpose, content, and frequency of publication should all be examined in terms of the needs of the target audience. The panel that originally identified the target audience can be again used to evaluate progress. Surveys and questionnaires also give useful information about how well a publication fulfills expectations. National magazines have found that even simple surveys can provide excellent insight into the interests of readers. To pretest the potential readership of planned articles, for example, a questionnaire can be prepared with a list of headlines, and a sample of the intended audience can be asked to say which articles they would read. An editor can thus get feedback about the probable success of stories.

**OCCASIONAL AND SPECIAL PUBLICATIONS**

Most organizations prepare publications on miscellaneous topics at irregular intervals. These take forms ranging from mimeographed one-sheet leaflets to books using professional writers. Responsibility for these often rests in

# PRACTICING PUBLIC RELATIONS

the personnel department, but other areas may become involved because of legal requirements, government regulations, or company policy. These publications generally can be divided into three categories, according to purpose.

*Orientation literature* indoctrinates new members in an organization. Such literature can help a new employee get off to a good start by setting forth the ground rules. Goals and objectives of the organization are often included. They give a sense of where the company is going and the employee's role in achieving that objective.

*Reference material* is designed to be kept for future use. Because of the nature of these publications, it is unlikely that anyone will ever read them from cover to cover, and they must therefore give fast and easy answers on any subject covered. This information sometimes changes and such publications should be designed for supplements or for material to be added later. Reference materials deal with such matters as benefit programs, insurance plans, and recreation programs.

*Position or special-topic publications* are put out only once. They deal with a specific subject or occasion. The subject can be any that an organization feels it should discuss. The free-enterprise system, charitable and social commitments, history, awards and scientific or technological developments are among the most frequently treated subjects. Occasional publications have more impact than a regularly scheduled newsletter, and give an organization the chance to convey a specific message. The same requirements of credibility and interest that apply to newsletters must be followed if special-topic publications are to state their message effectively.

**Leaflets, Inserts, and Enclosures**

Inexpensive publications which can be read and thrown away are often printed on a single sheet that can be folded to produce any of several formats. Leaflets or handbills can be typed on a good typewriter and duplicated on a copying machine, and are thus inexpensive and fast to prepare. With more attention to detail, these single-sheet publications can be folded into brochures for information racks, in-house distribution, or direct mail. Many organizations use them as inserts in pay envelopes to deal with immediate problems. Credit-card companies and utilities have proven inserts to be an effective and inexpensive means of communication with their customers.

**Booklets and Manuals**

Because of their expense, booklets and manuals are made to be read and saved for reference (*Figure 10-11*). Their greatest shortcoming is that they can be hard to read and use if not designed properly. Employee orientation manuals or insurance-plan booklets need indexes, and can benefit from the use of tabs or color-coded pages to improve accessibility of information. Regardless of how much information the book contains, employees will still be uninformed unless they can locate what they need when they need it.

**Figure 10-11**
Some Uses of Booklets
and Manuals

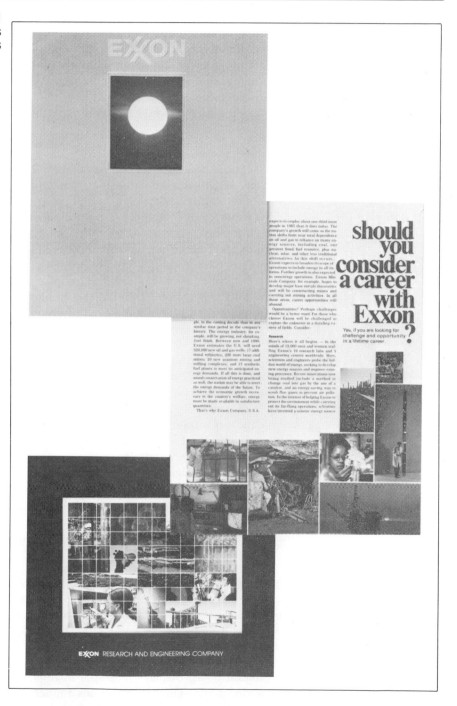

# PRACTICING PUBLIC RELATIONS

Booklets and manuals must be written with the needs of employees in mind. If management allows them to be written in technical language or the jargon of insurance, law, accounting, or finance, they will be useless. The reading levels and interests of the intended audience must be considered before copy is prepared for a booklet or manual. Too often, publications meet the regulations of insurance companies or government agencies rather than the needs of employees.

Some of the areas in which booklets and manuals can be used successfully are:

1. To orient new employees.
2. To explain the safety regulations as they comply with the Occupational Safety and Health Administration standards.
3. To explain the benefit plan and its value to the employee.
4. To explain company policies and their compliance with government regulations.
5. To explain the costs and benefits of the organization's insurance package.
6. To explain the company retirement plan and its requirements.
7. To give information helpful to the employee in his or her job.
8. To give information about social or community issues.
9. To explain organizational compliance with environmental standards.

## Printed Speeches and Position Papers

Speeches and position papers are sometimes distributed as occasional publications. Organization officials frequently speak to professional, community, or other groups. These speeches often concern topics of interest to employees (*Figure 10-12*). It may be useful to print them for distribution within the organization, since copies of the speeches have usually been made available to news media anyway.

Reprints of magazine articles of concern to the organization and its employees can be bought rather inexpensively. Magazine reprints have the advantage of outside credibility. If general-interest magazines are used, the readability of the articles will probably make them suitable for wide distribution. If the article is drawn from a more technical or professional publication, however, the style of writing may limit its use.

## MESSAGE DISPLAYS

A growing number of laws and regulations require the posting of notices where they are available to employees, and many organizations find that display messages are a quick, inexpensive medium for reaching large numbers of people. Message displays include posters, billboards, bulletin boards, information racks, and exhibits.

## Bulletin Boards

The bulletin board displays messages in regular locations with minimum effort and expense. The board remains a much-used and effective means of communication in organizations. It often does a supplementary or follow-

**Figure 10-12**
Reprint of Speech Given
by Exxon Company
Senior Vice President

# THE COURAGE TO WORK TOGETHER

Remarks By:
C.R. Sitter
Senior Vice President
Exxon Company, U.S.A.
Presented Before
American Council on Consumer Interests
San Antonio, Texas
April 27, 1979

up job. Notices that have been mailed or given out to employees can be posted as reminders. Details of announcements already made in meetings or in the house publication can be posted for those who wish more information. Bulletin boards are an appropriate location for information that is of value but does not warrant publication. And, of course, certain information is required by law to be posted on bulletin boards.

Bulletin boards are effective and fast when used and kept up properly. To insure credibility and readability, bulletin boards must be carefully planned.

*Location* is a primary consideration. No matter how professionally written and designed a board may be, if it is hidden in a corner it will not be read. Management must pick locations that meet the needs of most of those persons who should read a bulletin board. The convenience of the manager charged with keeping it current is secondary. Too many bulletin boards are outside supervisors' offices.

# PRACTICING
# PUBLIC
# RELATIONS

Bulletin boards should be placed in or near areas of heavy traffic. As many employees as possible should pass the message. The boards should be at eye-level where the reading light is good, and where employees can stop and read without blocking traffic. Bulletin boards should never be put where they present safety hazards.

*Neatness* will improve the readability. Order and arrangement invite reading. If a board becomes cluttered, even with important notices, it will no longer communicate its messages.

Someone should check each board regularly to be sure that it has not become overloaded and disorganized. Boards containing information on more than one topic should be organized so that all the messages on a given subject are together. When possible, have a separate board for each topic.

*Timeliness* is a key to credibility in bulletin boards. Out-of-date notices kill interest. If an organization's bulletin boards always have up-to-date information, many employees regularly check their contents. Constant attention is required to post current material and to take down outdated messages.

The "wear-out" potential of a message must also be considered. Even if the content is still current, the notice itself should be changed periodically. Once employees have read a notice, they are likely to skip over it when checking the board. If the information is "repackaged," it will once again attract notice. This method can keep employees alert to long-term issues.

*Interest* of the intended readers can be assured by picking messages that meet their needs. Like any other publication, posted items should reflect the interests of the intended audience. Messages posted must be significant to the employees. Personal items, advertisements, and entertaining odds and ends should be kept to a minimum. The presence of non-official information can create a relaxed atmosphere, but too many non-essential items destroy credibility.

*Responsibility* for the upkeep of each bulletin board should be fixed. One person must be charged with maintaining the condition of each board. Bulletin boards are important media. They should not be assigned to a secretary or clerk. Decisions about what should be posted and how it will be said are the job of public relations.

**Posters and Billboards**  Like bulletin boards, posters and billboards offer fast and effective communication. They are most appropriately used to give emphasis to an idea. They are not intended for careful reading or study. Posters and billboards provide messages that can be grasped quickly; details can be published in other media. Posters and billboards should be in high-traffic areas where they can be easily seen by most employees. "Wear-out" potential is also a consideration here. Messages should be changed or revised periodically.

**Information Racks**  You can combine the effects of posters, bulletin boards, brochures and booklets with an information rack. Such racks should incorporate a poster to draw attention and to invite the reader to take a copy of the material. Racks provide information on topics that cannot be handled in short messages. Because the booklets are selected by readers without pressure from management, interest is likely to be higher. There are economic advantages to information racks, in that only interested employees are likely to take material.

Information racks work best in areas where employees can look at the material in a leisurely way; Lunchrooms, break areas, waiting rooms, and dressing areas are good. Empty information racks suggest that management is uninterested, so regular attention is needed.

**Exhibits and Displays**   Exhibits and displays rely primarily on visual messages. Their effectiveness comes from seeing a sample or model of what is being discussed. Many organizations recognize the value of exhibits and displays at industrial meetings, or in sales-related contexts, but they are equally valuable in employee communication.

Exhibits and displays can be used to show how production facilities work, to display products, to honor those who receive awards, or to depict the history of the organization.

# CHAPTER 11 COMMUNITY RELATIONS

**PREVIEW**   Community relations refers to an organization's planned, active, and continuing participation within a community to maintain and enhance its environment to the benefit of both the organization and the community.

Recruitment, employee relations, waste disposal, energy use, design and maintenance of organizational buildings and grounds, marketing and advertising strategies, corporate philanthropy and many other organizational activities affect community relations.

The quality of an organization's employees, the cooperativeness of citizens and governmental agencies, the patronage of community members, the ability to attract financial support, indeed the success or failure of an organization can depend on the effectiveness of its community relations.

What people say behind your back is your standing in the
community in which you live.

—Henry Wadsworth Longfellow

In an age when marketing, technology, resource acquisition, and management are increasingly international in scope, and when the federal government seems the most conspicuous aspect of many organizations' operating
environment, concern for "community" seems almost anachronistic. Indeed,
certain sociologists and political scientists have maintained that our communities are dissolving in the face of increased mobility and communication.

But just as the community was about to be declared dead, some strange
things began to occur. Neighbors began to band together on small-scale
issues like schools, security, and community services. Back-to-the-city movements have repopulated many metropolitan areas; downtown businesses have
become active after years of inactivity; people have become interested in
genealogical and community "roots;" strong chauvinistic pride associated
with the cities and communities in which people live has become widespread.
Slogans modeled after the "I love New York" campaign have become com-
monplace, while the citizens of Buffalo, Cleveland, and Terra Haute rush to
the defense of their much-maligned hometowns.

The lesson for organizations in this revival is really simple: Regional, national, and international concerns may preoccupy you, but do not forget to
think about the folks next door. In the past, constructive community relations
programs were characterized by phrases like "corporate citizenship," or "good
neighbor." These terms still apply, but they oversimplify the complex relationships that exist between organizations and their communities. We expect
much more of major institutions than we do of the best of our neighbors.

The urban problems that were recognized as matters of public concern
in the 1960s cast "community relations" in a new light and forced institutions
to place new emphasis on their complex interrelationships with surrounding
communities. Equal employment opportunity and training, employment of
the disadvantaged, stimulation of minority business enterprises, elimination
of substandard housing, and many other community problems formed the
basis of greater involvement and activity throughout the 1970s on the part
of business and other institutions in dealing with community issues (for a
more in-depth discussion of these issues, see Chapter 21).

Of course, community relations significantly predates the 1960s as a business priority. Morrell Heald, in a history of the social responsibility of American business, points out that since the beginning of this century:

**American businessmen fully shared the social concerns and preoccupations
of their fellow citizens. Although they have often been depicted—indeed
caricatured—as single-minded pursuers of profit, the facts are quite other-**

wise. The nature of their activities often brought them into close contact
with the harsher aspects of the life of a rapidly industrializing society. Like
others, they were frequently troubled by the conditions they saw; and, also
like others, they numbered in their ranks men who contributed both their
ideas and their questions to redress social imbalance and disorganiza-
tion.  .  .  .

**From the outset, self-interest combined with idealism to foster sensitivity
to social conditions on the part of the business community.**[1]

An appropriate basis for institutional efforts toward good community relations is derived from an understanding of the nature of "community."
William Gilbert's definition provides some insight:

**A place of interacting social institutions which produce in the residents an
attitude and practice of interdependence, cooperation, collaboration and
unification .  .  . a web of social structures all closely interrelated.**[2]

Effective community relations depend on the recognition of the interdependence of institutions. George Sawyer puts it this way:

**The key elements for business management in establishing a social balance
with the local community are: (1) the recognition of the many ways in
which the business creates impacts on the community; and (2) recognition
of the basic business-community interdependence.**[3]

Of course, businesses are not the only organizations to practice community
relations. Schools, churches, hospitals, museums, and organizations like the
Red Cross and the Boy Scouts depend on community relations the way
businesses depend on marketing—it serves as the primary means by which
"customers" are attracted to such organizations. Prisons, military bases, and
universities (where "town versus gown" conflicts are common) must concern
themselves with community acceptance. Excepting the area of corporate
philanthropy, however, the process of community relations is the same whether
or not the organization seeks financial profit.

Every community has a vital stake in the economic health and prosperity
of its institutions. Every organization has a vital stake in the health and
prosperity of the community it inhabits. It is quite natural, therefore, that
organization and community should develop mutual interest in each other's
successful and effective operation. At this level the connection between institutional interest and public interest is most clear.

The clarity of this connection, however, does not imply that community
relations can be practiced without careful planning and execution. Effective
community relations does not just happen, nor is it an inevitable byproduct
of a well-run organization with civic-minded policies. It is not based on pure
altruism, but rather looks to the organization's self-interest. W. J. Peak offers
the best definition of community relations that we have seen:

Community relations, as a public relations function, is an institution's planned, active, and continuing participation with and within a community to maintain and enhance its environment to the benefit of both the institution and the community.[4]

In addition to considering the process and practice of community relations in this chapter, we will also deal with several subjects generally associated with the community-relations area, including corporate philanthropy, local government relations, business and the arts, and business and education.

**THE PROCESS AND PRACTICE OF COMMUNITY RELATIONS**

The process of community relations embraces all aspects of institutions. In some ways, good community relations simply means good performance. A company that offers poor products and unsatisfactory service is unlikely to enjoy positive community relations. Beyond this, Robert Ross explains, "good community relations consists of recognizing and fulfilling the organization's responsibilities in and to the communities in which it operates."[5]

Recruitment, employee relations, production processes, marketing and advertising strategies, design of the organization's buildings and facilities, and many other organizational activities affect community relations. Sawyer maintains that even the internal standards of the organization have a bearing on its community relations:

**A community becomes to a large extent an expression of the values, aspirations and achievements of its businesses. Thus, the internal standards a corporation sets for itself and for the members of its organization have an influence that carries down through the work force and out into the community.[6]**

Arguably, community relations is an organizational attitude or state of mind rather than any specific process or practice.

At the very least, organizations expect communities to provide adequate municipal services, fair taxation, good living conditions for employees, a good labor supply, and a reasonable degree of support for the plant and its products. In addition to employment, wages, and taxes, communities expect from their institutions attractive appearance, participation in the support of community institutions, economic stability, and a focus for hometown pride.

Good community relations not only aids in securing that which is needed from the community and providing what the community expects, but also helps to protect organizational investments, improve sales of products and stock, improve the general operating climate, and reduce costs of dealing with government agencies. Moreover, it can affect worker productivity through its effect community health and education, and because community attitudes frequently determine worker attitudes toward the organization.

In a very general sense, community relations seeks to inform the community about the organization, its products, services, and practices. It should correct community misconceptions and reply to criticism while gaining favorable community opinion and support. Other general community relations objectives include:

to obtain support for legislation that will favorably affect
   operating climate in the community;
to determine community attitudes, knowledge, and
   expectations;
to support community health, educational, recreational,
   and cultural activities;
to gain better local government;
to assist in the local economy by purchasing local
   supplies and services.

General objectives, however, will not suffice for specific institutions. Every community relations program should have a written policy clearly defining management's view of its obligation to the community. So that efforts can be coordinated and concentrated, specific community relations objectives should be spelled out. Failure to do these things kills too many community relations programs before they get started.

Community relations policies and objectives are not determined according to idealistic principles. They come about through an assessment of organizational needs, resources and expertise on the one hand, and community needs and expectations on the other. Before meaningful policies and objectives can be developed, the organization must know its community.

**Input Is Essential**   While community relations usually stresses communication from the organization to the community, the success of such efforts rests with the knowledge possessed by the communicator about the audience. The effective communicator always listens before acting. Stated simply: "A basic ingredient of every good community relations program is the necessity for officials up and down the line to know their community."[7]

Of course, it is useful for management to have standard information concerning the community. Demographic, historical, geographic, economic and other readily accessible data are essential knowledge. But real knowledge of the community is not found in almanacs or chamber of commerce fact sheets. The solid community relations program must be built on the answers to questions like these:

1. How is the community structured?
   A. Is the population homogeneous or heterogeneous?
   B. What are its formal and informal leadership structures?
   C. What are the prevailing value structures?
   D. How are its communication channels structured?
2. What are the community's strengths and weaknesses?
   A. What are the particular problems of the community?
   B. What is the local economic situation?
   C. What is the local political situation?

D. What are the unique resources (human, cultural, natural) possessed by the community?
3. What does the community know and feel about the organization?
  A. Do its neighbors understand the organization's products, services, practices, and policies?
  B. What are the community's feelings about the organization?
  C. Do misunderstandings about the organization exist?
  D. What are the community's expectations in regard to the organization's activities?

The answers to questions such as these are not necessarily easy to get. Moreover, answers change over time and thus require frequent monitoring. Good information can be acquired in several ways. Many organizations engage in survey research to determine community knowledge, attitudes, and perceptions. Professional polling organizations are often employed to provide such services. Close contact with community leaders is an extremely important source of information. Political officials; media editors; professional, civic, religious or fraternal leaders can generally be reached through common membership with institutional managers in local organizations or through face-to-face meetings on a variety of subjects. Some organizations formalize such inputs by including these individuals on organizational task forces or committees dealing with issues of importance to the community.

**GUIDELINES FOR EFFECTIVE COMMUNITY RELATIONS PROGRAMS**

Having established the means for ongoing community inputs, the following guidelines should be used to establish an effective community relations program:

1. There should be a careful effort to establish the objectives top management wishes to achieve. The organization may seek many objectives—reputation, experience with a potential future payoff, stability of environment, and so on—but whatever it seeks ought to be established in realistic and concrete terms.
2. Alternative strategies ought to be explored and choices made. If an organization wishes to improve housing conditions in a city in which it operates, for instance, possibilities for action range from partial funding of research into new ways to build low-cost housing, to actually building low-cost housing.
3. Impacts of community relations programs on the organization and the community should be anticipated. Offering training for jobs that will not exist when the training is concluded helps no one.
4. Attention should be paid to the likely total costs to the organization of a given course of not-for-profit action, and the volume of its resources which may legitimately be allocated to community relations. It is not to the advantage of the organization or the community to have the organization suddenly discover that a given program is costing much too much and then abruptly stop all community service.
5. Many managers have found that certain types of involvement in urban affairs require knowledge and understanding that go beyond the usual

managerial and technical business talents. Political skills, deep understanding of community problems, and an ability to settle problems in a
far different cultural setting are requisites for some activities. Special
expertise may have to be acquired.[8]

**ONE CORPORATION PUTS ACTION IN COMMUNITY RELATIONS**

Norton Simon Inc.'s commitment to community relations goes beyond good
words, high ideals and moral pressure. Based on performance in four areas
of community involvement, the company's managers' bonuses can be increased by as much as twenty percent.

The four areas of the company's concern are: equal employment opportunities; encouragement of minority businesses; charitable contributions; and
involvement of managers in community organizations. Norton Simon's managers are assessed on performance in these areas by their immediate supervisors as part of their normal performance appraisals. The company regards corporate citizenship as a central plank in its strategic plan. As such,
it provides an example of corporation-wide commitment to community relations backed by its resources and managerial experience.[9]

**AUDIENCES FOR COMMUNITY RELATIONS**

Community . . . . refers not only to a group of people
living in the same locality, but to the interaction of those
people. . . . In the past, the tendency was to treat a
community as a rather simple entity—a collection of
people, a 'home town.' Today we are beginning to
recognize each community as a complex dynamism of
diverse, constantly changing, often powerful, and always
important forces.[10]

There is no single audience for community communication. Messages reach
communities through employees and their families and local media. Other
important communication channels consist of a communities opinion leaders:
teachers, clergy, public officials, professionals and executives, bankers, union
leaders, and ethnic and neighborhood leaders. Caterpillar Tractor staged an
open house for barbers, bartenders and librarians because the company
found them to be significant spreaders of community information. Another
company hosted cabdrivers for the same reasons.

Local organizations are also an important method of communication in
communities. Fraternal, civic, service, and social clubs; cultural, political,
veterans, and religious organizations; and youth groups all provide platforms
for institutional messages and ample opportunities for informal communication. Organizational managers should be encouraged to belong to such
groups and should be available for public speeches to them as well.

The communication channels through which these audiences are reached
range from informal chats over lunch at a Rotary Club meeting to advertisements placed in local mass media. House publications, brochures and annual
reports can be easily shared with community leaders. Some organizations
create newsletters specifically for their neighbors. Upjohn Company, for in-

stance, distributed a special report on the company's economic and social involvement in its headquarters city (Kalamazoo, Michigan) to 20,000 people. Abbott Laboratories circulates 85,000 copies of its quarterly publication, *Commitment,* to employees, shareholders, customer groups, local, state and national leaders, and community groups. Institutions frequently make organizational movies available to local groups and set up exhibits at local airports, shopping centers, and civic centers.

**Open Houses**  A uniquely community-oriented method of organizational communication is the open house. Open houses can be very effective if well planned and executed. Successful open houses provide for tours of organizational facilities in small groups with knowledgeable guides. They include films, displays and brochures, and usually provide product samples or a memento of the event to take home. The major message of such activities, of course, is the interdependence between institution and community. In some cases, industrial or company tours become major tourist attractions. Tours of Heineken's Amsterdam Brewery, for instance, make the company "thousands of loyal friends who speak well of us throughout the world." [11]

**WHEN AN ORGANIZATION MOVES**  Community relations is particularly critical when an organization moves into a new community or leaves an old one. While virtually any major organization was once welcomed with open arms, communities now ask questions before they accept new business, industries, or even not-for-profit undertakings. Community response to an organization should be an important factor in the location decision.

Once the decision to move into a particular community has been made, it is essential to provide local media with factual information on appropriate events and project stages immediately. Key groups should be familiarized with the organization and its products, activities, policies, and people through all the media and methods discussed above.

Dependence of a community on its organizations is never clearer than when a plant or facility leaves a town. The organization that fails to prepare for its departure appropriately only invites greater public regulation to prevent irresponsible organizational activity in the future. General Foods and Olin Chemical provide examples of successful departures from communities highly dependent on them.

When General Foods' Jello Division left LeRoy, New York it provided full information on its plans. The company aided the community by supporting an industrial survey and the formation of an industrial development council to attract new industry to the town. Employees were offered their choice of transfer to the new plant in a neighboring state or a termination allowance and effective assistance in finding new jobs.

Olin Chemical was forced to close its Saltville, Virginia plant when new pollution regulations made production inefficient. The company carefully explained the reasons for its actions. Employees were offered the chance to relocate to other plants, and arrangements were made for special retirement and serverance benefits. According to *Life* magazine, "The people were disappointed but not bitter as the company left; the company dealt generously in its settlements with the town." [12]

**COMMUNITY ACTION**    Community relations goes beyond mere communication. It requires action on the part of organizations in relation to community health and welfare, education, government, culture, recreation and other areas.

**Local Government and Political Action**    While we will be discussing business/government relations in much greater depth and detail in Chapter 16, community relations and governmental relations clearly overlap in relation to local government and politics.

We have already stated that local political officials can supply invaluable input to corporate community relations programs. Corporations have a great stake in effective local government, since they are major taxpayers and users of municipal services. Part of the community relations effort, therefore, must be devoted to building solid relations with city officials, county commissions, and other agencies of local government. This is accomplished, in part, by making organizational expertise available to governments through loans of managerial personnel or through service on panels, commissions, or committees established by or for local government.

As political activity becomes more important to organizations, community relations plays a critical role. Institutions must mobilize on the local level those who recognize the importance of their contribution to the health and prosperity of the community and who will speak out for policies in the best interest of their community and its institutions. This is true whether the institution is a hospital, an art museum, a university, or a business. Moreover, political experts now recognize that strength in Washington is derived from organized, localized grassroots support. In an era when virtually all congressmen are looking out for their own districts and careers, local people making local demands and representing local interests are far more effective than Washington-based lobbyists. In this regard, community relations may be not only an end in itself, but an integral part of national efforts.

**Corporate Philanthropy**    Corporate philanthropy is a subject over which great controversy has raged for many years. Only in the past thirty years has corporate charity been recognized as a legal use of stockholders' funds. But even having its legality established, questions remain as to whether and the extent to which it is appropriate and useful. And beyond these issues are questions of the appropriate motivations, goals and criteria of corporate giving.

Some maintain that corporate managers have no business giving away profits that rightly belong to stockholders. If stockholders wish to donate their money to what they consider good causes, it is argued, it is their right—but managers should not take such decisions for them. One corporation solved this dilemma by making $2 per share available to stockholders to contribute to their favorite charities.

It is clear, however, that the corporate entity incurs obligations and responsibilities of its own, and needs to engage in activities traditionally considered philanthropic as a matter of long-term self-interest. W. J. Baumol explains:

**The company pays a high price for operating in a region where education is poor, where living conditions are deplorable, where health is poorly protected, where property is unsafe, and where cultural activity is all but dead. . . . These circumstances are all more expensive than corporate giving.**[13]

By law, corporations are permitted to donate up to five percent of earnings to charitable organizations. In practice, however, very few corporations give to the limit. Overall, about one percent of corporate profits is actually given away. Thus, while corporations could legally give more, they obviously feel that it is not in their interest nor in the interests of their stockholders to do so.

With these limits established, however, debates over the legitimacy of the practice have ended. As Richard Eells points out:

**The whole activity of corporate giving has now become an accepted part of good corporate management. The donative decision, as we are now coming to appreciate more and more, is part and parcel of the whole decision process in managing a business.**[14]

The motivations and goals for such decisions are, however, still matters of considerable debate. Despite the fact that the legal rationale for corporate donations rests on the notion of self-interest, some maintain that the term "philanthropy" be taken literally—that giving should be done strictly for the love of mankind. Irving Kristol represents the opposite view:

**Some corporate executives seem to think that their corporate philanthropy is a form of benevolent charity. It is not. An act of charity refines and elevates the soul of the giver—but corporations have no souls to be saved or damned. Charity involves dispensing your own money, not your stockholders'. When you give away your own money, you can be as foolish, as arbitrary, as whimsical as you like. But when you give your stockholders' money, your philanthropy must serve the longer-term interests of the corporation. Corporate philanthropy should not be, cannot be, disinterested.**[15]

In practice, research indicates that self-interest prevails. According to Baumol, surveys indicate that patterns of corporate giving fit in well with the doctrine that corporations should provide funds to causes that serve the broadly conceived interests of the firm.[16] Similarly, Neil Jacoby has found that "corporate giving is generally in proportion to the extensiveness of local public contracts which generate social pressures."[17] He points out the extensiveness of the charitable activities of banks as an example of this phenomenon.

Corporate giving can serve many corporate interests including recruitment, sales, and employee morale, but it inevitably serves that interest called public

relations. Consequently, corporate public relations personnel almost always
are involved in, if not responsible for, charitable decisions.

Unfortunately, in some cases corporate charitable decisions are still made
capriciously and without adequate planning. In developing a coherent approach to corporate giving, several factors should be considered.

1. *Do no harm.* Contributions should not be made to any cause that may
   be contrary to the best interest of the donor.
2. *Communication goes hand-in-hand with constructive contributions.*
   Effective grantmaking requires a close partnership between donor and
   recipient.
3. *Target contributions.* Gifts should be given based upon achieving maximum impact on the community while providing maximum benefits for
   the donor. In this regard, donations should be directed to those areas
   in which individual corporations have unique expertise not available in
   the voluntary, nonprofit sector.
4. *Contributions should be governed by specific statements of corporate
   policy.* Fully developed policies of this nature should include the charitable aims and beliefs of the company, the criteria to be used in evaluating requests for funds, the kinds of organizations and causes that will
   and will not be supported, and the methods of which grants will be
   administered.
5. *Budget.* Corporate giving should be tied to set percentages of net earnings.
6. *Inform.* Employees and the community at large should be fully informed
   of corporate charitable activities.
7. *Followup.* The corporation does a valuable service by demanding of
   recipients high levels of performance and proper financial accounting.
8. *More than money.* An effective corporate contribution requires more
   than "checkbook charity." Volunteer manpower, managerial expertise,
   and corporate leadership are essential elements of an effective program.

Two other trends in corporate giving hold the promise of making such
philanthropic programs more effective. Rather than reacting to public issues
and public pressures, more firms, particularly the larger ones, are taking
greater initiative in channeling dollars and corporate talent into problem
areas they deem significant and in which they wish to make an impact. Other
corporations are attempting to broaden their philanthropic programs through
decentralization and employee participation. By asking local managers of
corporate facilities to make decisions about allocation of donations, large
corporations ensure that they are in touch with the needs and desires of
local communities. Many corporations now match employee contributions
to educational institutions, museums, orchestras, public TV, hospitals, and
ballet, thus in effect, permitting their contributions to reflect those of their
employees. Xerox even gives employees paid leave to work on worthwhile
community projects. IBM encourages top executives to teach at colleges and
universities. In these ways employees can be the motivating force behind
their companies' charitable donations.

The vast bulk of corporate donations go to health and welfare organizations,
educational institutions, and the arts. Each of these is an appropriate area for

corporate giving, but gifts to each serve different objectives and suggest slightly different views of corporate responsibilities to communities.

**Health and Welfare.** The self-interest of corporations in their philanthropic efforts is perhaps most obvious in the area of community health and welfare. Donations to hospitals and medical schools are very common. Classic examples of corporate community action are found in relation to health and welfare. Professors Keith Davis and Robert Blomstrom offer the following example:

**In the first decade of this century, Birmingham, Alabama was menaced by serious health problems. Malaria, typhoid fever and other diseases were prevalent because of unsanitary community conditions. This city was the site of a United States Steel Subsidiary, Tennessee Coal and Iron Co., whose productivity was lowered by illness. Tennessee Coal and Iron organized a health department and hired a prominent specialist in the offending diseases from the Panama Canal Zone. In its first year of operation the health department spent $750,000 for draining swamps and improving sanitary facilities. This amount was 30 times the total health budget of the entire state of Alabama.[18]**

Health and welfare activities have come to encompass a broad range of activities dealing with employment, housing and the physical environment.

**Education.** Businesses have long made contributions to educational institutions. Again, aspects of self-interest in educational donations is evident. Skilled, intelligent workers and university-generated research are directly beneficial to business. A better-educated population creates a more congenial economic, political, and social environment for business. Corporate contributions to educational institutions can improve public relations, recruitment, and marketing. Increasingly, corporate contributions have specifically supported efforts to improve students' and teachers' understanding of the private-enterprise system.

Education is another area in which corporate support calls for more than money. With school budgets stretched to the breaking point, donations of materials for classroom and recreational use are extremely important. Examples of contributed materials include pencils and pads, automobiles for driver training, and sophisticated computers and equipment for advanced research. Businesses can also provide plant tours for student field trips, speakers for classes and assemblies, internships for high school and college students, and managerial and financial expertise for school administrators. Bridges built between the corporation and the classroom are among the most valuable available in any community.

**The Arts.** Only about five percent of all corporate contributions is devoted to cultural activities. This is the fastest-growing area of corporate philanthropy, however, and one in which corporations can make their most significant impacts. As government funds to support the arts are reduced, private-sector contributions will become even more important.

The arts as a target of corporate giving developed later than health and welfare or education because the advantage is less obvious. By the 1960s, however, business leaders like David Rockefeller were appealing to their colleagues' self-interest on behalf of the arts. "Support of the arts by business amounts to nothing less than a prudent investment in community survival and growth," Rockefeller claimed.

On a practical level, international cultural exchanges have paved the way for expanded trade relations. Theater, museums, dance, music, and architecture promote tourism. Bristol-Myers's Gavin K. MacBain points to the utilitarian aspects of art: advertising, packaging, design, and marketing. He maintains:

**The use of art to move products in the marketplace would be impossible if there were no art museums, composers, orchestras, painters, filmmakers, writers, playwrights, and choreographers who are dedicated exclusively to their arts.**[19]

Gideon Chagy puts his rationale for business support of the arts on a higher, more philosophical plane:

**If our society is to be both affluent and humane, the competitive drive and the sense of community must be kept in balance. Without a widely shared sense of community there would be nothing to restrain the logic and dynamics of business competition from leading to a system of exploitation. . . . While art is not a panacea for society's problems, it is a restorative for the sense of community.**[20]

But corporations become most directly involved in the arts when commissioning and designing products for themselves, as when new buildings are constructed.

Whether consciously or not, corporations routinely act as art patrons whenever they engage the services of an architect, and the community relations aspect of architectural decisions should not be overlooked. Cummins Engine has transformed Columbus, Indiana into an oasis of architectural excellence by paying fees of top architects to design new buildings and restore old ones in the town. Every company can make an important contribution to its community by considering appropriate location and design for their plants, warehouses, showrooms, and offices. The public is served well by distinctively designed buildings that enhance their surroundings.

Dayton-Hudson Corporation of Minneapolis has hired a full-time director of cultural affairs. Touche, Ross and Company makes its accounting and managerial expertise available to non-profit cultural organizations. J. Walter Thompson lends expertise in marketing research and advertising. Boston's National Shawmut Bank successfully combined support of the arts with marketing promotion. For every new $100 account or any addition of $100 to an existing account, the bank provided a six-month membership in any one of three Boston museums. The campaign resulted in $1.5 million in deposits for the bank and 5,921 members for the museums.

Community relations as an organizational activity is as diverse as the communities in which concerns are based and carry out their business. As the boundaries between community and organization become more permeable, the importance of the community relations function will continue to grow.

---

**CASE STUDY:**    **By R. Ferrell Ervin**
**PENNINGTON HIGH**    **Norfolk State University,**
**Norfolk, Virginia**

---

Pennington is a relatively small community located about one-hundred miles west of one of the nation's largest cities. The city has a rich history tied to its founder, Joshua C. Pennington, and his descendants. Many of those descendants are still active in the affairs of the community and are respected for their continuing civic role. Unlike some communities, the city has welcomed the addition of new industry and has kept pace with the needs of its citizens.

Now, however, there seems to be a change brewing. A new public school complex is being suggested to voters of the city, but support has not been as great as expected. Part of the reason may be due to the proposed change (from Pennington High to Midway Regional High); or the growing number of retired persons who have found the region to be ideal; or the fact that because of the industry in the area, this school would draw students from beyond Pennington alone; or that the city already has a higher tax cost to its citizens than any other city in the state; or that it would also welcome students from the area that might lower the quality of education that the school system now offers.

Whatever the cause, Joshua C. Pennington IV has publically voiced opposition to the project, and this has virtually sealed the coffin on the tax levy for the school.

If you had just been retained by the school system to encourage support, even though the balloting is only three weeks away, what method might you advise?

**Questions**    1. We often classify people according to their positions in society (upper upper class, etc.) or their willingness to accept new ideas (opinion leaders). How important are these classifications to the creation of a public relations program for the Pennington problem?

2. Typically we might suggest that extensive research be conducted on this issue but time prevents us from doing much in this case. However, some research is possible. What types would you suggest and what are their relative advantages?

3. How might we harness the local industrial leaders to our advantage? How important is such an educational institution to the continued success of local industry?

**NOTES**   [1] Morrell Heald, *The Social Responsibilities of Business: Company and Community,*
*1900–1960* (Cleveland: Case Western Reserve University Press, 1970), pp. 1, 2.

[2] William H. Gilbert, *Public Relations in Local Government* (Washington, D.C.:
International Management Association, 1975), p. 103.

[3] George C. Sawyer, *Business and Society: Managing Corporate Social Impact* (Boston:
Houghton Mifflin, 1979), p. 240.

[4] W. J. Peak, "Community Relations" in *Handbook of Public Relations,* ed Philip Lesly
(Englewood Cliffs, N.J.: Prentice-Hall, 1978), p. 65.

[5] Robert D. Ross, *The Management of Public Relations* (New York: Wiley, 1977), p. 170.

[6] Sawyer, *Business and Society,* pp. 316–317.

[7] Philip Lesly, *Handbook of Public Relations* (New York: Prentice-Hall, 1950), p. 150.

[8] Adapted from Jules Cohen, "Is Business Meeting the Challenge of Urban Affairs?"
*Harvard Business Review* (March–April 1970): 81–82. Reprinted by permission of the
Harvard business Review. Copyright © 1970 by the President and Fellows of Harvard
College. All rights reserved.

[9] Based on David Clutterback, "Bonus Pay-outs Linked to Social Responsibilty,"
*International Managment* (August 1978): 49.

[10] Peak, "Community Relations," p. 65.

[11] Gerard Tavernier, "Is Your Company Worth A Visit?" *International Management* (June
1974): 24–28.

[12] "End of a Company Town: The People of Saltville, VA, Lose Their Plant to Pollution
Laws," *Life Magazine,* 26 March 1971, pp. 37–45.

[13] W. J. Baumol, "Enlightened Self-Interest and Corporate Philanthropy," in *A New
Rationale for Corporate Social Policy,* eds. W. J. Baumol, R. Likert, H. C. Wallich, and
J. J. McGowan (Lexington, Mass.: Heath, 1970), p. 19.

[14] Richard Eells, "A Philosophy for Corporate Giving," *The Conference Board Record,*
January 1968, p. 15.

[15] Irving Kristol, "On Corporate Philanthropy," *Wall Street Journal,* 21 March 1977.

[16] Baumol, "Enlightened Self-Interest," p. 6.

[17] Neil Jacoby, *Corporate Power and Social Responsibility* (New York: MacMillan, 1973),
p. 199.

[18] Keith Davis and Robert L. Blomstrom, *Business, Society, and Environment,* 2nd ed.
(New York: McGraw-Hill, 1971), p. 277.

[19] Quoted in Gideon Chagy, *The New Patrons of the Arts* (New York: Harry N. Abrams,
N.D.), p. 87.

[20] Ibid., pp. 82–83.

PRACTICING
PUBLIC
RELATIONS

# TEN COMMANDMENTS FOR COMMUNITY RELATIONS

1. Review your organization's policies, practices, and procedures. Are they consistent with sound community relations?

2. Consider especially the following areas: waste disposal; employee recruitment; employment policies (lay-offs, compensation, overtime); noise or traffic problems; maintenance of organizational facilities and grounds; advertising, signs, and marketing; energy sources and energy waste.

3. Develop an organizational community relations policy. Spell out specific community relations objectives. Base the policy on assessment of organizational needs, resources, and expertise, and on community needs and expectations. Some sample objectives are: Attract more employment applications from women and minorities; improve community awareness of the organization's contributions; improve relations with local government; improve the local school system to make the community more attractive to potential executives and professional employees; improve the quality of local colleges for more effective recruitment; etc.

4. Know your community.

5. Utilize all means to communicate with the community. These may include: employees, local media, open houses, local clubs and organizations, local advertising, direct mail, newsletters, brochures, annual reports, movies, exhibits, etc.

6. Involve your organization in local organizations. This may be done by: sponsoring employees who wish to join civic and professional groups; providing speakers for meeting; lending facilities for meeting or activities; sponsoring contests and programs for youth; supporting fund raising activities; etc.

7. Offer aid to local governments. Make organizational resources available to governments by loans of employees and materials.

8. Use local merchants, banks, insurance agencies, lawyers, and other professionals for goods and services.

9. Distribute corporate donations according to community relations policies and objectives. Philanthropy is an important aspect of community relations.

10. Evaluate the community relations effort. Measure to determine the extent to which objectives have been achieved. Be prepared to developed new strategies if current programs fail to meet expectations.

**PREVIEW**    The media are businesses that gather, package, and sell information.

Journalists have mixed feelings toward public relations practitioners—suspecting them of manipulation while depending on them for information about their institutions.

Public relations practitioners view journalists as an audience, a medium through which to reach the broader public, and as gatekeepers representing and responding to the public's need to know.

Media relations can be particularly difficult for business organizations, despite the mutual dependency of business and media organizations.

The press will go after anything, and that is the way it
should be.

—Ben Wattenberg, Coeditor, *Public Opinion*

When some people consider the function of public relations their first
thought is: "Those are the folks who deal with the media." While public
relations does far more than deal with the media, that certainly is an important
aspect of the job. Media coverage of an organization can have significant
positive or negative impacts on every aspect of its operations. Public confidence in an organization and public support of its programs is often determined by the treatment it receives in the press and on radio and television.

If a public relations practitioner is to work effectively with the media, he
or she must understand how the media function and how reporters work.
Insights into journalists' views of public relations and into the working relationship of journalists and public relations practitioners are also essential,
particularly in relation to business organizations. Finally, public relations
practitioners must be prepared (and they must be prepared to prepare others)
to deal with the media face-to-face.

**UNDERSTANDING
THE MEDIA**

Most newspapers, magazines, and broadcasting stations are businesses. They
sell information. They gather and package information in such ways that
audiences will be sufficiently interested to spend money or time to read,
listen or watch. Journalists also tend to take their responsibilities to society
very seriously. They conceive of themselves as having a sacred public mission:
to serve as the public's eyes and ears; to be watchdogs on public institutions
doing the public's business; and to seek the truth, put it in perspective, and
publish it so that people can conduct their affairs knowledgeably.

That the media's goals of providing truth and making a profit are sometimes
in conflict is an issue that will not be pursued here. But anyone who deals
with the media must recognize that both these goals are constantly sought.

Journalists' devotion to these goals cause their view of "facts" to be quite
different from that of their sources of information. To the journalist, news
is a highly perishable commodity. The source is likely to be concerned about
the lasting impressions a news story makes. To the journalist, a story is a
transient element in the ongoing flow of information. The source is more
likely to consider a story about his or her organization as a discrete event,
and wants the story to cast his or her organization in a favorable light. The
journalist is uninterested in the positive or negative flavor of the story—just
as long as it fairly presents the facts.

Yet for all the concerns organizations manifest about how their stories are
covered, the power the media hold does not lie in their ability to slant material
one way or another. Rather it lies in whether they choose to define particular

words, deeds, events or issues as news. Douglas Cater, special assistant to President Lyndon Johnson and author of *The Fourth Branch of Government* put it this way:

**The essential power of the press is its capacity to choose what is news. Each day in Washington tens of thousands of words are uttered which are considered important by those who utter them. Tens of dozens of events occur which are considered newsworthy by those who have staged them. The press has the power to select—to decide which events go on page one or hit the prime time TV news and which events get ignored.**[1]

**The Reporter's Job**     The journalist's job has been greatly glamorized since reporters Bob Woodward and Carl Bernstein unraveled the political scandals of Watergate. On a day-to-day basis, however, the job can be highly demanding, stressful, and quite unglamorous. Working in a bullpen atmosphere without so much as a secretary or offices of their own, reporters need all the help they can get. Journalists have a tough job. Highly placed news sources, reporters maintain, are generally overly insulated, overly secretive, overly sensitive individuals who recognize neither the public's right to know nor the value of the media's role in exposing questionable organizational practices. They feel that those who complain about media coverage often engage in the ancient practice of seeking to slay the bearers of bad tidings. Besides, say journalists, we don't do much criticizing—we just report what others say.

Journalists maintain that they not only have the responsibility to provide information to the public, but also to provide feedback from society at large to the administrators of public institutions. As society has become more complex and as institutions have come to have greater impact on private lives, journalists have held that more reporting and investigating are necessary to determine the extent to which these institutions measure up to their social and moral obligations. This process, they argue, ultimately will have a positive effect on society as a whole.

Still, working journalists echo some of the complaints registered by the institutions they cover against their own employers. They recognize that they frequently have insufficient education and experience to adequately cover complex issues and institutions. They are frustrated by the lack of time, space, and staff needed to do their job thoroughly.

Reporters, in general, have an overwhelming desire to get "facts." Joseph Poindexter points out "to a reporter, a fact has an inherent worth, in and of itself. To a businessman, a fact is an asset to be invested."[2] Reporters hate anything and anyone who they perceive as standing between them and the facts. Anyone who seeks to keep a secret is regarded with deep suspicion. Organizations in business, government, and other fields which conduct themselves in ways considered less than open invite journalistic scrutiny.

In pursuit of "facts," etiquette, civility and even legality sometimes are foregone. It is important for public relations practitioners and others who deal with journalists to remember that when reporters ask nasty questions, it is not because they are antagonistic or ignorant; they are just being what are considered to be good reporters.

**Reporters' Views of Public Relations Practitioners**

A flack is a person who makes all or part of his income by obtaining space in newspapers without cost to himself or his clients. Usually a professional . . . they are known formally as public relations men. The flack is the modern equivalent of the cavalier highwayman of old. . . . His job is to say kind things about his client. He will not lie very often, but much of the time he tells less than the whole story. . . . Your job is to serve the readers, not the man who would raid your columns.[3]

In the common wisdom of the city room, public relations is a debased, manipulative art. Practitioners are referred to as "flacks" or worse.

A recent investigation of journalists' attitudes toward public relations practitioners revealed generally negative attitudes.[4] Closer examination of the data suggested, however, that in certain cases journalists' responses appeared to be contradictory. For instance, while a majority of journalists (fifty-nine percent) agreed that "public relations and the press are partners in the dissemination of information," they strongly disagreed (seventy-two percent) with the statement "public relations is a profession equal in status to journalism."

On the positive side, a sizable plurality of journalists (forty-six percent) agreed "the public relations practitioner does work for the newspaper that would otherwise go undone." A substantial minority (forty percent) felt that "public relations practitioners are necessary to the production of the daily newspaper as we know it." Nearly half (forty-eight percent) found that "public relations practitioners help reporters obtain accurate, complete and timely news."

At the same time, however, massive majorities of the journalists (eighty-four percent) believed "public relations practitioners often act as obstructionists, keeping reporters from the people they really should be seeing," and "public relations material is usually publicity disguised as news." Eighty-seven percent felt "public relations practitioners too often try to deceive the press by attaching too much importance to a trivial uneventful happening." Journalists sampled in this research seemingly recognized the dependency of the modern newspaper on the public relations profession, but at the same time they condemned what they seem to consider standard public relations procedures.

The same research indicated that journalists perceive public relations practitioners to be very different, even opposite to themselves in terms of their value orientation toward news. Moreover, while ranking themselves first in status among sixteen professional categories, they ranked public relations last.

These findings suggest that public relations practitioners are perceived as manipulators of the press and have low credibility. Such findings, in and of themselves, do not augur well for success in public relations practitioners' relationships with journalists. Before leaping to that conclusion, however, we had better take a closer look at the relationship between journalists and public relations practitioners.

**Relations Between Journalists and Practitioners**

Although journalists like to picture themselves as reticent to utilize public relations information, economic considerations make the use of such information essential. A news staff capable of ferreting information from every significant organization in a city without the assistance of representatives of these organizations would be prohibitively expensive. More specifically, the public relations practitioner makes the journalists' jobs much easier by saving them time and effort and by providing information that might otherwise be unavailable. Thus, the relationship between the public relations practitioners and journalists is one of mutual dependency.

Communication between certain public relations practitioners and journalists is massive. Some public relations offices send out news releases daily. Additionally, there may be personal contact and communication initiated by either party. The amount of communication between journalists and public relations practitioners is a measure of their dependency on one another. In some instances, public relations practitioners provide more useful information to specific media than do the journalists they employ.

Through the efforts of public relations practitioners, the media receive a constant flow of information free of cost. Information that journalists might not have acquired otherwise becomes available in packaged form. The journalist, as we noted above, can then decide what is newsworthy. As the editor of an Ohio daily newspaper remarked with relish, "I'm the guy who says 'yes' or 'no,' the public relations man has to say please."

His assessment of journalists' power is strictly accurate only when public relations practitioners and journalists share no dependency. When interdependency exists, journalists retain nominal veto power over incoming information, but they abdicate much of their decision-making responsibility to public relations practitioners, who select and control material given out. While journalists may reject one or another news release, they depend upon the constant flow of information from representatives of important institutions. To a large extent, journalists are processors of information—not gatherers of it.

Under these circumstances, journalists' primary means of control becomes their ability to refuse to deal with public relations practitioners who fail to meet subjective standards. But even such rejection is impossible when the public relations practitioner is firmly institutionally entrenched. As much as Washington journalists would have liked to avoid using material from Ron Ziegler, President Nixon's press secretary, they did not have that option.

From the public relations practitioner's perspective, the journalist is at once an audience, a medium through which to reach the larger public, and a gatekeeper representing and responding to the public's need to know. Some go so far as to say that the practitioner's livelihood depends on reporters' or editors' decisions to use his material.

Because of this dependency, practitioners' selection and presentation of information often conforms more to journalistic standards than to the desires of their superiors in their own organizations. In a sense, both the journalist and the practitioner, in dealing with each other, are caught between the demands of the organizations they represent and the demands of the opposite party. Public relations practitioners, as boundary spanners, are often caught in the middle between journalistic and other institutions, trying to explain each to the other.

To a considerable extent, the purposes of the news outlet and the public relations practitioner overlap. Both wish to inform the public of things which affect them. This provides the basis of a cooperative system for the dissemination of information. It is in this sense public relations practitioners function as extension of the news staff. They play a specific, functional, cooperative role in society's information-gathering network, even though they owe no loyalty to specific news outlets, are not paid by them, and may never set foot in the building in which the news is produced.

## The Impact of Public Relations on the Media

The total impact of public relations on the media is unmeasureable, but unquestionably massive. Several public relations scholars have attempted to measure or estimate specific aspects of public relations' contribution. Schabacker found almost half of the local news items in Milwaukee's daily newspapers to be of public relations origin.[5] Steinberg similarly suggested a figure of fifty percent but he found it also applied to all news carried in newspapers and wire services.[6] Other estimates (for instance those of Cutlip,[7] Chase,[8] and Mullaney[9]) have ranged from 25 to 80 percent. Aronoff found that 48.7 percent of local news items were derived from news releases or other public relations sources.[10]

## Results of Organization/Public Relations/Media Relationships

All of these relationships between organizations, public relations and the media have a variety of effects upon the institutions involved and the public at large. Institutions have become more aware of public opinion as a significant factor in their conduct. "Not only communications specialists, but all managers realize that none of their operations can be wholly effective unless they consider the potential media impact when making major decisions," explains Muriel Fox.[11] David Finn points out the benefits of this realization:

**Business conducts itself today with the awareness that all of its activities may be subjected to public scrutiny at any time. This is a healthy and positive characteristic of our society. The fruitful results of this process are reflected in positive modifications of corporate behavior in almost every industry that has been subjected to criticism. Some companies have stepped up affirmative-action programs because of public criticism. Other corporations have developed extensive public-service programs to provide support for specific segments of the community because articles in the press have suggested a corporate bias. There are many examples of companies which have improved their management structure or established needed quality-control procedures or improved the design of their products because of critical articles in the media.[12]**

But when the relationship between public relations practitioners and journalists is taken into consideration, we see that the media do not have a monopoly on power or benefits. In examining this process we find substantial economic benefits to the media. They get free information and can hire far fewer journalists because of the work done by public relations people. Public relations people and their clients come out ahead by reaching the public through the media.

No one can tell who gets the best of this bargain. Weighing economics against information in this contest is like comparing apples and oranges. One can note, however, that as journalists lose control of the flow of information reaching the public, the public becomes more liable to manipulation by established institutional interests. As *New York Times* editor and columnist Tom Wicker points out: "The American press tends to be an institutionalized press. It covers institutions and processes—anything that has official spokesmen and official visible functions." [13]

To the extent that the needs and goals of journalists, public relations practitioners and the institutions they represent, and those of the public coincide, this system of information processing can operate efficiently. When these goals do not coincide, however, the public is liable to manipulation by self-interested institutions.

**BUSINESS/MEDIA RELATIONS**

The American republic has prospered because of two interdependent marketplaces which, to an extent greater than in any other nation, have been maintained as free in their operation. These are, of course, the marketplace of ideas and the marketplace of goods and services. The relatively unrestricted operation of the marketplace of ideas is maintained through freedoms of press and speech guaranteed by the First Amendment to the Constitution. The marketplace of goods and services, more regulated than in the past but still characterized by broad individual discretion, is a system of free or private enterprise not guaranteed in law but deeply ingrained in the American ethos and American institutions.

In the course of two centuries the meaning of terms like "free enterprise" and "the free press" have changed with social, cultural, economic, and (particularly) technological changes. The technology and economics of "mass," as in "mass production" and "mass media," have restricted access to both the marketplace of ideas and the marketplace of goods and services. Where any printer could become the publisher of a substantial newspaper by the standards of the early 1800s, it now takes an investment of tens of millions of dollars to compete in a major media market. As access has become restricted, freedom of the press and freedom of enterprise, once provinces of the many, have become privileges of the few. Competition, which once supposedly assured that from the babble of many voices truth would emerge and that resources would be optimally allocated in relation to societal needs and values, has become less effective as a source of regulation as fewer entities have had the ability to compete.

The fundamental processes of press freedom and private enterprise have been concentrated and centralized. Today we see these processes not as characteristic of all participants of our socioeconomic system, but as the venue of institutionalized segments of society called "the media" on one hand and "business" on the other. This is not to say that either business or the media is a monolithic entity, but simply to suggest that this is the context in which the relationship between these institutions must be considered.

In many ways business and the media are kindred spirits. At the most obvious level, as we have already noted, the mass media in the United States with very few exceptions are profit-seeking organizations offering information as a commodity. The mass media are part of the corporate world, replete with accounting, marketing, and labor problems. Editors and publishers of newspapers and magazines, owners and managers of television and radio stations are prominent members of the Chambers of Commerce, the Rotary Clubs, and the United Appeals—in short, the business establishment—in virtually every city and town in America. These groups have been called "conservative," and rightly so, for they have a vested interest in the status quo.

Another area in which business and the media share common experience is that each has been the object of devil theories—both have been easy targets to blame for various evils and ills experienced by individuals or society. Where once people held the devil responsible for adversity, we have now seen them blame successively and cumulatively robber barons, Wall Street, Madison Avenue, and the mass media.

A third, more subtle, commonality is found in business and the media response to reduced competition in their respective marketplaces. As the marketplace of ideas has become less self-regulating, other forms of regulation have emerged. Protected from governmental regulation by the First Amendment, the media in general and print media in particular have increasingly accepted the idea of social responsibility, a form of individual self-regulation based not on the marketplace, but on some editorial conception to the common good. The idea that journalism should be objective, a relatively recent development in the history of journalism, is an example of this trend. Social responsibility has also become a key concept of the business world, where it also has a self-regulatory function based on managerial conceptions of the public good, and is often used to prevent or forestall governmental regulation.

Finally, business and media consistently play in each other's ballparks. Just as the media compete in the marketplace of goods and services, so business competes in the marketplace of ideas. On one level the competition is strictly commercial—the ideas are about what to buy. Primarily the venue of advertising, this level is by no means a trivial one. Information is the stuff of free economic decision making. Moreover, when the allocation of societal resources is made through numerous private economic decisions, the effectiveness of the marketplace depends on those decisions being well informed. Thus, as individuals and as a society our economic well-being depends upon a free flow of information.

On another level, however, the role business plays in the marketplace of ideas is more profound and, in the long run, more significant in the maintenance of a predominantly private-enterprise economy. Because private enterprise is not established by the Constitution, its ultimate support is public opinion. In effect, private enterprise is an idea that competes with other ideas about the manner in which society should allocate its resources.

As business once learned to deal with labor, politicians, and regulators, it now seeks to learn to deal with the media in their adversarial role. Businesspeople are irked by the public exposure of what was once private information. They are angered by the seeming inability of reporters to understand and accurately report on business and economic issues. They are frustrated by the inadequacy of their own efforts to influence public opinion.

**Journalism Spotlights Business**    In years past, the media devoted their resources to reporting on the courts, city hall, politics, legislatures, disasters, and wars. In newspapers, for instance, if business and economics were covered at all, such news was confined to a business page, which usually served as a boundary between sports and the classified ads.

But the 1970s saw business and economics raised from the occasional and arcane to what NBC anchorman John Chancellor called the decade's most important running story. Inflation, unemployment, taxes, energy shortages, international trade imbalances, farm production, and business behavior jumped from the back page to the headlines. In the process, the media have been subjected to blistering criticism from business, which in turn is writhing under the unfamiliar glare of spotlights.

Recognizing the paramount importance of business and economic news in the 1970s, journalists were forced to report on an area in which they sometimes had little experience or expertise. In many cases journalists claim that their job has been made more difficult by those who demand better coverage; business executives are often described by journalists as arrogant, inaccessible, unresponsive, manipulative, and insensitive to the requirements of the media.

The mass media make up the nation's public information system. The fact that business values the media as conduits through which the public can be informed is amply substantiated by the billions of dollars spent annually on advertising in print and broadcast media. The vast potentials of the media have motivated business institutions to begin to develop new strategies for using the media to reach the public, while countering what many business people consider an attack by the media themselves. As public opinion toward business deteriorated in the 1970s, business tended to blame the media, and went as far as to claim that the media—intentionally or unintentionally— were undermining the private enterprise system.

Various advocates of business allege that the media are guilty of excesses in the reportage of business failures, errors, and improprieties, and that they ignore the role of business in building a society unparalleled in both freedom and material wealth. Sensationalism, failure to provide background information, oversimplification, taking events out of context, and even alleged anti-business bias are supposed to contribute to the unbalanced reporting which results in a lack of public confidence in business. Boiled down, the accusations fall into five major areas:

Anti-business bias
Definition of news/overemphasis on bad news
Insufficient coverage of business/oversimplification
Distortion and inaccuracy
Susceptibility to manipulation by those opposed to
    business

**Anti-business Bias**   Some advocates of business have felt systematically attacked and have publicly concluded that the media have an anti-business bias. Some have gone so far as to accuse the media of engagement in a leftist conspiracy. Media critic Edith Efron, discounting the conspiracy theory, maintains that the media reflect certain cultural values. "No one living in the United States," she says, "need be told that for about ten years there has been a steady drumbeat of media reports informing us that American industry and modern technology are inducing disease and death . . ."[14]

Others dismiss such accusations. According to Curtis MacDougall, one of the nation's most honored journalism educators:

the journalistic media are a bulwark of the establishment, the status quo, the capitalistic system, because they are part of it . . . To charge that . . . high-powered financiers who happen to own journalistic enterprises . . . are interested in undermining or seriously changing the political and economic system of this country is palpably absurd.[15]

Likewise, broadcasting executive Elmo Ellis maintains:

there is no justifiable reason to conclude—as some business leaders have been inclined to do—that the media represent one of free enterprise's biggest enemies and greatest threats . . . To indict the media for bearing bad news is rather like condemning a doctor for advising a patient that he is ill.[16]

It is highly unlikely that a conscious, systematic anti-business bias exists among the media. Rather, as Ellis suggests, the media are simply playing out their role as bearers of bad news. Other critics, however, grant that the media are not meanly motivated. They focus instead on the means by which the media do their jobs and the quality of their work.

**Definition of News and Overemphasis on Bad News**   According to a recent Louis Harris poll, nine out of ten businesspeople feel that the media are basically out to report bad news and wrongdoing when dealing with business subjects. To some, the media are out to get business. Others say that the media accentuates the negative. Scott Cutlip suggests that "the media's definition of 'news' is at the heart of the problem."[17] At times the journalistic media seem to reverse the old dictum "no news is good news." To them, good news is no news. A plant opening is a local story at best; a plant closing can be national headlines and network news.

Cutlip explains:

**The struggle between the media's definition of "news" and an institution's definition of "truth" creates tension between news gatherer and news source . . . The basic conflict lies in the media's never-ending quest for exciting news, in their efforts to keep the news stream uncontaminated, and the need to deliver advertisers. On the other side are individuals, institutions and industries that find it imperative to have their stories told to the public with accuracy and fairness.**[18]

There is little question that the sensational stories of business wrongdoing get better play than routine good news of business. Moreover, it is media's job to play a watchdog role in American society. As Ellis points out: "If the media did not investigate questionable business dealings and share their suspicions and their findings with the public, they would be derelict in their duty and open to attacks on their own credibility."[19]

John Lawrence, former chief of business and economic coverage for the *Los Angeles Times,* suggests, "The problem often is vantage point, with the businessman suffering from being too close almost as much as the media from being too far away."[20] In fact, the problem is at least in part one of business perception. A high percentage of daily business news is favorable. And indeed, polls indicate that the public believes the media biased in favor of rather than against business. Lawrence maintains: "I believe that the media are far more guilty of being too soft on business rather than being too hard."[21]

Ellis questions the motivation of businesspeople who attack the media on the grounds of "bad news." "In principle, the business community wants the truth told about how it conducts its business but . . . no commercial enterprise relishes having its mistakes widely publicized."[22] He poses this question:

**Is the business community seriously worried about the quality of news coverage it is getting, or is it mainly indulging in the all-American habit of griping because it doesn't always receive the kind of treatment it wants?**[23]

Cutlip agrees with Ellis:

**It's high time that business leaders quit whining about the media and face up to the realities of why business gets so much unfavorable coverage . . . The fault . . . is not in media reporting, but in corporate performance.**[24]

It has long been established that media gatekeepers are highly subjective in their definition of news. Moreover, bad news has more journalistic appeal than good news does. But business is not the only interest group to claim to suffer as a result. Perhaps, in fact, what negative coverage there is reflects better on business than we realize at first. The media serve to point out deviance from societal norms. They point to the bad because good is assumed to be normal. If they ever begin systematically to point out the good, it will be because our society has become so bad that good is abnormal.

**Insufficient Coverage and Oversimplification**

Another accusation leveled at the media is that of insufficient and oversimplified coverage. On this score, Cutlip sides with the business community. "Businessmen can justly quarrel with the superficiality of much of today's news coverage of the corporate and economic life of the nation,"[25] he says. "The news media cover business and economics in the same manner they cover all other public matters—in an episodic and often superficial fashion."[26] Both oversimplification and insufficient coverage stem from two sources: the fact that reporters present information in packages to be sold, and inadequacy of journalistic resources.

"The press and television communicate information that can be selected, packaged, and sold as marketable commodities," explains communications economist William H. Melody.[27] That information that cannot be "sold" (which fails to hold audience interest) or that information which does not "fit" into the package (which exceeds the space or time available) goes unreported.

In the broadest sense, however, oversimplification and insufficient coverage occur because of the inadequacy of journalistic resources. Other than a few of the biggest and most financially secure newspapers, the business staff usually consists of one or two people. They can do little more than keep up with the incoming press releases. Moreover, those people often have inadequate training, have too little time or space in which to report their stories, and must deal simultaneously with an apathetic audience and defensive or even evasive businesses.

**Distortion and Inaccuracy**

The media are also accused of distortion and inaccuracy, a charge more serious than that of oversimplification. Such accusations are particularly troubling to journalists who think of themselves as objective and accurate above all else.

W. Lee Burge, chairman of Equifax, Inc., a company raked over the coals by CBS's "60 Minutes," feels that distortions and inaccuracies in the media's coverage of business have been directly harmful:

> Public ideas about corporate profit margins are incorrect, largely because businessmen have been characterized by the media as profitmongers . . . (but) perhaps the greatest area in which the media have failed to accurately picture business to the public is their portrayal of business as a defendant on trial.[28]

The reasons suggested for distortion and inaccuracy vary. Some attribute the problem to reporters' lack of business knowledge. Ellis maintains that the blame should be shared by "incompetent reporters and uncooperative business representatives."[29] David J. Mahoney, chief executive officer of Norton Simon, Inc., points to the attitudes of reporters:

> The too-promotional reporting of business a generation ago has been replaced by a too-suspicious attitude today. The wave of distrust in political life has spilled over into the world of business, and the result distorts what is happening in our economy.[30]

There is certainly truth in each of these explanations and certainly a degree of distortion and inaccuracy exists in business reportage. Again, however, what one sees as distortion depends on one's vantage point. And again, these complaints about the media are far from unique to business.

**Manipulation of the Media**

Even if the media are not harmful to business in and of themselves, say certain accusers, they allow themselves to be manipulated by its opponents. "The media have been consistently and effectively utilized by outside observers, investigators and critics of the American business community," Ellis observes.[31] The media are subject to such manipulation for two reasons. First, they are reflective. Much of the time they pass on to the public what others are saying. Deeper social changes are invisible to the media until someone brings them to the media's attention.

Second, reporters ascribe greater credibility to those who do not materially gain from communicating information and, like most other Americans, they tend to pull for the underdog. In this case, the underdog is almost anyone arrayed against "big business." Burge comments on this issue:

I am . . . somewhat baffled by what appears to be an inordinate acceptance of information handed to the media by government agencies. . . . Journalists should be as skeptical as they feel they need to be with businessmen. But they should be equally skeptical of governmental and "advocacy" groups.[32]

Muriel Fox, executive vice president of Carl Byoir & Associates, makes a similar point.

Business news must be more fascinating and its spokespeople more charismatic to receive the same hearing as a noncommercial organization might expect . . . because business messages reflect the profit motive, in contrast to the various motives of other interest groups, the press responds more cautiously.[33]

Harold Davis, a journalist, educator, and historian, maintains that "manipulation of the media in America commonly occurs as a result of a process that is almost mechanical."[34] Davis explains that the media's orientation toward conflict leads individuals or groups to stage provocative acts in order to draw attention to an idea or grievance. The media are thus at the mercy of the provacateurs. The Ayatollah Khomeini and his relations with American media in late 1979 exemplify Davis's point. Until recently, those who have taken advantage of process described by Davis have not been businesspeople. "They have been consumer groups, environmental groups, labor unions, and civil rights groups, to name a few," he says.[35]

But Davis does not hold that the media's susceptibility to manipulation must always work against business. "It would be an inept public relations person who could not suggest interesting ways by which corporations and institutions could play this rather cynical game to their own advantage."[36]

When the needs of the mass media and of journalists are understood, and when organizations prepare themselves to deal with those needs, print and broadcast media can be great resources to organizations. If the media are not understood and if organizations are not prepared to deal with the media, they can be extremely dangerous. Good media relations are the result of good organizational operations and management. The well-run organization, fulfilling its appropriate goals in appropriate ways, can only be aided by attention given it by the media.

These lessons are particularly valuable to business organizations. There is a tendency on the part of the media toward insufficient coverage, oversimplification, and a degree of distortion and inaccuracy in relation to business coverage. Moreover, the media's definition of news predisposes negative coverage of business and makes the media subject to manipulation by those who oppose business activities and practices.

| CASE STUDY: INSURANCE FOR WHAT? | By R. Ferrell Ervin Norfolk State University, Norfolk, Virginia |
|---|---|

In the early fall of 1977, heavy rainfall hit the Kansas City, Missouri area. Extensive flooding occurred. Nineteen people were killed. Property and businesses were severely damaged. The governor requested federal disaster aid.

As people assessed the losses suffered, they naturally turned to their insurance agents for financial settlements of their personal or property losses. One of those agencies responded to the claims with speed that matched their advertised message which guarantees that you are insured by "the good hands people."

Several months later, however, an investigative report by a local television station showed that the company paid for the damages to autos, asked people to sign over their car titles, and then sold the cars to local dealers. The action, in and of itself, was not unusual, but the cars were not identified as flood damaged. Car firms were selling flood damaged cars as used cars at near book value.

It appeared that the insurance company knew this might occur but did nothing to prevent it. The reporter from the television channel asked a company representative about the issue but was told "no comment." When the footage appeared on the news it gave the impression that the insurance firm had something to hide.

As a regional public relations director of the insurance company, you almost fall out of your chair while watching the news; the television report takes you unawares. You know that this incident might turn people away from your firm. What do you do now?

**Questions**  1. How might a previous doubt about the ethics of insurance companies be seen as confirmed by this flood situation?

2. Even if the insurance company were to be found innocent of any wrong-doing by the general public, how might the company still be in serious trouble with state authorities and still suffer long range consequences?

3. After a representative or spokesman has seemed to be evasive, how can a company overcome that problem by "straight talking" at a later time?

4. Is the flood situation made more serious by the deaths that were caused even though the issue under discussion concerns only the insurance coverage of cars?

---

**NOTES**   [1] Douglas Cater, *Press, Politics and Popular Government* (Washington, D.C.: American Enterprise Institute, 1972), pp. 83–84.

[2] Joseph Poindexter, "The Great Industry-Media Debate," *Saturday Review,* July 10, 1976, p. 22.

[3] *Associated Press Managing Editors Guidelines,* p. 44.

[4] Craig E. Aronoff, "Credibility of Public Relations for Journalists," *Public Relations Review* (Fall 1975); 45–56.

[5] W. Schabacker, "Public Relations and the News Media: A Study of the Selection and Utilization by Representative Sources" (M.A. thesis, University of Wisconsin, Madison, 1963).

[6] C. S. Steinberg, "Public Relations as Mass Communication," *Public Relations Journal* (June 1971); 13–14.

[7] Scott M. Cutlip, "The Press vs. The Publicist," *Nieman Reports* (April 1951); 20–22.

[8] W. H. Chase, "Public Relations in Modern Society," *Public Relations Quarterly,* 1962, pp. 12–20.

[9] T. E. Mullaney, "The Basic Change in Press Relations," *Public Relations Journal,* pp. 6–8.

[10] Craig E. Aronoff, "Predictors of Success in Placing Releases in Newspapers," *Public Relations Review* (Winter 1976); 45.

[11] Muriel Fox, "Business/Media Influence: Who Does What to Whom?" in *Business and the Media,* ed. Craig E. Aronoff, (Santa Monica: Goodyear Publishing Co., 1979), p. 152.

[12] David Finn, "The Media as Monitor of Corporate Behavior" in Aronoff, *Business and the Media,* pp. 128–129.

[13] Tom Wicker in *The Press and Public Policy* (Washington, D.C.: American Enterprise Institute, 1975), pp. 10–11.

[14] Edith Efron, "The Media and the Omniscient Class," in Aronoff, *Business and the Media,* p. 15.

[15] Curtis D. MacDougall, "Business's Friend, The Media," in Aronoff, *Business and the Media,* p. 46–47.

[16] Elmo Ellis, "The Media: Business Friend or Foe?" in Aronoff, *Business and the Media,* p. 87.

[17] Scott Cutlip, "The Media and the Corporation: A Matter of Perception and Performance," in Aronoff, *Business and the Media,* p. 135.

[18] Ibid., pp. 133-134.

[19] Ellis, "Media: Friend or Foe?" p. 91.

[20] John E. Lawrence, "The Press: Too Soft on Business?" in Aronoff, *Business and the Media,* p. 77.

[21] Ibid., p. 77.

[22] Ellis, "Media: Friend or Foe?" p. 98.

[23] Ibid., p. 96.

[24] Cutlip, "Media and Corporation," pp. 140–142.

[25] Ibid., p. 138.

[26] Ibid., p. 136.

[27] William H. Melody, "Mass Media: The Economics of Access to the Marketplace of Ideas," in Aronoff, *Business and the Media,* p. 217.

[28] W. Lee Burge, "Fair Information Practices: Some Imperatives for the Media and Business," in Aronoff, *Business and the Media,* pp. 175–176.

[29] Ellis, "Media: Friend or Foe?" p. 89.

[30] David J. Mahoney, "On Ending an Adversarial Relationship," *New York Times,* July 7, 1977.

[31] Ellis, "Media: Friend or Foe?" p. 93.

[32] Burge, "Fair Information Practices," pp. 177–180.

[33] Muriel Fox, "Business/Media Influence: Who Does What to Whom?" in Aronoff, *Business and the Media,* p. 153.

[34] Harold Davis "Conflict, Consensus, and the Propaganda of the Deed; or One Sure Way to Manipulate the Media," Aronoff, *Business and the Media,* p. 34.

[35] Ibid., p. 41.

[36] Ibid., p. 41.

PRACTICING
PUBLIC
RELATIONS

# WORKING WITH THE MEDIA

With a basic understanding of the complex relationships between public relations practitioners and journalists, we can outline a few general principles to use in working with the media. In the first place, organizational managers must reconcile themselves to the legitimacy of the media's role in monitoring the performance of all public institutions and leaders. Managers and institutions must understand and accommodate the unique position of the media, realizing that, on one level, adversary relationships with the media are normal.

The best advice in dealing with the media is to give journalists what they want in the form and language that they want. Respond quickly and honestly to media requests for information. By working to establish a relationship of mutual trust with particular journalists, you can defuse many potentially antagonistic encounters.

**PREPARING TO MEET THE MEDIA**

A reporter calls your office at 9 A.M. She wants to see you for an interview at 11 A.M. She wants your company to respond to allegations made by a source that she is not at liberty to disclose. She says that the charges deal with corporate finances and questionable conduct of certain corporate officials. That is all she will say.

As the public relations director of a major private university, you decide to hold a press conference to announce the initiation of a major fundraising effort. A prominent alumnus had donated $5 million to kick off the campaign. You know that there has been recent critical coverage of the university's budgetary problems, tuition hikes, and "incursions" into neighborhoods around the school which displaced poor people and eroded the community tax base.

You are the community relations director of the local police force. A reporter calls to request a meeting with your chief about low police morale resulting from to the city's inability to meet rank-and-file demands for pay raises. When you attempt to arrange the interview for the following afternoon, the chief berates you, saying: "It's your job to keep the press off my back. Why can't you handle the guy's questions?" You convince the chief that the reporter would not talk to you because he said he was tired of the chief hiding behind his "flack." You tell him that departmental integrity and morale depends on his willingness to deal with the press. You tell the chief that you will help him prepare. He reluctantly agrees to the interview.

In each of these cases, a meeting with the media represents a critical challenge to the organization. Some organizations see such challenges as problems to be overcome. It is more constructive, however, to view them as opportunities. Every media contact is an opportunity to get feedback, to tell your story, to create a positive response to your organization. Of course there are dangers—but what opportunity presents itself without risk? And what opportunity can be taken without preparation?

Preparation to meet the media is essential for both individuals and organizations. Preparation means more than getting psyched up about a particular interview, because when the opportunity comes, there may be little time for specific preparation, as the cases above suggest. In the first example, a company official had only two hours to gather information and prepare strategy to deal effectively with some very sensitive issues.

Before anyone in the organization meets with the media, the first step is to develop the proper set of attitudes. Meeting the media *is* an opportunity, not a problem; therefore, defensiveness is not appropriate. There is no need to feel intimidated—particularly if your objective is worthy. In the case of the university's fundraising campaign the purpose of the press conference was kept firmly in mind. The public relations director refused, in a friendly way, to be dragged by reporters' questions into subjects other than the donation and campaign.

The attitude of the interviewee should be one of hospitality, cooperation, and openness. However the interviewee should realize that the reporter need not be the person in control. A positive mental attitude is essential. Once this attitude is established among everyone in an organization who may be called upon to be interviewed, it becomes much easier and less traumatic to perpare for specific interviews. Once the chief of police completes his interview successfully, the next occurrence will be more easily handled.

**PREPARING FOR SPECIFIC INTERVIEWS**

The first step in preparing for a specific interview is to determine exactly what message you want to get across to the ultimate audience—those who will read the article or listen to the news on radio or television. You want to establish in your own mind the major point of the interview, *the bottom line*. In the examples presented earlier in this section the bottom line in the first case might be that the company takes great pride in its honesty and integrity and will take every step to maintain its good name. In the second case, the bottom line might be that the university is a great institution that makes significant contributions to its community and is deserving of the support of all its publics. In the third case, the bottom line might be that there may well be a morale problem but that the city's police consider themselves to be professionals devoted to safety and service.

Once the bottom line for the interview is established, gather information to support the position. Plan to relate all items of information to the basic message. Organize your material for the interview around your major point. Be prepared to return to it consistently. In this way you have the opportunity to control the interview rather than allowing it to control you.

# PRACTICING PUBLIC RELATIONS

Second, consider your audience—both the particular journalist who may be conducting the interview and the ultimate audience who will read or listen to what the journalist writes. Does the reporter have a particular approach, hypothesis, or philosophy? How can you phrase your messages to appeal to the interests and needs of the reporter and the ultimate audience?

Third, anticipate the interview. Many organizations even rehearse interviews—with the public relations practitioner playing the reporter while the executive who is to be interviewed plays herself or himself. Remember the reporter's basic questions: who-what-when-where-why-how. Try to organize your material like a journalist would. Do not consider a chronologically ordered presentation. Rather, try to think in the reporter's inverted pyramid style with the broadest, most important points first followed by the details. Try to visualize the first paragraph of an article developed from your interview as it would appear in print.

Fourth, have as much information as you can accumulate at your fingertips. It is almost impossible to overprepare. Develop alternative angles and back-up facts. Also be prepared to suggest the names of other people to whom the reporter might talk and tell those people that you will be using their names so that they can prepare.

Finally, develop your interview strategy. This will depend on the nature of your material and the interview situation. Do you want to take a balanced approach? How will you deal with the negatives? How explicit and specific do you want to be? How can you demonstrate the practical consequences of the issues being discussed?

In summary, keep these guidelines in mind:

1. Start with the news, then provide the details.
2. Answer direct questions directly—do not hedge or be evasive. But if you feel a question is unfair, you may say so. If you do not know an answer, say so—but promise to get the answer and follow through on your promise. Remember, an interview is a goal-oriented conversation, it is not a cross-examination. You are not on the witness stand.
3. Do not lie or exaggerate.
4. Do not argue with reporters—even if you win the argument, you will lose in the long run.
5. Do not let reporters put words in your mouth. Frequently reporters ask "Would you say . . .?" Either a "yes" or "no" leaves you open to an embarrassing quote. It is better to respond: "You said that, I didn't."
6. Do not talk off the record. Reporters use off-the-record information in a variety of potentially damaging ways beyond the control of the interviewee.
7. Approach the topic from the viewpoint of your public's interest, not from that of your organization. Do not talk about "capital formation," for instance; talk about jobs instead.

**8.** Follow up. Be sure to provide promptly any additional information you may have promised. Do not be pushy or meddlesome, but if you think a point needs clarification, do not hesitate to provide it.

You will never be satisfied with every interview as it is published or broadcast. But then, you cannot expect to hit a home run every time you go to the plate. Your ability to take charge of an interview and control it, however, depends on preparation of attitude and information. If you take the time and make the effort to prepare, your batting average will be significantly higher.

**HOW TO REACH THE MEDIA**

There are essentially three direct ways of intentionally reaching the media: a release, a discussion (conversation, phone call, meeting, or interview), and a media conference. Each has advantages and disadvantages, and these should be taken into account when the method is chosen.

The media release, as we discussed in Chapter 8, is the simplest and least expensive route. Releases can be duplicated and sent to dozens, even thousands, of news outlets. It should be used when the news is routine, to provide potential feature or background material, or to provide follow-up information.

Discussions should be used to establish contact with reporters, to deal with issues in greater depth, or to present complicated issues.

Media conferences should be used very rarely. They are appropriate for subjects or broad interest, when many journalists must be reached simultaneously, and when issues are controversial or complicated enough to need significant background material. When used, they should be carefully planned and prepared, and should provide all necessary support material in a well-organized and easily accessible format.

 LUTHERAN SOCIAL SERVICE
OF MINNESOTA

 American Public Radio Network

# SECTION IV  PUBLIC RELATIONS: NOT-FOR-PROFIT

The practice of public relations is not limited to private business. All organizations have constituent groups from which they must derive support. Although nonprofit organizations may not manufacture and sell a product, they do produce services that are consumed by their citizens, members, or clients. In addition, they are affected by the same social issues that corporations must deal with. Therefore, the principles of public relations are no different whether they are practiced in private enterprise, government, or nonprofit organizations. All the issues, skills, techniques, theories, and practices discussed elsewhere in this book also apply to government and nonprofit organizations.

We choose to discuss these two classes of organization separately in this section because they do present some different challenges to public relations practitioners. Certainly they are not all alike. There are at least as many different types of government bureaus, agencies, branches, and services as there are associations, societies, educational institutions, unions, hospitals, charities, and religious organizations. We shall attempt to point out both their general and individual characteristics as they relate to the practice of public relations today.

# CHAPTER 13  NONPROFIT ORGANIZATIONS

**PREVIEW**  Communication with members, government, and other publics is the bottom line for many nonprofit organizations.

Maintaining a positive public image, fund raising, and cost containment are crucial public relations issues facing nonprofit organizations in general.

Membership recruitment and retention is the chief public relations objective of many associations and religious organizations.

Labor unions, and trade and professional organizations sometimes prefer to work behind the scenes to influence government regulation rather than address issues in more public forums.

Health care organizations are peculiar in that physicians occupy the dual role of customer and manager.

Dealing with volunteers requires more attention to motivational factors than is required for typical employee groups.

In elementary and secondary schools, parents, alumni, and school board members represent both internal and external publics.

The value of higher education may be the single most important public relations issue facing colleges and universities in the 1980s.

Fund raising is a primary public relations function in most nonprofit organizations.

Nongovernmental organizations that do not seek to make a profit as the result of their activities are becoming more prevalent in our society. Numerous associations, societies, and labor unions promote the interests of their members and impose ethical, professional, or contractual obligations on those individuals or organizations they represent. Hospitals and religious and volunteer organizations serve various constituent groups in our society while relying on a broad range of support in order to survive. Educational institutions, both public and private, must maintain effective relationships with a variety of professional and nonprofessional publics while serving society as a whole. Successful performance of these missions depends to a great extent on the quality of the relationship a nonprofit organization is able to maintain with its publics. Fundraising is a common problem shared by all these organizations, and often becomes a priority of public relations practice.

## COMMUNICATION IN NONPROFIT ORGANIZATIONS

For many nonprofit organizations, communication is their primary mission. Most associations, societies, unions and religious organizations see communication as their reason for existence. Communication with members, government, and other groups becomes the basic product of many nonprofit organizations. Even those that have missions other than the dissemination of information find communication a necessary prerequisite to the accomplishment of their announced objectives. Hospitals, charities, and educational institutions also find themselves devoting a great amount of time and energy to communicating ideas and communicating the need for volunteers and funds. We discussed in Chapter 9 the need to relate public relations effectiveness to bottom line objectives of the organization. In nonprofit organizations, the bottom line is frequently measured in terms of new and retained members, dues collected, or funds raised. Effective communication programs are generally seen as the key to success in these basic areas.

In a recent survey of nonprofit organizations, the *Journal of Organizational Communication* reported that while a range of techniques are used to communicate with members, employees, volunteers, and special audiences, the most prominent were print media.[1] Publications were cited most frequently, and news releases and meetings were also mentioned. All three of these are traditional areas of expertise for public relations practitioners. When compared with corporate public relations activities, nonprofit organizations rely much more strongly on publications. The predicted trend is toward greater use of new communication technologies such as management information systems, word processors, and video telephones, nonprofit organizations have not branched into these areas as rapidly as their business counterparts have.

Formal communication programs with written goals and objectives are also less prevalent in nonprofit organizations than in corporations. In their survey, the *Journal of Organizational Communication* reported that sixty-six percent of the corporate chief executive officers (CEOs) responded affirmatively when asked if their organization had a formal communication plan. By comparison, only forty-one percent of the CEOs of nonprofit organizations could respond positively to that question.[2] There was also a distinct difference between for-profit and nonprofit organizations with regard to the issues they believed should be addressed through their communication program. High on the corporate list of key issues were inflation and compensation, government regulation, and equal opportunity. Nonprofit organizations pointed to maintaining a positive public image, fundraising, and cost containment. Table 13-1 lists the areas of concern to nonprofit organizations which they feel can be addressed through their communication efforts.

**Public Relations Jobs in Nonprofit Organizations**

In the same survey, nonprofit organizations indicated that their departments charged with public relations functions were called either public relations (twenty percent), communication (twenty-one percent), public information (sixteen percent), or public affairs (sixteen percent). In 46% of the 81 organizations included in the survey the public relations function reported directly to the CEO, nineteen percent reported to a vice president, and twenty percent to a director.[3] The size of the public relations staff varies as widely as the size of the nonprofit organizations themselves. It should be noted from Table 13-2, however, that thirty-five percent of the organizations surveyed reported a staff exceeding ten persons.

Although there are some differences in application, public relations is alive and well in nonprofit organizations. In fact, it could be argued that public relations is the business of many nonprofit organizations. While the salaries for practitioners in these organizations have traditionally been lower than those in corporations (*Table 5-3*), they represent excellent opportunities for many professionals. We will discuss some of the differences and opportunities specific to certain types of nonprofit organizations in the remainder of this chapter.

**ASSOCIATIONS AND UNIONS**

Both labor unions and the various trade or professional associations have one important factor in common: membership. Representing the interests of members to a number of different publics is the business of these nonprofit organizations. Recruitment and retention of members is also a major function. Therefore, publics for both unions and associations can be divided into essentially two groups: members and nonmembers. Member publics must be constantly kept informed about new developments in the field or area of interest they represent. Nonmember publics must be informed about the importance of the group to society and the beneficial effects of following their recommendations. Many associations and all labor unions mount strong efforts to influence local, state, and federal legislation. While membership

**Table 13-1**
Issues for Nonprofit
Organizations

**What are the areas of present concern facing your organization that you feel can be improved through your communication program (for your various publics)?**

| Areas of Concern | Times Mentioned |
|---|---|
| Organization's public image | 30 |
| Fund raising | 29 |
| Cost containment | 29 |
| Building and maintaining membership | 25 |
| Winning public support on issues | 24 |
| Influencing legislation action and lobbying | 20 |
| Keeping abreast of professional developments | 18 |
| Legal issues | 18 |
| Increasing public expectations | 17 |
| Labor relations | 13 |
| Reaching special audiences such as minorities, the handicapped, etc. | 11 |
| Training | 10 |
| Accountability/credibility | 7 |
| Government regulation | 7 |

*(All other items mentioned 5 times or less)*

Rae Leaper, "CEOs of Nonprofit Organizations Agree: Communicate or Perish," *Journal of Organizational Communication* 4 (1980): 17. Reprinted by permission.

may be the single most important factor all these organizations have in common, it also accounts for their diversity.

**Associations and Societies**

Associations can be divided into two categories: professional and trade. Professional associations such as the Public Relations Society of America and those listed in Table 13-3 work to enhance the public image of the profession and disseminate knowledge among the membership and to society at large. In addition, many professional associations establish legal and ethical requirements for practice and certify the proficiencies of practitioners. Therefore, the public relations function of an association can be complicated considerably when it plays the dual roles of advocate and regulator of a professional group. Besides professional associations there are many learned societies, such as the International Communication Association or the Academy of Management, which promote a field of knowledge without exercising any

**Table 13-2**
Size of Nonprofit Public
Relations Staffs

**What is the size of your communication staff?**

| Staff Size | Times Mentioned |
|---|---|
| One | 3 |
| Two | 3 |
| Three | 4 |
| Four | 13 |
| Five | 6 |
| Six | 2 |
| Seven | 2 |
| Eight | 3 |
| Nine | 4 |
| Ten | 3 |
| More than 10 | 29 |

*Note: the numbers indicate the actual number of times a particular response was mentioned in relation to the following audiences: members or volunteers, the public, employees, and other specific groups.*

Rae Leaper, "CEOs of Nonprofit Organizations Agree: Communicate or Perish," *Journal of Organizational Communication* 4 (1980): 16. Reprinted by permission.

regulatory powers. Members of these organizations are both individuals and organizations involved in research, practice, or teaching in the field. Learned societies for the most part do not employ public relations professionals.

Trade associations (*Exhibit 13-1*) primarily represent organizations engaged in producing a common product or service. Sometimes ethical and legal standards are enforced by a trade association such as the television and radio codes established by the National Association of Broadcasters. More frequently, trade associations promote the product or service of its member organizations and attempt to affect legislation and government regulations in ways that will benefit its members. Sometimes these efforts are perceived as working against the broader interests of society. For example, the American Dairy Association conducted a massive television, radio, and print media campaign advertising milk as "the perfect food." After this campaign was in full swing it was widely reported that drinking milk could in fact pose a threat to the health of some individuals, primarily members of several minority groups, who did not have an enzyme necessary to digest milk products. The Dairy Association and its member cooperatives were suddenly in the position of promoting a product that could be harmful to minority children.

**Table 13-3**
Special Interest
Groupings of U. S.
Associations

| Type of Association | Percentage of Total |
|---|---|
| Trade | 22% |
| Culture | 9.8 |
| Health or Welfare | 9.2 |
| Education | 7.8 |
| Scientific, Technical, Religious, Agricultural and other Specialties | 43.7 |

William H. Jones, "Trade Associations Flourish," *Washington Post,* July 4, 1976, p. F-1. Reprinted by permission.

**Association Diversity.** Many associations and societies are divided into local, state, national, and sometimes international organizations. Frequently each of these levels has a separate staff. Table 13-3 divides associations and societies into categories by purpose. While such statistics demonstrate the variety of types of associations, the diversity that exists among the members of any broad-based group is not apparent. For example, The National Rifle Association has become well known for its opposition to gun control laws, but not all its members support these efforts, and this has caused criticism and even loss of membership within the organization. Member organizations in a trade association may range from small family businesses to giant conglomerates. Obviously these organizations will not see all issues the same. Public relations skills must therefore be used within associations as well to retain members and ensure that all points of view have a chance to be represented.

**Public Relations Practice in Associations.** Some associations take very aggressive action to promote the interests of their members (Figure 13-1). Many, like the American Dairy Association, spend millions of dollars on advertising. The Grocery Manufacturers of America bought time and space to inform consumers about the percentage added to the costs of food by growers, shippers, wholesalers, and retailers as food prices began to rise sharply. The Toy Manufacturers of America have also spent considerable sums to increase consumer confidence in the safety of its members' products.

Other organizations prefer to work behind the scenes to promote the welfare of their members. Frequently their efforts take the form of attempts to influence legislation and regulation. Lobbying has become a major activity of many associations ranging from the American Medical Association to the National Association of Homebuilders. Many organizations maintain offices in Washington, D.C. as well as some state capitals to support continuous efforts to communicate their point of view to lawmakers and government officials. At times such efforts exceed legal limits. During the Nixon administration[4] three of the country's largest dairy cooperatives were convicted of making illegal campaign contributions in exchange for higher milk price supports. Public relations professionals must be able to advise policy makers concerning the possible damage such activities in support of organizational

---

**Exhibit 13-1**
A Sample of the Many
Different Trade and
Professional
Associations

American Bar Association
American Dental
   Association
American Management
   Association
American Library
   Association
American Institute of
   Architects
American Association of
   University Professors
American Society of
   Association Executives
American Society for
   Personnel
   Administration
American Society for
   Training and
   Development
American Home
   Economics Association

Canadian Home
   Economics Association
Canadian Nurses
   Association
Credit Union Executives
   Society
Music Educators National
   Conference
National Association of
   Realtors
National Secretaries
   Association
Women in
   Communications, Inc.
Young Presidents
   Organization
National Association of
   Manufacturers
Retail Council of Canada
Texas Motor
   Transportation
   Association

Agricultural Institute
   of Canada
American Hospital
   Association
American Hotel and Motel
   Association
American Iron and Steel
   Institute
American Bankers
   Association
Canadian Bankers
   Association
Canadian Pulp and Paper
   Association
International Association
   of Chiefs of Police
National Association of
   Home Builders
National Industrial
   Recreation Association

---

objectives may do to an association's image, whether the action is technically legal or not.

Communicating with members occupies the time of professionals in many associations. The need to attract new members and retain current ones is a constant problem facing most organizations of this type. The majority of their budgets and professional talent may therefore be spent on association meetings and publications. Of course large associations engage in membership recruitment, lobbying, advertising, and other activities simultaneously. According to the Public Relations Society of America, practitioners in professional and trade associations can expect to participate in the following activities:

• **Preparation and distribution of news and informational material to the press, radio and television.**

• **Preparation and dissemination of technical and educational materials (publications, motion pictures and audio-visual aids) to other publics.**

• **Sponsoring conventions, meetings, educational seminars and exhibitions.**

• **Government relations, including the interpretation of the legislative and administrative actions of government agencies in terms of members' interests.**

• **Compilation and publication of business and industry statistics.**

**Figure 13-1**
Sample Association
Publications

**Figure 13-2**
Sample Hospital
Publications

- Public service activities (such as health or safety matters).

- Preparation and enforcement of codes of ethics or professional standards.

- Cooperative research (scientific, social and economic).

- Institutional and/or product advertising to better acquaint various publics with the products or services represented. Most of these activities underscore two basic values and functions of the association in America's economy and society.

- Wide variations exist in the activities of associations or societies.

First, they provide a means of *experience sharing* by individuals and entities engaged in the same activity or having a common interest. The benefits of this shared experience accrue to all members, and might otherwise be unobtainable.

Second, they make possible—through voluntary, cooperative support—beneficial programs that in most instances could not be undertaken by individual companies or persons. Many medical, engineering, scientific, technological and social advances affecting the lives of all Americans exist only because of such programs.[5]

**LABOR UNIONS**   In many ways the public relations practitioner in a labor union finds her or his role to be a great deal like those in professional and trade associations. Communication with current members, the recruitment of new members, and influencing legislation and regulation are all objectives of labor unions. The public relations professional, therefore, will be involved with union publications, news releases, and lobbying efforts. Some unions, such as the International Ladies' Garment Workers' Union, have undertaken campaigns to encourage consumers to buy products with the union label.

   For the most part, however, unions have avoided public discourse in favor of lobbying efforts and member communication. These tactics have been successful in making the labor movement, which represents only twenty percent of the country's workforce, the major voice of working people in the United States. But, although the voice of labor is powerful in political circles, its popularity with many publics has suffered in recent times. Many of the economic problems of inflation and deficits in trade have been blamed on organized labor. A Gallup survey taken at the end of an economic downturn in 1976 placed labor unions last among institutions in public confidence.[6] These data suggest that the labor movement itself may face a greater confidence crisis than big business. It may be necessary for labor unions to become more interested in communicating with publics other than government and their own members if this lack of confidence begins to lead to pressure for increased regulation of union activities and/or loss of membership. But sensitivity to public opinion does not appear to be spreading fast in the labor movement. In the summer of 1981 the Teamsters elected Roy Williams as their international president in spite of the fact that he had just been indicted by a federal grand jury for allegedly bribing a senator and was widely reported to have connections with organized crime.

Unions have traditionally looked to their own ranks for professional services. Frequently those who make public relations policy in organized labor are promoted from the rank-and-file with little or no formal training in the field. This practice appears to be changing, however, and more professionals are being employed by unions. As a result the aversion of labor unions to broader public discourse may also change.

**HEALTH-CARE, RELIGIOUS AND VOLUNTEER ORGANIZATIONS**

**Hospital and Health-Care Public Relations**

Hospital public relations, like all other aspects of hospital administration, is a relatively new field. Not many years ago professional managers in hospitals were very rare. Instead, hospitals were typically managed by a board of physicians with one named as director. These physicians gave more attention to patient care than they did to details of administration, and hence, as hospitals became larger and more complex, the managerial duties were turned over to professionally trained administrative personnel. As hospital management has become increasingly professional, a need for public relations practitioners was perceived and met.

Hospitals, nursing homes, convalescent care centers, health maintenance organizations, emergency care clinics and all other health-care organizations have been caught in the bind of rising patient expectations for services. It takes only a quick review of recent trends in malpractice law to realize that health-care organizations and the people who work in them are coming under increased criticism for the services they provide. No one would dispute the fact that health care has improved phenomenally over the past twenty-five years. Health-care practices that were considered advanced a few years ago are now obsolete. Yet scientific, technological and clinical advances have in fact contributed to the problems of health-care organizations. In a situation in which the state of the art changes so rapidly, hospitals and other organizations are under constant pressure to update their services. The same publics that call for continuous updating of services, however, are shocked by the rapid rise in the cost of treatment.

When the fact that people today know more about their own health and the treatments available than ever before is added to the cost/service dilemma, the credibility problems of health-care organizations can be better understood. In spite of the tremendous advances in the practice of medicine, physicians are no longer relied upon completely as they once were. Today it is not unusual for a patient to ask for a second opinion on a diagnosis or treatment—something almost unheard of only a few years ago. In this rapidly changing environment hospitals and other health-care organizations need help communicating with a variety of publics (Figure 13-2).

*Nonprofessional employees* in hospitals and other health-care organizations are increasingly joining unions to help them gain better working conditions. Traditional union issues such as pay and benefits are not the only complaints of this employee group. Under the administration of physicians, hospitals seemed to have little regard for the importance of employees in support areas such as housekeeping, laundry, food service, and clerical service. As a result, many of these groups have felt out of touch with the decision makers in their organizations. Only recently have health-care organizations attempted to make nonprofessional employees feel a part of the patient care team.

The lingering vestiges of this negative organizational climate create a number of employee communication problems. Many hospital managers have found that they need to use all the methods of effective employee communication, with special emphasis on the needs of nonprofessionals, to overcome these problems (*see Chapter 10*).

*Professional employees* such as nurses and specialized technicians that staff health-care organizations have also been turning to unionization to solve their problems. Like their nonprofessional coworkers, they have often felt out of touch with the decision makers in their organizations. Nurses have long complained that doctors do not recognize their professional abilities and training. Nursing organizations and schools have launched massive efforts to make physicians and patients alike aware of the expertise of nurses. Lack of recognition for the skills of professional staff is not the only problem in dealing with this important public. A nationwide shortage of nurses, especially in critical areas such as intensive care units, puts additional stress on the relationship between hospitals and professionals. Hospitals are beginning to respond by incorporating more opportunities for professional recognition into nursing roles. Public relations practitioners must help their organizations respond to the needs of these employees by helping to create effective channels of communication that will recognize their professional contributions. Building new, more effective relationships between physicians and other professional as well as nonprofessional employees will ultimately help to produce increased public confidence in health-care organizations.

*Physicians* form a unique public for health-care organizations that has no counterpart in profit-oriented businesses. While some hospitals and health maintenance organizations have staff physicians that are professional employees, most physicians are independent business persons who use the services of the institution. Doctors, therefore, represent a client group for hospitals and many other organizations. Hospitals provide the facilities, support staff, and technology necessary for the physician to practice. In fact, many argue that doctors, rather than patients, are the real customers of hospitals. It is frequently the physician who decides where a medical procedure will be performed—the patient has little or no voice in the decision. Thus, while patients pay the hospital bills, their physicians make the decisions concerning which hospitals will get their business. Because of this, and because physicians have traditionally been highly esteemed in health-care organizations, they are probably the single most powerful public of hospitals and other medical institutions.

On the other hand, physicians function in hospitals and other health-care organizations in much the same way employees do. They work side by side with the organization's employees, usually in the role of supervisor or work director. Many hospital employees come to regard them as managers in the organization rather than customers. Frequently employees take their complaints, suggestions, or questions to physicians rather than their supervisors. This produces confusion about appropriate channels of communication and tensions between employees, administrators, and physicians. To establish effective internal communication systems in health-care organizations, public relations practitioners must communicate effectively with physicians. In addition, the accomplishments of physicians who practice at a hospital can represent an excellent opportunity for external publicity on a local, national, and even international scale.

*Patients,* as we have already discussed, are a unique class of consumers. Most people do not elect to enter a hospital or other health-care facility. They are usually there at their physician's direction. Most hospitalized patients are unhappy to begin with; because of their condition they may feel that they have no voice in what happens to them. The routine of hospital work seems cold and unfeeling to patients. Many hospitals are responding to patients' psychological as well as physicial needs. Numerous special publications are made available to patients regarding their stay in the hospital, their condition, and the treatment they can expect to receive. In addition many hospitals have responded to the demands of consumer-advocate groups to produce a patients' bill of rights to inform patients of the choices that are available to them and the information they can request. Hospitals also have special teams of nurses to educate patients and their families in health care. Another factor in patient relations can be the closed-circuit television system many hospitals already have installed. As we discussed in Chapter 8, many of these hospitals are finding creative new ways to communicate with their patients through video programming.

*Volunteers* are an important part of the operation of most hospitals and nursing homes. Volunteers are typically motivated by a sense of civic and/or organizational pride or compassion for those who need their services. Most health-care organizations rely upon organized groups to provide the volunteers they need. These groups may serve only one institution or they may be an outside organization that offers its services. Public relations practitioners are frequently responsible for establishing workable communication links with these organizations. Their leaders must be kept informed about what types of services are needed and where extra personnel can be accommodated. In addition, each volunteer must be able to see the results of their work and be made aware of the fact that the administration, professional staff, physicians, and patients appreciate their help. Maintaining effective communication channels with a number of different groups and perhaps hundreds of individuals becomes a major public relations effort.

Even though public relations plays an obviously important role in the operation of health-care organizations the number of full-time practitioners employed is still rather low. However, as the professionalization of health-care administration increases, the opportunities for public relations professionals in these organizations will likely increase also. Public relations practitioners are needed to advise administrators and professional employees in a variety of matters such as internal, community, and media relations.

**Religious and Volunteer Organizations**    Churches and other religious and charitable organizations depend upon positive public images for their very lives. All organizations of this type have very few employees which forces them to rely on volunteer labor. The vast majority are funded solely by contributions from their members, public fund-raising drives, and/or philanthropic gifts. Public relations is an important part of the day-to-day operations of these organizations, but only the largest have full-time practitioners on their staffs.

**Religious Organizations.** The goal of most religious organizations requires a great many activities that can be considered public relations. Churches and synagogues must communicate with their memberships as well as local and even national publics regarding doctrinal and social issues. In the early 1970s decline in church membership and rising prices forced many of the larger Protestant organizations to cut back their mission operations and staffs. This helped some of these denominations realize their need for professional help in public relations.

Recently a number of religious organizations have begun to expand their communication activities, especially those involving mass media. The influence some of these organizations have been able to exert has been considerable. The Moral Majority, a conservative group of fundamentalist Protestant churches, became active in the 1980 presidential elections and is widely believed to have been instrumental in the election of Ronald Reagan. Other organizations, such as the church in the following mini-case, have found that public relations skills and techniques can help them accomplish their traditional missions better.

---

**Mini-Case 13-1
Advocacy Advertising
for a Church in
Trouble**

An Episcopal Church in Minneapolis, Minnesota found that techniques borrowed from corporate advocacy advertising campaigns could turn a dying congregation around. Their first set of ads was so successful that they have prepared a second campaign as follow-up messages (see Figure 13-3).

The Episcopal Ad Project sold about 200 sets of ads nationwide to other churches of several denominations. "They just stuck their own name in place of ours," said the Rev. George Martin, pastor of St. Luke's Episcopal Church.

St. Luke's was a shrinking church in a shrinking town two years ago when it decided to advertise itself, "break out of the church advertising mold of just the sermon topic and time of services," Martin said. The project came up with ads that brought in both new church members and national awards for the effort.

"Now, we're a congregation with a good mix of 300 families and growing in a city that lost 100,000 people over the past few years," Martin said. The first ads were aimed at "what people are doing on Sunday morning .   . they had striking visuals like a line drawing of Dante's Inferno with short messages."

The church placed the ads in neighborhood newspapers.

The new set of four ads is aimed at people who "seem to fear any religious involvement, worrying they might turn into some kind of religious fanatic," or will lose themselves in church trappings, he said.

One of the ads shows a picture of Jesus with the caption: "He died to take away your sins. Not your mind."

Perhaps the most striking of the new ads again concerns television religion, raising the question: "Have you ever seen a Sony that gives Holy Communion?"

Martin said that while researching the new set of ads, "We were also concerned with what was happening to young people involved with some of the cults." The resulting ad notes: "There's only one problem with religions that have all the answers. They don't allow questions."

Tom McElligott Jr., with the Minneapolis office of the national advertising firm of Bozell and Jacobs, worked on the ads, saying it was part of the free public service work "we feel we should do."

Adapted with permission of Knight-Ridder Newspapers.

---

The number of public relations practitioners employed in churches, synagogues, and other religious organizations is still very small. However, the fact that the church is no longer the center of local communities and cannot automatically count on large weekly attendance means that things may have to change. Indeed, examples like those cited here appear to indicate a new era of religious communication.

**Volunteer Groups.** It has been estimated that there are some 500,000 gift-supported organizations in the United States other than hospitals, churches, and colleges.[7] Most of these organizations depend upon gifts of time and expertise as well as money to survive. Unfortunately volunteers, like church members, can no longer be taken for granted. Families move so frequently that they may never become a permanent part of any community; more and more women are entering the workforce—these two facts are among the reasons volunteerism is declining in the United States. Although volunteers are still an important factor in the life and economy of many organizations, their future is uncertain.[8] To continue attracting volunteers in the numbers necessary to carry out their programs, these organizations will need to take some innovative approaches to communicating with their publics. The following is a list of just a few of the many large volunteer organizations in the United States:

| | |
|---|---|
| American Heart Association | Sierra Club |
| American Cancer Society | Salvation Army |
| American Lung Association | Girl Scouts of America |
| American Red Cross | Boy Scouts of America |
| American Humane Association | Junior Achievement |
| Advertising Council | YMCA |
| National Foundation March of Dimes | YWCA |

**Figure 13-3**
The Episcopal Ad Project

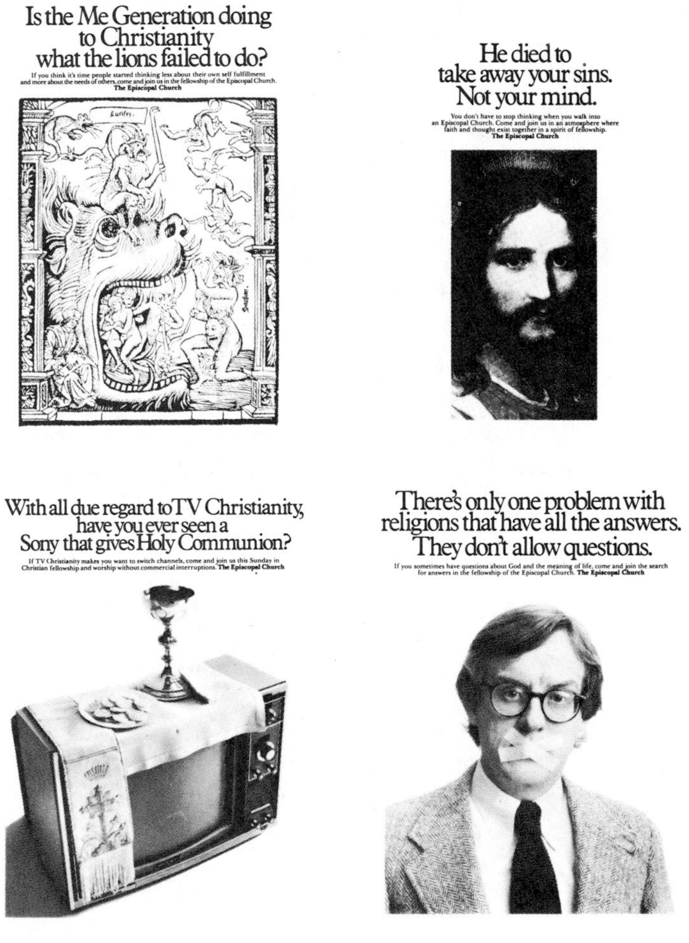


The Episcopal Ad Project, a ministry of St. Luke's Episcopal Church, Minneapolis, Minnesota, 1981. Reprinted by permission.

While their full-time staffs are small compared to the size of the organizations, volunteer organizations represent an excellent opportunity for public relations students to gain experience. Volunteers with communication and other public relations skills are always needed and the problems to be faced are good preparation for full-time careers.

## EDUCATIONAL INSTITUTIONS
### Public Schools

Anyone who doubts the need for public relations practice in the administration of elementary and secondary schools today need only glance at the headlines. School-bond issues are being voted down, teachers are striking, students are suing schools because they have graduated and still cannot read, parents are demanding that school curricula return to the "basics," students and teachers are being attacked in the classroom; the list of problems in our schools could go on. Most large school districts have now come to realize that part of their responsibility as a publicly-funded agency is keeping taxpayers and other publics informed about their operations.

In some communities, few issues are as volatile as those relating to the public schools. The recent history of bussing and other issues related to desegregation of the public schools has proven in every region of the country that changes in the schools can result in catastrophic upheavals in society. Any issue that affects public schools is likely to affect large segments of the community; even people who do not have children attending the public schools in their community may have an interest in the school system because their taxes support it and because it is a focus of civic pride and concern. Most people in our society feel they have a right to know what goes on in the public schools and to have a voice in what happens there. As the educational level of society continues to rise, more and more people seem to feel they not only have the right, but also the qualifications to express their opinion concerning every phase of public education. Some of the many publics that must be addressed by a school public relations effort are:

*Internal*
- Teachers
- Students
- Local school administrators
- Other employees
- Parents
- Alumni
- School board members

*External*
- Taxpayer advocate groups
- Service and civic clubs
- Local business and industry leaders
- School neighbors
- Churches and religious organizations
- Athletic boosters
- Legislators
- Local, state, and federal government agencies
- Teacher's organizations and unions

While each of these publics affect schools in a variety of ways, certain groups are of particular importance and must receive special attention.

*Teachers* have become a well-organized and influential force in many areas of the country. Teachers' unions and professional organizations are concerned with every phase of public school operation. These groups also exert influence with other publics such as legislators, government agencies, and parents. The political nature of public-school administration and the enormous size of many school districts has strained the naturally cooperative relationship that should exist between teachers and administrators. With every other segment of the population demanding a greater voice in what goes on in the classroom, many teachers feel deprived of authority. Like many other employee groups, teachers have increasingly turned to unions to gain a voice in what happens where they work. Any effective public relations effort in a school district must recognize the importance of the professional input teachers can offer and take appropriate steps to bring them into the communication system.

*Students* even at the elementary and secondary school level have become more active and vocal. Various student groups have demanded a greater voice in the decisions that affect their educational environment. Individual students have brought suit against school districts over policies they considered to be discriminatory or unreasonable. Public relations efforts must be designed to inform students about the reasoning behind decisions that affect them. In order to be responsive to student needs, however, school public relations programs must be able to assess student opinion and reaction to decisions before they are made.

*Parents* function as both internal and external publics. Because of their intense interest in everything that affects their children, parents are frequently as knowledgable about events in schools as students are. Many parents become volunteer workers in their local schools through the parent-teacher organization or other programs. They often feel as involved in the school as the staff does. But because they do not take part in school activities full-time, they must be kept informed about those things in which they do not directly participate. Teacher organizations are quick to point out the necessity of parental cooperation in providing good education. Public relations programs must be designed to win parental approval and cooperation in a team effort to educate children.

*Residents* of the school district are concerned about public-school operations even if they do not have children who attend school. The quality and reputation of local schools have a great deal of influence on the property values of a community. In addition, the preparation of young people to become productive citizens of our society is an issue that affects everyone. School public relations programs must be sensitive to the impact their efforts have outside of the classroom. Those who pay taxes and vote on school bond issues must be kept informed about the needs, concerns, and contributions of local schools to their community.

**Higher Education**   The practice of public relations is well established in higher education. Colleges and universities, both public and private, have long understood the necessity to cultivate favorable public opinion. The Council for Advancement and Support of Education (CASE), a national organization concerned with public relations, alumni relations, and fund raising, goes back to 1917.

In spite of its long history, however, public relations in higher education may be facing its most difficult era. The student activism of the 1960s brought numerous changes to college and university operations. Curricula were changed to meet the interests of politically and socially active students. Rules and entrance requirements were relaxed due to student pressure. By the mid-1970s students were changing and so were their expectations of higher education. Many found that the reforms of the 1960s were no longer relevant to the needs of students and society. The question of whether or not a college education was really worth the time, effort, and expense involved was raised. Books such as Caroline Bird's *The Case Against College* pointed to the fact that many college graduates were not trained in fields where they could find jobs.[9] During the same period, two researchers at the Massachusetts Institute of Technology published the results of their analysis of college as an investment, concluding that the economic status of college graduates was deteriorating,[10] at about the same time colleges and universities were experiencing a decline in enrollments due to slowed birth rates and other factors.

This situation has been further complicated by the pressures on state governments to increase funding for highways, social services, mass transportation, and other important services. Funding of public colleges and universities has in many instances been reduced, and this in turn has put demands on private institutions. Colleges and universities have had to face funding reductions, cutbacks in curricula, and even some layoffs of tenured faculty.

In the late 1970s and early 1980s higher education began to respond to these pressures by offering new degree programs that were career-oriented. In addition, colleges have begun to look for students other than the traditional eighteen-year-old high-school graduate. Both degree offerings and non-degree continuing-education programs have been expanded to meet the needs of students in all age ranges. Higher education has become a lifelong process instead of a brief training period. Continuing to meet the needs of a changing society without sacrificing quality will be the toughest challenge faced by colleges and universities in the 1980s. Public relations practitioners must help institutions of higher learning communicate their changing programs and needs to a changing audience. Some of these varied publics are:

*Internal*
- Students
- Faculty
- Administrators
- Alumni
- Parents
- Trustees

*External*
- Federal government agencies
- State government agencies
- State legislators
- Professional associations and learned societies
- Accrediting agencies
- Textbook publishers
- Business and industries which employ graduates
- Local community

In the 1980s college and university public relations professionals must help their institutions justify the value of a college education, the institutions' emphasis on teaching and research, and the workloads of faculty.

**A Profile of One University's Public Relations Function.** Clodus R. Smith, Vice-President for University Relations at Cleveland State University, describes the function of his division as follows:

Cleveland State University is a maturing institution of higher education which has a rare opportunity for interaction with a cosmopolitan urban community. In its pursuit of excellence, the University stresses its commitment to the community by sharing traditional and innovative programs of instruction, research, and service. In return it asks for public understanding, acceptance, and support.

Basic to the University's need for understanding and support are effective channels of communication between the institution and its many publics. To this end, the Cleveland State University Division of University Relations was created and given the responsibility for representing the University in matters of governmental relations, development, and alumni and community relations. The Division meets its responsibility by interacting with these publics, informing them about the University's aspirations and accomplishments and providing feedback on their reaction.

To help his division meet its responsibility, Smith has formulated a comprehensive plan for university relations that incorporates specific objectives for each subunit and measurable indicators by which their accomplishments can be determined. This program has become a model for many colleges and universities and helps to illustrate the diversity of responsibility usually placed upon public relations professionals in higher education (*Exhibit 13-2*).

**FUND RAISING: A COMMON PROBLEM FOR NONPROFIT ORGANIZATIONS**

All nonprofit organizations face a common problem: the recurring need to raise funds to support their operations. Even public institutions such as universities and hospitals discover that in these inflationary times they cannot continue to develop without a source of private funds. Institutional advancement (or development) programs have become big business in the United States. A great deal of the effort of most nonprofit organizations goes toward raising the funds necessary to carry out their mission.

Frequently the job of coordinating fund-raising efforts falls to the public relations function of an organization because of the communication expertise required for such efforts. John Price Jones, a pioneer professional fund raiser, noted that: "Fundraising is public relations, for without sound public relations no philanthropy can live long . . . . It takes better public relations to get a man to give a dollar than it does to convince him to spend a dollar. Favorable public opinion is the basis upon which American philanthropy has been built."[11]

Successful development campaigns require close attention to many details. Because they are such massive projects, organizations frequently employ

**Exhibit 13-2**
Introduction to
Cleveland State
University's Plan for
University Relations

# DIVISION OF UNIVERSITY RELATIONS

### Concept

The Division of University Relations, as the interpreter of Cleveland State University policies and programs, is responsible for informing the University's many publics of the institution's programs, activities, achievements, and needs. The Division provides a planned communications link through a comprehensive program of activities conducted by the departments of Development, Graphic Services, University and Community Relations, and the Office of Governmental Relations.

The guiding principles which generate the goals and objectives of the Division recognize the qualities of effective leadership needed to improve the image and stature of the University, the need to present to its many constituencies the perspective of the institution as a sound investment worthy of public trust and private support, and the essential nature of involving members of the academic community in the University's quest for excellence.

The Division provides the supportive environment which unifies, motivates, and guides its several units toward successful achievement of University and Division goals and objectives.

### *Goal*

*To create an environment which fosters understanding, confidence, and respect between the University and its diverse publics and which will facilitate the fulfillment of the institution's mission and gain support for its academic, research, and service programs.*

### Objectives for 1976-1977

**Develop** and expand the capabilities of each of the Division's administrative officers and increase through education the abilities and effectiveness of professional staff members to further enhance the credibility and integrity of the Division and the acceptance of its functions by the University community.

**Improve** the administration of and expand the University's development programs.

**Conduct** a study of publications programs at comparable institutions and recommend changes as determined by the findings of the study.

**Initiate** additional community programs, establish new communication channels, review publications and recommend changes to increase their effectiveness in promoting a positive image of Cleveland State University.

**Lead** Division staff to create, accept, and apply more effective indices of measurement to evaluate the productivity of each department, office, and unit.

### Indicators of Achievement

Valid measurement of the progress of the Division requires assessment in terms of the stated goals of the individual units it administers. The effectiveness of the administrative leadership provided by the Division can be measured quantitatively by the increased production of its offices and departments. Qualitative assessment is based on the improved techniques implemented by these units and the creativity and innovativeness of ideas generated by the professional staff as determined by public acceptance and support of these efforts.

Reprinted by permission of Clodus R. Smith, Vice-President of University Relations, Cleveland State University.

professional fund-raising firms to provide counsel or even to manage the entire campaign. John W. Leslie, Vice-President for Development of the University of Houston System and an international authority in fund raising, enumerates nine steps for a successful institutional advancement program: [12]

*Step 1:* Identify broad objectives and policies for the institutional advancement program. In this first step, the broad objectives and governing policies should be outlined for all activities designed to advance the understanding and support of the institution. Objectives, broad and specific, are designed to assist in the achieving of already established institutional goals. (We are assuming, of course, that the institution has a current concrete, understood, and accepted statement of purpose and goals.) Resulting from this first step is a plan with both long- and short-range objectives.

*Step 2:* Define relevant trends which might affect the program. The conscious consideration of trends which might affect the institutional advancement program activities will assure that the implementation of the plan will be as pertinent as possible to the existing conditions. Examples of trends and external influences which would affect elements of the program are: relations with various components of the institution's constituency, condition of the national economy and of various industries important to the particular institution, congressional and legislative attitudes, current and anticipated campus problems, etc.

*Step 3:* Identify specific communication and financial support activities and group them into program elements. All institutional advancement programs are composed of a number of activities through which objectives of the program are carried out. All activities (regardless of departmental direction) should be itemized as to which are designed to communicate and ensure the financial support of the institution's educational goals. Activities may be singular and nonrecurring, such as a special event. Or they may be ongoing, such as securing and distributing institutional news.

A program element is a logical grouping of related activities established for management and budget control. A program element is administered by a director who supervises the activities and personnel within the program element.

*Step 4:* Determine the basic approach and designate the administrator for each activity within the program elements. Plan and outline, in a broad way, the purpose, basic approach, and audience emphasis of each activity within each program element. The primary concern should be the determination of the type (personnel, funds, etc.) and amount of resources required within each program element.

When converting to a programmatic planning and budgeting analysis (using information acquired from conventional accounting methods) managers need to keep several points in mind. Arbitrary allocation of staff time and expenditures will often have to be made for various activities. Travel, telephone, and printed materials are examples of expensive items which often serve multiple activities but which usually are accounted for in lump sums.

Further, it should be expected that, in the beginning, allocation estimates will be crude. The key to effective program planning and budgeting in the future is to set up procedures to validate, as well as possible, the initial allocation estimates. Much literature and experience exists in the maintenance of staff time records. For persons who divide their time among several activities, the easiest classification method would be to use the various activities as broad time-category headings. To repeat, procedures need to be established, but the assessing of time devoted to specific activities is not difficult; in fact, it is routine among consulting firms, advertising agencies, and similar groups which provide services to a number of clients.

Each major activity should be under the responsibility of one administrator. It is not always possible or desirable to limit activity administration to professional staff personnel. More than likely one person will administer several activities, but this has been common to management of institutional advancement programs for some time.

*Step 5:* Designate a director for each program element. The designation of a person to direct and coordinate the various activities within a program element is crucial to the success of the overall program. The decision will depend upon:

Nature, purpose, and audience of the key activities
Principal source of funding of the key activities
Knowledge and experience deemed desirable
Management skills

Each program element director will report to the program manager for purposes of coordination and direction of the various activities for which they are responsible—regardless of whom they report to in the departmental chain of command. Procedures must be established which will facilitate smooth working relationships and transfer of funds (when necessary) among budget authorities.

*Step 6:* Establish objectives of various program elements. Program element directors, in conjunction with the program manager, should determine long- and short-range objectives for each program element. Objectives should be as specific and quantitative as possible and must reflect similar objectives of other program elements.

*Step 7:* Review and revise various activities to conform to objectives of their respective program elements. The entire rationale for engaging in programmatic planning and budgeting is contained in this step. Undoubtedly Step 6 will point up a number of duplications—and probably some oversights—in programming. If increased effectiveness, along with greater efficiency, is to be gained, it must start in the streamlining of the activities composing a program element. The cost in staff time and institutional funds of each activity has to be assessed in relation to exact results achieved—or the estimated results you hope to achieve. Likewise, the relative merit of each activity within a program element must be analyzed. Undoubtedly, opportunities for revision—and probable elimination—of an activity will be obvious to analytical judgment. Objective scrutiny and the courage to streamline decisions are crucial to success of program planning and budgeting as a management tool.

*Step 8:* Develop revised plans for each activity with program elements. Program element directors will need to work with each activity administrator in the revision and formulation of new plans and procedures for the various activities composing each program element. The program element director must make certain that objectives established by his or her particular element will be met by the sum of the results of the activities. Directors and the manager may discover that a realignment of activities might be advantageous.

Revised program element plans will need to include resources required, source of those resources, job descriptions, space requirements, time schedule, results expected, evaluation procedures, and revisions and modifications expected in the future in light of long-range objectives.

*Step 9:* Establish a control system. The control system needs to be designed to provide a periodic, systematic review of performance in relation to objectives. The control system is the manager's chief method of assessing progress toward the realization of objectives.

Managers must allow sufficient calendar time—not continuous time—for the implementation of a program planning and budgeting system. Procedures must be thoroughly tested, and personnel will have to understand and become adjusted to the new methods.

Programmatic planning and budgeting is a management tool. It must not be confused with a philosophy of management. Its strength is its flexibility, but programmatic planning does not replace imagination, intelligence, and initiative.

**Fund Raising—A Public Relations Problem**

While no one questions the need for nonprofit organizations to raise funds, the methods they employ can become public relations problems. Burnout is always a problem in massive fund drives that employ mass media, direct mail or telephone communication channels. Another issue that can cause adverse public reaction is the percentage of the funds raised that are spent on the campaign. Some national campaigns cost as much as twenty-five percent of the total funds raised. Unfavorable publicity about campaign costs can hurt future efforts for all organizations that depend on public generosity. Most professional fund-raising organizations advise that costs should not exceed twelve to fifteen percent of the amount raised.

Nonprofit organizations by their very nature rely on public relations for their survival. In spite of this, many of these organizations have been slow to develop the public relations function within their professional staff. Increasingly, however, the realization of the necessity for more consistency in their relationships with various publics is causing many nonprofit organizations to expand their public relations efforts.

---

**CASE STUDY: THE CHILDREN WERE WAITING**

By James W. Anderson
Department of Advertising and Public
Relations, University of Florida,
Gainesville, Florida

---

The Cook County (Illinois) Regional Office of the Illinois Department of Children and Family Services was desperate. It needed immediately some 600 volunteer families to open their homes to wards of the state.

The courts were placing increasing numbers of children, from newborns to teenagers, in the department's custody. Tragically, at the time, private and religious orphanages and other institutions on which the agency had depended over the years were closing down and refusing for financial reasons to take in any more wards of the state.

Wards of the state are children who have been orphaned, abandoned and/ or abused by their parents or guardians. In some cases, both parents are in the hospital or jail. Other children suffered various diseases, deformities, deficiencies, or the effects of abuse. All were innocent victims of their circumstances and none were delinquents or law-breakers of any sort.

To the extent feasible, the state placed most of these children in available foster homes or private and religious orphanages and paid for their support. However, there were no state-owned and operated homes of this type and too few volunteer foster parents to accommodate all the children who needed them.

About 600 children were, as a last resort, being held in juvenile delinquent facilities along with murderers, rapists, muggers, addicts and criminals of every description. It was appalling, but unavoidable.

One social worker, in addition to her heavy caseload, was given the extra duty of recruiting foster parents. There was no budget for this task and she had no training in public relations.

Unable to accomplish anything by herself, she sought help in the public relations and public affairs offices of major Chicago corporations and media organizations.

Ultimately, she talked with Jerome Schmitt, Director of Corporate and Employee Communications at Inland Steel Company. Schmitt was horrified to learn about the problem. He set out to solve it by organizing several dozen volunteer public relations and public affairs executives from establishment organizations into what he named the Businessman's Task Force.

This group, operating with no money, donated time, services, and "clout," and launched what was to become a major public relations campaign. It involved a variety of public relations tools and techniques and significantly, all Chicago media from radio, television and newspapers to car cards. The initial results were encouraging as first dozens, then hundreds of Chicago families volunteered to become foster parents.

A breakthrough came midway through the campaign. CBS-TV donated a full hour of prime time on a Friday evening for a documentary.

The Task Force and the Agency worked feverishly with the CBS Public Affairs Department in Chicago to produce what, ultimately, became an Emmy-award-winning program entitled, "The Children Are Waiting." In contrast to the usual "Isn't it awful?"-type documentary, the second half of this show urged members of the audience to take direct action in helping to solve this major social problem. It asked them directly to pick up the phone, call in, and volunteer to be foster parents.

No one involved knew what to expect.

Preparations had been made for success. Illinois Bell had installed a 100-telephone setup in anticipation of viewer calls. Some 300 volunteers waited with bated breath in the Inland Steel Company cafeteria. When the call-in number first flashed on the television screens, the crowd swallowed hard in unison. Then, in one joyous instant, all 100 phones lit up like a Christmas tree. It was spine-tingling. One could literally feel love pouring in from all over Chicagoland. Euphoria filled the room as 3,043 requests for information were received before midnight that evening.

More than 7,000 families called in during the next three days wanting to hear more about how to become foster parents. Ultimately, after some exasperating problems with government red tape, this big-city social problem was completely solved using public relations techniques with no cost to the taxpayers.

The 600 children being held in juvenile delinquent facilities were all placed in foster homes and there was a waiting list of qualified foster homes available to any future children to be deemed wards of the state.

The Businessman's Task Force helped wring Chicago's heart. That heart opened wide and the children wait no more.

**Questions**

1. Why did the social worker turn desperately to corporate and media public relations offices for help?

2. What kinds of research were needed before the effective documentary program could be produced? What needed to be put on the screen to make people want to volunteer to become foster parents?

3. Can you think of other situations in which a volunteer group of public relations practitioners could be called upon to solve a social problem?

---

**NOTES**

[1] Rae Leaper, "CEOs of Nonprofit Organizations Agree: Communicate or Perish," *Journal of Organizational Communication* 4 (1980): 9–17.

[2] Ibid., p. 16.

[3] Ibid., p. 16.

[4] "16 in Probe of Milk Fund Got Co-Op Cash," *Chicago Tribune,* 5 June 1974, p. 1.

[5] Reprinted from *Association Public Relations,* with permission from Association Section, Public Relations Society of America.

[6] James J. Kilpatrick, "Populaces' Confidence on Upbeat," *San Diego Union,* 5 January 1977, p. B-6.

[7] Scott M. Cutlip and Allen H. Center, *Effective Public Relations* (Englewood Cliffs, New Jersey: Prentice Hall, 1978), p. 467.

[8] Leaper, "Communicate or Perish," p. 12.

[9] Caroline Bird, *The Case Against College* (New York: David McKay, 1975).

[10] Richard Freeman and J. Herbert Hollomon, "The Declining Value of Going to College," *Change* 7 (Sepember 1975).

[11] John Price Jones in *The Engineering of Consent,* ed. Edward L. Bernays (Norman, Oklahoma: University of Oklahoma Press, 1955), p. 159.

[12] John W. Leslie, *Seeking the Competitive Dollar: College Management in the Seventies* (Washington, D.C.: American College Public Relations Association, 1971), pp. 44–46.

**PREVIEW**  Governmental public relations plays a crucial role in keeping the public informed about issues, problems, and actions of their governments.

Government public information officers seek citizen approval of government programs, help explain what citizens want from their government, strive to make government responsive to citizen's wishes, and attempt to understand and affect public opinion.

Public information officers in government face problems not encountered by their counterparts in the private sector: their mission and legitimacy are questioned more extensively; constituents are forced through taxation to provide financial support; red tape and internal bureaucratic situations hinder professional efforts; political pressure; and limited career development opportunities.

The framers of the United States Constitution believed that the people of the nation were capable of governing themselves, provided that they were fully informed of the issues and problems confronting them and of actions taken by their government. Despite this belief, they provided no specific method by which such information would be disseminated, nor any assurance that citizens would be informed. It was assumed that government would maintain open communications channels with the public and provide information of sufficient quality and quantity to enable citizens to make intelligent decisions about the policies and activities of the government.

To a certain extent these ideals are in fact realized, through a system evolved in response to public needs. The mass media struggle to serve our "right to know." In providing information to the public about government affairs, they draw upon the public relations arm of government—local, state, and federal—which offers the media a constant flow of information.

Government public relations practitioners are often called public information officers (PIOs) to suggest that they simply transmit information in an objective and neutral fashion. In fact they are neither neutral nor objective.

Since the success and stability of democratic governments ultimately are determined by continuous citizen approval, public information officers seek to ensure such approval. Since in the democratic system it is assumed that government will respond to the wishes of the governed, public information officers work to determine the wishes of the governed and strive to make government responsive to those wishes. Since public opinion provides the climate in which public officials, agencies, and institutions succeed or fail, public information officers seek to understand and affect public opinion. Since a multitude of institutional interests coexist in any society, public relations practitioners both inside and outside of government represent a similar variety of perspectives. As a consequence, much of the significant dialogue needed to insure democracy's proper functioning is generated, molded, and enunciated by public relations practitioners.

In short, in government—as in any other kind of organization—public relations is a management function that helps to define objectives and philosophies while facilitating the organization's ability to adapt to the demands of its constituency and environment. Public relations practitioners, though referred to as public information officers, still communicate with all relevant internal and external organizational publics in order to make organizational goals and societal expectations consistent. Public information officers, like their counterparts in business and industry, develop, execute, and evaluate organizational programs that promote the exchange of influence and understanding among the organizations' constituent parts and publics.

Of course, because they work in a different context, with different constraints and problems, government public relations specialists operate somewhat differently than their private-sector counterparts. In this chapter, we will explore the ways in which government public relations is practiced, as well as its history, functions, importance, and responsibilities.

**A BRIEF HISTORY OF PUBLIC RELATIONS IN AMERICAN GOVERNMENT**

As we stated in Chapter 2, leaders have always courted the sentiments of their people. In this sense, public relations has been practiced by governments since the reign of the Pharaohs. In the United States, however, its integration into local, state, and federal government programs has occurred largely since World War II. Before this time, public relations practice was confined to the upper levels of the federal government.

As previously discussed, Amos Kendall served Andrew Jackson in the various capacities of pollster, counselor, ghost-writer, and publicist. Use of such counsel did not become established until the administration of Theodore Roosevelt. From that time forward, "Strong U.S. presidents have utilized the expertise of public relations to exploit the mounting power of the news media .   .   . to mobilize public support for their policies."[1]

Public relations pioneer Edward Bernays recognized that his own expertise could be applied to government and politics as well as to business and philanthropic endeavors. Having served as advisor to Presidents Coolidge and Hoover, he recommended in the 1930s the creation of a cabinet-level Secretary of Public Relations. His suggestion was not acted upon; nevertheless, press secretaries of some recent presidents, although formally ranked as presidential staff rather than cabinet officers, have been more influential than cabinet officers. Gerald Ford's first appointments on taking office were a personal photographer, a new press secretary, and a chief speechwriter.

Frequently presidents have been conscious of the public relations aspects of their highly visible job. Teddy Roosevelt talked of the presidency as a "bully pulpit." Harry Truman was characteristically more blunt; in a letter to his sister, Mary, dated November 14, 1947, he wrote: "All the President is, is a glorified public relations man.   .   .   ."

Outside of the presidency, public relations had tougher sledding. In 1913 the U.S. Civil Service Commission announced an examination for a "Publicity Expert." On October 22 of that year, Congress passed the Gillett Amendment (38, U.S.C. 3107) which stated:

**No money appropriated by any act shall be used for the compensation of any publicity expert unless specifically appropriated for that purpose.**

Despite the law, the public relations function continued to be performed. Most notable among government's early public relations endeavors was George Creel's World War I Committee on Public Information.

Public relations in the federal government came of age during the New Deal, when the creation of the so-called alphabet agencies "precipitated a flood tide of publicists into the channels of government." [2] The Office of War Information, created during World War II, gave further federal support to the profession. When the war was over it became the United States Information Agency (USIA), now known as the International Cummunication Agency (ICA). During the late 1940s, public relations activity was increasingly evident in state and local government. By 1949, nearly every state had established a state-supported public relations program to attract both tourism and industry.

**THE IMPORTANCE AND SCOPE OF GOVERNMENTAL PUBLIC RELATIONS**

Despite the limits placed on public relations activity by Congress, there has always been a need for government publicity, if for no other reason than to inform citizens of the services available and the manner in which they may be used. With the developing complexity of government there was a corresponding increase in publicity.[3]

It is impossible to estimate the number of people involved or the money spent in government public relations. As William Gilbert states, "If you are in government, you are in public relations .   .   . (There is a) public relations element in all the things .   .   . government .   .   . does." [4]

Government public relations ranges from simple publicity to global propaganda. The government spends more money on audio-visual services than does any film studio or television network. It prints over 100,000 different publications each year. K. H. Rabin quotes *U.S. News and World Report* in putting the size of the federal government's public relations expenditures in perspective:

**The federal government spends more money each year trying to influence the way people think than it spends altogether for disaster relief, foreign military assistance, energy conservation and cancer research.   .   .   .**[5]

It is similarly difficult to know the numbers of people involved in federal public relations. Government public information officer Don Brown puts it this way:

**The Civil Service Commission officially classifies slightly more than 6,000 federal employees in two major public affairs/information categories. However, there may be as many as three times that amount who perform government information tasks under a whole host of other job titles.**[6]

As impressive as these figures may be, they do not include the personnel or expenses involved in city, county, state, or regional governmental agencies, programs, or authorities. Nor do they recognize that the inputs provided by these tens of thousands of public relations officials grow more influential every year.

**THE FUNCTION OF GOVERNMENTAL PUBLIC RELATIONS**

Government public information officers, like any other public relations practitioners, seek to achieve mutual understanding between their agencies and publics by following the four-step process explained in Section II of this book. They must gauge public opinion, plan and organize for public relations effectiveness, construct messages for internal and external audiences, and measure the effectiveness of the entire process.

Like all organizational boundary spanners, public information officers must jointly serve two masters—their publics and their employers. On the one hand, they provide the public with complete, candid, continuous reporting of government information and accessible channels for citizen inputs. On the other hand, Scott Cutlip maintains:

**The vast government information machine has as its primary purpose advancement of government's policies and personnel . . . The major objective is to gain support for the incumbent administration's policies and maintain its leaders in power.**[7]

Currently, public information officers serve neither master very well, as evidenced by the fact that millions of Americans view their "government as distant and unresponsive, if not hostile."[8] Both would be better served if public information officers can provide more active input for governmental decision makers. In his seminal 1947 report, *Government and Mass Communication,* Zachariah Chafee, Jr., held that:

**Government information can play a vital role in the cause of good administration by exploring the impact of new social forces, discovering strains and tensions before they become acute, and encouraging a positive sense of unity and national direction.**[9]

The most basic function of government public relations is to contribute to the definition and achievement of government program goals, enhance government responsiveness and service, and to provide the public with sufficient information to permit self-government. The goal of public information officers is to promote cooperation and confidence between citizens and their government. This, in turn, requires governmental accessibility, accountability, clarity, consistency, and integrity.

Cutlip and Center suggest the following objectives for planned, continuous governmental public relations programs:

1. To win consent for new laws and reforms necessitated by changes in our dynamic society.
2. To overcome citizen apathy and relieve public bewilderment with new and complex functions and forms of government.
3. To provide reliable information for the voter seeking to make intelligent decisions.
4. To continuously inform citizens about services provided by government to facilitate their ability to participate and gain full benefit from them.
5. To give citizens the means to communicate directly with government administrators.

6. To interpret public opinion to rule makers so that laws and regulations will be realistic and acceptable.

7. To encourage noncoercive compliance with laws, regulations and rules by demonstrating to citizens the need and sense of such programs.

8. To build a reservoir of support for an agency or program to be used when conflict develops with other agencies, the legislature or the public.[10]

## THE PRACTICE OF GOVERNMENTAL PUBLIC RELATIONS

While the practice of public relations in government is much like that in other institutions, government information officers do face some difficulties unique to their area. Because they are paid with public funds, the mission and legitimacy of public relations practitioners is questioned more in government than in private organizations. Gilbert points out that "the citizenry . . . regards government public information activities as wasteful of the taxpayers' money and essentially propagandistic."[11] This is why the Gillett Amendment has never been repealed and why government public relations practitioners ply their trade under euphemisms like "information officer," "public affairs officer," or "education officer."

Unlike the customers of corporations, the constituents of governmental entities are forced to support financially those entities through taxes. Thus, while government may be responsive to political forces, it is not directly responsive to market forces. "Government red tape" has become a sadly accurate cliche and a serious public relations problem.

Brown points out other problems of public information officers: internal bureaucratic situations that hinder professional efforts; weak job standards; political pressure; and little career development or recognition. Moreover, he states, government public relations specialists are considered "after-the-fact-operators, expected to put out fires started by others, or to implement information about programs that we strongly feel will not stand the muster of the media."[12] Increases in the complexity of government policies, rules, and practices, the widening chasm between citizens and their government, and the escalation of citizen demands without their understanding of political, legal, and financial constraints placed on government, are additional difficulties faced by public information officers.

To deal with these problems particular to government public relations practice, public information officers should adopt several strategies. First, they should strive to be generalists in both public relations and management skills while becoming expert in the language and discipline of particular fields within government (health, education, transportation, welfare, defense, etc.).

Second, they should practice preventative maintenance. Public information officers should provide policy guidance before programs are approved. This requires that public information officers enter governments' management mainstream as we discussed in Chapter 4.

Third, government public relations must develop a service orientation—responding to the public in their role of consumers of government. Moreover, public relations should strive to foster this perspective in all government employees through established channels and media of internal communication.

Fourth, government public information officers should concentrate on inputs as well as outputs. As Rabin suggests, "The proverbial general audience . . . . will be identified more and more as a consumer public." [13] This calls for the acquisition of direct feedback through citizen participation, surveys and questionnaires, and community meetings to be used in adjusting programs, messages, and media.

Finally, as the downfall of the Nixon administration so aptly demonstrated, there are great hazards confronting any governmental attempts to hide failures, ineptitude, or mistakes. Openness is essential to effective government public relations.

**EMPLOYEE AND MEDIA RELATIONS IN GOVERNMENT**

While employee and media relations are processes important to all institutions, there are aspects of these that are specific to government public relations practice.

**Employee Relations**

The impression that citizens have of their government, particularly of local government, is often formed through the routine day-to-day contacts that occur between government employees and members of the public. Gilbert points out, "One dissatisfied employee can, by his or her deeds and words, do irreparable harm . . . . If such actions are multiplied by several . . . the result can be devastating." [14]

Practitioners must work to foster attitudes of goodwill and respect for the public among governmental employees and officials. Particular attention should be given to the conduct of face-to-face contacts, correspondence, and telephone conversations. Reception areas should be pleasant and well maintained, and public vehicles should be driven in a safe and courteous fashion.

Rabin puts it this way:

> If the image of the government is to be enhanced, the process must take place at the level of the individual employee—his or her productivity, and how he or she conducts encounters with individual citizens . . . . Focus will be more and more on internal communications . . . employees . . . will be seen more and more as media for communicating with external publics. [15]

Chapter 10 on employee communication provides further discussion of the rationale and means of employee communication.

**Media Relations**

Some commentators seem to believe that media relations has lost some of its importance among the methods of public information officers, and the public increasingly receives government information in direct forms. J. M. Perry, writing in the *Wall Street Journal,* observes, "The press release is more or less a decaying institution in Washington . . . . Government communicators have turned more and more to sophisticated tools—orchestrated advertising campaigns, television commercials, videotape cassettes, full-color brochures and glossy magazines." [16] Although government information encompasses an ever-broadening range of media and techniques, plain old media relations still gets tremendous attention. Indeed, without government information officers, the news media could not function as effectively and as economically as they do in reporting on government.

Government public information officers outgun reporters in numbers and resources. Moreover, reporters often feel lost in local, state, or federal bu-reaucracies. Under these circumstances, says Cutlip, "an ever-increasing share of news content . . . is coming, often unchanged from the government officer's typewriter. More and more of the governmental news reporting task is abandoned to the practitioner who supplies the information in professional ready-to-use packages." [17] The public information officer thus has enormous opportunities for media access. It also means accepting the responsibility not to abuse that access.

**The Presidential Press Secretary**

The single most conspicuous and important government public relations practitioner is the presidential press secretary. As the chief public relations spokesperson for the administration, he communicates policies and practices to the public while providing input into governmental decision making. The unfortunate wounding of President Reagan's press secretary, Jim Brady, shows that the job even carries an element of danger. Descriptions of the job give indications of the practice of government public relations in general.

According to William Safire, a speechwriter for President Nixon who be-came a political columnist for the *New York Times,* "A good press secretary speaks up for the press to the President and speaks out for the President to the press. He makes his home in the pitted no-man's-land of an adversary relationship and is primarily an advocate, interpreter and amplifier. He must be more the President's man than the press'. But he can be his own man as well." [18] This description, of course, is a nearly classic definition of the boundary-spanning role discussed in Chapter 3.

Gerald Ford's two press secretaries give differing perspectives on the relationship that should exist between the practitioner and the president. Gerald terHorst quit after Ford pardoned Nixon, commenting, "A spokesman should feel in his heart and mind that the Chief's decision is the right one so that he can speak with a persuasiveness that stems from conviction." [19]

Ron Nessen, who replaced terHorst, took a different view. "A press sec-retary does not always have to agree with the President. His first loyalty is to the public, and he should not knowingly lie or mislead the press." [20]

Whether or not a practitioner must agree with her or his boss is a matter of personal conscience. Loyalty to the public and an ability to foster com-munications in both directions, however, are essential aspects of the job, just as they are for all public relations professionals.

**THE IMPACT OF GOVERNMENT PUBLIC RELATIONS**

The success of many government programs depends on the adequacy of information about those programs reaching relevant publics. The President and the policeman, the legislator and the librarian, all depend on public information officers to do their jobs effectively and efficiently as possible. Governmental programs ranging from soil conservation to crime prevention, from anti-litter campaigns to army recruitment to use of zip codes depend upon public relations for their success.

R. L. Rings demonstrated the dramatic impact of governmental public relations in a study of seventy Ohio city school districts. Rings analyzed thirty-five school districts which had public information officers and thirty-five school districts which did not. Those districts with public information officers received significantly more news coverage. Moreoever, where there were public information officers, the news focused on student and public affairs. Without public information officers, the news coverage consisted mainly of sports and administrative news.

The most telling findings, however, had to do with the finances of the school districts.

**Financial records indicated that the director systems' current average operating millage was two mills above the state mean, whereas the nondirector systems average operating millage was four mills below the state mean. In local support per pupil, the director sample averaged $375 to the nondirector sample average of $275.[21]**

While it could be argued that more affluent school districts could afford to hire public relations directors, it is probable that public relations directors in Ohio have some impact on public support of education which directly translated into financial support.

Public relations is just as critical to governmental organizations as it is to other institutions. Since government activities depend so much on public opinion, public relations is the stuff of government. Rather than seeking to ban public relations from government, citizens should recognize its legitimacy, and public relations specialists should work toward making its practice ever more professional, responsible, and efficient.

**CASE STUDY:** **By S. Carlton Caldwell**
**URBAN UNRENEWAL** **Assistant Dean, College of**
**Journalism, The University of**
**Maryland, College Park, Maryland**

The state Urban Renewal Office for a large midwestern city has requested a grant of $60 million from the state to rebuild a poverty-stricken area of the city. The Public Affairs Officer (PAO) for that office receives a memo from the departmental director saying that the governor expresses confidence that the legislature will allocate funds. The PAO sends out a press release describing the plans for renovation.

A group of slum landlords who own the buildings in this area are very upset by the proposed renovation because the state would assume ownership of the newly constructed units. The landlords would receive a minimal assessed-value for their property. These men also happen to be major contributors to the governor's reelection campaign and have also donated large sums of money to the campaigns of some prominent state senators. They have informed the governor and the senators that if they would like to receive future contributions, they had better halt the project.

When the bill for the grant comes before the state senate, it is amended as recommended by the governor, so that the city would match every dollar. The city has no funds available for urban renewal. An Urban Renewal Office staff meeting after passage of the bill decides to scrap plans for renewal on a public-financed basis, and instead to try to lure private investors to the area.

The governor, a close personal friend of the director, meets with him to explain the situation, but advises the director to keep quiet. Two local newspaper reporters, with whom the PAO has spent years developing his credibility, as well as close personal relationships, receive anonymous letters outlining the reasons behind the amendments. They go to the PAO and ask him to tell the story. He tells them that he has no knowledge of the story, but will get back to them the next day with what he can find out. They arrange to meet in his office.

He goes to the director, tells him of the inquiry, and asks him to verify or deny the facts at hand. With great remorse the director fully explains the pressures put on the governor and the senators as the reason for the amendment of the bill.

**Questions**   1. If you were the PAO and had to write a press release for the two reporters, what would you say?

2. What is the legal situation facing the PAO?

3. How could the PAO handle the situation without having his/her name appearing in the papers?

---

**NOTES**   [1] Scott Cutlip, "Public Relations in Government," *Public Relations Review* (Summer 1976): 10.

[2] William H. Gilbert, ed., *Public Relations in Local Government* (Washington, D.C.: International City Management Association, 1975), p. 9.

[3] Ibid., p. 8.

[4] Ibid., p. 5.

[5] K. H. Rabin, "Government PIOs in the '80s," *Public Relations Journal* (December 1979): 21.

[6] D. H. Brown, "Information Officers and Reporters: Friends or Foes?" *Public Relations Review* (Summer 1976): 31.

[7] Cutlip, "Public Relations in Government," p. 12.

[8] Final Report of the 32nd American Assembly, Columbia University.

[9] Zachariah Chafee, Jr., *Government and Mass Communication*, 2 vols. (Chicago: University of Chicago Press, 1947), 2: 736.

[10] Scott Cutlip and Allen H. Center, *Effective Public Relations,* 5th ed., (Englewood Cliffs; NJ: Prentice-Hall, Inc., 1978), p. 498.

[11] Gilbert, *Public Relations in Local Government,* p. 11.

[12] Brown, "Information Officers and Reporters," p. 33.

[13] Rabin, "Government PIOs," p. 23.

[14] Gilbert, *Public Relations in Local Government,* p. 20.

[15] Rabin, "Government PIOs," p. 23.

[16] J. M. Perry, "Federal Flairs . . .", *Wall Street Journal,* 23 May 1979, pp. 1ff.

[17] Cutlip, "Public Relations in Government," p. 15.

[18] William Safire, "One of Our Own," *New York Times,* 19 September 1974, p. 43.

[19] Robert U. Brown, "Role of Press Secretary," *Editor and Publisher,* 19 October 1974, p. 40.

[20] I. W. Hill, "Nessen Lists Ways He Has Improved Press Relations," *Editor and Publisher,* 10 April 1975, p. 40.

[21] R. L. Rings, "Public School News Coverage With and Without PR Directors," *Journalism Quarterly* (Spring 1971).

Northwestern Bell

National Car Rental

Munsingwear

General Mills, Inc.

Ford

NCR

DANA

BURLINGTON NORTHERN RAILROAD

# SECTION V: PUBLIC RELATIONS IN BUSINESS

Public relations serves all types of organizations. But historically it has served business, particularly big business, more than any other kind of organization, and continues to do so today. Business has embraced public relations and set it to work, recognizing it as a means of increasing organizational effectiveness in a complex and changing environment.

To operate effectively within business organizations, the public relations practitioner must be thoroughly aware of all that we have discussed in this book to this point: the process of communication; public relations role in organizational decision making; the four-step public relations process; and the primary publics of public relations. Practitioners must also recognize the problems and publics that are specific to public relations in business.

In this section we first look at attitudes toward business in the United States, particularly in reference to such matters as corporate credibility, business's human scale, and public understanding of private enterprise. This discussion provides the foundation for considerations of the relations between business, government, and the financial community.

# CHAPTER 15  ATTITUDES TOWARD BUSINESS

**PREVIEW**  Public relations efforts designed to improve public attitudes toward private enterprise must address: the credibility of corporations; corporate concern for individuals on a human scale; public understanding of economic realities; and corporate willingness to lead society toward change.

Renewed business credibility must be built on a firm foundation of honest performance, open communication, removal of inconsistencies between performance and communication, commitment to problem solving, and avoidance of creating expectations that cannot be met.

In the effort to restore public confidence in business, public relations should be business's eyes and ears, receivers of the subtle information that signals societal demands, and providers of information that moves management toward effective response.

During the 1970s it became increasingly apparent that public sentiment toward business and business people was deteriorating. Coverage of business in the media became more negative, consumers complained more frequently about products and services, and economic boycotts and mass protests were organized. Harris, Roper, Hart, Yankelovich, Opinion Research, and other polls provided statistics supporting the drop in confidence toward business. Business people were quick to interpret the trend as a large-scale rejection of the private enterprise system.

Various reasons were offered to explain the unpopularity of American business: communist plots and socialist conspiracies; the unresponsiveness of business to customers; mass media's treatment of business (as was discussed in Chapter 13); general distrust of institutions and power; the failure of business to tell its own story; unrealistic expectations of business; crimes, misdemeanors and corporate misconduct; so-called economic illiteracy, a lack of public understanding of profits, productivity and the laws of supply and demand; and many others. Most explanations contained some truth, but no single reason is sufficient to explain the phenomenon.

The potential consequences of public opinion adverse to private enterprise are many and diverse. Business executives recognize that private enterprise enjoys no constitutional guarantee—that private and corporate business are carried out at the public's pleasure. The ballot box, the media, and the marketplace are mechanisms through which the members of American society express their approval or disapproval of the ways, means and institutions by which this nation's business is conducted.

To some, the environmental and consumer movements, governmental regulations, calls for social responsibility, and more, are direct consequences of negative public attitudes toward private enterprises. The election of Ronald Reagan as president, some claim, marked a positive change in attitudes toward business. Others maintain that the demise of American capitalism is the ultimate conclusion as public opinion continues its present course.

In any case, the problem has been defined as one that public relations might appropriately address. Since public opinion is at the heart of the issue, the move is not surprising. It does, however, represent a substantial shift in orientation for the public relations practitioner. Instead of working on behalf of a particular and specific institution, organization, individual, product or idea, the practitioner is asked to promote what could best be described as a way of life.

In this chapter we will explore public attitudes toward private enterprise; how corporate management has responded to those attitudes; what corporations, trade associations and others are doing about the problem; and what else might be done. We hope to produce an accurate picture of the problem and to suggest a role public relations can play in its solution.

**WHY THE CONCERN?**   Concern about negative public opinion toward private enterprise surfaced among pollsters, business media, and business executives in the early 1970s. Louis Harris Associates found that public approval of business dropped from 55% in 1966 to 27% in 1972. Opinion Research found that one person in five felt cheated by business and that respondents estimated business profit on sales at an average of 28%, far above the actual 5% figure.[1] In a 1972 speech presented to the Public Relations Society of America, then General Motors CEO Richard Gerstenberg noted that the percentage of people who thought business was doing a good job of balancing profits and service had declined from seventy percent to twenty-nine percent in the preceeding six years.[2] In 1973, Opinion Research Corporation completed another survey and found startling declines in attitudes toward the utility of profits, corporate size and the morality of corporate executives.[3]

In 1974, when Compton Advertising was developing an "economics understanding" campaign for the Advertising Council, their marketing research found a mixed bag of attitudes. While fifty-six percent of those surveyed wanted more government regulation of business, the report concluded: "No evidence was found of any widespread overt feeling that fundamental structural changes are needed."[4] Still, in his 1975 survey Louis Harris found that confidence in business leaders had further declined, to nineteen percent.

By this time, America's corporate leaders were convinced that a problem existed. In a 1976 Conference Board survey, 107 of 185 chief executive officers cited "growing distrust of business on the part of the general public" as the key problem of corporate external relations.[5] The intensity of their rhetoric underlined their concerns. Luther Hodges, CEO of North Carolina National Bank, stated: "Public erosion of confidence in capitalism as we know it is such that the future of the system is now in doubt."[6]

A petroleum company executive cited in the Conference Board study said: "Upon the success of companies like ours in stemming or reversing the deterioration of relations with publics and governments, depends the retention of anything like the freedom of action historically enjoyed by private enterprise."[7] The late Richard Darrow, then chief executive officer of Hill and Knowlton public relations, commented, "It is the lack of . . . public understanding in a democracy . . . That is so perilous to business."[8]

By the mid-1970s, new data and reexamination of old data began to suggest that the situation, while in need of improvement, might not be quite so drastic. In 1975 Walter Barlow and Carl Kaufman reported, "The U.S. public already is overwhelmingly sold on the system in principle, but there is considerable misinformation in circulation and people are critical of what they regard as deficiencies in the way the economy works."[9]

Writing in *Finance* the following year, Aronoff maintained:

**When the polls, quoted so often to show that the public has turned against business, are examined more closely, one finds strong support for the private**

enterprise system as a whole.   .   .   . Business people delude themselves when they claim the problem to be the American public's loss of confidence in the private enterprise system. If anything, Americans seem to be of the opinion that it is big business that has abused the system.[10]

Somewhat later *U.S. News and World Report* issued a report of research indicating that Americans were critical of business, but that business was on the defensive for the wrong reasons.[11]

Taylor Humphrey, Louis Harris & Associates president, concluded in March 1978: "The target for this hostility is not what it seems. It is not the free, competitive marketplace. Nor, in the main, is it business as such. The hostility is directed squarely at *big* business."[12]

It is safe to conclude that public relations efforts designed to improve public attitudes toward private enterprise as a whole will not work. The real issue is not private enterprise. To be effective, public relations efforts must focus on the following factors:

1. The credibility of corporations and corporate management.
2. Demonstration of corporate concern for individuals on a human scale.
3. A more thorough public understanding of the economic realities of corporate life including profits, productivity, pricing, and the distribution of the sales dollar.
4. A willingness on the part of business to lead American society toward change.

**CORPORATE CREDIBILITY**

If business and private enterprise are to regain their good standing in American society, they must find the means by which they can be perceived by the public as trustworthy. In a sense, businesses have and always will have one strike against them in this respect. Research into techniques of persuasion clearly demonstrates that disinterested parties are perceived as more credible than interested ones. As long as the profit motive drives business (that is, as long as business is business) business spokespersons will be perceived as self-interested. Today, *caveat emptor* is directed as much toward business's words and deeds as it is toward its products. Hill and Knowlton Vice-Chairman William A. Durbin says simply: "The single most critical problem facing [business] today is .   .   . lost credibility."[13]

Other reasons for the lack of corporate credibility include a record of evasion, disclaiming responsibility (as in the Ford Pinto, Allied Chemical Kepone, and Firestone 500 cases), exaggerating facts, or overpromising results. Perhaps the most devastating cause is the systematic violation of public expectations of business behavior, largely built an image projected by business itself. Business, in effect, has not lived up to the standards expected of it by the American public. According to George A. Steiner, "Society expects business to help society improve the quality of life, and expectations are running ahead of reality."[14]

**Mini-Case 15-1**
**How to Destroy**
**Corporate Credibility:**
**The Case of the**
**Firestone 500**
**Radial Tire**

"Did you ever have one of those days when you felt like you were driving down the highway of life in a Ford Pinto on Firestone 500 radials?"

What turns a good company into a bad joke?

In today's world a corporation's success is a function not only of how it manufactures and markets its products, but also of how it is viewed by its publics.

Firestone Tire and Rubber Company, second largest in the industry, lost its credibility—and did damage to the credibility of business as a whole—in what has come to be known as the "500 Fiasco." Shortly after Firestone introduced its "500" line of steel-belted radial tires, questions began to be raised regarding the safety of the product.

Federal authorities charged that the tires were prone to blowouts, tread separations and other dangerous deformities. Thousands of customer complaints, hundreds of accidents and at least thirty-four deaths formed the basis of their allegations. In the process, profits became losses as customers deserted the company; millions of tires were recalled; stock prices plummeted; takeover attempts, once unthinkable, were sought.

Meanwhile, the company had been hit with over 250 lawsuits. As of August 1978, Firestone had lost nine, won twenty-two, and settled sixty-four cases—for as much as $1.4 million in one case—out of court. Through it all, Firestone steadfastly maintained that the company was unjustly accused, that nothing was fundamentally wrong with the tire, and that tire failures can be blamed on consumer neglect (overinflation of tires) and abuse (hitting curbs).

Firestone made every effort to avoid negative consequences in the situation. In fact, the company made too many efforts, and became its own worst enemy. By failing to cooperate with government agencies, by attempting to thwart government investigations by regulatory agencies and by Congress, by attempting to publicly impugn investigator motives, and by legalistic maneuvering and hairsplitting—all of which was widely reported in the mass media (to which Firestone officials told blatant lies)—Firestone provoked hostility and doubt. In spite of all the company's efforts, the government eventually forced recall of all "500" radials on the market.

Even before the massive recall occurred, Firestone had lost not only the battle but the war. It now stands as an example to some of why government regulation is desirable and necessary. It is also an example of how not to deal with the government and the public.

Business's failure to meet public expectations run the gamut from economic performance (as it relates to improving living standards, combating poverty, controlling business cycles, fostering employment, etc.), to social performance (rebuilding cities, eliminating discrimination, promoting world peace, etc.), to scientific and technological performance (finding cures for disease, controlling pollution, reducing accidents, etc.). Table 15-1 shows the

**Table 15-1**
Has Business Been Taking Leadership in Key Social and Economic Areas . . . Should It?

| | 1973 | | | | Change in Gap from 1966 (%) |
|---|---|---|---|---|---|
| | Has Been (%) | Should Be (%) | Gap (%) | 1966 Gap (%) | |
| Rebuilding our cities | 60 | 92 | −32 | + 7 | −39 |
| Raising living standards around the world | 52 | 80 | −28 | +18 | −46 |
| Eliminating racial discrimination | 50 | 84 | −34 | −11 | −23 |
| Finding cures for disease | 47 | 76 | −29 | + 8 | −37 |
| Enabling people to use their talents creatively | 41 | 81 | −44 | − 8 | −36 |
| Eliminating economic depressions | 41 | 88 | −47 | − 8 | −36 |
| Giving a college education to all qualified | 40 | 75 | −35 | − 6 | −29 |
| Controlling air and water pollution | 36 | −92 | −56 | −34 | −22 |
| Wiping out poverty | 35 | 83 | −48 | − 6 | −42 |
| Cutting down accidents on highways | 29 | 72 | −43 | −21 | −22 |
| Eliminating religious prejudice | 28 | 63 | −35 | − 3 | −32 |
| Controlling crime | 23 | 73 | −50 | 12 | −38 |
| Raising moral standards | 21 | 70 | −49 | −10 | −39 |
| Controlling too rapid population growth | 21 | 44 | −23 | − 6 | −29 |
| Reducing the threat of war | 18 | 68 | −50 | 32 | −18 |
| Cutting out government red tape | 11 | 57 | −46 | 15 | −31 |

Louis Harris, "The Public Credibility of American Business," *The Conference Board Record* (March 1973): 37. Reprinted by permission.

gap between the public's view of what role business should play in relation to societal problems and what role it is perceived as playing. The table demonstrates a significant perceived performance gap in terms of leadership exerted in social problem areas, including racial discrimination, air and water pollution, crime, and moral standards. Moreover, the data show a widening gap in all of these areas.

Richard Darrow explained that the public's inflated expectations are the result of what he referred to as business's "five big mistakes." He argued that business took credit—or permitted the American public to give it credit—for material prosperity:

1. Furnished by mass production and mass marketing of products, some of which contained defects that were only gradually detected;
2. Energized by a speculative stock market;
3. Based on underpriced fuel and raw materials from less developed countries, many of whom have ceased to cooperate;
4. Provided at the cost of mismanaged solid, liquid and gaseous wastes;
5. Measured largely against the illusory statistics of spiraling wage and price inflation.[15]

In short, American business made promises it could not keep, accepted credit for accomplishments which were not really its own, pushed costs and problems into a future that has begun to arrive, oversold and underdelivered, and kept score with a crooked measuring stick. Whether such mistakes and misdemeanors are intentional or not, and whether business is the perpetrator or the victim of these circumstances, is not the point. What matters is that public and consumer expectations have been pumped up in thousands of small ways—through corporate statements, through advertising, through marketing techniques, and through public relations—and that those expectations have not been fulfilled.

In the early 1930s President Hoover and American business promised that "prosperity is right around the corner." When the promises proved false, the American public invited Franklin Roosevelt and the New Deal to change the face of American business, government and society. Such is the power of promises perceived to be broken.

**Restoring Credibility**  Credibility once lost is difficult to regain. Nevertheless, a number of policies implemented and practiced by businesses individually and collectively can substantially contribute to the reestablishment of public trust.

As a first step, tear down the walls. The notion that public relations can be used as a shield is passé. The idea that the corporate domain is impervious to the prying eyes and ears of consumers, competitors, the media, and the regulators is an illusion. Honesty is no longer just the best policy, it is the only policy when even painful truths cannot be securely and permanently hidden.

Complete candor and forthrightness is the only way to achieve credibility. But this candor must be active rather than passive. It is not enough to say "I will answer any question" when you know, in effect, that your audience does not necessarily know what questions to ask. Instead, businesses must listen to their constituents (including employees, customers, regulators, and the public in general) and respond to their incompletely articulated questions and concerns.

American corporations, represented by their upper-level executives, must reach out into their communities directly and through the media on a regular and continuing basis, responding to public concerns and explaining the impacts and rationales for corporate actions and decisions. Chief executive officers should play a leading role in public outreach, following the examples of Pfizer, Inc., Chairman Edmund T. Pratt, who spends up to twenty-five percent of his time on public affairs, and former General Electric Chairman Reginald H. Jones, who spent half his time on "externalities."

---

**Mini-Case 15-2**
**Speaking Out at**
**Union Carbide**

In the late 1960s and early 1970s, Union Carbide fought public and government efforts to enforce control of the air pollution produced by several plants in West Virginia.

In 1978, an OSHA official complimented Union Carbide for its cooperation in the agency's investigation into a company product suspected of causing urinary disorders among workers. EPA praised Union Carbide for releasing the results of a study, not exactly favorable from a company perspective, that described patterns of public attitudes about cancer and its environmental causes.

The differences in these before-and-after snapshots of a $7.5 billion company are a result of Carbide's deliberate policy decision to speak out as a responsible corporate citizen before regulators, legislators, educators, the media, and the public.

In 1976, all the company's public affairs activities were placed under one person who was charged with discerning the popular will and tailoring the company's interest to that sentiment. Crucial issues are identified (currently international trade, energy, health, safety, the environment, taxes, and capital formation), policies are worked out, then multifaceted communication programs are developed.

A cadre of 200 Union Carbide managers, led by Chairman William S. Sneath (who devotes a quarter of his time to external activities), busy themselves with presenting speeches, lobbying, writing articles for newspaper op-ed pages and otherwise speaking out. Their approach is to pursue reason, avoiding strident, self-serving polemics. While the executive time commitment is large, top management is convinced that the results are worth the effort. According to an article in *Fortune,* the company "is undoubtably beginning to build a store of good will and credibility with regulators and administrators at the federal and state levels." [17]

In responding to the public's desire and "need to know," businesses must go further than ever before in releasing what had previously been considered confidential information. Marshall C. Lewis, who heads Union Carbide's communication department, states:

**I think we have no choice but to accept less confidentially as the quid pro quo for greater credibility. Openness has become the name of the credibility game.  .  .  .[16]**

Openness, in this case, refers again to many publics. Employees need more information on the finances, economics, and policies of their employers. Members of communities in which businesses operate should be informed in many cases of decisions and actions that may affect them before the actions are taken or the decisions made. Corporations have already painfully learned that voluntary disclosures of corporate problems, mistakes or wrongdoing hurt far less than discoveries of cover-ups by regulators or the media.

The second step in restoring the credibility of business is to remove some of the glaring contradictions of business behavior. Too often what business says and what it does fail to correspond. There is a gap between mouth and movement, code and conduct, espoused theory and actual practice. These inconsistencies undermine business credibility. Examples of such inconsistencies include:

The promise that private enterprise rewards on the basis of ability rather than birth—yet, being "born on the wrong side of the tracks," being born to a poor family rather than a rich one, black or white, male or female, or having an accent still affects individual opportunities. What you get, good or bad, still fails to correspond, in many cases, with what you do.

Some businesspeople who preach free and open markets at the same time seek to restrict freedom and act in secrecy. Even some of those who claim to fear for the future of private enterprise only fear the loss of privileges currently enjoyed through abuse of that system.

Some businesspeople who publicly crusade against government intervention and regulation are quick to rush off to Washington or to the state capital to seek favorable legislation, treaties, tariffs, regulations and policies. A steel company that resists the Environmental Protection Agency on ideological grounds one day but that insists on protective tariffs on pragmatic grounds the next day appears self-serving at best and hypocritical at worst.

Third, if business is to be treated and trusted as a central force in American society, it must address itself to issues perceived as crucial to society. Although we will discuss this matter at greater length later in this chapter, we should note here that for the sake of credibility business must be visibly involved in public business, making substantial commitments in time, energy, resources and disciplines to solving problems of public importance.

In a sense, the focus of corporate concerns needs to be redefined. William M. Agee, Bendix Corporation chairman, put it this way in *Business Week:*

**Companies like ours are public institutions with several publics to account to—not just shareholders. This requires a different type of informational approach. Part of my job is to be a public figure and to take positions on public issues, not just company activities.**[18]

Mini-case 15-3 demonstrates how a relatively small action aimed at the social problem of urban housing can build credibility and sales.

---

**Mini-Case 15-3**
**GM: Being a Good**
**Neighbor**

In June 1978, General Motors Corporation began quietly to acquire titles to rundown houses in a square-mile area adjacent to the company's headquarters in the decaying midtown area of Detroit. By September, 130 houses, almost seventy percent of all houses in the area, had been acquired. *Newsweek* broke the story nationally in its September 25 issue. GM, it was reported, planned to renovate the homes, at a cost of about $10,000 apiece, and then allow their former owners the chance to rebuy them at GM's original price. The company hopes that its investment will spark further investment in the area, encouraging private parties who build new apartments and establish retail stores.

According to *Newsweek,* GM officials hope the $1.3 million program will do for midtown Detroit what Ford's $337 million Renaissance Center did for the city's downtown and, equally important, provide a model for other firms with headquarters in distressed cities.

Expecting dissent from shareholders, GM chairman Thomas Murphy was prepared to reply: "We're doing it because it's right." GM's motivation is really a moot point. In a letter to *Newsweek,* a reader's response indicates that the company's action was an excellent marketing technique, as well as an expression of social responsibility. "General Motors Corp.'s commitment to improve the lives of its Detroit neighbors," she wrote, "does more to cause me to buy a GM car than all the millions of dollars that the company will spend on advertising this year."

This quiet, responsible action—at a cost of only .38 percent of the amount Ford invested in Renaissance Center (in a move widely and loudly touted)—places General Motors on the list of major businesses actively addressing crucial social

problems. No single action will restore the credibility of
business, but systematic and continuous actions of this sort
will go a long way toward that end.

Finally, business must strive to offer the public a better understanding of
what it can do, what it cannot do, how it does what it does, and the constraints
upon its operations. Public expectations must be brought into line with reality.
This process is especially crucial at a time when the public is showing signs
of disaffection toward government and is beginning to look more favorably
at business as a problem solver. The temptation is, again, to oversell business,
but doing so would invite the pendulum's next swing.

Renewed credibility must be built upon a firm foundation of honest performance, open communication, removal of inconsistencies between performance and communication, reemphasis of commitments to problem solving in areas usually considered beyond the purview of business, and avoidance
of the creation or encouragement of expectations that cannot be met.

Restoring business credibility is, however, only a first step in the overall
"rehabilitation" of public attitudes toward business.

**FROM THE
IMPERSONAL TO THE
PERSONAL: THE
HUMAN SCALE**

Most people's attitudes toward business are developed neither by reading
stories about business in the newspaper nor by listening to the pronouncements of business executives in public forums. Most people develop attitudes
toward business, at least in part, as a result of their own experiences with
business—as consumers, employees or investors. Every interaction between
buyer and seller, or employee and employer, is in a sense not only an
economic act, but an educational and political act as well.

Polls have shown widespread belief that business lacks concern for the
consumer. Harris found in 1973 that seventy-one percent of the population
agrees that business will do nothing much to help the consumer if that
reduces profits—unless it is forced to do so.

But it is really not necessary to go to the pollsters to discover consumer
dissatisfaction. Everyone these days has not one but several horror stories
about their experiences as customers with business: battles with computers,
insensitive salespeople, false and misleading advertising, abusive repair services, warranty problems, and on and on. At the heart of all such difficulties
is a perceived lack of concern and unresponsiveness on the part of business
toward the consumer. Business, on too many occasions, reinforces these
feelings of depersonalization and alienation—the feeling of being just a
number. It is in this fertile ground of hostility and alienation that the roots
of the consumer movement have grown.

At some point the people say (as they did in the popular film *Network*)
"I'm mad as hell and I'm not going to take it any more!" While we will discuss
the consumer movement at some length in a later chapter, we will touch
here on its relation to the improvement of public attitudes toward private
enterprise.

Researchers Z. V. Lambert and F. W. Kniffin analyzed the concept of alienation and concluded that it "provides important insights into the propelling

forces behind consumerism." And in looking at the feeling of powerlessness that is an important component of alienation, they found that:

**From a consumer standpoint, powerlessness is a feeling or belief held by a person that as an individual he cannot influence business behavior to be more in accord with his needs and interests.**[19]

Since many dissatisfied consumers feel that they cannot obtain redress through the offending company, they either live with their anger or make their complaints and seek resolution at the institutional level. They turn to the courts, regulatory agencies, or the mass media for action. Consequently, when businesses are systematically unresponsive and insensitive to the problems of individual consumers, they invite public attitudes and actions that tend to restrict business freedom and private enterprise.

Standard public relations techniques cannot address these problems—nor will "educational" efforts designed to inform consumers about their real clout in the marketplace. Lambert and Kniffin offer a five-point program, which could be called "point-of-sale public relations." It addresses problems of consumer alienation by making it possible for even very large corporations to respond to individuals as individuals. The program includes:

1. A corporate mechanism and willingness to implement consumer proposals;
2. An information system that monitors consumer concerns and irritants;
3. Corporate conditioning and mechanisms for rapidly alleviating consumer dissatisfactions;
4. A control system to prevent practices that inadvertently produce consumer dissatisfaction; and
5. Employee training, evaluation and compensation methods that are incentives for satisfying consumers.[20]

If attitudes toward business are to be positively influenced, the quality of average individuals' daily experiences with business must be improved. Public relations' role in this effort is to advise top management of appropriate responses to the problem and to assist in all ways in the implementation of point-of-sale public relations.

**PUBLIC UNDERSTANDING OF PRIVATE ENTERPRISE**

Many polls have shown that Americans severely overestimate average business profits on sales. While ten percent was considered a just and reasonable profit on sales, actual average profit on sales is less than five percent.

When a poll stated "excessive profits are one of the most important causes of inflation today," seventy-four percent agreed with the statement. Equal numbers agreed and disagreed with the statement: "The country would be a lot better off if the government put a tight lid on the percentage of profit any business can make." A plurality of forty-five percent agreed that "most companies could afford to raise wages ten percent without raising prices" (twenty-nine percent disagreed).

When these opinions are analyzed, it appears obvious that they are based on erroneous information about the size of profits. This widespread misinformation, together with the inflated expectations of Americans, suggests that mass economic education might remedy negative public attitudes toward private enterprise.

**Conveying Information**

The need for improved understanding of business and economics has been demonstrated by several surveys showing that many people lack the knowledge and skills to make intelligent individual decisions in the marketplace, let alone to comprehend or appreciate the private enterprise system as a whole. The term "economic illiteracy" is now widely used to describe this condition. Sylvia Porter has labeled this illiteracy as "a fundamental threat to the survival of our capitalistic systems." [21] Still other surveys underscore the need for economic education by showing a strong correlation between people's attitudes toward private enterprise and the amount of economic information they have.[22]

The battle against economic illiteracy is being waged on several fronts. Centers for economic education and chairs of private enterprise have been established, with the support of thousands of businesses, at colleges and universities throughout the United States and abroad to develop objective economic understanding among teachers, students and others. Many states have recently mandated economics for high-school curricula. The Advertising Council has mounted a multi-million dollar public-service advertising campaign on "The American Economic System . . . . And Your Part In It." The Chamber of Commerce of the United States and the National Association of Manufacturers have developed programs responding to this need, as have hundreds of major corporations, using their advertising and employee communications. In effect, economic education has itself become a minor industry.

In turning to education as a means to combat negative attitudes toward business, businessmen and educators demonstrate tremendous faith in the underlying principles of American political economy. If we have an enlightened electorate, the reasoning goes, votes cast both with dollars in the marketplace and ballots in the voting booth will ensure the future of this nation. As Senator Russell B. Long put it during congressional hearings on economic education in 1967:

**A widespread understanding of the operations and problems of the American economic system is essential if our people are to meet their responsibilities as citizens, voters, and participants in a basically private enterprise economy.**[23]

Although it is difficult to assess the effect of all the activity aimed at reducing economic illiteracy, two conclusions can be drawn:

1. Those who claim that economic education is sufficient to correct the problem of negative public attitudes are mistaken. Economic education as a remedy can be effective only in the context of the people's overall

economic experience. Credibility and individual responsiveness must be restored if economic education is to achieve its desired ends.

2. Those who claim that economic education is inherently inappropriate for achieving goals of improved public opinion toward business are also mistaken. Real gaps of knowledge and understanding do exist; these gaps have helped to create public attitudes; and depending on the means and methods by which it is pursued, economic education can be an effective antidote to negative public opinion.

Public relations, always charged with providing information and building public sympathy for organizations and their activities, is in the thick of corporate efforts to improve public understanding of private enterprise in terms of advising corporate management, developing programs, and dissemating information. Unfortunately, much of the economic education effort to date has been ineffective. The remainder of this section will be devoted to exploring the problems of economic education efforts made thus far and means by which such efforts can be made more effective.

**Preaching to the Choir**   Too often economic education efforts have been directed toward audiences that already understand and agree with the points being made. While such activities reinforce communicators, making them feel good, they serve very little useful purpose in relation to the goal of improved public understanding. "A lot of business people want to preach to the choir" says Richard A. Condon, west coast director of public relations for TRW, Inc. "That does no good whatsoever." [25]

Perhaps even worse is the tendency to communicate as though you were preaching to the choir when in fact you are not. Such activities have allowed critics of economic education to label the effort as propagandistic indoctrination. Preaching the "gospel of private enterprise" to nonbelievers will result in rejection of messages at best, and at worst, in reinforcement of negative attitudes.

Who are the nonbelievers? Many business people think that the major market for economic education is students, and are content to support academics and teachers in their traditional roles. In fact, the far bigger market consists of those who have already left school. It may be, in fact, that the primary audience for economic education is business and its employees.

Economic understanding programs for employees should be built on the specifics of corporate finances, activities, and economics as these affect the individual employee. Bethlehem Steel, Dart and Kraft, Dow Chemical, Firestone, GTE, Kemper, OwensCorning Fiberglas, Pitney-Bowes, TRW, and other companies have done or are doing just that.

To be effective for any audience, economic education must be communicated in an objective, "the facts speak for themselves" way. Moreover, the facts must be presented in ways that are meaningful to the audience, and relate to their needs and values. Finally, while facts are important, they are insufficient. Most attitudes are at least in part emotionally derived. Consequently, affective as well as cognitive dimensions of learning must be addressed. In a strike situation, for instance, all the facts a company can muster will pale before the sight of one striker's suffering family. Economic education must be exciting and alive, appealing to the emotions as well as the intellect, while walking the thin line between propagandistic manipulation and relatively objective presentations of economic reality.

**Cowboys and Indians**    Too much of what passes as economic education in some circles is in fact scare tactics in which the so-called enemies of private enterprise are reviled while the "heroes" are stridently defended. The enemies may be communistic conspiracies, creeping socialism, consumer activitists, government regulators or simply critics of business behavior. It is important to remember, however, that there is little sentiment in the United States for either communism or socialism. Consumer activism and government regulation are arguably necessary checks on business behavior. Critics sometimes express legitimate grievances of the public. In any case, defensive postures lack both credibility and persuasiveness.

Moreover, if economic education is to be believable, it must resist the temptation to equate private enterprise with big business as it is practiced in the United States. As we noted earlier, opinion polls indicate that private enterprise has broad support. Private enterprise is in danger at least in part because it is too often equated with huge corporations—that is, collective organizations that are not private, involve little entrepreneurship, promote dependency and conformity, and that have, on many occasions, sought to avoid risk and responsibility. If private enterprise is to be presented in ideal terms, economic education must also point out those areas in which the ideal is not being achieved.

It is not the function of economic education to paint business as the good guys in white hats. In fact, effective economic education will facilitate public recognition of abuses of the private enterprise system, whether they come from government, business, or some other institution. Individuals educated in economics and business will recognize and point out monopolistic and other unfair business practices. They will demand information and openness from business, not only about products but also about the ways in which businesses are managed.

In short, business takes risks when undertaking the economic education of the American public—it risks increasing scrutiny, demands that promises be honored, and most of all, it risks change.

**First, Do No Harm.** We have repeatedly mentioned polls showing that the public has an exaggerated notion of business profits. Where do people get their ideas about businesses' profits on sales? Some have suggested that respondents have not understood the distinction between profit and markup. A more obvious source, however, is to be found in recent trends in business reporting. In the rush to impress investors with reports of quarterly earnings, public relations staffs can undo years of careful nurturing of economic understanding.

A clue was to be found in a 1976 newspaper headline which read, "GM Profits Up 273 Percent" (other sources put the increase at 173 percent; reporters sometimes have trouble working percentages). During the next few days, corporations' second-quarter earnings were reported in newspaper and magazines in similar terms: Ford's profits were up 313 percent; Eastern Airlines was up 499 percent; Schlitz Brewing was up 123 percent; Celanese was up 109 percent; DuPont, up 430 percent; Hercules, up 947 percent. It was reported in various sources that all industries enjoyed an average profit increase variously reported as thirty-one to thirty-six percent.

Those with business experience understand these figures and can immediately put them in perspective. Indeed, these statistics are designed to impress stockholders and investors who understand such things. But these astronomically high figures also reach the general public who interpret big numbers as big, even "obscene" profits.

Admittedly, those who know what they are looking for and who are willing to search for information or to apply a calculator to a newspaper article can dig out the real story. One can learn, for instance, that GM's return on sales rose from 3.6 percent to 7.3 percent, figures that are impressive to the trained eye, but not inflammatory to the untrained eye. Of course, even these numbers can be manipulated. The increase can still be expressed by claiming a 103 percent increase in profit as a percent of sales, or simply expressed as an increase of 3.7 percent in profits as a percent of revenues. Disraeli was right about lies, damn lies, and statistics.

Aetna Life and Casualty offers another example of inflammatory rhetoric, reporting "operating earnings . . . almost four times greater than . . . a year earlier." The consumers, who do not understand the statistics which follow this claim, consider their higher insurance premiums and conclude they are being ripped off. With the help of a calculator, however, we can conclude that Aetna's margins rose from .92 percent to 2.57 percent. Informed emotional responses can go from hostility to sympathy. But Aetna cannot assume that the consumer will understand.

If we want the public to understand profits or private enterprise, we first must do no harm. We must see to it that communications present information in terms that the public can understand. If statistics are used, they must illuminate, not exaggerate. Here again, public relations practitioners should heed the basic tenets of their creed: consider your audience, carefully consider the actual message of your communication, and be consistent. We cannot hope for public economic understanding if such understanding is blocked not with lies, but with statistics, generalities, technical language, or the like. Frequently such communication does more harm than good.

## BUSINESS LEADERSHIP IN SOCIETAL PROBLEM SOLVING

As we mentioned in our discussion of credibility, the public expects business to play a leading role in working toward solutions to societal problems, and has been disappointed when business has not lived up to expectations.

There was once a time in this country when business was broadly perceived as benevolent. From 1850 to 1887 there was probably less regulation of business in America by the government than in any other time or nation. Business will never again be viewed in such a way—never again will business be seen as the means by which society's ills will be solved as a function of the simple pursuit of profit. Society now expects business to improve the quality of life in ways that go beyond serving narrowly-defined, if enlightened, self-interest. The popularity of business or government in the public mind is ultimately less important than society's choice of institutions to fulfill the role of problem-solver. Since the New Deal, we have chosen government. With the Reagan Administration, business is getting another chance. More even than transitory public opinion, the long-term efficacy of business and the well-being of private enterprise depend on the society seeing business not as a problem, but as a problem-solver.

Business must adjust to a changing world. It must realize that capitalism can no longer be based on an economy of unpaid costs. Profit must be measured by more than a bottom line that does not account for human and environmental costs. Business has to find profitable solutions to such social problems as pollution, health care, housing, and urban decay. This will call for unparalleled creativity on the part of business and the private-enterprise system.

If business begins to solve such problems, the old relationship of government aiding business rather than business serving government may be re-established. The trend toward increasing government encroachment in the marketplace will be reversed if business demonstrates that it can fulfill the goals and aspirations of the American public.

Ultimately, the case for private enterprise must be made in the marketplace. The present and the future of private enterprise depends upon its abilities to meet societal demands. Its ability to meet those demands, in turn, rests upon the receptiveness, the responsiveness, the flexibility and abilities of those who are engaged in private enterprise. If business fails, it will go the way of any single business that fails to meet market demands. It will be bankrupt.

In the effort to restore public confidence in American business, the public relations practitioner must seek to reestablish business credibility, reintroduce the human dimension to business corporations, and facilitate public understanding of business and economics. But most importantly, public relations must be business's eyes and ears, receivers of the subtle information that signals societal demands, and the prod that moves management toward effective response.

---

| CASE STUDY: "UNFORTUNATE DEATH," SAYS GAS COMPANY SPOKESMAN | **By Nancy M. Somerick Department of Mass Media-Communications, The University of Akron, Akron, Ohio** |

---

The body of an elderly man is found in his home. He had frozen to death.

Police report that when found the man was wearing two sweaters, two jackets and two pairs of pants. Police also report finding $80 in one of his pockets.

Neighbors describe the man as friendly but solitary. He lived alone in a home which he had owned for decades.

Several months before the man's death, the gas company had cut off service to his home for nonpayment of a $60 bill.

A reporter contacts the gas company. According to the reporter, a company official states that it's unfortunate about the man's death. Since he's dead, the company probably won't be able to collect the money he owed.

The resulting story appears to emphasize the gas company official's concern about his inability to collect the overdue bill.

Later, the official insists his statements were taken out of context. The reporter denies it.

**Questions**  1. What do you think about the way the gas company official handled the situation?

2. How would you have handled it?

3. What ramifications could there be from this situation?

---

**NOTES**  [1] Cited in *Iron Age,* 9 November 1972, pp. 52–53.

[2] Richard Gerstenberg, "Free Enterprise and the Power of Public Opinion" (speech delivered to the Public Relations Society of America, Warren, Michigan, 14 November 1972).

[3] Hill and Knowlton Executives, *Critical Issues in Public Relations* (Englewood Cliffs, N.J.: Prentice Hall, 1975), pp. 10–11.

[4] *National Survey on The American Economic System* (New York: The Advertising Council, 1975), p. 13–17.

[5] Phyllis S. McGrath, *Managing Corporate External Relations* (New York: The Conference Board, 1976), p. 2.

[6] Luther H. Hodges, "The New Challenge for Public Relations," *Public Relations Journal* (August 1975); 8.

[7] McGrath, *Corporate External Relations,* p. 4.

[8] Hill and Knowlton Executives, *Critical Issues,* p. 3.

[9] Walter Barlow and Carl Kaufman, "Public Relations and Economic Literacy," *Public Relations Journal* (Summer 1975); 14.

[10] Craig E. Aronoff, "In Defense of Free Enterprise," *Finance* (February 1976); 4–5.

[11] Reported in *Advertising Age,* 25 October 1976, p. 100.

[12] Humphrey Taylor, "Creeping Socialism: Fact or Fiction?" *Executive* (March 1978); 9.

[13] Hill and Knowlton Executives, *Critical Issues* p. 223.

[14] G. A. Steiner, *Business and Society,* 2nd ed. (New York: Random House, 1975), p. 72.

[15] Hill and Knowlton Executives, *Critical Issues,* p. 4.

[16] Marshall C. Lewis, "How Business Can Escape the Climate of Mistrust, " *Business and Society Review* (Winter 1975); 70–71.

[17] Hugh D. Menzies, "Union Carbide Raises Its Voice," *Fortune,* 25 September 1978, pp. 86–90.

[18] *Business Week,* 22 January 1979.

[19] Z. V. Lambert, and F. W. Kniffin, "Consumer Discontent: A Social Perspective," *California Management Review* 18 (1975): 36–44.

[20] Lambert and Kniffin, "Consumer Discontent," p. 37.

[21] "Sylvia Porter Blasts Economic Illiteracy," *The Ann Arbor News,* 17 October 1975, p. 26.

[22] See W. Barlow and C. Kaufman, "Public Relations and Economic Literacy," *Public Relations Review* (Summer 1975): 14–22; and *National Survey on the American Economic System* (New York: The Advertising Council, 1978).

[23] Senate Resolution 316, 89th Congress, 2nd Session.

[24] "The Corporate Image: PR to the Rescue," *Business Week,* 22 January 1979, p. 50.

# CHAPTER 16  BUSINESS/GOVERNMENT RELATIONS

**PREVIEW**    The relationship between business and government in the
United States is so contradictory as to seem schizophrenic.
The two institutions interact both as partners and as
adversaries.

Business's task of dealing with government can be described
as a very complex sequence of information acquisition,
processing, and dissemination.

Corporate political activities fall into three broad categories:
electoral, legislative, and regulatory.

Which of the following positions is true:

POSITION I: In the United States in the 1980s, government has become a pervasive presence. Its bureaucracy, spewing red tape, reaches everything, everywhere, and everybody. Through its regulatory mechanisms government sticks its nose where it does not belong, makes life miserable for business, and is generally ineffective in achieving its aims while adding substantial burdens of costs to businesses and consumers. Moreover, these costs are not just monetary—they come at the price of freedom.

POSITION II: Government seeks to stimulate business through laws and regulations benefiting their interests. Extensive governmental research and data-gathering supports business decision making. Exports are facilitated through international diplomacy, while loans, loan guarantees, and tax incentives benefit domestic commercial concerns. Moreover, government is the largest single consumer in America today. Consequently, it is businesses' largest customer. Finally, government seeks to protect businesses from natural disaster, foreign competition, and even domestic competition. Tariffs, loan guarantees, cheap loans, and other programs offer protection, as do regulations over certain industries (transportation, communications, banking) and certain legislation (e.g. fair trade laws). Some charge that government constantly attempts to artificially stabilize the economic environment to benefit business. In fact, there are many who claim that government and business are in bed together.

Which picture is true? They both are. The relationship between business and government in America today is very nearly schizophrenic. And it is not at all clear which elements of the relationship harm or help society at large. What is very clear, however, is that government can and does have enormous impact, both positive and negative, on specific businesses and industries. Government has become one of the most important variables determining the success of business. Before we study governmental impact on business and suggest ways that business can deal with government, however, let us look at the historical development of the relationship between these institutions.

**BUSINESS AND GOVERNMENT IN AMERICAN HISTORY**   The founding fathers were strongly influenced by the economic philosophy enunciated by Adam Smith. Nevertheless, since its beginnings government has exerted more power over economic activity than is considered acceptable in classical capitalistic theory. The prevailing attitude in the fledgling nation was that government best serves by inducing economic prosperity. Political and social ends were fostered by creating economic strength. Under such circumstances, government interceded in the marketplace in ways that benefited business. In those early days, business eagerly accepted a favorable partnership with government and was quite happy to use political devices to achieve its goals when market devices were unavailable. Never in the history of this country has business refused government largesse on ideological grounds. As a consequence, arguments against government restrictions for ideological reasons have a distinct odor of hypocrisy about them.

Business leaders of the young United States saw government as a tool to be used in the pursuit of profit. Theirs was a pragmatic rather than a doctrinaire approach. They were pleased by the government's promotional predispositions: tariffs, stimulation of transportation, land grants, and loans.

Although the founding fathers took care to protect political freedoms, they did not deem it necessary to protect economic freedom. Consequently, the preconditions for government regulation of business activities were present at our nation's birth.

The happy partnership of business and government was little questioned until late in the nineteenth century. In the period between 1850 and 1887, there was probably less regulation of business by the United States government than at any other time, in any other nation. This was the era of McCormick, Remington, Westinghouse, Swift, Armour, Pabst, Schlitz, Duke, and Rockefeller. Contemporary commentators like Herbert Spencer observed that Americans' "sole interest" was "the interest in business." Lord Bryce noted, "It is natural that in the United States, business . . . should have come more and more to overshadow and dwarf all other interests, all other occupations . . . Business is king." In 1853, *Harper's New Monthly Magazine* reported "to the vast majority of Americans, success has long since come to mean achievement in business and making money."

"Among the nations of the earth today," wrote a sober journalist, "America stands for one idea, business, for in this fact lies, potentially the salvation of the world."

"What is the finest game?" he continued. "Business. The soundest science? Business. The truest art? Business. The fullest education? Business. The fairest opportunity? Business. The cleanest philanthropy? Business. The sanest religion? Business."

This extreme position was perhaps understandable in an age of invention and westward expansion. But the euphoria could not last. All was not right with the world, nor was all right with American business.

The passage of the Interstate Commerce Act in 1887 marked the beginning of a spate of regulatory legislation aimed at curbing monopoly, stopping debilitating business practices and controlling outright competition. Unions were organized in response to abysmal working conditions; and, strikebreaking, violence, murder, corruption of public officials, watered stock and monopolistic practices were constantly in the public eye. Moreover, a nation of small individual businessmen was rapidly becoming a nation of employees.

Winston Churchill's observation of nineteenth-century Britain held equally for America. "Trade was free. But hunger, squalor, and cold were also free . . . and people wanted something more than liberty." The remarkable achievements of the nineteenth century created a kind of revolution of rising expectations. As deTocqueville observed, "The evil which was suffered patiently as inevitable, seems unendurable as soon as the idea of escaping from it crosses men's mind."

Captains of industry came to be known as robber barons. For the first time in this country, business found out what it was like to be unpopular. By the turn of the century muckrakers and trust-busters, socialists and populists made business their targets in the courts, the voting booths, the streets. Still, Woodrow Wilson proclaimed, "Business underlies everything in our national life." And Calvin Coolidge claimed that "The business of America is Business."

Gradually, a moderate position emerged which held that while the game was basically good, some of the rules needed modification. In the pursuit of economic gain, valid social ends were being overlooked. As a result legislation was passed in areas including anti-trust, labor relations, child labor, food and drug purity, copyrights and others. Government took upon itself a new function—that of rulemaker and referee. It plays the role with even greater zeal today.

Popular support of business returned to relatively high levels in the 1920s, but it was short-lived. The Depression shook business prestige as well as profits. The bankruptcies, mass unemployment, and economic stagnation engulfing the country seemed to suggest that the American Dream was counterfeit. Business reached a low ebb of popular and political approval. When business failed to perform as it had promised and as was expected, older values were called into question and new solutions were found. Government, along with business, became the engine of the economy. And government took up the responsibility for stimulating business activity, correcting abuses directly and relieving distress. Franklin Delano Roosevelt, considered a socialistic devil in some quarters of the business community, was more widely considered a saint because under his administration the government broke from its traditional role. Where once government sought simply to maintain a society in which individuals could pursue their own goals, it now accepted the direct responsibility for providing them sustenance.

The New Deal was the demarcation point for all American socio-economic activity since that era. It is a great watershed of American history, separating the culture of the self-regulating economy and its individualistic society from that of the mixed economy and its mass society. The alphabet soup of agencies engendered by New Deal legislation made impersonal government bureaucracy a permanent fixture of American life.

But let us not fool ourselves that the New Deal was some sort of plot foisted on innocent business. Both business and the public were unwilling to endure the vagaries of a free market pulling itself ever so slowly from depression. By mutual consent, the principle: "that government is best which governs least" was abandoned. Herbert Hoover observed, "the business world threw up its hands and asked for government action."

World War II institutionalized government's new roles and functions. These were explicitly reaffirmed with the passage of the Employment Act of 1946 by a Congress with a conservative majority. The federal government accepted responsibility for policies that would maintain employment and generally oversee the nation's economy.

The Act read in part:

**To coordinate and utilize all its plans, functions, and resources for the purpose of creating and maintaining in a manner calculated to foster and promote free competitive enterprise and the general welfare, conditions under which there will be afforded useful employment opportunities, including self-employment, for those able, willing and seeking to work, and to promote maximum employment, production, and purchasing power.[1]**

In the 1960s American society experienced increased complexity, an increasing velocity of change, greater risks than had previously been confronted, and the fragmentation of social norms and goals. Both businesses' and government's economic engines were at full throttle. Social goals began to go beyond materialism with demands for racial and sexual equality and the rise of environmentalism, consumerism and other causes. Government began to use business to seek social as well as economic goals.

In relation to business and the economy, government now plays a variety of roles: stimulant, referee, rule maker, engine, pursuer of social goals, defender, provider, controller. To be successful, business must be prepared to deal with government in any of these roles. That is the critical importance of governmental relations and why it has become, in the last dozen years, a crucial dimension of public relations.

**WHY GOVERNMENT RELATIONS? THE CHANGING RELATIONSHIP**

From our historical review, it is obvious that business interests have been involved in politics and government from the earliest days of our nation. By the late 1970s, however, governmental relations were being pursued as never before in terms of resources, executive involvement, sophistication, and openness. Corporate political activity has in effect grown up and come out of the closet.

To some extent, business realizes that it could no longer even pretend to be above the political fray. Fundamentally, ours is a pluralistic society in which various interests compete in the political arena. Under these circumstances, business has recognized that its interests, indeed its survival, require political acumen.

**The profit-seeking corporation . . . has no choice but to be as politically influential as the law . . . and its resources . . . permit. Hedged in by a multiplicity of local, state and federal regulations affecting building, zoning, health, safety, insurance, employment, workmen's compensation, social security, wage and hour standards, equal opportunity rules, securities issuance, financing, fees and taxes, product and advertising standards, et cetera, corporate business naturally takes political action to defend the freedom of action that remains to it.[2]**

While business and government have always had a partnership, government used to be a silent partner. Government's increased willingness to take an active hand in business management and the enormous power of government's hand when it becomes active are further pressures for corporate involvement. Some have described the new and complex link between business and government as "a second managerial revolution . . . one in which the locus of real control over the corporation shifts from private executives to public officials."[3]

A recent article in *Time* pointed out government's power and the vigilance required to deal with that power. "A single clause tucked away in the Federal Register of Regulations (this year's version has already grown to a mountainous 32,000 pages) can put a small-town manufacturer out of business or rejuvenate an industry that was on the brink of bankruptcy."[4] As a consequence business's presence in Washington has increased rapidly. In 1968, about 100 companies had Washington offices. By 1978, over 500 maintained such offices and in most cases, Washington staffs had been considerably expanded.

Another change in the relationship is the posture of business's political activity. Traditionally, business reacted to the threat of government action, whether through taxation, regulation, legislation or the actions of labor, public-interest groups or even other business groups. Not until the danger was apparent did business, as a rule, enter into political activity (see Figure 16-1).

Recently, however, business has realized the value of developing continuing relationships with government at all levels that permit early involvement in the development of issues, policies, regulation and legislation. Advance notice can be a critical factor in political effectiveness. Moreover, when there has been early involvement there is no need for crisis management when a critical bill is coming to a vote.

Finally, the business/government relationship is changing because business senses changes in public attitudes toward government. As public attitudes toward government become more critical and negative, business success in specific and general political activity becomes more likely. F. Clifton White, president of Public Affairs Analysts, Inc. states:

**Because of growing negative attitudes toward government, it should be possible to convince people that the solution to specific economic and social problems does not lie in the direction of governmental action, but is quite the reverse.**

**CHANGES IN MANAGEMENT AND PUBLIC RELATIONS** The increasing importance of government relations and business political activities has had substantial impacts on management in general and public relations in particular. Grover Starling maintains, "The direct and indirect influence of government action on business changes the kinds and mix of skills that one needs to succeed as a manager."[5] The effect on top management, he feels, is even more pronounced. "Top managers must now be as concerned about public policy as they are about anything else they do."[6] Today no public relations program is complete unless it includes provisions

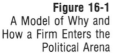

**Figure 16-1**
A Model of Why and
How a Firm Enters the
Political Arena

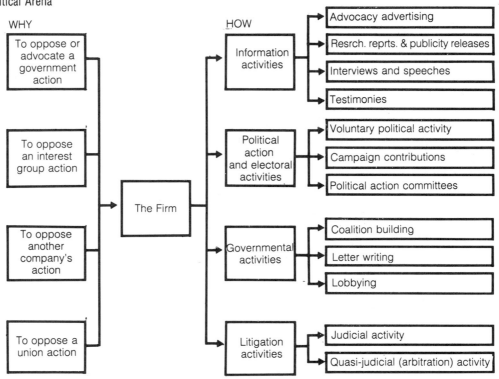

Grover Starling, *The Changing Environment of Business: A Managerial Approach*, p. 517. © 1980 by Wadsworth, Inc. Reprinted by permission of Kent Publishing Company, a division of Wadsworth, Inc., 20 Providence St., Boston, MA 02116.

for dealing with government. The job of dealing with government is, in part, a complex sequence of information acquisition, processing and dissemination. In gathering information, practitioners often do essentially the same thing as journalists.[7] Fact finding and serving as a listening post may be the most important aspects of governmental relations.

Having gathered information, government relations specialists weigh and evaluate it for its impact on the company or industry. Information is then disseminated to corporate decision makers, employees and stockholders, and the public. At the same time, government relations people move information from the corporation to legislators, regulators, congressional staffers, potential political allies, and the public.

Many, but not all, government relations activities resemble other kinds of activities undertaken by public relations practitioners on a daily basis.

Finally, public relations is sometimes called upon to fight fire with fire on the government relations front. Investigation and publicity lack the force of law, but they are clearly among the weapons which government uses to influence business. "Leaks" to the media by "high-level sources," walking tours of supposed infractions, staged public hearings, and the like, may be used against business by government officials. Businesses' public relations specialists are required to compete in the marketing of ideas. They work in competition with the public information machines of government and the public relations operations of a variety of special interests. Honest and forceful public communication is a crucial aspect of the government relations process.

**TYPES OF CORPORATE POLITICAL ACTIVITIES**   In a general sense, corporate political activities fall into three broad categories: electoral, legislative, and regulatory. Electoral activities have to do with the election of candidates favorable to business and the development of plans for contributing to and supporting selected political campaigns.

**Figure 16-2**
Two-Way Flow of
Political Information

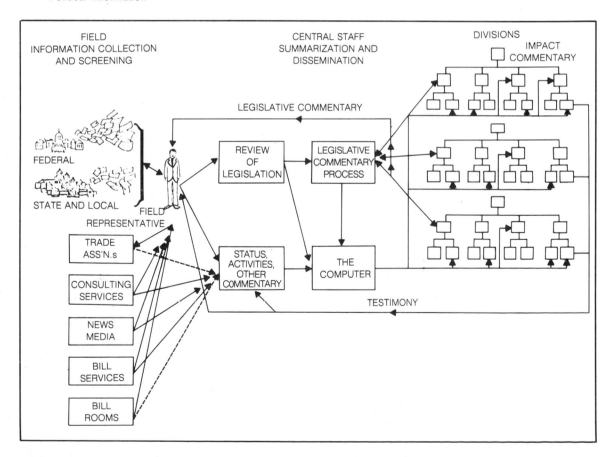

Phyllis S. McGrath, *Action Plans for Government Relations*. New York: The Conference Board 1977, p. 29. Reprinted by permission.

Political action committees are the major vehicle for fundraising efforts. Legislative activities involve efforts to create or gain support for favorable legislation and moves to build opposition to unfavorable activities. Lobbying is the major avenue by which legislative activities are pursued. Regulators are more difficult to lobby because they are rarely elected officials. The primary goal of regulatory activities from a public relations point of view is to foster an understanding of the day-to-day problems of a particular business or industry. Nonetheless, much of corporate regulatory activity takes a form quite similar to lobbying.

**Electoral Activities**     Although political action is often conceived of in electoral terms, business actually places less emphasis on electing candidates than it does on working with the winner after the election is over. Recently, however, the Federal Election Campaign Act legitimized the role of corporations and business-related groups in federal elections, greatly improving their position vis-a-vis labor and other special interests.[8] The law allowed the formation of business political action committees (PACs).

A PAC is a group of people who raise or spend at least $1,000 in connection with a federal election. Federal Election Commission requires that PACs submit financial statements for review. In 1982, corporate and other business-related PACs contributed almost $80 million to congressional candidates.

Corporate PACs get their money from the employees or stockholders of the business. Thus, if a PAC is to be effective, the business "must first educate its own people and motivate them to participate."[9] Raising PAC funds requires careful planning, top management involvement, and careful selection of PAC solicitors. By their nature, PACs generate political awareness and involvement by employees who get together to hash out which candidates should receive PAC money and why.

The money generated by corporate PACs goes to politicians of divergent views. The American Trucking Association PAC has given almost exclusively to incumbents. Coca-Cola and Grumman PACs have favored Democratic incumbents. Ford and General Motors have tended to give to both incumbents and challengers. Amoco and Corning Glass Works have favored Republicans. "Overall business-related PACs split their donations about equally between Democrats and Republicans with most of the money going to senior incumbents in both parties."[10]

This pattern of PAC donations indicates that corporations recognize that in most cases they cannot "buy elections." Senator Edward Kennedy has claimed that PACs "are doing their best to buy every senator, every representative, and every issue in sight."[11] In fact, PACs recognize that senators are generally not for sale for the price of a $5000 campaign contribution. PACs are attempting to buy only one thing—access. A campaign contribution opens the door to a legislator's office. Therefore, the most important function of business electoral activities is to provide support for business legislative activities.

**Legislative Activities**     Most political decisions of importance to corporations are made outside of the electoral process. Consequently, business firms concentrate their efforts on affecting legislation and regulation in relevant areas. These activities are known as lobbying.

Lobbying has been defined as "the practice of trying to influence governmental decisions, particularly legislative votes, by agents who serve interest groups."[12] Although the term has acquired an unsavory connotation of graft and influence peddling, the practice has long been recognized as legitimate. James Madison, writing in 1788, held that an essential characteristic of a representative democracy is that the various interest groups in society are permitted to compete for the attention of government officials.

In recent years lobbyists have cleaned up their acts. Business lobbyists have adopted more restrained practices regarding gifts and entertainment. Old-time Washington business lobbyists have been replaced by carefully selected professionals with business acumen, a thorough grasp of sometimes highly technical information, and lots of political savvy. Henry Ford II sums up the new attitude: "The problem with 'lobbying' activities is not to conceal their existence, nor to apologize for them, but to make sure they are adequate, effective and impeccably correct in conduct."[13] *Time* estimated in 1978 that 8,000 to 15,000 lobbyists worked their trade in Washington, spending $1 billion to influence capital opinion and $1 billion to affect public opinion across the nation.[14] *Fortune* magazine's Walter Guzzardi calls lobbying "the country's great growth industry."[15]

The lobbyist's function is critical from the perspective of business. Starling maintains:

**Because many government policies can have a sizable effect on company profits, the business manager who neglects the lobbying function is every bit as irresponsible as one who ignores the company's capital structure or level of employee motivation.[16]**

The job done by the lobbyist has become essential to the functioning of Congress. The mass of legislation introduced in Congress each new session is so large that congressional staff simply cannot handle the load. Senators and representatives cannot judge the impact of legislation without the imputs of lobbyists who analyze proposed bills and point out potential consequences. *Time* assesses the impact of the lobbying process this way:

**On balance the relationship between the governors and the governed, even when the lobbyist does represent one of the nation's many special interest groups is often mutually beneficial, and perhaps indispensable, to the fullest workings of democracy. The increasingly knowledgeable and competent Washington lobbyist supplies a practical knowledge vital to the writing of workable laws.[17]**

What do lobbyists do? Many things. They inform corporate executives about developments in legislation, report on the introduction and progress of specific bills, offer or arrange testimony to Congressional committees, file statements, communicate with legislators, analyze policies and legislation, inform legislators about the potential effects of legislation, educate legislators about business and economics, help draft laws, publicize testimony, and develop strategy to support or oppose specific legislation. Specifically, lobbyists dig out information from officials and records to transmit to corporate executives, persuasively inform government officials, promote or oppose legislation or other governmental action, and obtain governmental cooperation. Much time is devoted to creating contacts and programs to improve communication with government and monitoring activities of legislators regarding statutes and laws.

Lobbyists involve themselves in the earliest stages of the legislative process. Recognizing that lobbying only works until the legislator makes up his or her mind, lobbyists provide information before bills are drawn up. The emphasis in lobbying is on information and advocacy, not pressure. Often working through congressional committee staff or legislative assistants, lobbyists seek to define issues in terms of the legislators' constituency and the public interest. They provide briefly stated, neatly organized facts that answer questions.

The facts must be presented in a truthful, straightforward and helpful fashion. Honesty is essential because credibility is the lobbyists' most important asset. Guzzardi says, "Without credibility, try suicide." [18] Those lobbyists who achieve credibility come to be relied upon by senators and representatives and their staffs. When such relationships are established, the lobbyist is in a position to suggest legislation, prepare speeches, line up witnesses for congressional hearings, and provide research and position papers. Under such circumstances, it is difficult to tell where legislator leaves off and lobbyist begins.

Lobbying activities are carefully organized and integrated into corporate planning. Figure 16-3 shows the organization of Atlantic Richfield's Washington office.

Perhaps even more important than establishing the order of the staff is establishing an order of issues. The legislative battles must be carefully chosen and related to the overall objectives of the corporation. Figure 16-4 shows Atlantic Richfield's governmental issues list (as of May 1, 1977) and clearly established priorities and responsibilities for the Washington staff.

Of course there is considerable overlap between legislative and regulatory activities. But there are significant differences as well.

**Lobbying from the Grass Roots.** "The chief weapon (for) all successful lobbies today is the mobilizing of support at the grassroots level." [19] As we have mentioned in other chapters, businesses increasingly seek to organize employees, stockholders, community leaders and others as potent weapons in the political arena. Washington lobbyists must demonstrate that their positions are those of the congressman's constituents. To accomplish this, the constituents must be organized to make their voices heard.

Many different people may be mobilized to communicate in a variety of ways; the grassroots approach may consist of flooding Congress with mail or of getting just the right people to give their representative a call. Grassroots lobbying means establishing an organization at the local level by which support can be activated when needed. Associated General Contractors, for instance, maintains a legislative network among its 113 chapters across the country. At least one person in each chapter personally knows his senator or representative. This network was invaluable in defeating a labor law reform bill.

**Figure 16-3**
Atlantic Richfield's
Government Relations
Coordination and
Policies

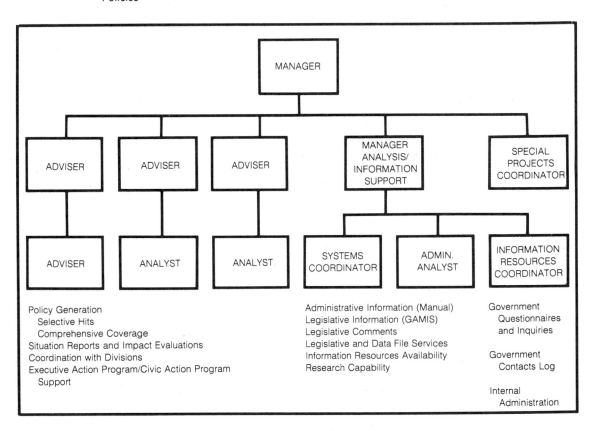

Phyllis S. McGrath, *Action Plans for Government Relations.* New York: The Conference Board, 1977, p. 29. Reprinted by permission.

In 1977, Penneys and Sears Roebuck asked their store managers to write letters to their representatives about a bill that would increase the ability of individuals to initiate class-action suits. They argued that if such suits were allowed, the courts would be jammed with irresponsible litigation benefiting gunslinging lawyers seeking to get rich off legitimate businesses. The provision was defeated. The American Bankers Association asks congressmen which bankers they want to hear from. Then the ABA asks those bankers to transmit the ABA's position on specific legislation. The ABA has 1200 designated "contact" bankers, many of whom served as campaign treasurers, worked on campaigns, or know members of Congress.

The most incredible aspect of grassroots lobbying is the mail it generates. Congressional mail has more than tripled in the past decade. House Speaker

**Figure 16–4**
Governmental Issues
List—Atlantic Richfield

## Environmental/Transportation Cluster

*Adviser 1/Analyst 1*

| *Priority 1* | *Priority 2* | *Priority 3* |
|---|---|---|
| Clean Air | Land Use | Nuclear Fuel Assurance, Nuclear |
| Vessel Safety | Consumer Communications |   Power |
| Coastal Zone Management |   Reform Act | Deepwater Ports |
| Coastal Commissions | Air Resources Boards | General Environmental and |
| State Energy Policy | Utility-type Regulations |   Conservation Issues |
| State Lands Commissions | Utility Rates | Safe Drinking Water |
| National Energy Policy | Pacific Northwest (Coastal Zone | Solid Waste Disposal |
|   (Conservation Aspects |   Management, Tankers, Supply) | Noise Pollution |
|  | Economic Planning | Lobbying Reform |
|  | Full Employment | Campaign Contributions and Reform |
|  | Facilities Sitting | National Health Insurance |
|  | Other Selected State Regulatory |  |
|  |   Issues/Responses |  |
|  | Energy Conservation |  |
|  | Water Quality |  |

## Resources/Tax Cluster

*Adviser 2*

| *Priority 1* | *Priority 2* | *Priority 3* |
|---|---|---|
| North Slope Crude Pricing | Mineral Leasing Act | Strategic Reserve Implementation |
| West Coast Crude Disposition | Alaska Gas Pipeline | Miscellaneous Chemical Issues |
| Surface Mining (Coal) | Synfuel Loan and Subsidies | Federal Energy Projects—Revenue |
| Natural Gas Pricing | Naval Petroleum Reserve #4 |   Sharing |
| Outer Coastal Shelf Issues |   Development | Law of Sea |
| Trans Alaska Pipeline System | Federal Oil and Gas Company | International Energy Agency |
|   Rate Base |   Variations | Miscellaneous Synthetic Fuel Issues |
| National Energy Policy | Amendments to Emergency |  |
| Import/Export Policy |   Petroleum Allocation Act |  |
| Alaska State Tax | Antitrust Improvements |  |

*Adviser 3*

| *Priority 1* | *Priority 2* | *Priority 3* |
|---|---|---|
| State Regulatory Agencies | FTC Litigation Liaison | Ad Valorom Taxes |
| Taxation (General) | Property Tax (Split Roll) | Social Security |
| FEA Related items | State Taxes | Capital Formation |
| Energy Information | Investment Tax Credit |  |
| Crude/Product Decontrol | Tax Equity Act of 1977 |  |
|  | Gasoline Tax and Mass Transit |  |
|  | Severance Taxes |  |
|  | Windfall Profit and Plowback |  |

**Corporate Issues Marketing Cluster**

*Adviser 4/Analyst 2*

| *Priority 1* | *Priority 2* | *Priority 3* |
|---|---|---|
| Franchise Legislation | Common Situs | Sunset and Sunrise in Government |
| —Dealer Day in Court | Self-Serve Restrictions | Consumer Protection |
| —Mandatory Rack Pricing | Octane Posting | Copyright |
| —Company Operation | Marine Cargo Preference | Employee Stock Option Plans |
| Restrictions | FTC Retail Credit Consent Decree | Arts and Humanities |
| Joint Ventures | Board of Director Composition | Code of Conduct—Multinationals |
| Divestiture | —Interlocking Directorships | Government Reorganization |
| —Horizontal | —Public Members | Workers' Compensation |
| —Vertical | —Employee Representation | ERISA Regulations |
| —Marketing | Federal Corporate Chartering | Black Lung Benefit |
| Toxic Substances | Anti Boycott | |
| National Oil Pollution | Questionable Corporation Payments | |
| Liability and Compensation Act | | |
| Slurry Pipeline | | |
| Bulk Plants | | |
| Right to Privacy | | |

Phyllis S. McGrath, *Action Plans for Government Relations* (New York: the Conference Board, 1977), pp. 32–33. Reprinted by permission.

Tip O'Neill received 55,000 pieces of mail in four hours on the common situs picketing bill. As much as fifty per cent of congressional staff time is devoted to constituent mail.

If mail campaigns are to be effective, the letters have to make an impression. Letters that receive notice are those from a constituent, a local community leader, or a friend, or those dealing with a subject of particular interest to the congressman. Personal, persuasive, fact-filled letters from individuals are far more effective than canned or preprinted letters. "We are more impressed by personal correspondence than by mass produced, engineered campaigns," says California Senator S. I. Hayakawa.

In general, letters to legislators should be brief and address only one subject. The issue or legislation in question should be clearly identified. Of course, the letter should be typed, neat, and follow all rules of spelling, grammar, and punctuation. Your case should be stated positively and politely, without criticism or threats. Ask the legislator to state his position in his reply. Timing is perhaps the most important factor in determining the clout of your correspondence. If the letter arrives after the vote, it is useless. Letters should be timed to arrive during the early stages of consideration of pending legislation.

**Regulatory Activities**   In an era of governmental growth, it is in the area of government regulation that the most dramatic expansion has occurred. During the 1970s twenty-two new regulatory agencies were created, including the powerful Environmental Protection Agency (EPA), Consumer Product Safety Council (CPSC) and the Occupational Safety and Health Administration (OSHA). A total of

120 major regulatory laws were passed during the decade. There was a 537 percent increase in regulatory outlays while regulatory staff increased from 27,600 to 87,500 in ten years. (*Figure 16-5*)

"We have become a government, not of laws passed by elected officials . . . . but a government of regulation," claims Congressman Elliot H. Levitas (D-Ga.). "A Congress . . . . will enact 500 laws during its two-year tenure. During that . . . . time, the bureaucracies will issue 10,000 rules and regulations."[20]

Almost every facet of business activity is subject to the rules, standards, or other controls of one or more federal agencies which have the power to review, inspect, modify or even reject the work of private industry. Robert Lane explains business's response:

**Business objects to regulation not just on economic grounds but because it challenges the manager's belief systems, questions his judgments, deprecates the importance of his role, limits his autonomy, and creates anxiety by introducing new uncertainties into an already unpredictable environment.[21]**

A recent Conference Board study showed that the country's major corporations are seeking to reform the federal regulatory structure. Although they accept the need for virtually all regulatory agencies, "the vast majority of firms are demanding that companies and industries be given a larger voice in the formulation and execution of regulations."[22]

Business activities meant to affect regulation are more the purview of the corporation's legal function than that of its public relations function. The reasons for this lie in the structure of the regulatory process and in the way that opportunities for challenge or intervention present themselves. For an example, let us look at the government's attempt to develop safety standards for power mowers.

The Consumer Product Safety Commission began working on lawn mower regulation in August 1973. For six years lawyers, economists, engineers, and technicians conducted research, oversaw oral presentations, attended public

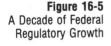

**Figure 16-5**
A Decade of Federal
Regulatory Growth

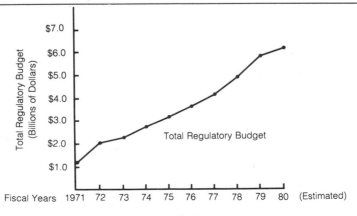

Source: Center for the Study of American Business

meetings, and debated foot-probe requirements and thrown-object tests. Having accumulated 35,000 pages of official record on the subject, CPSC decided to require that walk-behind power mowers be equipped with a clutch that stops the blade three seconds after the operator's hand comes off the handle. The commission said this would prevent 60,000 injuries and cost $190 million per year. Of course, the industry had provided inputs during the investigative process. As soon as the CPSC published its requirements, however, the Outdoor Power Electric Institute, a trade association, sued the commission, challenging its data, conclusions, and every aspect of the proposed regulation. The Fifth Circuit Federal Appeals Court heard this case on April 1, 1980—seven years after the regulatory process began. Their decision was appealed.

"This saga is fairly typical of the way federal regulation works—or, to put it more accurately, doesn't work."[23] Ultimately, regulations on lawn mower safety will not be made by Congress, the president, the CPSC, or the industry. The final regulation will be handed down by federal judges. In this process, public relations may prepare testimony or publicize a corporation or industry position, but the final job is usually the lawyer's.

## INTERNAL POLITICAL COMMUNICATION

We have already discussed political action committees as a means of promoting employee and shareholder political awareness and involvement. Beyond PAC activities, however, a public relations practitioner whose position requires monitoring government relations can also provide political instruction, use in-house publications and other media to increase employee awareness of political issues, and encourage employee political involvement.

Corporations have generated employees' political awareness in a variety of ways. Bliss and Laughlin Industries of Oak Brook, Illinois, provides worksheets along with employees' W-2 forms so that they can calculate how much of their wages went to taxes, what percent of income goes to taxes, and how long each must work to support the cost of government. The employees learned that their biggest expense was not shelter or food, but taxation.

Dow Chemical maintains an extensive public affairs program for employees. The program rests on four objectives:

1. Informing employees about national and local issues that potentially affect the firm;
2. Making employees aware of governmental processes and legislative procedures;
3. Encouraging employees to take part in the political process and giving specific examples of approaches they might use;
4. Advising employees of the value of political contributions and providing the opportunity to do so through political action committees.

Budd Company gives its managers a "discretionary bonus" of up to several thousand dollars based on evaluation in eleven categories, including "involvement in government affairs." Managers are judged on their ability to get their people involved in political campaigns, their willingness to write to government officials on issues affecting the company, and their ability to organize in-plant political education committees. All of these companies recognize that if business intends to remain a viable part of society, its leaders must encourage employee participation in the political process.

**DOES BUSINESS CONDUCT ITS GOVERNMENT RELATIONS PROPERLY?**

Some claim that American corporate business holds inordinate political power. Undeniably, corporations have the organization, financial resources, access, and prestige which tend to increase political effectiveness. It is important to remember, however, that business is only one of many "interests" seeking political favor. And indeed, from the mid-1960s through the late 1970s, businesses were notably unsuccessful in their political efforts. Moreover, as Neil Jacoby points out, "At any given time, business corporations are split on many national issues; there does not appear to be a monolithic 'business interest.' "[24]

Perhaps a more serious charge is that of "crosstown estoppel" or corporate political doubletalk. Corporations seriously jeopardize their position and their image when they contradict themselves. *Business Week* warned: "Companies that have made conflicting statements to federal agencies could find those contradictions coming back to haunt them, and cited the case of the Sharon Steel Corporation as an example. When the Environmental Protection Agency moved to bar the company from government contracts because of non-compliance with federal regulations, Sharon Steel claimed that the penalty was "so severe that its imposition may destroy a going business." Yet in a prospectus filed with the Securities and Exchange Commission, the company said that if it were blacklisted, it "does not anticipate that the resulting loss of business, if any, would have a material adverse effort on its consolidated sales or results of operations.[25]

Sharon Steel was lying to someone, and unfortunately, it is not the only company that engages in "crosstown estoppel." Such corporate behavior gives opportunities to business's political foes, invites congressional scrutiny, and almost begs for additional regulations.

The relationship between government and business has been described in many ways. Depending upon the observer's perspective, the pair are partners, adversaries, or strange bedfellows. In fact, as we have seen, the relationship is far more complex than any of these imply. It might be summed up as mutual dependence in structural terms and mutual hostility in emotional terms. The complexity and the schizoid nature of the dealings between government and business are not likely to lessen. The importance of government in the business environment however, is undeniable. For business and for public relations, the challenge is clear.

---

**CASE STUDY: PORTER'S CLEANERS vs. OSHA, NIOSH, CPSC AND EPA**

**By Craig E. Aronoff**
**Georgia State University, Atlanta, Georgia**

---

John T. Porter feels surrounded. All he is trying to do is run his dry-cleaning business in Shreveport, Louisiana, but it seems like every agency in Washington is out to get him.

First, the Occupational Safety and Health Administration (OSHA) established in-plant exposure levels for the dry-cleaning solvent perchlorethylene, a chemical used in seventy percent of retail dry-cleaning plants in the United States. To comply with OSHA requirements, Porter bought expensive vapor absorbers.

Next, the National Institute of Occupational Safety and Health (NIOSH) recommended stiffer standards for perchloroethylene. If the standards were adopted, the vapor absorbers would have to be scrapped and a different and even more expensive system would have to be installed.

But at the same time, the Consumer Product Safety Commission (CPSC) was attempting to ban the substance. CPSC claims, based on a single test on one animal species, perchloroethylene is a possible carcinogen.

Porter would like to stop using perchloroethylene, but there are only two alternative cleaning solvents in existence. Both of those substances, however, are under attack by the Environmental Protection Agency (EPA).

At times Porter feels like throwing in the towel. But he decides not to go down without a fight. He decides to call a professional public relations counselor for advice.

**Question**   If you were that public relations professional, what would you recommend?

NOTE: Based on a statement read at the New Orleans Open Forum of the White House Conference on Small Business on December 8, 1978, by John T. Porter, president of Porter's Cleaners, Shreveport, Louisiana.

---

**NOTES**   [1] 15 U.S.C. 1021 (1946).

[2] Neil H. Jacoby, *Corporate Power and Social Responsibility* (New York: Macmillan, 1973), p. 150.

[3] Grover Starling, *The Changing Environment of Business* (Boston: Kent Publishing Company, 1980), p. 95.

[4] "The Swarming Lobbyists," *Time*, 7 August 1978, p. 15.

[5] Starling, *Changing Environment of Business*, p. 96.

[6] Ibid., p. 516.

[7] R. C. Born, "Corporate CIA: In Washington, It Helps to Meet Business' Need to Know," *Barron's*, 19 March 1979.

[8] Edward M. Epstein, "An Irony of Electoral Reform," *Regulation* (May/June, 1979).

[9] Edie Fraser, "PACs: The Political Awakening of Business" (Washington, D.C.: Fraser/Associates, 1980), p. 2.

[10] Ibid., p. 5.

[11] Ibid., p. 5.

[12] Starling, *Changing Environment of Business*, p. 531.

[13] "The Swarming Lobbyists," p. 15.

[14] Ibid. p. 15.

[15] Walter Guzzardi, "Business is Learning How to Win in Washington," *Fortune*, 27 March 1978, p. 54.

[16] Starling, *Changing Environment of Business*, p. 538.

[17] "The Swarming Lobbyists," p. 22.

[18] Guzzardi, "How to Win in Washington," p. 55.

[19] "The Swarming Lobbyists," p. 17.

[20] Elliot H. Levitas, "Bureaucracy Stifling America's Right to Self-Govern," *Atlanta Business Chronicle*, 9 June 1980, p. 4.

[21] Robert E. Lane, *The Regulation of Businessmen: Social Conditions of Government Economic Control* (New Haven: Yale University Press, 1954).

[22] Alan Jenks, "Memos," *Atlanta Business Chronicle*, 2 June 1980.

[23] "Lawn Mower Regulations Taking Years to Develop," *Atlanta Journal*, 5 June 1980, p. 28-A.

[24] Jacoby, *Corporate Power*, p. 155.

[25] "A U.S. Drive to Curb Corporate Doubletalk," *Business Week*, 12 May 1980, p. 35.

# CHAPTER 17  FINANCIAL RELATIONS

**PREVIEW**    Financial public relations works to create and maintain investor confidence by building positive relationships with the financial community through the provision of corporate information. Strong financial relations programs, characterized by responsiveness, openness, and regular communications, help to lower the cost of capital to businesses.

Major tools of financial relations include annual reports and annual stockholder meetings.

Effective financial relations results in increased support of company management, higher stock prices, and greater ease in attracting new capital for a business.

The success of any organization depends upon its ability to attract resources from its environment. Among the most important of these resources is capital—the money with which other resources can be purchased. Corporations raise money in a variety of ways: selling stock, issuing bonds, and securing loans from financial institutions. In all cases, businesses can attract capital only if investors have confidence in the business and its management. It is the task of financial public relations to create and maintain investor confidence, building positive relationships with the financial community through the dissemination of corporate information. Corporations that fail in this regard are unable to attract capital investment, and may become subject to takeovers by unfriendly outsiders.

Financial public relations is much easier to relate to the proverbial "bottom line" than are other kinds of public relations. Relative stock prices, bond ratings, and interest rates are direct measures of confidence in a company. When confidence is high, stocks are worth more; bonds and borrowing cost less. In relation to stock prices, for instance, Hill and Knowlton executive vice president Richard E. Chaney maintains:

**The price-earnings ratio is equal to the integrity of a company's financial communications plus its perceived future prospects diminished by the risk of the specific business the company is in and the risks of the marketplace at a given time.**[1]

Investors bet fortunes on what they believe to be true about a particular enterprise. Fraud and deception could be used to part gullible investors from their funds. These dangers have been largely (but not completely) eliminated by government law and regulation, stock exchange policies, and the voluntary disclosures of corporate management. The importance of corporate information to investor decisions, however, points out the importance of the second major aspect of financial public relations: prompt provision of public information required by law, regulation, and policy.

**PURPOSES AND OBJECTIVES OF FINANCIAL PUBLIC RELATIONS**

The practice of financial public relations touches upon such diverse areas as finance, accounting, law, public affairs, community relations, marketing, and employee relations. Consequently, the list of objectives for financial public relations is a lengthy one. Practitioners are charged with:

Building interest in the company
Creating understanding of the company

Selling company products
Broadening the stockholder base by attracting new
   investors
Stabilizing stock prices
Winning stockholder approval for management
Increasing the company's prestige
Creating favorable attitudes in the financial community
Developing political sensitivities of stockholders for issues
   relating to the company
Improving employee relations
Building loyalty of stockholders

Arthur Roalman best sums up the purpose and rationale for financial public relations:

An individual is not likely to invest money . . . in a corporation's stocks, bonds, commercial paper, or other financial pledges unless he believes strongly that he understands fully what is likely to happen to that corporation in the future . . . most investors' willingness to invest in a corporation is influenced by their trust in its management. Trust isn't built overnight. It is the result of long-term actions by the corporation to provide factual financial information in proper perspective.[2]

He continues:

Strong investor relations programs emphasizing a full and continuous flow of information about the company can help lower the cost of capital in the securities markets and develop and maintain goodwill among shareholders.[3]

**PROVISION OF PUBLIC INFORMATION** Many aspects of financial public relations are affected by law and regulation. The Securities Act of 1933 was passed "to provide full and fair disclosure of the character of securities . . . and to prevent frauds in the sale thereof. . . ." The Securities Exchange Act of 1934 supplemented the act of the previous year and was intended "to secure for issues publicly offered, adequate publicity for those facts necessary for an intelligent judgment of their value." These and other Securities and Exchange Commission (SEC) regulations apply to all companies listed on any of the thirteen largest United States stock exchanges, or with assets of $1 million and 500 stockholders. Other regulations require that corporations should "act promptly to dispel unfounded rumors which result in unusual market activity or price variations."

Policies of various stock exchanges also influence the task of financial public relations. The New York Stock Exchange states, for example, that "news on matters of corporate signficance should be given national distribution."[4]

SEC regulations are copious and subject to frequent changes. It is therefore impractical to present them all here. The commission routinely requires submission of three kinds of reports: Annual Reports (Form 10-K); Quarterly Reports (Form 10-Q); and Current Reports (Form 8-K). Form 10-K includes descriptions of a corporation's principal products and services; assessment of competitive conditions in its industry; the dollar amount of order backlog; source and availability of raw materials; all material patents, licenses, franchises and concessions; and the estimated dollar amount spent on research. The form also requires reporting of the number of employees; sales and revenues for the last five years in principal lines of business; description of principal physical properties; list or diagram of parent and subsidiary firms; pending legal proceedings, and changes in outstanding securities.

Other information required by Form 10-K consists of the names, principal occupations and shareholdings of the corporation's directors; remuneration, including amounts accrued in retirement plans, of each director and principal officer; stock options outstanding and exercise of stock options; and interest of officers or directors in material transactions. All of this information must be accompanied by corporate financial statements prepared in accordance with SEC accounting rules and certified by an independent public accountant. Moreoever, the entire form must be submitted to the Commission no later than 90 days from the close of the fiscal year. Finally, 10-K must be made available free of charge to anyone requesting one.

The 10-Q Quarterly Report is much less detailed. Its primary reporting requirements include the corporation's summarized profit and loss statement; capitalization and stockholder's equity at the end of the quarter; and sale of any unregistered securities.

In its effort to gather all relevant investment-related information on a continuous basis, the SEC also requires Form 8-K, the Current Report. Filing of this document is required on the occurrence of an unusual event of immediate interest to investors. Such events might include the acquisition or sale of significant assets or changes in the amount of securities outstanding.

These documents are prepared largely by accountants and lawyers. We have described them in detail, however, because public relations professionals should recognize the extent to which SEC-regulated corporations must share information, should understand the kinds of information deemed significant by investors, should realize the extent of federal regulation in this aspect of business, and should avail themselves to the kinds of information contained in these forms.

One other SEC regulation of particular interest to the public relations practitioner is Rule 10B-5, which makes it unlawful "to make any untrue statement of a material fact or to omit to state a material fact . . . in connection with the purchase or sale of any security." In *SEC v. Texas Gulf Sulphur Co.* 401 F.2d 833 (2nd E.r. 1968), this regulation was found to apply to press releases.[5] In subsequent suits, public relations counsel has been named as a defendant when press releases and other materials "contained false and misleading statements and omitted to state material fact."[6]

**AUDIENCES FOR FINANCIAL RELATIONS**

In addition to the Securities and Exchange Commission, those interested in a corporation's financial information include stock exchange firms, investment counselors, financial writers, brokers, dealers, mutual fund houses, investment banks, commercial banks, institutional buyers, employees, individuals currently holding corporate stock, and those individuals who may purchase stock in the future. For the purposes of discussion, however, we can lump all of these various categories into three broad audiences: individual stockholders; financial analysts; and the financial press. We will examine the nature of each group, their informational needs, the means by which to reach them, and methods of best securing positive relations with them.

**Individual Stockholders**    Some consider a corporation's stockholders as a vast untapped resource of potential customers and grass-roots support for management on political and financial issues. Harrison T. Beardsley recommends that the major thrust of the financial relations effort, particularly of smaller companies, concentrate on stockholders rather than financial analysts.[7] Others dismiss them as investors who purchase stock for income and profit holding that stockholders are best ignored. John Kenneth Galbraith says simply "The typical stockholder does not identify himself with the goals of the enterprise." In either case, a combination of factors have made stockholders a group that must be communicated and reckoned with.

As we discussed above, the Securities and Exchange Commission requires that companies keep their investors fully informed. Management has learned the hard way that uninterested stockholders may be quick to sell their shares even to the most unfriendly entity attempting takeover. Moreover, the stockholders themselves have become more vocal and active—initiating proxy fights or raising financial, social and ethical questions concerning managerial action in relation to environmental issues, sex discrimination, corporate political activities at home and abroad, labor relations, apartheid, and many other problems. Most corporations now recognize that "a company's foremost responsibility is to communicate fully anything that can have a bearing on the owner's investment."[8] The extent and quality of their efforts vary widely, however. Informative and meaningful annual and quarterly reports, and well-organized annual meetings with follow-up reports are the basic tools of stockholder relations. We will discuss both of these in detail later in this chapter.

Sound stockholder relations are built on three principles: learn as much as possible about your stockholders; treat your stockholders as you would your important customers; and encourage investor interest in your company from people who are predisposed toward you. A basic principle of communication is "know your audience." Consequently, learning as much as possible about your stockholders makes excellent sense from a communications perspective. The stockholder survey, which may ask for demographic and attitudinal information, is a readily available tool to use for gaining such information, and too few United States corporations actually use it.

Treating your stockholders as you would treat important customers has a number of implications for financial relations officers. Communicating in readable, nontechnical language is a must. Welcoming new stockholders and writing to express regret when stockholders are lost is a good business practice, just as it would be with customers. Prompt and appropriate response to stockholder correspondence is another requirement for maintaining positive relations.

Sun Company is an example of comprehensive stockholder relations. The company believes that "shareholders are our business partners. It's helpful to us if management gets an insight on what they think of us." Each new Sun stockholder gets a welcoming note from the company's chairman. A very readable newsletter goes out with every dividend check. About one hundred shareholders are selected at random six or eight times a year and invited to a dinner at which a top company executive speaks. Sun also maintains a toll-free telephone line to make corporate news available to stockholders and invites them to call the shareholder relations department collect with questions or complaints.

Sometimes going beyond the call of duty in stockholder relations reaps excellent benefits. Consider the case of Mr. William Comptaro of Pittsburgh, Pennsylvania, owner of one hundred shares of Louisiana-Pacific. Mr. Comptaro was dissatisfied with management's decision to acquire Flintkote Corporation, and expressed his views in a letter to Louisiana-Pacific's president. Mr. Comptaro received a reasonably prompt response from a woman in the stockholder relations department in which she explained how much confidence she had in the company's officers and invited a phone call if there were other questions. Mr. Comptaro wrote a letter of thanks and considered the matter unsatisfactorily closed.

But here the story takes an unexpected twist.

One evening Mr. Comptaro's phone rang. The president of the company was calling to explain in detail why he considered Flintkote a good buy.

Louis Rukeyser, who reported Mr. Comptaro's story in his nationally-syndicated column, made these comments:

**You don't have to be a skeptical professional securities analyst in order to recognize that there are plenty of other factors that ought to be considered by a potential investor, other than extraordinary courtesies shown him by the company's president . . . but surely there is a lesson here . . . for all those arrogant corporation bureaucrats whose cold form-letter responses frequently feed public cynicism.**

Rukeyser continues:

**If capitalism is to survive in the face of ideological competition and muddled political management, it had better look to its own followers—and to its own failings. And while the company president can't be on the phone all day every day, a little more of the kind of communication related here could win the system a lot more friends.[9]**

Finally, just as a company should seek new customers among those segments of the population most likely to become customers, it should seek stockholders among those predisposed toward buying stock. Employees, suppliers, dealers, members of communities in which the corporation has facilities are the most likely prospects. They should receive annual reports and other materials which might encourage investment.

**Financial Analysts**    Financial analysts include investment counselors, fund managers, brokers, dealers, and institutional buyers—in other words, the professionals in the investment business. Their basic function is to gather information concerning various companies, to develop expectations in terms of sales, profits and a range of other operating and financial results, and to make judgment about how securities markets will evaluate these factors. They gather quantitative and qualitative information on companies, compare their findings to statistics from other companies, assess opportunities and risks, and then advise their clients. Corporate financial relations assists analysts by providing information and, in so doing, may positively influence expectations and judgments. The New York Stock Exchange gives its listed companies the following advice:

**Securities analysts play an increasingly important role in the evaluation and interpretation of the financial affairs of listed companies. Annual reports, quarterly reports, and interim releases cannot by their nature provide all of the financial and statistical data that should be available to the investing public. The Exchange recommends that corporations observe an "open door" policy in their relations with security analysts, financial writers, share-owners and others who have a legitimate investment interest in the company affairs.**[10]

Maintaining relations with professional analysts somewhat is analogous to the practice of industrial marketing. The basic method is to identify the prospects, meet them, establish interest and understanding, and then maintain the relationship. All dealings with professional analysts should be characterized by responsiveness, openness, and regular communication, but care should be taken not to overcommunicate.

Information desired by analysts includes background—the nature of the business; an understanding of the primary factors affecting the business; a clear picture of current operating conditions; and estimates of future outlooks for the industry. They are also vitally interested in management forecasts, pricing data, capital expenditures, financial data, labor relations, research and development, and any other information which may materially influence the quality of investment.

The relationship with the financial analyst is not, however, all one way. Analysts can provide very valuable information to companies as well. In communicating with financial analysts, first of all be prepared to listen. Significant feedback may be offered on your financial relations program in terms of adequacy, credibility, and sufficiency of information provided. Perhaps even more importantly, this is an opportunity for the company to understand market perceptions of the company's strengths and weaknesses and of the behavior of the business as a whole.

**The Financial Press**   The third major audience of financial relations is the financial press. "The financial press provides a foundation and backdrop for any corporation's financial communication program," says Hill and Knowlton executive Stan Sauerhaft. "It develops credibility and it can add impressive third-party endorsement."[11]

Financial public relations practitioners deal with the media much as other public relations specialists do. The major difference lies in the specialized nature of the financial media. Major daily newspapers have business sections that carry financial items of local, regional, or national interest. Weekly newspapers generally carry items of local interest. The business press includes *The Wall Street Journal, Forbes, Barron's, Business Week, Fortune* and other publications serving national audiences, as well as various local business-oriented publications (like the *Business Chronicle* in Houston, Atlanta, Los Angeles, San Francisco, and other cities). These are primary outlets for financial news, but they are deluged with information, so it is very important not to clutter channels of communication with trivia or fluff. Do not overlook the financial columnists. The Dan Dorfmans and Louis Rukeysers of this country carry great weight, and can offer unique perspectives on particular companies. Trade magazines, which are usually devoted to particular industries, occupations, or professions are also important outlets. They may reach such likely prospects as suppliers and producers. Television and radio are limited but growing outlets for financial news. Certain programs (and even entire stations in major cities) are devoted specifically to business, however. Public Broadcasting's *Wall Street Week,* Cable News Network's financial programs, and Associated Press Radio's *Business Barometer* are examples of such programs. News operations on network or major-market local levels generally should be approached only if the information has news value transcending the business community and affecting the community at large. Finally, specialized financial media are extremely interested in company news. Market newsletters (often published by brokerage firms), investment advisory services, and statistical services (like Standard and Poor's, Value Line, or Moody's) often carry the greatest weight with potential investors.

**COMMUNICATION STRATEGY IN FINANCIAL RELATIONS**

Strategies for communicating financial information, like those for implementing other plans (see Chapter 7) must grow out of management's long-term view of the corporation. Strategy must be developed on the basis of company goals (where you are trying to go) and perceptions of the company by relevant publics (where you are now). Communication strategy is a plan for getting from where you are to where you want to be. The methods available to use in implementing strategy include personal meetings, financial literature (correspondence, quarterly and annual reports, dividend enclosures), financial news releases, and annual meetings. Whatever your current status or ultimate objectives, your financial relations communication strategy must be characterized by responsiveness, regularity and openness. Communication should never be evasive and must include bad news as well as good. Financial openness means "willingness to communicate honestly and forthrightly with its employees and external constituencies regarding economic matters."[12] Credibility is the key to a strong financial relations program.

**ANNUAL MEETINGS**

Annual meetings are a kind of mandated ritual in which the actual owners of a business have an opportunity to consider and vote on the effectiveness of management. In theory, stockholders possess the power to do what they please (within the law) with their company. In practice, issues are rarely discussed and even more rarely voted on, because management collects proxies in advance in support of its positions, appointments, and decisions.

Views on the annual meeting ritual are widely divergent. "At one end of the spectrum are those who regard the annual meeting as a hallmark of corporate democracy and an expression of our free enterprise system," says Arthur Roalman. "At the other are those who look upon the function as a meaningless corporate exercise."[13] The view taken by management will influence the nature of a given corporation's annual meeting. Whatever the case, the annual meeting presents certain opportunities and entails genuine risks. To take advantage of the opportunities and to avoid the potential pitfalls, careful planning and orchestration are essential.

The annual meeting should attract, inform, and involve the audience of stockholders. It enables corporate management to reach all stockholders through pre- and postmeeting communication. It provides a showcase and a focus for corporate publicity. It permits personal contact between executives and stockholders through which actions can be explained, accomplishments recognized and feedback offered. It is a marketing tool when products are displayed in their best light. It is a safety valve by which stockholders can let off steam. But the democratic nature of the meeting makes the company vulnerable. There is the possibility of organized dissent, sometimes from stockholders who have bought a few shares of stock specifically to gain this platform. They may intervene or disrupt by confronting management with embarrassing questions, and draw the attention of the news media to their actions.

J. P. Stevens and Company, the controversial textile giant which has been fighting unionization for twenty years, was faced with the possibility of confrontation in its 1980 annual meeting. A proposal on the agenda made by thirteen Catholic organizations owning company stock sought establishment of a review committee to advise on management/employee relations. The union was also staging a countermeeting to make public their grievances against the company. Media attention was focused on the potential conflict. Management, in this case, stuck by its guns and explained its position once again. The proposal was defeated. The union's effort drew less than 100 to the meeting's South Carolina site.

Deloitte, Haskins and Sells, one of the "Big Eight" among accounting firms, has published a guide for corporate managers on how to cope with issues that may arise at corporate annual meetings. Among other issues, they cover political stability of nations where companies have foreign operations; impacts of inflation, energy costs, and governmental actions; employee representation in corporate decision making; political action committees; and environmental compliance.

Commenting on J. P. Stevens's annual meeting, *Atlanta Journal* business editor Tom Walker observed tongue-in-cheek that corporations should retain consulting sociologists, "especially during the annual meeting season when managements are forced to line up before their shareholders and give an account of themselves."[14] Financial public relations actually plays the role that Walker would give to sociologists. By anticipating the concerns, issues, and even the mood of stockholders—based on continuous interaction—financial public relations should be able to prepare management for most situations that could arise. With careful planning, the positive potentials of the annual meeting may even be realized.

**ANNUAL REPORTS**     American companies spend around $150,000,000 per year on annual reports. Gulf and Western spent $5 million to publish its entire 1978 report into the February 5, 1979, issue of *Time.* Emhart Corporation tried a video version of its 1979 annual report and played it on cable TV in eight states. H. J. Heinz Company, the food processing giant, published its 1979 report in five languages for use as a worldwide marketing tool. The pharmaceutical company Pfizer, Inc. sends copies of its annual report to every physician in the United States. Oscar Beveridge calls the annual report "unquestionably the single most important public document issued by a publicly-held corporation." [15] Writing in *Fortune,* Herbert Meyer states: "Out of all the documents published by a Fortune 500 corporation, none involves so much fussing, so much anguish—and often so much pride of authorship—as the annual report to shareholders." [16] In short, the annual report is the keystone of a company's financial relations program.

The Borden Company published the first corporate annual report in this country in 1854. It was a simple document, but its appearance was shocking to corporate leaders, who considered stockholders among those covered by the statement "the public be damned." By 1899, the New York Stock Exchange required listed companies to publish at least once a year "a properly detailed statement of its income and expenditures . . . and also a balance sheet, giving a detailed and accurate statement of the condition of the company at the close of its last fiscal year."

In 1903, United States Steel published what could be considered the first "modern" annual report. Its sixty pages included thirty-six pages of facts and figures and twenty-two pages of photographs. By the mid-1950s the typical annual report was a slick, magazine-style publication. In 1964 Litton Industries went so far as to commission Andrew Wyeth to produce a painting for the cover of its report. What were once management scorecards have become management showcases.

**The Purpose of**     Fundamentally, the annual report fulfills a company's legal requirements of
**Annual Reports**     reporting to stockholders. As such, it becomes the primary source of information about the company for current and potential stockholders, providing comprehensive information on the condition of the company and its progress (or lack thereof) during the previous year.

Some companies leave it at that. But nearly all large companies carry their annual reports considerably further, treating the report as an opportunity to reinforce their credibility, to establish their distinct identity, and to build investor confidence, support, and allegiance. In this sense, the annual report becomes the company's calling card, a summary of what the company does and what it stands for. By accident or by design, the report usually conveys much about the personality and quality of the corporation's management.

Some companies get further service from their annual reports by using them for marketing, public relations, employee recruitment and orientation, an informational resource for financial advisors, a "backgrounder" for business editors, even an educational tool for teachers, librarians, and students. General Motors uses its report to advertise its products. Goodyear Tire and Rubber puts out a special edition for classroom use. Increasing numbers of companies produce special editions of the annual report for employees to gain their loyalty and support, build morale by stressing their contribution, and improve their understanding of company operations.

Another purpose of the report for some companies is to serve as an accounting of activities and social responsibility or political positions. Paine Webber recently devoted part of its report to an essay extolling the virtues of economic growth and warning of the dangers of increased taxation. Columnist James J. Kilpatrick calls for much broader efforts of this nature:

> I have complained before, and will keep on complaining, about annual reports and other messages to stockholders. The annual reports that flow across my desk are often beautiful specimens of the graphic designer at work. There are four-color photos, pie charts that glitter like Keno wheels, the last word in typography. But only a handful of top executives seize the opportunity to mobilize a constituency of stockholders, who presumably have some political clout, in support of the company's political positions. I am mystified by this failing.  .   .[17]

Some disapprove of the many faces of the annual report. James H. Dowling, for instance, maintains that annual reports have only one purpose: to help investors decide whether to become or remain stockholders in a company.[18] Another dissenter is former SEC chairman Harold M. Williams, who claims that annual reports "often appear to reflect the results of a conflict between the desire to create a promotional document and the need to provide full and fair disclosure."

Herbert Meyer takes the opposite view:

> What some people see as the great weakness of annual reports—their use as a soapbox to sell products, build managerial egos, and blast off against government regulations—is in a very real sense their considerable strength. Annual reports have become wonderfully clear windows into the personalities of corporations and the executives who manage them.[19]

While accountants may decry verbal and pictorial embellishment of their ciphers, the opportunity to communicate presented by annual reports is too important to pass up. Moreover, with the costs of preparation and distribution at over $2.00 per copy, financial considerations practically demand that these publications be put to double duty. There is at present no likelihood that annual reports will return to the minimum level of information required by the government.

**Planning and Producing the Annual Report**

Preparing the annual report is an elaborate undertaking requiring creativity and coordination. It is a product of the joint efforts of people specializing in public relations, financial relations, accounting, law, photography, graphic design, and general management. Aspects of the report may require consultation and input from marketing, personnel, research and development, public affairs or others. Although public relations may have overall responsibility for creating, producing, and distributing the annual report, it is necessarily a corporate effort.

The first step in the process of planning and producing the annual report is to establish its objectives. What message should the document communicate? The objectives should be defined as specifically as possible. Once these are chosen, the means of achieving them must be selected. Often a theme is established. Products, employees, social responsibility, foreign operations, and new facilities are examples of the kinds of themes that can be used to achieve the report's objectives.

The third step in planning and production is the establishment of a schedule and budget. Budgets for annual reports vary tremendously and depend largely on corporate means and desires. At least three months should be allowed for gathering material and information for the report, writing the copy, graphic designing, collecting photos, and obtaining financial statements. Corporate attorneys and management must approve the copy. Adequate time for printing and distribution must be allowed.

Much of the effort devoted to annual reports is aimed at producing a document that attracts readers. F. C. Foy explains: "The annual report needs more than figures and tables, or even graphs, charts, or pictures. It needs candid, specific, readable statements of objectives, of difficulties and problems and how they are being attacked, of new products or services, and of how management envisions the future of the business." [20] Tulsa's Parker Drilling Company was candid, specific, and readable in its annual report. In bright red letters the report's front cover read: "The first half of 1980 was lousy.    .  .  ." Those who read the report found that the second half of the year was much better. Good design and clear writing contribute greatly to the attractiveness and readability of the publication.

The planners and producers of the annual report must be ever mindful of the needs of its potential audience. It is well to remember, however, that annual reports reach a variety of audiences. Primary audiences, of course, are investors and the investment community. Generally speaking, the investing community is most interested in the auditor's report, financial highlights, changes in financial position, debt and other data. Even among investors, however, desires for information differ. Potential and current employees also constitute an audience, but they maybe more interested in the president's letter or the graphic presentation.

How can various audiences be served by one document? Some companies, as we have noted, produce special editions for employees or students because they feel a single report cannot serve their needs. Other companies, however, recognize that annual reports should not be designed to be read from cover to cover. Instead, these companies' reports present information in "layers" so that various readers can take what they want. The layers consist of 1) cover, pictures and captions; 2) the president's letter and financial highlights; and 3) detailed information about operations and financial developments, including the footnotes. In this way, the reader can decide just how deep he or she wants to go.

**Contents of the Annual Report**

The typical annual report consists of a cover; president's letter; financial and nonfinancial highlights; balance sheet and income statement; description of the business (products and services); names and titles of corporate officers; names and affiliations of outside directors; location of plants, offices and representatives; address and telephone number of corporate headquarters; and reference to stock exchanges on which company stock is traded. The report may also include the company's history (particularly in anniversary issues), discussion of company policies, request for support of a corporate stance on a political issue, results of stockholder survey, and other reports or features.

Photographs, graphic art, and color are increasingly important in annual reports. Award-winning Michael Watras, president of Corporate Graphics and producer of annual reports for companies such as H. J. Heinz and Chase Manhattan Bank, explains, "Annual reports are more visual today than they were a few years ago. We're using larger pictures and more of them, and much more four-color.   .   .   . Photographs are more likely to be tied into an overall theme."[21]

Annual reports should always put corporate earnings in perspective, and spell out prospects for the next year. It should answer these questions:

What is the major thrust of our company?
Where do we excel?
What are our weaknesses?
Why has the company performed as it has?
What are we doing about the future?

Financial highlights are a well-read aspect of annual reports. They generally include figures representing net sales, earnings before taxes, earnings after taxes, net earnings per common share, dividends per common share, stockholders' equity per common share, net working capital, ratio of current assets to current liabilities, number of common shares outstanding, and number of common stockholders. Some highlights also include profit margin, percent return on stockholders' equity, long-term debt, and number of employees. Report designers are concerned not just with the numbers, but how they look. Financial data is now more often integrated into the entire report and presented in interesting or unusual ways.

Herbert Rosenthal and Frank Pagani list eight elements of what they call "big league annual reports:"[22]

1. A meaningful or provocative pictorial cover
2. A well-designed format
3. Complete and understandable graphics
4. Unstilted photographs and art work
5. Comprehensive text
6. Comparative figures
7. Tasteful presentation of products
8. Stylish printing

**EVALUATION OF FINANCIAL RELATIONS**

The annual report is out. The annual meeting is over. Good communication links are established with financial analysts and editors. Stockholder correspondence is operating smoothly. But how can you evaluate your efforts?

Good financial relations usually result in increased proxy response, reduction of stock turnover, better attendance at stockholder meetings, appropriate price-to-earnings ratios, and greater ease in selling new stock issues.

And if you do not achieve this kind of success, you can always blame the economy.

---

**CASE STUDY: BALL CORPORATION**

**By Charlotte R. Hatfield**
**Ball State University, Muncie, Indiana**

---

Stability certainly wasn't the problem: Ball Corporation had been successful for almost 100 years before its shares began trading on the New York Stock Exchange in 1973. That year company executives traveled the big-city analyst-house circuit telling their story, but the stock did not sell as the company hoped it would.

In examining the situation, company officials recognizezd two immediate problems affecting the sale of public shares. First, sixty percent of the company stock was still in the hands of the Ball family or corporate officers. Over 900,000 shares were available for outside purchase, too small to be attractive to large or institutional investors who routinely purchase large blocks of stock.

The second problem was the perception of the company by financial professionals. Most were familiar with Ball Corp. as the producers of Ball canning jars, an American tradition ranking near baseball and apple pie, but were not aware of the corporation's international involvement in space exploration and defense contracting; glass and metal container manufacture for the food and brewing industries; plastics products for electronics, computers, medical uses; zinc, lead, and chemical products; or the production of computer-related, irrigation, and petroleum equipment.

For a century the company had been growing and diversifying but had not felt it necessary to publicize that information. Now the need was clear—if its stock was to sell, the company had to tell its story.

Utilizing the U.S. Census Report, demographics studies, population and income studies, and New York Stock Exchange shareholder surveys, Ball determined its most logical shareholder to be the middle-class, age 40–70 years, rural or suburban-oriented American who knows of the canning jar's quality and is interested in investing money into a company with Ball's tradition and stability. Ball decided the best way to reach these individuals was through stockbrokers, the people directly in contact with potential shareholders.

The effort to reach brokers began in 1977 and is built around face-to-face meetings. The program reached forty-eight cities and approximately 2000 brokers the first year. Brokers or "registered representatives" in a target city receive an invitation to attend a breakfast, lunch, or cocktail hour four weeks before the scheduled meeting time. Before the day of the meeting, Ball Corporation employees contact each individual again by mail, including in the mailing a copy of the book *A Collector's Guide to Ball Jars,* and later by telephone if a response to the invitation had not been received.

The day of the meeting the director of public relations and the treasurer of Ball Corp. are on hand to greet the brokers and conduct the program. The usual format includes general remarks about the history and growth of the company and a ten-minute film concentrating on the corporation's major markets followed by a short presentation exploring financial data and a question and answer session for the brokers. The focus of the message is on the selling points of the company: ideas the brokers can use to sell their customers on Ball stock.

In addition to the printed information given to the brokers at the meeting, each is presented with a special-edition pint Ball canning jar embossed with the Ball signature on one side and the bull and bear symbols of the stock exchange on the other. Sealed inside the jar is the business card of Ball's director of public relations.

In the six years the investor relations program has been in existence, over 200 meetings have been held with an average of 35–40 brokers attending each meeting.

Although direct attribution of stock sale is difficult to make, Ball Corp. found that in the first year of the effort 2000 new investors joined Ball's shareholder ranks, approximately one for each broker attending the meetings that year. In the ensuing years, stock sales have continued to attract new investors, guaranteeing a long-term commitment to the program.

**Questions**
1. Had the company been delinquent in its public relations efforts prior to 1973? What type of an external communications effort might have eased the problems encountered between 1973 and 1977?

2. What considerations may affect the format and timing of the meetings? Also discuss the location for the meeting, the food and beverage choices, and other details which would affect the brokers' reactions to the meeting/ message.

3. Prepare a timetable for a Ball Corporation investor relations meeting. The timetable should begin eight to twelve weeks before the meeting and should include details on acquiring mailing lists, meeting formats, facilities contacts, mailings to brokers, materials to be used at the meeting, travel plans for Ball executives, and other appropriate information.

**NOTES**  [1] Richard E. Cheney, "Catch 23 for Regulated Companies" in Hill and Knowlton Executives, *Critical Issues in Public Relations* (Englewood Cliffs, N.J.: Prentice-Hall, 1975), p. 29.

[2] Arthur R. Roalman (ed.), *Investor Relations Handbook* (New York: AMACOM, 1974), p. iii.

[3] Ibid., p. 31.

[4] NYSE Company Manual, August 1, 1977.

[5] Henry Rockwell, "A Press Release Goes to Court," *Public Relations Journal* (October 1968).

[6] G. Christman Hill, "Financial Public Relations Men Are Warned They're Liable for Clients' Puffery," *Wall Street Journal,* 16 March 1972, p. 30.

[7] Harrison T. Beardsley, "Problem Solving In Corporate Financial Relations," *Public Relations Journal* (April 1978): 23.

[8] Oscar M. Beveridge, *Financial Public Relations* (New York: McGraw-Hill, 1963), p. 68.

[9] Louis Rukeyser, *Atlanta Journal,* 28 February 1980, pp. 12–13.

[10] Roalman, *Investor Relations Handbook,* p. 190.

[11] Stan Sauerhaft, "Won't Anybody Listen?" in Hill and Knowlton Executives, *Critical Issues,* p. 37.

[12] Frederick D. Sturdivant, *Business and Society: A Managerial Approach* (Homewood, Ill.: Irwin, 1977), p. 358.

[13] Roalman, *Investor Relations Handbook,* p. 43.

[14] Tom Walker, "J. P. Stevens Fights Catholics' Proposal," *Atlanta Journal and Constitution,* 2 March 1980, p. 10.

[15] Beveridge, *Financial Public Relations,* p. 137.

[16] Herbert E. Meyer, "Annual Reports Get An Editor in Washington," *Fortune,* 7 May 1979, p. 219.

[17] James J. Kilpatrick, "A Short Course in Media Relations," *Nation's Business,* June 1979, pp. 17–18.

[18] James H. Dowling, "Main Job of the Annual Report: Wooing Investors." *Dunn's Review,* September 1978, p. 127.

[19] Meyer, "Annual Reports Get Editor," p. 222.

[20] F. C. Foy, "Annual Reports Don't Have To Be Dull," *Harvard Business Review* 51 (January–February 1973): 49–58.

[21] "Annual Reports Help Sell Organizations," *IABC News,* December, 1981, pp. 1, 11.

[22] Herbert C. Rosenthal and Frank Pagani, "Rating Your Annual Report," *Public Relations Journal* (August 1978): 12.

NISSEN

# SECTION VI  PUBLIC RELATIONS: CRITICAL ISSUES

Public relations practitioners in all sorts of organizations are called upon to deal with a baffling variety of issues and problems. Indeed, as the concept of public relations has expanded it has increasingly included the notion of responsiveness to the broad concerns of organizational publics.

Since the late 1940s the phrase "social responsibility" increasingly has become a part of the vocabularies of organizational managers and public relations practitioners. Questions of accountability and legitimacy have become constant concerns of administrators of profit and non-profit organizations. To be considered socially responsible, accountable, and legitimate in modern society, organizations must deal with matters other than their central mission. Businesses have been forced to deal with matters other than profits, schools address issues that seem to be far removed from education, hospitals involve themselves with situations apparently unrelated to health care, because various crucial constituencies demand it. Of course, public relations practitioners often provide links between organizations and their constituencies, and thus find themselves squarely in the middle of organizational efforts toward social responsiveness.

In this section we first look at the concept of social responsibility to better understand its impact on contemporary public relations practitioners and organizational management. Then we discuss some of the specific issues arising from the general concept of social responsibility in which public relations practitioners have been actively involved. These issues include environmentalism, consumerism, urban problems, and international public relations.

# CHAPTER 18  THE CONCEPT OF SOCIAL RESPONSIBILITY

**PREVIEW**    Public relations can be defined as those aspects of our personal and corporate behavior that have a social rather than purely private and personal significance.

The theory of profit maximization argues that individuals can best serve society by pursuing their own self-interest.

The idea of trustee management maintains that the management of an organization must establish a balance in decision making between the various publics served by the organization.

The concept of enlightened self-interest allows management to make decisions in the interest of society that may have little or no obvious relationship to profit.

Public relations must function as a two-way channel of communication between an organization and its publics if it is to be socially responsible.

Recent research indicates that the public feels that appropriate areas for the expression of organizations' social responsibilities include insuring quality products and services, fighting inflation, promoting minority hiring, and improving human resources on the job.

Public relations practitioners must be able to function as sensors of social change, policy makers, communicators of corporate policies both internally and externally, and internal monitors of social responsibility.

Since its inception, public relations has been concerned with issues involving the social responsibilities of business and other organizations. As we discussed in Chapter 2, the practice of public relations can trace its beginnings to pressures for business organizations to be more responsible to the society they serve. At its best the response of public relations to these demands has been to make corporate management more keenly aware of the needs of society and inform the publics involved about management's response to their needs. At its worst the role of public relations has been to help management cover up, confound, and avoid the critical issues of our society.

Edward L. Bernays, an early public relations practitioner, was one of the first to point out that the function of public relations is to establish some common ground between the organization or individual represented and society.[1] Harwood Childs, in defining public relations, tied the practice tightly to the exercise of social responsibility:

Public relations may be defined as those aspects of our
personal and corporate behavior which have a social
rather than a purely private and personal significance
.   .   . Public relations as such, is not the presentation of
a point of view, not the art of tempering mental attitudes,
nor the development of cordial and profitable relations
.   .   . It is simply a name for activities which have a
social significance.[2]

Although it is easy to see that the practice of public relations is directly involved with the concept of organizational social responsibility, that concept is not easy to define. Social responsibility pertains to all organizations; because they do not pursue profit, the activities of public institutions are erroneously assumed to be consistent with the public interest. Considering the pollution flowing from certain municipal water systems, racial or sexual discrimination in government bureaus, or public housing authorities that operate as little more than slumlords, however, it is clear that social responsibility is a concept relevant to all organizations. The material in this chapter can be applied to all types of organizations whether or not they make a profit. It is more difficult to isolate the nature of social responsibility. What is considered to be a socially responsible activity by some is labeled poor management practice by others. Even among those who agree that business has a social responsibility, the concept is an evolving one that eludes any fixed definition.

In this chapter we shall attempt to trace the evolution of the concept of social responsibility in business and define its relationship to public relations. We have already discussed the interdependence of institutions in our society and the role of public relations in spanning the boundaries between them (Chapter 3). Now our focus will be on the relationship between the organization and its various publics, both internal and external. At the center of this relationship is the two-way communication function of the public relations practice.

## DEVELOPMENT OF THE CONCEPT
### Profit Maximization

The guiding principle of American business from its inception has been the belief that the primary rightful objective of every firm is to maximize profits. This principle is deeply rooted in the concept of free enterprise upon which the economic system of this country is based. Profit maximization has been closely associated with the ideas of rugged individualism which have shaped western society. In the late eighteenth century Adam Smith suggested that social responsibility was a natural effect of profit maximization.

**Every individual is continually exerting himself to find out the most advantageous employment for whatever capital he can command. It is his own advantage, indeed, and not that of the society, which he has in view. But the study of his own advantage, naturally, or rather necessarily, leads him to prefer that employment which is most advantageous to the society . . .**

**As every individual, therefore, endeavours as much as he can both to employ his capital in the support of domestic industry, and so to direct that industry that its produce may be of the greatest value, every individual necessarily labours to render the annual revenue of the society as great as he can. He generally, indeed, neither intends to promote the public interest, nor knows how much he is promoting his own security; and by directing that industry in such a manner as its produce may be of the greatest value, he intends only his own gain, and he is in this, as in many other cases, led by an invisible hand to promote an end which was no part of his intention. Nor is it always the worse for the society that it was no part of it. By pursuing his own interest he frequently promotes that of the society more effectually than when he really intends to promote it. I have never known much good done by those who affected to trade for the public good. It is an affection, indeed, not very common among merchants, and very few words need be employed in dissuading them from it.**[3]

Adam Smith's proposal that individuals could serve society best by pursuing their own self-interest has been a guiding philosophy for American business. While other perspectives have developed since 1776, the view that business serves society by doing what it does best (making profits for its shareholders) is still a popular notion.

### Trustee Management

Another point of view regarding the social responsibility of business was advanced during the 1930s. At that point in the development of western industrialization, individual ownership of business was being replaced by group ownership following the crash of 1929. Managers of corporations, even those in the highest offices, were employees rather than entrepreneurs. Ownership of these large organizations was vested in numerous shareholders, most of whom had never even seen the company offices. As a result of this diffusion of ownership, many observers began to point out the changed role of management from owner to trustee. Under trustee management, the top executives of a corporation play the role of mediator between various points of view. Management must maintain a balance in its decision making between the interests of the various publics served by a company (stockholders, employees, customers, suppliers, and the general public). This philosophy of social responsibility maintains that business must balance the goals of its owners (stockholders) against those of several other groups in society which affect and are affected by the organization. Decision makers might therefore elect to sacrifice some profits to meet the needs of another public directly related to the organization. Thus, while short-range profits might be lower, the belief is that long-range profits will be increased.

The same period of time that produced the trustee management philosophy also saw the maturation of public relations practice. The period betwen the end of World War I and the start of World War II saw the spread of public relations counselors in corporations and the creation of many new public relations firms. The careers of many of the pioneers of public relations span this period: Ivy Lee, George Creel, Carl Byoir, Edward L. Bernays, John W. Hill, and Don Knowlton.[4] In addition, scholarly interest in areas related to public relations began to take shape. University courses in public relations were established, and several books were published in the field.

It is no accident that the practice of public relations developed and matured as new concepts about the social responsibility of business were taking shape. As trustee managers began to realize the nature of their tasks and feel the pressures exerted by the various publics related to their organizations, they could no longer concern themselves with profit alone. Other issues which fell outside the boundaries of profit and loss statements had to be considered. These considerations required new managerial skills that had not been necessary before. To supply these skills the top management of many corporations began to employ public relations professionals either as consultants or managers.[5] As we discussed in Chapter 2, one such professional was Arthur W. Page, former vice-president of AT&T, who said: "All business in a democratic country begins with public permission and exists by public approval."[6]

**Enlightened Self-Interest**    With the social unrest of the 1960s a new philosophy of social responsibility for business began to develop. It was felt by some managers that economic success should not take priority over the social and physical environment of the society in which an organization exists. This philosophy, often described as enlightened self-interest, maintains that major business actions can be undertaken that do not have any direct relationship to profit. Therefore, management may decide to "invest" the resources of the organization in social programs, charities, environmental protection, and other activities that do not directly increase and may even reduce profits.[7]

Enlightened self-interest differs from the philosophy of trustee management in that it permits decisions that lack obvious relationship to either long-

or short-range profit. Although profit may not be the primary consideration, actions taken are believed to be in the ultimate best interests of the firm. Therefore, an organization that contributes to colleges and universities may not be able to quantify its investment in terms of net profit. But, to the extent that the organization draws its future managerial and technical talent from college-educated people, it will ultimately benefit. Likewise, the environmental and social improvements funded by a corporation may result in a better climate for its business activities. Certainly publicized social actions by an organization can enhance its public image and result in many benefits that are difficult to measure adequately. Actions and policies calculated to reap this type of nonquantifiable benefit for organizations have always been the forte of public relations professionals.

As we consider the evolution of these three distinctly different schools of thought concerning the social responsibility of business, it is useful to study the parallel evolution of public relations practice. Under a profit maximization system of management, the role of public relations is one of pacification and sometimes obfuscation. If an organization's primary operating philosophy does not recognize any responsibility other than the enrichment of its shareholders, it will be in constant need of press agents who can manage the inquiries of media representatives and create volumes of positive publicity to offset the negative opinions stimulated by unresponsive management. In this role the public relations practitioner is an employee hired to aid management in the implementation of its policies. Public relations considerations are not part of the information processed to reach managerial decisions. Instead, public relations practitioners are informed of decisions and instructed to release them in the most positive context possible. Under profit maximization, public relations functions to secure the acceptance of managerial decisions but has no role in making them.

The practice of trusteeship management brings the public relations practitioner into a legitimate managerial role. This philosophy of social responsibility recognized the influence of groups other than the immediate consumer on the short- and long-term profits of the organization. Public relations information becomes an important input into the decision making process. Public relations experts are placed in senior managerial roles where their knowledge of public opinion and communication can be used in the planning process to avoid actions which result in negative opinion. Trusteeship management is still concerned with profit, but recognizes the need to balance long- and short-term gains. The public relations manager is an important decision maker in this process.

Under the philosophy of enlightened self-interest, public relations practitioners often assume more complex roles. Managers with public relations expertise are often called upon to represent the interests of various publics inside corporate decision making circles. Frequently, public relations practitioners assume the role of advocate or ombudsman on behalf of consumers, minorities, environmentalists or other publics. In this role the public relations practitioner is asked to be completely familiar with the needs and views of these publics and press their cause within the organization structure. This type of internal advocacy may or may not have an obvious link with the company's profit situation. It is the philosophy of management, however, that such constant attention to social problems will lead to responsible policies and actions that will ultimately benefit the organization and society even if profits are reduced. Within organizations that operate under the philosophy of enlightened self-interest, the responsibility for public relations expertise is spread to most, if not all, top managers. Several specialized departments, such as consumer affairs and community relations, may be established to deal with those publics which the organization views as most critical.

## THE CURRENT STATE OF SOCIAL RESPONSIBILITY

Although the three philosophies of social responsibility discussed here evolved in a chronological sequence, all exist today. In fact, a single organization could conceivably operate under all three philosophies. Extremely large, diversified corporations may employ profit maximization in one division or area while adopting trusteeship management and enlightened self-interest in other segments of the business. Even within the same division or unit, management may shift from the implementation of one view to another depending upon the situation. Most organizations, however, do adopt an overall approach to social responsibility that can be categorized under one of these three headings. Public relations practitioners must be able to discern this governing philosophy, whether it is the stated one or not, in order to determine their role in the organization.

### The Business of Business

Although it is the oldest concept of social responsibility, the profit maximization view is still a popular one. Those who believe that the "business of business is business" are supported by some highly persuasive arguments from very different points of view.

Noted economist Milton Friedman argues that managers are employees of the owners (that is, stockholders) of corporations and have no right to spend resources on projects that do not have the potential to increase profits. The only responsibility corporate executives have, according to Friedman, is to conduct the business in accordance with the desires of its owners, and that generally means to make as much money as possible. He believes that to ask an executive to restrict the price increases of his organization in an effort to curtail inflation is not in the best interest of the owners. The same holds true for programs such as those designed to hire and train the unemployed. Friedman believes that those who recommend a responsibility for business in the promotion of socially desirable outcomes are advocating socialism.[8] The only social responsibility of business is:

. . . to use its resources and engage in activities designed to increase its **profits so long as it stays within the rules of the game, which is to say, engages in open and free competition, without deception or fraud . . . Few trends could so thoroughly undermine the very foundations of our free society as the acceptance by corporate officials of a social responsibility other than to make as much money for their stockholders as possible.**[9]

Others argue from a very different point of view that business not only does not have a responsibility to become socially involved, but that society must prevent it from doing so. Theodore Levitt is among those who are afraid that the significant involvement of business leaders in matters of social significance will lead to the domination of our values by those of big business. Levitt acknowledges the need for action to solve society's problems:

But at the rate we are going, there is more than a contingent probability that, with all its resounding good intentions, business statesmanship may create the corporate equivalent of the unitary state. Its proliferating employee welfare programs, its serpentine involvement in community, government, charitable, and educational affairs, its prodigious currying of political and public favor through hundreds of peripheral preoccupations, all these well-intended but insidious contrivances are greasing the rails for our collective descent into a social order that would be as repugnant to the corporations themselves as to their critics. The danger is that all these things will turn the corporation into a twentieth-century equivalent of the medieval Church. The corporation would eventually invest itself with all-embracing duties, obligations, and finally powers—ministering to the whole man and molding him and society in the image of the corporation's narrow ambitions and its essentially unsocial needs.[10]

**What is Business?**   The important question to many observers is simply this: what is the business of business? Critics of the notion of social responsibility tell us that corporations must stick to business and not become involved in affairs that do not concern their objectives (profit). As we have already discussed, however, many social issues do affect either the short- or long-range profits of a company. Frequently it is difficult to know how significant such effects will be at least until after they have occurred. For this reason a number of informed observers and executives have argued that business must assume certain responsibilities as a corporate citizen in society which may not have direct relationship to profit. According to John W. Hill, the late chairman of Hill and Knowlton, "Corporate enterprise operates under franchise from public opinion, and that franchise can be modified or withdrawn by the people's representatives in government at any time they so wish."[11]

The Committee for Economic Development, an organization of prominent business leaders, concluded that ".   .   . it is in the enlightened self-interest of corporations to promote the public welfare in a positive way."[12] In support of this statement, they argued that:

there is broad recognition today that corporate self-interest is inexorably involved in the well-being of the society of which business is an integral part, and from which it draws the basic requirements needed for it to function at all—capital, labor, customers. There is increasing understanding that the corporation is dependent on the goodwill of society, which can sustain or impair its existence through public pressures on government. And it has become clear that the essential resources and goodwill of society are not naturally forthcoming to corporations whenever needed, but must be worked for and developed .   .   .[13]

While pointing to the fact that society expects business to become involved in more than its own profit-making activities, the CED makes it clear that private corporations cannot be expected to solve all the problems of society. Those who manage socially responsible businesses must strike a balance between profit and responsibility—"no company of any size can willingly incur costs that would jeopardize its competitive position and threaten its survival." [14]

Steiner sums up the difference between those who feel business must concern itself only with profits and those who argue for social responsibility as follows: "The older [profit maximization] was often irresponsible self-interest; the newer is enlightened in that it reaches out to benefit society while at the same time favoring the company. The new self-interested businessman sees that justice, due process, and concern for employees can harmonize with the company's best interests." [15]

Many of the responses of business to the needs and expectations of society have been listed in Exhibit 18-1. This extensive list provided by the CED in its 1971 report could be updated with the addition of categories such as product safety, advertising, consumer affairs, and community affairs. While the response of business to social problems has been significant and comprehensive, the results have not always been acceptable to either side. There is a need for more careful study of the proper role of business in solving society's problems in the wake of what were often massive but carelessly planned programs in the 1960s and '70s.

---

**Exhibit 18-1
Ways in Which
Business Has Tried
to Meet its Social
Responsibility**

**Economic Growth and Efficiency**

Increasing productivity in the private sector of the economy

Improving the innovativeness and performance of business management

Enhancing competition

Cooperating with the government in developing more effective measures to control inflation and achieve high levels of employment

Supporting fiscal and monetary policies for steady economic growth

Helping with the post-Vietnam conversion of the economy

**Education**

Direct financial aid to schools, including scholarships, grants, and tuition refunds

Support for increases in school budgets

Donation of equipment and skilled personnel

Assistance in curriculum development

Aid in counseling and remedial education

Establishment of new schools, running schools and school systems

Assistance in the management and financing of colleges

**Employment and Training**

Active recruitment of the disadvantaged

Special functional training, remedial education, and counseling

Provision of day-care centers for children of working parents

Improvement of work/career opportunities

Retraining of workers affected by automation or other causes of joblessness

Establishment of company programs to remove the hazards of old age and sickness

Supporting where needed and appropriate the extension of government
accident, unemployment, health and retirement systems

### Civil Rights and Equal Opportunity

Ensuring employment and advancement opportunities for minorities
Facilitating equality of results by continued training and other special
programs
Supporting and aiding the improvement of black educational facilities, and
special programs for blacks and other minorities in integrated institutions
Encouraging adoption of open-housing ordinances
Building plants and sales offices in the ghettos
Providing financing and managerial assistance to minority enterprises and
participating with minorities in joint ventures

### Urban Renewal and Development

Leadership and financial support for city and regional planning and
development
Building or improving low-income housing
Building shopping centers, new communities, new cities
Improving transportation systems

### Pollution Abatement

Installation of modern equipment
Engineering new facilities for minimum environmental effects
Research and technological development
Cooperating with municipalities in joint treatment facilities
Cooperating with local, state, regional, and federal agencies in developing
improved systems of environmental management
Developing more effective programs for recycling and reusing disposable
materials

### Conservation and Recreation

Augmenting the supply of replenishable resources, such as trees, with more
productive species
Preserving animal life and the ecology of forests and comparable areas
Providing recreational and aesthetic facilities for public use
Restoring aesthetically depleted properties such as strip mines
Improving the yield of scarce materials and recycling to conserve the supply

### Culture and the Arts

Direct financial support to art institutions and the performing arts
Development of indirect support as a business expense through gifts in kind,
sponsoring artistic talent, and advertising
Participation on boards to give advice on legal, labor, and financial
management problems
Helping secure government financial support for local or state arts councils
and the National Endowment for the Arts

### Medical Care

Helping plan community health activities
Designing and operating low-cost medical-care programs
Designing and running new hospitals, clinics, and extended-care facilities

Improving the administration and effectiveness of medical care
Developing better systems for medical education, nurses' training
Developing and supporting a better national system of health care

**Government**
Helping improve management performance at all levels of government
Supporting adequate compensation and development programs for
     government executives and employees
Working for the modernization of the nation's governmental structure
Facilitating the reorganization of government to improve its responsiveness
     and performance
Advocating and supporting reforms in the election system and the legislative
     process
Designing programs to enhance the effectiveness of the civil services
Promoting reforms in the public welfare system, law enforcement, and other
     major governmental operations

Social Responsibilities of Business Corporations, New York: Committee for Economic
Development, 1971, pp. 31–40. Reprinted by permission.

**SOCIAL RESPONSIBILITY: A PUBLIC RELATIONS ANALYSIS**

As the political and social turmoil of the mid-'60s and early '70s began to calm, business executives and other analysts were taking a fresh look at the concept of social responsibility and the specific ways it had been practiced. It was clear that while much had been accomplished, a great deal of waste had also occurred. Management must remember that profit and positive cash flow are still essential considerations. If an organization assumes social costs that are beyond its reach, the results can be just as devastating as those associated with growth that is too rapid. An example is the $40 million pretax loss suffered by Boise Cascade as a result of promoting a minority company in the heavy construction industry. Boise Cascade was forced to reconsider its actions after a sixty-point drop in the price of its stock.[16]

If an organization overextends its abilities in attacking social problems, it is likely to do more harm than good to society. The economic welfare of the United States depends upon a healthy business climate. Ultimately it does no good to invest large sums in programs designed to solve society's problems if such efforts cripple the economic growth of the company. Some of the worst failures of social responsibility involve organizations that have begun inner city branches, training programs for the unemployed, or support for minority enterprises without adequate potential for profit. When these business ventures are curtailed, the effects on the communities and people involved are frequently worse than if the effort had not been made.

Expenditures for socially responsible activities must still be judged in the harsh light of business reality. Businesses cannot spend money on social programs to the extent that they impair their ability to survive. On the other hand, in present-day society companies that neglect their social responsibilities will be forced to pay costs that could drive them from the marketplace.

This tenuous situation calls for careful analysis and planning before an organization commits to a course of action.

Because most of the real benefits and dangers of social responsibility policies and actions have their basis in public relations, they need to be analyzed from this perspective. Public relations expertise is needed at the uppermost levels of organizational decision making. The need for managers who possess public relations skills and knowledge is critical to most large corporations. Likewise, the organization must be structured to allow the public relations function to be a two-way channel of communication between the organization and the publics with which it must deal. Burson summed up the critical nature of these decisions as follows:

**Those corporations which have reacted promptly and voluntarily to social change, are by and large, those which are generally regarded as socially responsible . . . Timing is important. The corporation that reacts too quickly may find itself penalized in relation to its competition, since a response to social change usually involves an added cost. On the other hand, the corporation that responds too slowly may also be penalized, since failure to act may carry economic penalties.**[17]

It is possible to take socially responsible actions which do not produce any benefit for the organization because the public being aided does not feel a need for the help provided. Providing support for a child-care facility for working parents in disadvantaged neighborhoods is certainly a socially responsible action. However, if the unemployment rate in that neighborhood is extremely high because people are untrained, have no reliable transportation, and there are no employment opportunities in the area, providing child care is a useless exercise and will have little positive effect. Likewise, an organization that spends millions of dollars annually on charitable causes and other socially responsible actions can still appear irresponsible if its publics are not made aware of these actions.

Effective social responsibility must combine a correct assessment of the needs of the target publics and an adequate method for communicating the organization's response to them. These are the areas where the special expertise of the public relations manager is needed. An organization faced with the almost endless possibilities for socially responsible action listed in Exhibit 18-1 must be able to select those courses of action which will prove most effective. Public relations management should be able to focus attention on the most significant publics and their expectations of the business community. A study by James Grunig, one of the few scientific attempts to discover what publics actually expect from business, produced some interesting results that should lead to a critical evaluation of many corporate social-action programs. Grunig concluded that "respondents in this study generally did not believe business should be involved in social problems such as education, support of charities, or decay of the cities not directly related to business."[18] Even the respondents most committed to social change did not feel that organizations should be involved in social programs unrelated to their business. The study did show that all the publics surveyed believed business should be more involved in actions designed to ensure quality products and services, to fight inflation, to promote minority hiring, and to improve human resources on the job.

Many of the socially responsible actions of American business listed in Exhibit 18-1 would be better left to government or joint government-business ventures, according to the Grunig study. There are indications that corporate management is beginning to respond to the expectations of their publics. A survey of top-level and operating-level executives from the *Fortune* 500 list of corporations produced the following list of areas of social responsibility in order of their perceived priority:[19]

1. Equal opportunity hiring and promotion
2. Pollution control and environmental impact
3. Employee safety
4. Resource conservation measures
5. Responding to government guidelines
6. Reacting to consumerism
7. Community improvement
8. Foreign investments
9. Purchasing from minority-owned enterprises

The role of public relations management in generating information about publics for use in corporate decision making is treated at greater length in our discussion of measurement techniques (see Chapter 9).

## CORPORATE SOCIAL RESPONSIBILITY AND PUBLIC RELATIONS

As we have already established, the role and function of public relations has developed in relation to the practice of enlightened self-interest in management. As corporations have become more aware of their social responsibilities, they have come to require new expertise and knowledge from public relations practitioners. In a lecture sponsored by the Foundation For Public Relations Research and Education, Hale Nelson, former vice-president of Illinois Bell Telephone, outlined the nature of this new public relations role.[20] Nelson asserted that important socio-political information is now missing from the "decision-making mix" of most organizations. American business has been very quick to respond to the need for increased information concerning production, personnel, market characteristics, and economic climate, but little has been done to improve the input of socio-political data. To correct this information gap, Nelson recommends an internal structure designed to gather socio-political data and distribute it within the decision-making components of the organization. This function should be headed by a senior officer, vice president for public relations, who can process this input and apply it at the highest levels of executive decision making, according to Nelson:

A department, captained by a vice president-public, or similar generic title, heads up a corporate intelligence system which obtains and applies political and sociological information—processed for the business mind—to all important phases of business operations. That same input will mold the communications output, which in the new age must be marked by candor, integrity, and helpful information. [20]

A similar view was expressed by the chairman of Burson-Marsteller Public Relations, Harold Burson:

**In assessing and responding to social change the public relations function must play a central role. It is the responsibility of the public relations professional to convince his management that there is, indeed, a ground swell of public opinion sufficiently significant to lead to social change. And it is his responsibility to participate in the policy determination that will lead to an effective response.[21]**

The public relations manager must function as a sensor of social change, policy maker, communicator of corporate policies both internally and externally and internal monitor of corporate response to its social responsibility.

This complex role of intelligence gatherer, policy maker, communicator, and ombudsman is already finding its way into the structures of many major corporations. In the closing chapters we present some specific social issues requiring the attention of public relations specialists and we will discuss the various organizational structures used to gain this input.

---

**CASE STUDY:**
**A COMPLEX**
**PROBLEM IN ETHICS**

**By J. Carroll Bateman**
**Associate Professor, College of**
**Communications, The University of**
**Tennessee, Knoxville, Tennessee**

---

It is the year 1959. Both the United States and the Soviet Union have been testing atomic weapons in the atmosphere for several years, and this caused a considerable amount of radioactive fallout in the Northern temperate zone. One of the radioisotopes in the fallout is strontium 90.

You are director of public relations for a national association of milk producers and dealers, and the matter of the strontium 90 fallout is of considerable concern to you for the following reasons:

Stratospheric winds carry the fallout around the earth without regard to national boundaries. Eventually, the various radioactive substances, including strontium 90, fall to earth. The other elements are of little consequence, but when the strontium 90 lands in the lush dairylands of the northern United States, Canada, and other countries around the world, it is consumed by the milk cows. In the cow's body, the strontium 90 locks on to calcium and appears in the milk that is given. As the milk is consumed by humans, especially babies and young children, it is absorbed into the bone structure along with the calcium. Since the strontium 90 has a "half-life" of twenty-eight years, it remains radioactive throughout the life of the individual. If it collects in the bone structure in sufficient quantities, it destroys the bone marrow which creates the red blood cells, and this leads to leukemia.

Government tests show that the radioactive element is present in the milk in all parts of the United States, and that in some areas it is at relatively high levels. There are two schools of scientific thought about strontium 90. One school holds that, below certain levels, the strontium 90 is not dangerous to humans. The other school holds that any level of strontium 90 in the body is dangerous.

Unfortunately, there is no means by which the strontium 90 can be removed from the milk, except on a small scale in a laboratory by a complex process. But this process is not feasible for removing the radioactive element from tens of thousands of gallons of milk as it is processed daily in the milk bottling plants.

The Atomic Energy Commission and the U.S. Public Health Service have been very cooperative in providing information on the problem to the milk industry. As director of public relations for the industry's national trade association, it is your responsibility to recommend a course of action to your member companies.

**Questions**

1. What are your responsibilities to the public on this matter? (Keep in mind that there is a great danger of creating public panic if the facts are dealt with carelessly or irresponsibly.)

2. What are your responsibilities to your member companies? What should they be told? Assuming you decide to inform them of the facts, how can this best be done? What would you recommend to them, with reference to their communications to their customers?

3. What responsibility do you think the government has in this matter? What, if anything, should it tell the public?

4. Prepare a written plan for dealing with the problem, keeping in mind that eliminating the cause is something that only the governments of the U.S. and the U.S.S.R. can do. (As a matter of historical fact, this situation eventually led to an agreement between the two governments to ban atmospheric tests of atomic weapons.)

**NOTES**   [1] Edward L. Bernays, *Biography of an Idea: Memoirs of Public Relations Counsel Edward L. Bernays* (New York: Simon and Schuster, 1965).

[2] Harwood Childs, *An Introduction to Public Opinion* (New York: Wiley, 1940).

[3] Adam Smith, *Wealth of Nations*, Book IV, Chapter 2 (1776), as quoted in E. Bakke et al., *Unions, Management and the Public*, 3rd ed (New York: Harcourt Brace Jovanovich, Inc. 1967), p. 22.

[4] Scott M. Cutlip and Allen H. Center, *Effective Public Relations* (Englewood Cliffs, New Jersey: Prentice-Hall, 1978), pp. 84–87.

[5] Cutlip and Center, *Effective Public Relations*, p. 87.

[6] George Griswold, Jr., "How AT&T Public Relations Policies Developed," *Public Relations Quarterly* 12 (Fall 1967): 13.

[7] Robert D. Hay, Edmund R. Gray, and James E. Gates, *Business and Society* (Cincinnati: South-Western, 1976), p. 11–13.

[8] Milton Friedman, "The Social Responsibility of Business is to Increase Its Profits," *The New York Times Magazine,* September 13, 1970.

[9] Milton Friedman, *Capitalism and Freedom* (Chicago: University of Chicago Press, 1962).

[10] Theodore Levitt, "The Dangers of Social Responsibility," *Harvard Business Review* (September–October 1958); 44. Reprinted by permission of the Harvard Business Review, Copyright © 1958 by the President and fellows of Harvard College. All rights reserved.

[11] Norton Clapp, "Corporate Responsibility to the Community," *University of Washington Business Review* (Spring 1968): 7.

[12] Committee for Economic Development, *Social Responsibilities of Business Corporations* (New York: CED, 1971), p. 25.

[13] CED, *Social Responsibilities,* p. 28.

[14] Ibid., p. 70.

[15] George A. Steiner, *Business and Society* (New York: Random House, 1975), p. 164.

[16] Hay, Gray, and Gates, *Business and Society,* p. 182.

[17] Harold Burson, "The Public Relations Function in the Socially Responsible Corporation", in *Managing the Socially Responsible Corporation,* ed. M. Anshen (New York: Macmillian, 1974), p. 230.

[18] James E. Grunig, "A New Measure of Public Opinions on Corporate Social Responsibility," *Academy of Management Journal* 22 (1979): 761.

[19] Lyman E. Ostlund, "Attitudes of Managers Toward Corporate Social Responsibility," *California Management Review 19* (Summer 1977): 40.

[20] Hale Nelson, "The Public Problems of Business—Crucial Test of the Seventies," quoted in Raymond Simon, *Public Relations: Concepts and Practice* (Columbus, Ohio: Grid, Inc., 1976), pp. 64–65.

[21] Harold Burson, *Burson-Marsteller Report,* May 1973.

# CHAPTER 19  ENVIRONMENTALISM

**PREVIEW**   Public relations has played substantial roles on every side in the great debates on the environment and has helped to develop the consensus on the issue that now exists.

Environmental issues and problems give public relations executives outstanding opportunities for input into organizational decision making and policy creation.

Effective environmental public relations requires acquisition of special scientific and legal knowledge, creation of an inventory of an organization's environmental activities and problems, public relations inputs to organizational decisions about environmental issues, and communication links with enrivonmental activists.

An activist is the guy that cleans up the river, not the guy
who concludes it's dirty.

—H. Ross Perot

Controlling pollution in the environment is one of the issues where corporate interests, public opinion, and government regulation overlap and often
conflict. Public relations has played important roles on every side of environmental issues fostering public awareness and understanding of company
position, providing inputs into decision- and policy making, building organizational credibility by publicizing environmental successes, and rebuilding
the images of organizations exposed as polluters. Consequently, it is essential
that public relations practitioners understand the dimensions of the controversy past, present, and future. In this chapter, we will attempt to put pollution
in its public relations perspective, help the public relations practitioner to
prepare for environmental public relations, and discuss the roles of public
relations in communicating environmental information to employees, management, the media, environmental groups, and the public.

**POLLUTION IN
PERSPECTIVE**
Two basic, interrelated facts are essential to understanding the issue of pollution. First, pollution is not a new problem. It is as old as humankind.
Second, pollution is a by-product of living. From these facts it may be argued
that it usually is erroneous to condemn a single organization or operation
as the "cause" of environmental damage.

Although local smoke control regulations were on the books one hundred
years ago and water pollution was addressed in 1899, the contemporary
concerns over the physical environment began in earnest in the 1960s. Many
point to the publication of Rachel Carson's *The Silent Spring* in 1962 as a
turning point in environmental activism. During the 1960s two concepts—
ecosystems and externalities—became much more thoroughly understood.

The study of *ecosystems* deals with the ways in which the members of
ecological systems relate to each other and their physical environments. The
idea of ecosystems helps us to recognize our dependence on fragile biological
and physical systems and the inadvertent harm done to those systems by
society's habits of production and consumption. The term *externalities* is
applied to those aspects of production and consumption that have costs not
assumed by the producer or consumer but passed into the environment
instead. In the past, such externalities could be ignored with relative safety
because nature's ability to renew itself was not overly taxed. Because of
pressures created by increased population and industrial growth and concentration, however, externalities have become increasingly unacceptable
both economically and politically.

An understanding of the concepts of ecosystems and externalities led the Council on Environmental Quality to the identification of the following causes of environmental problems:

**Our past tendency to emphasize quantitative growth at the expense of qualitative growth; the failure of our economy to provide full accounting for the social costs of environmental pollution; the failure to take environmental factors into account as a normal and necessary part of our planning and decision making; the inadequacy of our institutions for dealing with problems that cut across traditional political boundaries; our dependence on conveniences, without regard for their impact on the environment; and more fundamentally, our failure to perceive the environment as a totality and to understand and to recognize the fundamental interdependence of all its parts, including man himself.**[1]

**An Emerging
Consensus**

In one sense, the pollution debate is over. To pollute or not to pollute is no longer the question. Today the controversy takes place on much subtler levels, involving methods of pollution abatement, avoidance of future problems, the balance of social and economic benefits against environmental costs, and the levels at which natural systems can cleanse themselves.

William D. Ruckelshaus, former head of the Environmental Protection Agency, maintains that a four-point general consensus has emerged relating to the environment:

1. Pollution will not go away by itself and action must be taken to reduce pollution and correct past damage. Major questions about which actions, how fast and how actions should be taken, however, remain.
2. We have realized that the environment cannot be cleaned up instantly and that it cannot be restored to its original "pristine state."
3. The return of clear, clean, free flowing waters, fresh blue skies, noise abatement and management of solid waste are not cheap. They must be paid for in terms of taxes, higher prices and giving up certain hallowed but wasteful habits.
4. Plans to clean up the environment must be devised so that the end of one problem is not the beginning of another.[2]

Although a degree of consensus has been achieved, many unresolved problems and questions remain. Significant progress has been made in the areas of air and water pollution, but the problems of solid waste disposal (including disposal of toxic, chemical, and nuclear waste) and cancer associated with environmental hazards are only just beginning to be addressed.

**The Role of
Businesses**

Environmental quality is frequently a problem that confronts management, simply because wastes occur at all points in the cycle of production, distribution and consumption. In the past, business has operated in a socioeconomic situation in which degradation of the environment was costless while stopping such degradation was expensive. Business is not the only institution that pollutes. Government-owned Tennessee Valley Authority power plants and dams have the same environmental impact as those owned by private sector utilities. The Interior Department and Army Corps of Engineers come under frequent criticism from environmental activists. Municipal water and sewage systems are now the largest factor in pollution of rivers and streams. But businesses' responses to pollution problems serve as models for any organization in similar situations.

When environmental abuse first became an issue, business response was very mixed. In Pittsburgh, in the years immediately following World War II, business leaders played a major role in the development of an effective air pollution control program. Consequently, there were no fines, no orders to cease production, and no unrealistic deadlines for compliance.

Most businesses, however, tended to treat environmental activism as a faddish movement that would fade with time. Businesses often ignored environmental problems until they were confronted with unfavorable publicity, at which time they issued denials or statements skirting the issues involved.

In a few cases, corporations deliberately gave out misleading information on environmental issues. Potlatch, Inc. ran an advertisement in 1970 with a stunning landscape photograph and a headline reading: "It cost us a bundle but the Clearwater River still runs clear." *Newsweek* found that the picture had been taken fifty miles upstream from the company's pulp and paper plant and reported that downstream the river looked like a cesspool.[3]

In general, business has reacted to environmental problems rather than taking the initiative, and thus allowed environmentalists like Ralph Nader and Barry Commoner to direct the debate. As Carl Thompson of Hill and Knowlton pointed out:

**By the time industry . . . was ready to get into the game, the other players were already on the field, the rules were set, the officials chosen, and the grandstands were wildly cheering the ecologists—freaks and otherwise. Then industry showed up, saying the game was being played wrong, the officials were biased, the rules should be changed, and the fans should be more sympathetic.[4]**

This may overstate the case somewhat, but it is true that the environmental legislation of the 1970s contains a number of flaws and inadequacies that might have been avoided had industry taken a leadership role. Too little attention is given to cost/benefit comparisons; too much power is vested in regulatory agencies; too little room is left for negotiation and compromise in particular cases; too often environmental legislation and regulations overlap and conflict.

But it is also true that laws are becoming more fully developed and tested; environmentalists are becoming less emotional and more rational; and the impact of the energy crisis, in particular, has made us more conscious of the costs of environmental initiatives. Neil Orloff describes the current environmental legislation situation as fluid, and maintains that business has the opportunity to explore new approaches to environmental protection including modification of priorities, adjustment of required abatement levels, postponement of compliance schedules, and greater flexibility in requirements.[5]

How business can be most effective in influencing environmental legislation will be addressed later in this chapter.

**Costs of Environmental Controls**

There is no question that the bill for environmental cleanup and pollution control is very large. The Council on Environmental Quality (CEQ) projects total expenditures on pollution control in the decade between 1976 and 1985 at $289.1 billion. In 1977, the CEQ estimates that $40.6 billion was spent—2.1 percent of the gross national product, or $187 for each and every man, woman and child in this country.[6]

Other costs of pollution control are less easily quantified. Unemployment is considered a tradeoff in this regard. CEQ says that pollution control costs were significant in the decision to close 107 plants employing 20,138 people between 1971 and 1977.[7] Stahrl Edmunds estimates that because of expenditures on pollution control, national unemployment has been increased between .05 percent and 1.0 percent.[8] Others maintain that employment is increased by the effort to clean up the environment with between 500,000 and 1,000,000 workers employed by what has become a pollution control industry.[9] Inflation and diminished capital supply are other frequently cited results of pollution control; while there is certainly some impact in these areas, it is perhaps less than some have claimed.

These costs, of course, must be weighed against the benefits of better health and reduced property and crop damage, as well as aesthetic and convenience benefits. Environmentalists maintain that the issue is one of the survival of the human species, and that no cost is too great.

**PREPARING FOR EFFECTIVE ENVIRONMENTAL PUBLIC RELATIONS**

Several things are necessary if an organization is to create an effective approach to environmental public relations. In addition to all of the other public relations skills discussed elsewhere in this book, successful treatment of environmental issues requires special kinds of knowledge and special procedures.

Environmental public relations responsibilities include understanding of science and the law as they apply to specific industries, communities and processes. Furthermore, the public relations practitioner must be thoroughly knowledgeable concerning any organizational activities that may be related in any way to pollution or potential pollution.

**Scientific Knowledge**

In order to address environmental issues effectively and credibly, the public relations practitioner must have some scientific understanding of ecological problems. Knowledge of biology, botany, chemistry, physics, meteorology, and other sciences may be relevant to particular environmental issues, but of course the public relations practitioner cannot be expected to master all or any of these areas. Nonetheless, an organization's public relations staff should have sufficient scientific background to understand the environmental issues that might affect their particular organization. They should be prepared to talk about the organization's pollution problems and achievements in depth and with authority. This process is facilitated by maintaining close

liaisons with appropriate scientists and engineers either within the organization or from a university or research center. (It is usually advisable to check
the expert's scientific credentials and political beliefs and to talk to more
than one source. Science may be objective, but scientists are human.)

**Environmental Law**   Dealing with environmental issues requires familiarity not only with science,
but also with the law. One must be knowledgeable about existing local, state,
and federal legislation and regulations in order to assess and defend the
organization's compliance (a synopsis of environmental legislation appears
in Table 19-1). One must keep abreast of any changes in legislation or
interpretation and help to interpret the impact of such changes on organizational activities. Finally, one must be prepared to counsel management on
the public relations ramifications of any legal initiatives undertaken by the
organization in relation to environmental issues. Many corporations have

---

**Table 19-1**
A Synopsis of Major
Environmental
Legislation

**Water Pollution Laws**

1899   *Rivers and Harbors Act*—prohibits direct discharge of any wastes into navigable
       waters without prior permit.

1924   *Oil Pollution Act*—prohibits dumping of oil into coastal waters.

1948   *Water Pollution Control Act*—treats water pollution as a local problem but requires
       the U.S. Public Health Service to provide technical information and coordinate
       research.

1956   *Water Pollution Control Act*—regulates discharges into interstate waterways.

1961   *Amendments* to the 1956 law broaden federal jurisdiction and shorten time for
       establishing standards and prosecuting offenders.

1965   *Water Quality Act*—creates a Federal Water Pollution Control Administration in the
       Department of Health, Education and Welfare.

1966   *Clean Water Restoration Act*—improves controls over oil discharges and creates
       an agency to establish regional clean water standards.

1970   *Water Quality Improvement Act*—regulates mine wastes and sewage discharges
       from ships and boats.

1972   *Water Pollution Control Act*—establishes the goal of the elimination of all water
       discharge; limits discharges to best practical technology in 1977 and best available
       technology in 1983.

1974   *Safe Drinking Water Act*—provides for the establishment of regulations relating to
       public health, and the taste, odor and appearance of drinking water; and citizen
       suits against any party believed to be in violation of the act.

1977   *Amendments* to the 1972 act—provides new classifications of pollutant types with
       different requirements for each category with greater emphasis on toxic pollutants;
       promotes new waste treatment technology including recycling, reuse of pollution
       control by-products, energy conservation, and multiple use of lands and waters
       used as components of waste water treatment systems.

**Air Pollution Laws**

1881   Chicago and Cleveland pass smoke control laws.

1955   *Air Pollution Control Research and Technical Assistance Act*—provides support for research and data collection; extended in 1959.

1963   *Clean Air Act*—provides for federal regulation of discharges causing interstate pollution; amended to become more stringent in 1966 and 1970.

1965   *Motor Vehicle Air Pollution Control Act*—authorizes federal government to establish automobile emission standards.

1967   *Air Quality Act*—establishes air pollution control as a national objective.

1969   *National Environmental Pollution Act*—mandates environmental-impact statements for projects using federal money.

1970   *Environmental Quality Improvement Act*—increases federal enforcement activities.

1977   *Clean Air Act Amendments*—reaffirms 1970 law's intents, sets or strengthens standards, guidelines or programs.

**Other Environmental Laws**

1972   *Noise Control Act*—mandates the environmental protection agency to set standards in relation to products which constitute major noise sources.

1976   *Resource Conservation and Recovery Act*—encourages improved practices in solid waste disposal; establishes regulatory control of hazardous waste; establishes resource conservation as the preferred solid waste management approach.

1976   *Toxic Substances Control Act*—makes the entire chemical industry subject to comprehensive federal regulation.

---

gone to court seeking to delay or overturn legislation or regulations in the environmental arena. In the main, such suits have made corporations appear defensive, self-serving, and unconcerned with public health and well-being, and have not achieved their intended relief. This is not to say that organizations should completely refrain for public relations reasons from taking legitimate grievances to court. As Bernard M. Kostelnik, Anaconda Company's environmental affairs officer, puts it:

**If (industry) is convinced that a particular set of standards is just completely erroneous and unachievable and that they have a strong technical and legal position, they ought to stand pat and litigate.   .   .   .**[10]

From a public relations perspective, organizations should take issue with environmental law or regulations on behalf of the public, and should be prepared to demonstrate dramatically, without appearing defensive or stubborn, that they are acting in the public interest. This position is best achieved by a cooperative attitude that stresses the organization's expertise gained through a long record of environmental sensitivity, initiative, and action.

**Environmental
Inventory**

Public relations practitioners must be aware of all of their organization's environmental activities and problems. To accomplish this, an environmental inventory should be maintained. The inventory should begin with a clear statement of the organization's environmental policy, and include a review of all environmental initiatives undertaken by the organization, its plans for the future, and the goals, objectives and schedules of such programs. Carl Thompson suggests that understandable background papers be maintained on research being supported, on technical problems being tackled, and on the complexities of yet-unsolved problems.[11]

To prepare such an inventory, the environmental impacts of all organizational activities must be thoroughly considered. Some, like smokestacks or effluent discharges, will be obvious. Others, like paper waste disposal or the emissions of a fleet of delivery vans, may be more difficult to identify. Checklists of sources of air, water, noise, and waste pollution should be maintained for every organization facility and should include relevant abatement activities, priorities, costs, and schedules. The inventory should also list what other organizations are doing about similar problems. Once the inventory is established, it should be updated at least quarterly.

There are multiple benefits to such an inventory. It can help to pinpoint opportunities and needs for environmental actions. It provides ready access to information about all environmental activities and problems within the organization. It helps the public relations staff to assess the organization's real, potential, and perceived environmental hazards and progress. It points out to the public relations staff areas for further research and helps them to identify questions requiring answers or information from scientists or lawyers.

**AFFECTING
ENVIRONMENTAL
DECISION MAKING**

Throughout this book we have stressed the crucial role public relations can play in organizational decision making. The development of organizational policies, strategies, and action in response to environmental issues has demonstrated the critical importance of public relations input and thereby contributed to the elevation of public relations in the corporate hierarchy. One effect of our society's coming to grips with environmental problems has been a tendency towards more nebulous, difficult, and complex decision making within corporations. Keith Davis and Robert L. Blomstrom, noted scholars in the area of business social responsibility, suggest:

New decision tools and organizational units will need to be brought to the situation. New values and ways of thinking will be involved. . . . business will need to adjust its procedures, organizational units and lifestyles in order to improve both its social inputs and outputs. Business intelligence particularly needs to become more sensitive to inputs beyond economic ones. . . . [business must] develop thorough inputs from the social system and respond thoughtfully to them. . . .[12]

R. J. Mockler makes a similar point:

A plan to solve a water pollution problem must take into account internal company factors such as the company's size and financial resources, its public image, and the social responsibility values of the company's management.[13]

Public relations is best able to represent a company's public image in such planning efforts, and to a large extent can provide certain social inputs of the kind recommended by Davis and Blomstrom. For these reasons, environmental concerns give public relations executives outstanding opportunities for input into organizational decision making and policy creation.

One structural mechanism through which corporations address environmental issues is the environmental affairs committee. These committees, which take many forms, serve to coordinate the variety of elements needed to produce enviornmental policy. Leonard Lund, in *Corporate Organization for Environmental Policy Making,*[14] outlines several actual organizational structures that provide for the role public relations plays in various organizations' environmental policy making. In some cases, a high-level environmental officer uses the environmental committee as an instrument for interweaving other company operations into the environmental policy (Figure 19-1).

Lund found the most common practice among companies is to view action on environmental matters as an exercise of corporate social responsibility, and to assign responsibility for such issues to the public relations division (*Figure 19-2*).

Sometimes the committee is used to provide environmental insights into other company operations (*Figure 19-3*).

Finally, Lund reports that a number of companies handle their environmental problems within regular operating structures. Figure 19-4 is a production-oriented example.

Having seen how public relations can function within organizational policy, strategy, and decision-making capacities, we can now turn to public relations

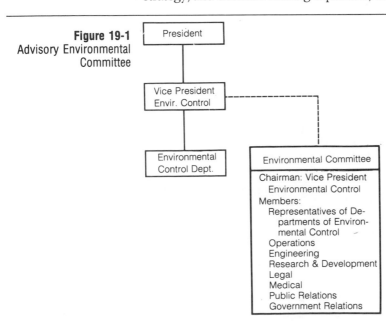

**Figure 19-1**
Advisory Environmental
Committee

President

Vice President
Envir. Control

Environmental
Control Dept.

Environmental Committee

Chairman: Vice President
    Environmental Control
Members:
    Representatives of Departments of Environmental Control
    Operations
    Engineering
    Research & Development
    Legal
    Medical
    Public Relations
    Government Relations

in its function of communicating environmental information to various organizational publics.

**COMMUNICATING ABOUT THE ENVIRONMENT**

Virtually all corporate audiences have needs for information about environmental activities. Stockholders must be kept informed about expenditures on pollution abatement and must be convinced that such expenditures are appropriate and necessary. Internal corporate communication directed toward employees and their families should demonstrate responsible corporate citizenship by providing information about new pollution-abatement facilities, research and development on products or processes that combat pollution, company policies related to the environment, and practical advice on how individuals can control pollution at home and on the job. Other audiences include community groups and governmental officials. We will concentrate here on two extremely important audiences: the mass media and environmental activists. Whatever the audience, however, it is necessary to remember that the single most important ingredient in a successful environmental communications program is complete candor.

**The Mass Media**

Certain environmental problems are highly visible. Smoke, fish kills, noxious odors, roaring motors or the like attract attention of those close enough to smell, hear, or see. Such problems can also attract media coverage, carrying the unpleasant sensation to individuals far removed from the event. Severe environmental problems, particularly those in which the circumstances and the source are clear, can make big, bad news. By the same token, however,

**Figure 19-2**
Environmental Control as an Aspect of Public Affairs

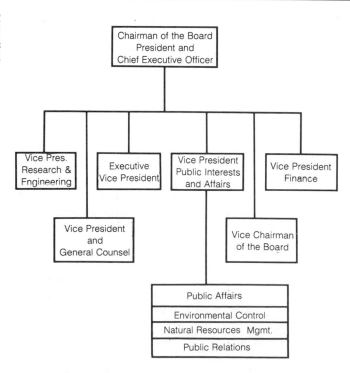

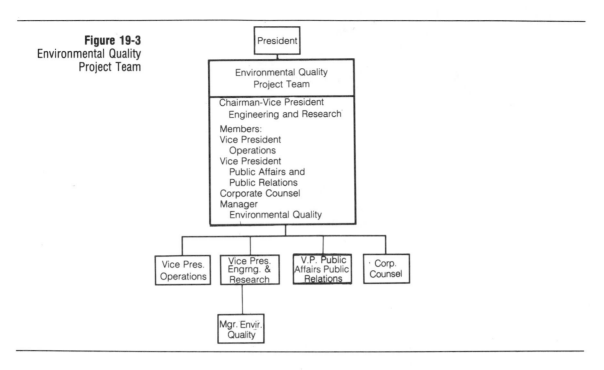

**Figure 19-3**
Environmental Quality
Project Team

the media serve as avenues to inform the public of corporate innovations or progress in the area of pollution control. Many companies make use of their efforts to solve pollution problems in building their public image.

Although environmental problems have, on occasion, provided fertile fields for muckrakers, the media seldom investigate environmental problems on their own.[15] In fact, research indicates that environmental stories come from press releases or official sources more often than other kinds of news do. According to David Sachsman, journalists rarely question the reliability of press releases dealing with environmental matters, do not investigate substantial numbers of them, and rely on press releases from environmental groups or government agencies for the other side of the story.[16]

Reporters who cover environmental issues have a difficult job, at best. They must be science writers, business writers, and political writers rolled into one. As Rubin and Sachs put it:

**The environmental reporter [is] hobbled by his lack of scientific expertise, the enormity of his beat, the rippling ramifications of everything he reports, and the nonhuman or inanimate nature of most of his news sources. . . .[17]**

Rubin and Sachs go on to describe this reporter as "a slave to the pseudo-event," who depends heavily on conservation groups and government agencies as sources of information. "Although industry public relations men supply newsmen with as much or more material than do conservationists," they find, "the reporters apparently give more credence to the conservationists."[18] Jim Grunig maintains that the media "are quite willing to use press releases

**Figure 19-4**
Environmental Control
Within Regular
Operating Structure

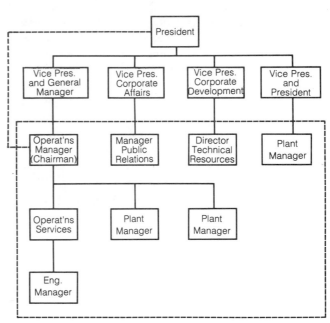

ENVIRONMENTAL CONTROL COMMITTEE

from industry sources," but at the same time "will print negative information about local firms . . . if it comes from government sources or from a pseudo-event created by environmental groups."[19]

Given the nature of environmental reporting, then, corporate public relations staffs are well advised to brief journalists on the environmental activities of their organizations before any crisis situations develop. The environmental inventory discussed earlier in this chapter should prove very useful in this regard. When reporters have been given background information, they are more likely to approach environmental stories open-mindedly and knowledgeably.

**Environmental Activists**

Perhaps the greatest threat to corporations concerned about public and government reaction to pollution problems comes from educated activists with political savvy. Corporations should devote much of their effort to communicating with these activists. It is far more effective to reach environmental activists directly, through personal contact, than indirectly through the mass media. Furthermore, corporations must be as concerned about listening and learning as they are about getting their own points across. With legislation and litigation, a few sophisticated and vocal activists can handcuff the giant corporation which is unwilling to listen and learn about concerns, problems, and avenues of compromise.

Environmental activists can only rarely be convinced or converted through confrontation. Their very real power can be channeled toward constructive ends, however, by opening avenues of communication to them and even by incorporating their recommendations into environmental decision making. Some corporations have established citizens' advisory committees specifically for this purpose. Although this plan may sound extreme, such participation is less costly, time-consuming, and frustrating than enforced "participation" by courts, regulatory bodies, or legislatures.

As James Reilly, former president of The Conservation Foundation, commented, ". . . difficult decisions about our future economic and ecological goals and the trade-offs between them . . . will be the better if they are made on the basis of open exchange and reasoned analysis." [20]

The public relations practitioner can play perhaps his or her most vital role by providing the means and media for open exchange. In this manner, reasoned analysis can be brought to bear on an issue long dominated by myth, emotion, and confrontation.

---

**Mini-Case 19-1 Energy Through Communication** [21]   The citizens of Galveston understood the nation's energy needs and the positive economic impacts of the discovery of large deposits of natural gas in the region. They raised no objections to Mitchell Energy and Development Corporation's onshore drilling, but when the company proposed to tap a natural gas field 9,000 feet beneath the Gulf of Mexico off Galveston, community environmental groups and the local tourism and recreation industry posed stiff resistance.

Mitchell could have buckled down for the long, hard fight, but instead decided on a strategy of open communications emphasizing several basic points:

Energy is essential but we must never cease to consider and observe every ecological constraint;

Our plans will be better if they are thoroughly examined and criticized before being approved;

Personal communication with a diversity of publics at each step of the process is invaluable to achieving approval of the drilling project.

On these cornerstones, Mitchell Energy developed a communications program including the following elements:

● Mitchell respresentatives held personal meetings with publishers, general managers, and editorial staffs of newspapers and broadcasting stations to obtain understanding and support.

● Articulate and credible spokespersons appeared at meetings and hearings to explain technical and safety aspects of the project.

• The company sought approval from community groups including the local convention bureau, hotel and motel operators, restaurant owners, shrimp boat operators, labor unions, the city council, civic clubs, the Junior Chamber of Commerce and others.

• Political leaders and other influential citizens were given helicopter tours before, during, and after·drilling.

• A special well head was designed at additional expense to meet the ecological requirements of the project. A mockup of the well head was constructed and towed to the proposed drilling site to demonstrate that the working model would be practically invisible from the beach.

• Brochures, films, and mass media were used to demonstrate Mitchell's commitment to the environment, and to the existing tourism and fishing industries.

As a result of Mitchell's communication efforts, seemingly contradictory interests were reconciled. A responsible, concerned company tapped vital energy resources in an environmentally sound way with the backing and support of the community.

Adapted with permission from the December 1974 issue of *Public Relations Journal* © 1974.

---

**Mini-Case 19-2
Public Relations,
Pulp Mills and
Pollution** [22]

In 1968, the Escanaba Paper Company, a wholly-owned subsidiary of Mead Corporation, announced its intention to build a $100 million pulp mill and paper manufacturing facility on the pristine Upper Peninsula of northern Michigan, an area known for its clean air, natural beauty, high unemployment, and low per-capita income. Mead had a long history of good relations with the town of Escanaba. A policy of urging employees to be involved with local affairs resulted in the presence of two Mead employees on the county Board of Supervisors.

The first phase of construction—a huge paper machine—began without opposition and was well under way when the Delta County Citizens Committee to Save Our Air (SOA) was formed to oppose the second phase of construction, a paper mill. SOA raised questions about potential odor problems from the proposed pulp mill before the county Board of Supervisors, in the *Escanaba Daily Press*, and before the local Chamber of Commerce. The following statement exemplified the rhetoric used by those who opposed construction of the pulp mill:

**I would like to emphasize that I have always had the highest respect for the Mead Corporation as a responsible corporate citizen. Their support of charitable and civic projects in the community has always been open and generous. . . . For this reason, I have asked myself how they could do such a thing in Escanaba and my only conclusion is that in this case the economic considerations to the Mead Corporation override their demonstrated corporate good citizenship.**

When the local plant manager announced his company's decision on 28 April 1969 to proceed with the pulp mill, a complete communications plan was ready to be implemented, focusing on the fact that Mead would use the most advanced available air pollution prevention equipment and that $5 million would be spent on pollution-control technology.

On 19 May SOA passed a resolution calling for a guaranteed odorless mill and a county ordinance that would require permanent closing of the mill if it was not odorless. In an effort to build support for their position, the committee undertook a publicity campaign including newspaper advertisements, mass mailings, radio announcements, and news releases. In June, Mead responded to questions raised by SOA. The company explained that it delayed in answering questions about the pulp mill until it had investigated available technology and had been assured that it could build a pulp mill as free from odor as possible. Mead steadfastly refused to make promises it couldn't keep and allowed that malfunctions, errors, or climatic conditions could result in temporary odors.

In August, the Associated Press carried a story nationally that began:

**Citizens in this northern Michigan community are battling to save their clean air—air that gives off the fragrance of balsam fir and has been judged by one scientific study to be the cleanest in the U.S.**

**What has alarmed some townspeople is the proposed construction of a sulfate pulp mill. . . .**

**"It smells like rotten eggs, rotten cabbages, skunks and who the hell knows," said John T. Walbridge.**

On September 15, SOA staged a public rally attended by 400 to 500 people. The event was covered by CBS television.

Two days later, SOA presented their proposed ordinance to the Delta County Board of Supervisors. They claimed that it would safeguard "the health, safety, welfare and comfort of the people." In effect, it banned the pulp mill.

Mead felt that the ordinance was irresponsible and decided to oppose it, but made clear its willingness to cooperate enthusiastically in the effort to develop a reasonable ordinance. Publically, Mead's position was that a law which provided clear technical measures was indeed needed.

SOA continued its campaign, receiving an endorsement from the Episcopal Diocese of Northern Michigan and a complimentary article in *New Republic*. In the meantime, Mead maintained relatively low-key position, attempting to remain reasonable, cooperative, and open. An open house at the company's $2 million water treatment plant received favorable notice in the local press.

The Michigan Air Pollution Control Commission took the matter up at hearings in Lansing, the state capital. Mead was opposed by SOA, Friends of the Earth, the League of Conservation, the Environmental Action Council, and student groups from the University of Michigan and Michigan State University. All of these groups questionoed the company's credibility, maintaining that Mead would promise anything to get the plant built.

Mead's response was to refuse to promise unobtainable results, offering complete and understandable technical and economic data, and flying twelve community leaders to Lansing so that they could testify. The chairman of the county Board of Supervisors testified that "Mead has placed its integrity and excellent public relations on the line."

The Commission's staff established seven stipulations to be met by Mead before a permit would be granted. With minor modifications, and despite increased costs, Mead agreed to the stipulations. One of the commissioners concluded, "I'm satisfied that Mead is not going to violate our law." The permit was granted by a 7–1 vote on 28 April 1970, one year after Mead announced its intention to construct the pulp mill.

Adapted from John Collins and Donald De Salvia, "Escanaba Paper Company," in R. D. Hay, E. R. Gray, and J. E. Gates (eds.), *Business and Society* (Cincinnati: Southwestern Publishing Company, 1976), pp. 132–146.

CASE STUDY:  **By Jim VanLeuven**
THE CLEARWATER  **Associate Professor of**
RIVER  **Communication, Washington State**
**University, Pullman, Washington**

The national environmental protection mood of the 1960s collided head-on with the U.S. Army Corps of Engineers' announced intention to build Penny Cliffs Dam on the middle fork of Idaho's Clearwater River, one of America's few remaining free-flowing rivers.

Reaction to the announcement was quick. Landowners whose property abutted the river feared their land would be damaged by new water levels. Local businessmen recoiled at the prospect of losing the tourist dollars from campers, hunters, and fishermen. The Sierra Club summoned a task force to investigate potential environmental damage. Hunting club members in Montana, Idaho, and Washington began a scattershot letter-writing campaign. Even the membership of a Pacific Northwest mushroom collectors group fretted over changed in river bank composition.

Each of the groups realized that the Corps had all the legal machinery to build the dam and that only federal legislation would save the river for its existing recreational, logging, and residential uses. These pressure groups gave birth to the National Wild and Scenic Rivers program, a plan to set aside the land immediately adjacent to America's most scenic rivers.

Congress instructed officials of U.S. National Forest Service to mount a public information and public participation program testing support for the Clearwater's wild river designation. Unfortunately, no public information specialist was included in the planning process and none was employed in the area at the time. To assess support, the forest service staff talked to a few already-favorable civic groups, appointed a hand-picked public advisory body, and disseminated news releases announcing public meetings. Meanwhile a vocal group of riverfront landowners formed an organization to support the wild river idea only because that would effectively block dam construction. National media and outdoor magazine writers moved in and helped create a national audience.

Next came a management plan calling for expanded camping facilities, special road signs, and visitor information centers as well as restrictions on future building. A few months later Congress enacted the Wild and Scenic Rivers Act and designated the Clearwater Middle Fork the first of eight "instant" wild rivers.

All affected parties seemed pleased at the time, but gradually came to feel the government failed to deliver what the wild river program had promised. No special signs were placed along nearby roads and highways. No new recreational facilities were built. To make things worse, the U.S. Forest Service, which manages the area, was charged with applying one set of building and zoning requirements on nearby private lands while maintaining a separate standard on their own lands.

**Questions**     1. What could the public information officer now assigned to the Clearwater Wild River program do to inform tourists, landowners, and others about the wild river area?

2. What communication and public information techniques should have been used initially to reach local publics? What techniques should have been used to reach national publics?

3. How should the public information specialists acquire and use the complaints from the public about the lack of an ongoing public relations and wild river program?

**NOTES**     [1] Council on Environmental Quality, *Environmental Quality* (Washington, D.C.: U.S. Government Printing Office, 1970).

[2] William D. Ruckelshaus, "It's Time for Environmental Truth or Consequences," *Public Relations Journal* (May 1973); 6–8, 33.

[3] *Newsweek*, 28 December 1970.

[4] Carl Thompson, "Warning Flags (Still) Wave in Polluted Air," in Hill and Knowlton Executives, *Critical Issues in Public Relations* (Englewood Cliffs, N.J.: Prentice-Hall, 1975), pp. 105–112.

[5] Neil Orloff, "Payoff for Business Initiative on the Environment," *Harvard Business Review*, 1977, p. 8+.

[6] Council on Environmental Quality, *Environmental Quality*, Washington, D.C.: U.S. Government Printing Office, 1977.

[7] Ibid.

[8] Stahrl Edmunds, "Trade-Offs in Assessing Environmental Impacts," *California Management Review*, 1976.

[9] Gladwin Hill, "The Profits of Ecology: Cleaning the Stable Makes Jobs," *The Nation*, 17 April 1976, pp. 455–458.

[10] F. D. Sturdivant, *Business and Society* (Homewood, Ill.: Irwin, 1977), p. 323.

[11] Thompson, "Warning Flags," p. 111.

[12] Keith Davis and Robert L. Blomstrom, "Observations on Energy and Business Responsibility," *Arizona Business* (March, 1974) 19–26.

[13] R. J. Mockler, *Business and Society* (New York: Harper & Row, 1975), p. 184.

[14] L. Lund, *Corporation Organization for Environmental Policy Making* (New York: The Conference Board, 1974).

[15] J. E. Grunig, "Review of Research on Environmental Public Relations," *Public Relations Journal* (Fall 1977); 45.

[16] David B. Sachsman, "Public Relations Influence on Coverage of the Environment in the San Francisco Area," *Journalism Quarterly*, (1976).

[17] D. M. Rubin and D. P. Sachs. *Mass Media and the Environment* (New York: Praeger Publishers, 1973), p. 109.

[18] Ibid., p. 41.

[19] Grunig, "Review of Research," p. 45.

[20] H. J. Leonard, J. C. Davies III, and G. Binder (eds.) *Business and Environment* (Washington, D.C.: The Conservation Foundation, 1977), p. v.

[21] Based on Jack J. Yanovich "The Controversy Over Energy," *Public Relations Journal* (December 1974): 20–22.

[22] Adapted from John Collins and Donald DeSalvia, "Escanaba Paper Company," in R. D. Hay, E. R. Gray, and J. E. Gates (Eds.), *Business and Society* (Cincinnati: Southwestern Publishing Company, 1976): 132–146.

# CHAPTER 20  CONSUMERISM

**PREVIEW**   The relationship between consumer affairs and public
relations in an organization is a natural one because
consumers are one of the publics to which practitioners
respond.

While complaint handling must be effective and fast, this
cannot be the extent of an organization's response to
consumer issues.

Practitioners must find ways to improve two-way
communication between an organization and its consumer
publics.

Information from consumers and regarding consumer
problems must be communicated to manufacturing and
service areas if problems are to be prevented before they
affect public opinion.

Public relations practitioners must use their skills to help
organizations provide consumers the right kind of information
in a form that they can use.

*Populus iamdudum defatatus est.*
(The consumer has been screwed long enough.) [1]

A couple from Middletown, Pa. checked into the Holiday Inn Penn Center in Philadelphia for a relaxing weekend. Their forty-eight-hour holiday was plagued with numerous annoyances inconsistent with the price of the accommodations: too few towels, a bathtub that would not drain and a shower head that sprayed the ceiling. The final blow came when the desk clerk forgot their wake-up call and caused them to have to pay an overtime charge in the hotel garage. [2]

A letter to the corporate offices of Holiday Inn brought immediate action in the form of an apology from the manager of the hotel and an offer of a free return visit. Nevertheless, the experiences of this couple are typical of those being cited more and more by consumers who feel that big business in particular is insensitive to the needs and problems of its customers. In a broad sense, consumers can be defined as the ultimate users of any product or service. Therefore, the issue of consumer satisfaction applies to all organizations that provide a product or service for public consumption. Government and nonprofit organizations also face the problems of dealing with irate consumers and their representative groups. The types of goods, services, and problems that are the focus of consumer complaints vary widely. The following list illustrates the diversity in the nature and seriousness of issues that are brought to public attention.

The National Highway Safety Bureau reported that 1 out
   of 11 tires it tested failed to meet safety standards.
Some eyeglasses are made of highly flammable cellulose.
TV sets emit potentially hazardous radiation.
Unsafe pollutants have been found in municipal water
   supplies.
300 out of 4,000 drug preparations, according to the
   National Academy of Sciences, did not live up to the
   claims made for them.
A patient died during minor surgery because hospital
   personnel confused oxygen and gas lines in the
   operating room.
Shoppers make uneconomical purchases in supermarkets
   forty per cent of the time because of deceptive
   advertising; 3.25 ounce tube of toothpaste is labelled
   "medium" for one brand, "large" for another, and
   "giant" for another.

The FTC says that chances for "winning riches" in games
   is 3.4 in 1,000 for a $3.87 prize.
Manufacturers fail to fulfill "guarantees."
State or federal regulatory practices allow unsafe or
   undesirable practices by the industries they are
   supposed to regulate.
Instruction manuals on how to assemble products are
   incomplete or incomprehensible.
Consumers lack knowledge of what credit costs and
   interests costs really are.

Too often the response of the manufacturer or organization is to deny
everything. This reflex action often extends to the hiring of public relations
practitioners to change public opinion and remove the teeth from consumer-
protection legislation. Increasingly, however, organizations are realizing the
need to respond effectively to consumer problems.

---

**Mini-Case 20-1
Procter & Gamble
and Rely Tampons**

Even when an organization has factual grounds to deny
liability for consumer problems, an attempt to totally evade
responsibility may be more costly in the long run. For
example, when toxic shock syndrome (TSS) was isolated as
a disease in 1980. Procter & Gamble's Rely tampon was
linked in media reports to a number of cases. At first there
was no evidence that Rely directly contributed to the
development of TSS, but the product nevertheless became
the target of massive publicity surrounding the sudden
upsurge of the disease. Procter & Gamble has been working
both independently and in cooperation with the U.S. Center
for Disease Control in an attempt to isolate the source of the
disease. The results of this research showed no contaminants
in the product that would transmit the disease. In fact, the
materials used in the tampon appeared to retard growth of
the bacterium involved. Results of an early study by the
Center for Disease Control showed that Rely and other
tampons appeared to be equally linked with TSS.

Later, however, Procter & Gamble was notified by the Federal
Food and Drug Administration that a second study at the
Center for Disease Control indicated that Rely was more
significantly linked with TSS than any other tampon.
Immediate action followed. A task force consisting of
representatives of the corporation's top management, public
relations, scientific, legal, and medical advisors was formed.
Members of the task force began to shuttle back and forth
between Procter & Gamble headquarters in Cincinnati, Ohio
and FDA offices in Washington, checking the details of the
Center for Disease Control study. In addition, an independent

commission of scientific and medical experts was assembled to evaluate research data and advise the task force.

Only one week after notification from the FDA, Procter & Gamble's task force had determined that Rely must be permanently withdrawn from the market. Although the company felt that the research data was arguably inconclusive, the publicity about TSS had linked Rely to the disease in the minds of consumers, and numerous product-liability suits were being filed. Immediately, the decision to withdraw the product was announced to the media and the task force began working out the terms of a consent agreement with the FDA. Within a week, the agreement had been finalized. Procter & Gamble agreed to buy back any unused tampons from retailers and consumers and to mount a massive advertising campaign warning the public of the dangers of toxic shock and informing them of the withdrawal of Rely. Within one week, eighty-five percent of the stock had been removed from store shelves. Figures 20-1 and 20-2 are samples of the public relations effort that resulted from this decision.

In addition to avoiding the negative effects of a possible FDA-ordered recall of Rely, the action the Procter & Gamble task force took was successful in dealing with the concerns of consumers. Through its quick response, Procter & Gamble avoided any lingering damage to its public image and the image of its other brands. An independent research firm took two surveys of public opinion concerning Procter & Gamble and its other products. One survey, immediately after the withdrawal was announced, showed a significant negative reaction to Rely. The second survey, conducted in mid-October, revealed admiration for Procter & Gamble's quick response and no permanent effect on the organization's public image.

---

**CONSUMER AWARENESS**

As our society moved from an agricultural base to a structure that is service-oriented and highly interdependent, perceptions of business also changed. Where the corporation was once perceived as a private entity, it is now thought to be quasi-public in its responsibilities.

At a point in our history when the variety of products available was rather small it was possible for consumers to rely on face-to-face relationships with merchants and tradesmen. Trademarks, grading and other forms of standardized product identification were not needed because the relatively small product selection enabled both buyer and seller to be knowledgeable about their transactions.

**Figure 20-1**
Letter from the Public
Relations Department of
Procter & Gamble

THE PROCTER & GAMBLE COMPANY

PUBLIC RELATIONS DEPARTMENT                          P. O. BOX 599    CINCINNATI, OHIO 45201

October 24, 1980

To Our Educational Services/Consumer Affairs Contacts:

In the past, my colleagues and I have discussed with you such topics as Procter &
Gamble's Educational Services, our teaching aids, and most recently, the consumer
service provided by the addition of toll-free 800-lines to P&G's consumer product
packages.

The current controversy concerning tampons is good news to no one. But because
of our mutual interest in better-informed consumers, we thought you might want
to hear from us about the considerable publicity on tampons in general and P&G's
Rely in particular. I would like to share with you:

— special advertising P&G has developed in cooperation with the
   Food & Drug Administration (FDA) to inform women about toxic
   shock syndrome (TSS) and its suspected link with tampons.

— a copy of the statement on Rely made by Procter & Gamble's Chief
   Executive Officer at the annual meeting of Procter & Gamble shareholders on October 14, 1980. It is a long statement, but it contains all we know on the subject to date. We believe, therefore,
   that it will provide you with a reference which will be helpful in
   sorting out and evaluating the speculation that often surrounds
   such issues.

This subject will obviously remain under considerable discussion in the coming
months. But since we have worked together in the past on professional and educational
matters of mutual interest, we wanted you to have this information now to
share with your families, friends and professional associates.

We believe the events speak to our Company's commitment to do what is right. I
would be personally interested in your reactions to the course of action P&G has
followed. Use the enclosed reply envelope to send me your thoughts or any specific
unanswered questions you have.

Sincerely,

Edward B. Tetrault, Manager
Educational Services/Consumer Affairs

EBT:ml
cc:    Ms. J. A. Learn
       Ms. P. B. Sussman
       Ms. M. C. Ruffin

P.S.   The enclosed advertisement will also be helpful if you or your associates
       have any questions about how to obtain a refund for Rely still on hand.

Reprinted by permission: Courtesy of The Procter & Gamble Company

Toward the end of the nineteenth century, the relationship between seller
and buyer began to change. Manufacturers of consumer goods found it
necessary to expand their markets, and began to ship goods over great
distances, thereby separating the purchaser from the source. This lengthening
of the channels of distribution brought about the use of preservatives such
as formaldehyde and other harmful additives in food. A large segment of the
business community in the United States adopted the philosophy that customers have the responsibility to look out for their own interest. This philosophy of trade created a gap between buyer and seller that led to many
unethical business practices. Eventually, muckraking journalists exposed
unsafe and unsanitary conditions in many industries, especially food packing.
In 1906 the first pure food law was signed to correct a number of the problems
that had been revealed.

In the 1930s consumers became aware of corporate abuses in the areas
of food and drugs. More federal legislation was passed to remedy the prob-

**Figure 20-2**
Advertising Message
from Procter & Gamble

# A message to users of Rely tampons from Procter & Gamble.

Women who use Rely® tampons should stop using them and return the unused product to Procter & Gamble for a refund.

Government studies show that tampons are associated with an increased risk of Toxic Shock Syndrome (TSS). This is a newly-discovered disease that affects mainly women who use tampons during their periods.

Toxic Shock Syndrome can be very serious and is believed to be responsible for a number of deaths. Almost all women who have had the disease have recovered.

Some recent studies indicate that Rely was apparently involved with Toxic Shock Syndrome to a greater extent than other tampon brands.

Toxic Shock Syndrome was first reported in November 1978. It is believed to be caused by a toxin produced by a bacterial infection (Staphylococcus aureus). In June 1980, the U.S. Center for Disease Control (CDC) first linked it to tampon use. No one yet knows how or why tampons are associated with this disease.

In June, based on research conducted up to that point, CDC said that tampon use alone was not sufficient to cause the disease. CDC also said that no particular brand of tampon was more involved than others.

But on September 15, CDC announced a new study. It compared women who had Toxic Shock Syndrome with women who did not. The study confirmed that Toxic Shock Syndrome was associated with tampon use. It also indicated that Rely was apparently involved with more cases than any other brand. Here are the key data available to date:

**DEFINITE TSS CASES REPORTED TO CDC**

| | | Brands Used** | | |
|---|---|---|---|---|
| | # Cases Involved | Rely Brand | Other Identified Tampon Brands | Brands Unidentified |
| CDC Study #1 (completed June 20) | 52 | 17 | 43 | 2 |
| CDC Study #2 (completed September 12) | 50 | 35 | 22 | 0 |
| Other cases reported to CDC | 140 | 24 | 19 | 100 |
| Total CDC cases (through September 23) | 242 | 76 | 84 | 102 |

**Brands used** totals more than the number of cases reported because some women used more than one brand.

On September 21, P&G convened a scientific advisory group to review all known data relating to TSS. The group concluded that the available data were still fragmentary, but advised that the results of the latest CDC study should not be ignored.

Therefore, on September 22, Procter & Gamble announced it was suspending sales of Rely and that it would refund money to consumers who had Rely in their homes.

The Food and Drug Administration offers this advice to consumers:

"The current evidence indicates that women should stop using Rely. Women who want to reduce their risk of toxic shock even further may want to consider not using any tampons at all, or using napkins part of the time during their periods.

"Women using tampons who develop a high fever and vomiting or diarrhea during their periods should stop using tampons and see their doctors right away."

The FDA and CDC have said they will continue studying Toxic Shock Syndrome to find out what causes it and why it is associated with tampons. Procter & Gamble will participate with the government in this important effort.

In the meantime, Procter & Gamble advises women not to use Rely tampons and to return unused Rely for a refund.

**You should know these symptoms of Toxic Shock Syndrome:**
- High Fever (102°) and
- Vomiting or diarrhea

If you have these symptoms during your menstrual period, discontinue use of tampons and see your doctor at once.

**How to return Rely and obtain refund:**
Send your unused Rely tampons with your name and address to:
Rely,
Box 8448,
Clinton, Iowa 52736.
And you will receive a refund including cost of mailing.

*NOTE: You may see Rely advertisements in the November issues of various women's magazines. Unfortunately, these issues were already printed when the decision to suspend sales of Rely was made on September 22, 1980.*

© 1980, The Procter & Gamble Company

Reprinted by permission: Courtesy of the Procter & Gamble Company

lems that had been uncovered. The Sea Food Act of 1934, the Wool Labeling Act of 1939, the Flammable Fabrics Act and the Wheeler Lea Act provided government standards and regulations for the food packing, garment, and advertising industries respectively.

The 1960s saw a new rise of consumer activism marked by the scandal over the drug thalidomide and by Ralph Nader's successful campaign against the Corvair automobile. The concerns of this latest era of consumer awareness were articulated by President John F. Kennedy in the preamble to his consumer message to Congress in March of 1962. The four basic consumer rights which he stated then have formed the foundation of the American consumer movement to the present day.

*The Right to Safety*: Products should not damage or harm the user; they should live up to the maker's claims. Proponents based their views on the assertion that in an affluent nation, mass production and complicated distribution systems have increased the risk of danger to health and safety. They claimed that the consumer has a right to be protected against danger from inferior products and deceptive industry practices.

*The Right to be Heard*: Consumers' views should be given greater consideration by those responsible for marketing goods and services. Consumer advocates claimed that manufacturers are increasingly less responsive to consumers' opinions and complaints.

*The Right to Choose*: Rational consumer choice must be preserved based on the right of consumers to spend their money on any one of a diverse number of products.

*The Right to be Informed*: The consumer must have easy access to complete and accurate product information in order to exercise the first three rights. Critics contended that through its advertising, business often neglected to provide the information necessary to intelligent buying decisions.

## ISSUES OF MODERN CONSUMERISM

The decade of the 1960s was a period of general discontent that spread deep into the fabric of American society. This atmosphere of unrest proved to be a fertile breeding ground for the development of many new consumer issues as well as the revival of several old ones. The bigness of American business itself became a negative factor from the consumer's perspective. Consumers began to feel powerless in the buyer-seller relationship when dealing with giant companies, conglomerates, and multinational corporations. These feelings of powerlessness in buying-selling transactions produced further demands for consumer legislation. In the past, calls for reform had come from legislators or from journalists, but in the 1960s the movement was led largely by consumer advocates in the private sector.

## Consumer Advocates

The modern consumer movement has applied principles of social organizing to combat what is perceived as the ever-growing power and influence of the giant corporations that now dominate American business. Because of this consequent imbalance in the seller-buyer relationship, consumer advocates believe, every aspect of the American economic climate is biased in favor of big business. They claim that:

Legal remedies in cases of corporate liability or criminal action are insufficient.

Prototype research and development for safety and health of consumers is lacking.

Consumer information systems are inadequate.

Corporate executives are not required to answer to Congress on consumer issues.

Government has failed to provide for an effective system of handling consumer complaints.[5]

According to some of these activists a balance of bargaining power between buyer and seller can be restored only by replacing the traditional adage *caveat emptor* with the government-enforced requirement *caveat venditor*, "let the seller beware."

**Better-Educated Consumers** The rising educational level of American consumers has contributed to the development of the current consumer movement. Expectation levels have been raised along with awareness and knowledge. As this trend continues, consumers will:

Have greater and different expectations about the goods and services they purchase and the organizations which provide them.

Place greater emphasis on product performance, quality and safety.

Be more aware of their "rights" as consumers.

Be more responsive to political initiatives to protect these rights.

Have more self-esteem.

Want to be treated more as individuals.

Be far less tolerant of authoritarianism and organizational restraints.

Consumers today demand more information about the products and services they purchase and they demand more voice in business decisions that affect them.

**Product Defects** Almost every day consumers learn of product warnings, hazards, and recalls in the mass media. Manufacturers claim that although defective products are the exception, they make news while routinely good products do not. That may be true statistically, but every consumer has had a bad experience with a product of some type, and this makes it easy for them to identify with news reports about recalls and defects. In its 1970 report the *National Commission on Product Safety*, concluded that "the exposure of consumers to unreasonable consumer product hazards is excessive by any standard of measurement."[7] The report also noted that 20 million Americans are injured in the home each year in connection with consumer products. The commission estimated the annual cost of these product-related accidents to be in excess of $5.5 billion.

**Excessively Priced and Inadequate Repair Service.** Once consumers have braved the threat of product defects and recalls to make a purchase, they may encounter numerous frustrations in obtaining product repairs. Independent repair services have become difficult to monitor and control; incompetence and fraud appear to be equally widespread. In one survey conducted in New York City, twenty servicemen were called to repair a defective tube in a television set. Charges ranged from $4 to $30 for the $8.93 job. The researchers concluded that 17 of the 20 servicemen called were dishonest or incompetent.[8] Everyone has encountered this kind of problem in some form.

Several similar surveys have been conducted in various repair industries and indicate a strong probability that a consumer is either likely to be charged for service that was not performed or sold parts and service that were not needed. In response to this growing problem, many major manufacturers are attempting to provide their own service units.

**Inadequate or Unfulfilled Guarantees.** Product warranties have been the focus of numerous consumer complaints. It is claimed that manufacturers and retailers have carefully written warranties that guarantee nothing, or that they refuse to honor warranty statements. This problem, perhaps more than any other single concern, has created a credibility gap between American business and its consumers. The Presidential Task Force on Appliance Warranties and Service in 1969 reported that ".   . it is fair to state that in some instances the exclusions, disclaimers, and exceptions so diminished the obligations of the manufacturer that it was deceptive to designate the document as a warranty, because the remaining obligations were lacking in substance."[9] When the consumer who is unable to gain satisfaction from a dealer takes the complaint directly to the manufacturer, the task force found:

It is not uncommon for the manufacturer to ignore the appeal altogether and make no response. Some do respond and advise the consumer to contact the dealer.   .   . Others recommend contact with a distributor or area service representative. This often leads to what is described as the "run around" with a considerable exchange of correspondence, broken appointments, and nothing being done, with the manufacturer, distributor, and retailer all disclaiming any blame or ability to solve the problem.[10]

**Unfair and Deceptive Advertising.** Further compounding the deterioration of the buyer-seller relationship is the proliferation of unfair or deceptive methods for the promotion of products and services. Again the business community points out that deceptive advertisers are a minority that receive disproportionate attention, particularly from the mass media. Government-sponsored research seems to back up the claims that only a relative few use false or misleading advertising. Research done for the Federal Drug Administration in 1969 by an agency of the National Academy of Science found the vast majority of the drugs they tested lived up to the claims manufacturers made in their advertising. Only seven percent were found to advertise claims for effectiveness that could not be supported. Included in this group, however, were mouthwashes, which are widely used in the United States and gross more than $200 million in sales each year.[11] Therefore, even though only a small percentage of advertisers may have been guilty of false or deceptive practice, their fraudulent claims had a direct impact on the majority of American consumers.

The emergence of mass-marketing techniques and strategies has created a climate that allows a small percentage of American industry to have a major impact on public opinion. This situation has created a climate where otherwise small infractions can do major harm to an entire industry because of the large numbers of consumers affected. Statistically only a small percentage of manufactured goods cannot live up to their advertising, but enough consumers have had a bad experience with these few products to make it a common occurrence.

**PUBLIC RELATIONS AND CONSUMER AFFAIRS**

The result of the consumer-related problems we described in the first part of this chapter has been a steady decline in the public's opinion of American business in general. As we noted in Chapter 15, in 1960 about seventy percent of the consumers surveyed felt that business was striking a fair balance between making profits and providing service. By 1972 that view was held by only twenty-nine percent of the consumers surveyed.[12] In the early 1960s business began to feel the pressure of declining public opinion. Early efforts to counter this disturbing trend were based on quick, dramatic demonstrations of sympathy to consumer concerns rather than on long-term solutions. This shallow approach, coupled with the tendency of many business leaders to regard consumer awareness as a fad that would go away if ignored, led to a situation in which groups outside the firm identified consumer problems and forced managers to react to them. Recently corporate management has recognized the importance of consumer issues and realized the need for organizations to take the lead in identifying and solving their own problems.

Evidence of the importance business now places on consumer issues can be seen in the willingness of some organizations to take action against others that do not respond to consumer needs. Giant Foods has responded to the unwillingness of some of its suppliers to label their products properly by dropping those lines. This action has not only put additional pressure on those manufacturers who would not respond, but has also enhanced Giant Food's image.[13]

**The Corporate Response to Consumerism**

In the past two decades the corporate consumer affairs unit has become a fixture in most organizations with any direct link to consumers. A variety of names may be used to describe this function: public affairs, customer relations, consumer relations, consumer advocate, or public relations. Whatever the title, these units usually work on the outside to improve the organization's relationships and communication with consumers and on the inside to help the organization become more responsive to consumers by investigating and articulating consumer issues in the decision-making circles of management. Responsibilities of the consumer relations unit usually include resolving customer complaints, disseminating consumer information, advising management on consumer issues, and dealing with outside consumer-advocate groups.

Frequently consumer relations units are linked to the public relations function of the organization. This relationship is a natural one, since consumers are one of the publics that public relations practitioners have traditionally served. The exact placement and design of the consumer affairs units differ greatly depending upon the size and nature of the organization and the diversity of its products or services. One common characteristic does appear among the different approaches to consumer affairs—the vast majority of the units report directly to top management. This provides the autonomy necessary to investigate issues and identify problems before they blow up, as well as easy access to those who make policy decisions.

**Organizational Structure**

Figure 20-3 illustrates the placement of the consumer relations unit at J. C. Penney. The Educational and Consumer Relations Department is a separate unit under the supervision of the public relations manager, vice president of public relations, and vice president of public affairs. This organizational substructure includes all of the other functions and staff specialists that are normally associated with public relations functions. The advantage of a separate consumer relations unit within the public relations area is the responsiveness and ability to follow up that is possible with a specialized group. Within the Educational and Consumer Relations Department there exist three functional groups. One group is concerned with various publications dealing with consumer issues sponsored by J. C. Penney. A second group is charged with the coordination and development of annual consumer issues programs for educators operated through local stores. A third consumer relations team is responsible for organizing and developing various informational programs in which consumers can participate.

The Chase Manhattan Bank's Consumer Affairs group has even greater access to the top, as Figure 20-4 shows. Organized under the public relations vice-president and director and the corporate communications senior vice-president, consumer affairs at Chase Manhattan has a direct line to the chairman and chief executive officer. Because of this structure, the consumer affairs division operates as a consumer consulting service to top management as well as handling complaints that are directed at senior management. Fre-

**Figure 20-3**
Organizational Structure
for J. C. Penney
Company, Inc.

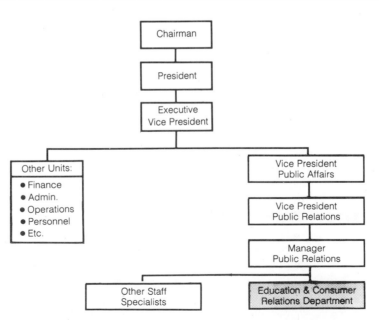

*The Consumer Affairs Department: Organization and Function.* The Conference Board, 1973. Reprinted by permission.

quently the complaints it receives are those which have already gone through regular channels without resolution. In these situations consumer affairs can deal directly with the vice president in charge of the division where the complaint originated.

Most divisional firms like Chase Manhattan have chosen to locate their consumer affairs group at the corporate level rather than in the divisions. This provides a consumer voice in organization policy that affects the entire organization. In this way the consumer affairs unit becomes more than a complaint department. A few very large organizations have consumer affairs groups at both the corporate and divisional levels.

**Consumer Affairs
Staff**
Staffing of consumer affairs units varies tremendously. Some organizations have only one consumer affairs specialist while others have in excess of a hundred employees assigned to their consumer affairs group. Frequently the staff is divided into groups responsible for certain functions such as complaint handling, publications, consumer education, and so on. The activities of these groups are frequently integrated with those of other public relations groups with similar functions in the organization.

Most often organizations choose personnel with extensive experience within the company to staff their consumer affairs unit. This background is considered necessary because staff members must handle complaints and investigate problems that require a thorough knowledge of the organization.[14] Frequently these staff members are selected from various other public relations positions. One recent study revealed that among chief consumer affairs officers public relations was the area of previous experience most often cited.[15]

**Figure 20-4**
Organization and
Structure for The Chase
Manhattan Bank

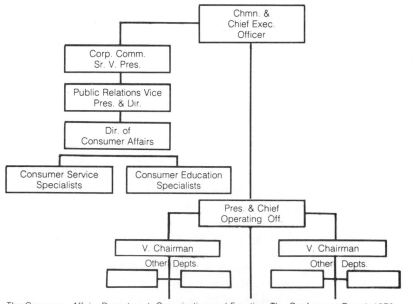

*The Consumer Affairs Department: Organization and Function.* The Conference Board, 1973. Reprinted by permission.

**Complaint Handling**   While customer complaints are a primary concern of most consumer affairs units, this is only one aspect of their growing list of responsibilities. Even the rare units that are not directly involved in handling complaints from consumers do participate in policy decisions that establish the procedures for complaint routing and response. These departments are also concerned with monitoring the effectiveness of policies and procedures and their effect on consumers.

In an attempt to ensure fast and uniform processing of consumer complaints, many organizations have developed elaborate complaint control systems. Consumer affairs specialists feel that:

1. All complaints should be logged when received.
2. The complaining party should be notified at receipt with a statement about how the problem will be handled.
3. Action to resolve the complaint should follow quickly.
4. Company personnel and departments that are affected should be notified promptly and their response monitored.
5. On going analyses should be made to determine the pattern of complaints received to look for possible preventive action.

The operation of the consumer affairs unit of the Chase Manhattan Bank is an example of how such a comprehensive system works. The office monitors various types of complaints, dividing them into about twenty-five categories and preparing monthly reports on the effectiveness of each division and the entire company. From these analyses, recommendations are made for preventive measures. A summary of typical complaint letters, including direct quotations, is also prepared and submitted with these monthly reports. Top management has found these summaries to be particularly revealing and informative. For example, one such analysis revealed that the tone of collection letters sent out by the bank's credit department was perceived as irritating. The bank's management reasoned that irritating a customer was not likely to speed up payment and would only harm the bank's image, and steps were taken to revise the letter so that it was firm but reasonable in tone.

Frequently the consumer affairs unit at Chase Manhattan attempts to deal with grievances which have not been expressed. For every letter that arrives, there are probably many more dissatisfied customers who complain to others but not to the bank. In an attempt to discover these hidden complaints, questionnaires are sent out with letters over the president's signature to customers of each branch bank (*Figure 20-5*). The information collected in this form is compiled in a statistical summary and reviewed by top management. Organizations with more progressive consumer affairs policies are integrating this kind of information into their production and service decision-making structures.

Responding to consumer letters concerning product performance prevented a major loss of customers for Chesebrough-Ponds, Inc. Letters from customers regarding Wipe 'n Dipe baby washcloths complained that the oil was settling to the bottom of the package. The manufacturer promptly reworded the labels to recommend that consumers turn the package upside

**Figure 20–5**
Questionnaire Sent to
Customers of Chase
Manhattan Bank

CONSUMER RELATIONS SURVEY:

Please check ONE answer in each of the following categories:

| | In–person at Branch | By Mail | Quick Deposit Box | Drive–in Window |
|---|---|---|---|---|
| 1. How do you currently do your banking | ( ) | ( ) | ( ) | ( ) |

| | Daily | Weekly | Twice a Month | Not Applicable |
|---|---|---|---|---|
| 2. How often do you come into the branch? | ( ) | ( ) | ( ) | ( ) |

Other (specify) : _____

| 3. How would you rate our tellers on: | Very Good | Satis-factory | Poor | Not Sure |
|---|---|---|---|---|
| a) Courtesy | ( ) | ( ) | ( ) | ( ) |
| b) Accuracy | ( ) | ( ) | ( ) | ( ) |
| c) Speed of service | ( ) | ( ) | ( ) | ( ) |
| d) Knowledge of job | ( ) | ( ) | ( ) | ( ) |
| e) Helpfulness | ( ) | ( ) | ( ) | ( ) |

| 4. How would you rate our officers on: | Very Good | Satis-factory | Poor | Not Sure |
|---|---|---|---|---|
| a) Courtesy | ( ) | ( ) | ( ) | ( ) |
| b) Accuracy | ( ) | ( ) | ( ) | ( ) |
| c) Speed of service | ( ) | ( ) | ( ) | ( ) |
| d) Knowledge of job | ( ) | ( ) | ( ) | ( ) |
| e) Helpfulness | ( ) | ( ) | ( ) | ( ) |

| | over 5 years | 2–5 years | 1–2 years | under 1 year |
|---|---|---|---|---|
| 5. How long have you had your account at this branch? | ( ) | ( ) | ( ) | ( ) |

| | Very Good | Satis-factory | Poor | Not Sure |
|---|---|---|---|---|
| 6. How would you rate the convenience of banking hours at your branch? | ( ) | ( ) | ( ) | ( ) |

| 7. How would you rate the appearance of your banking office? | Always | Some-times | Seldom | Not Sure |
|---|---|---|---|---|
| a) Clean | ( ) | ( ) | ( ) | ( ) |
| b) Orderly | ( ) | ( ) | ( ) | ( ) |

8.  If applicable at this branch,
    how would you rate our

| | Very Good | Satis-factory | Poor | Not Sure |
|---|---|---|---|---|
| a) Express Line Service | ( ) | ( ) | ( ) | ( ) |
| b) Drive–in Window | ( ) | ( ) | ( ) | ( ) |
| c) Safe Deposit Service | ( ) | ( ) | ( ) | ( ) |
| d) Quick Deposit Service | ( ) | ( ) | ( ) | ( ) |

9.  To further help us in this survey,
    please check:

| | AGE: | under 25 | 25–34 | 35–50 | over 50 |
|---|---|---|---|---|---|
| Male   ( ) | | ( ) | ( ) | ( ) | ( ) |
| Female ( ) | | ( ) | ( ) | ( ) | ( ) |

10. What other services do you use at
    this branch?

Safe Deposit          ( )
Savings Account       ( )
Christmas Club        ( )
Other: _____

We welcome your suggestions on specific areas where we may improve our services and any other
comments you may have: _____

_____

Name _____Address _____

(Name and address are not essential, but you may fill it in, if you wish.)

_____

down periodically to redistribute the oil. Letters from consumers to Scott
Paper Company stating that their paper napkins emitted a strange odor started
an investigation that turned up a leaking valve. At Coca-Cola, advice from the
director of consumer affairs was heeded and Tab labels were changed to
read "less than one calorie per 10 ounce serving" instead of the potentially
deceptive statment "$\frac{1}{16}$ of a calorie per ounce." In each situation a potentially
costly mistake was averted or corrected before it got out of hand by quick
attention to information from the consumer affairs unit.[17]

**Consumer Information**   The major tenet of the consumer movement is that consumers do not have
adequate information for making purchasing decisions. The proliferation of
products and services, combined with greatly lengthened lines of distribution,
have helped to create this problem. It is also true that consumer problems
often are the result of product misuse, improper maintenance, or purchase
of the wrong product for the intended use. Consumer relations units have
responded to the need for fuller and clearer information through simplified
warranties, clarified product-use instructions, and educational programs to
help consumers select the right product for their needs and use it properly.

J. C. Penney has launched a massive consumer information effort consisting
of improved labels, publications to explain how labels and warranties should
be read, educational programs for consumers at local stores and programs
to help educators obtain information and materials.

**The Corporate**
**Ombudsman**
The consumer affairs role within corporations has become that of consumer spokesperson to management. Most consumer affairs specialists see it as part of their job to take an active role in decision making by speaking out for the consumer in all levels of management. They actively solicit consumer opinions and make management aware of the effects various decisions will have on consumers. The in-house ombudsman must seek a balance between the needs of the actual customers, the demands of consumer activists and the goals of the organization. This role as liaison has always been the highest calling for public relations professionals.

Those who understand the role of public relations realize that the practitioner must do more than echo the company line. Public relations professionals must help senior managers to stay in touch with the various publics of the organization.

---

**CASE STUDY:**    **By Charlotte Hatfield**
**CONSUMER INPUT**    **Ball State University, Muncie, Indiana**

---

Effective consumer relations means not only providing consumers with current product information, but also being aware of and responsive to consumer concerns. Public utilities, particularly the nation's telephone companies, have recognized this necessity. These businesses face a particular challenge because their consumers are the general public—people of all ages, professions, ethnic and special interest groups, and from every economic and education level. As one part of its consumer communications program, Indiana Bell Telephone established in 1979 a Consumer Advisory Council to facilitate two-way communication between the company and its customers through a representative panel of telephone company consumers.

The fifteen council members reflect the geographical area served by Indiana Bell and include representatives of the following groups: teenaged student; family; senior citizen; handicapped; low income; minority; urban; suburban; rural; small business; and nonprofit organizations. Remaining panel members are from consumer-professional, theoretical-technical, and consumer-user groups. The latter members serve as independent "resident experts" in areas nearest their own professional or personal interests, although they do not represent any organized interest groups. The council is moderated by a university professor who acts as an independent representative, and the only company representative is the consumer affairs specialist, who serves as secretary to the group.

The council's stated purpose is to:

1. Establish dialogue between consumers and Indiana Bell on issues of mutual concern.
2. Promote understanding of company and consumer positions on the issues.

3. Explore policy alternatives and compromises.
4. Formulate recommendations to the company.
5. Identify potential issues of concern with particular focus on implications for the future.

The panel members agree to follow certain guidelines. The appointment provides no monetary honorarium, beyond reimbursement for members' expenses. Meetings are conducted informally and are closed to the public, except selected Bell personnel or invited experts. Neither panel members nor Indiana Bell will make public statements about the proceedings of the council meetings. Panel members are appointed to the council for one year, although appointments can be renewed.

In bi-monthly meetings, the council discusses a wide range of subjects, including how Indiana Bell meets the needs of small business; utility rate making; advertising policy; service and equipment for disabled and elderly persons; local measured service; directory assistance charging; and the Bell System Statement of Consumer Rights.

Two council recommendations regarding Yellow Pages advertising have been implemented by the company. The first, concerning false claims by advertisers regarding business history and services offered, prompted Indiana Bell to actively solicit input from local Better Business Bureaus, consumer protection agencies, and individuals regarding accuracy and honesty in the advertising. As part of this effort, Better Business Bureaus were provided copies of the Advertising Codes and Standards for Bell Telephone companies.

The second recommendation by the council was to emphasize to consumers that the Yellow Pages are strictly a form of advertising. The recommendation led the company to insert a "Buyer be aware" message in the Yellow Pages section of telephone books.

Bell officials see the Consumer Advisory Council as an important source of input into the decision-making process. The minutes of the meetings are distributed internally to upper-level management and department heads.

**Questions**

1. Why is it in the best interests of both the advisory council and Indiana Bell to keep a low profile on the activities of the council?

2. How would Indiana Bell go about selecting council members? What are some of the concerns for balancing the group and continuing their term on the panel?

3. The consumer advisory council is only one part of the Indiana Bell Telephone Consumer Relations Program. What other consumer-related activities might the company be involved in to benefit and communicate with consumers?

**NOTES**   1 "The Heat is On", *Newsweek,* 5 March 1973, p. 60.

2 "Disgruntled Customers Finally Get a Hearing," *Business Week,* 21 April 1975.

3 Robert D. Hay, E. R. Gray and J. E. Gates, *Business and Society* (Cincinnati: South-Western, 1976), p. 297.

[4] S. E. Cohen, "How Business Lobby Swang Defeat of Consumerist Bill," *Advertising Age*, 20 February 1978.

[5] Hay, Gray, and Gates, *Business and Society*, p. 300.

[6] Ibid., p. 301.

[7] National Commission on Product Safety, *Final Report Presented to the President and Congress* (Washington, D.C.: U.S. Government Printing Office, June 1970).

[8] E. G. Weiss, "The Corporate Deaf Ear," *Business Horizons* (December 1968): p. 14.

[9] Presidential Task Force on Appliance Warranties, "Presidential Report of the Task Force on Appliance Warranties and Service," mimeographed, (Washington, D.C.: January 8, 1969).

[10] G. A. Steiner, *Business and Society* (New York: Random House, 1975).

[11] E. F. Cox, R. C. Fellmeth, and J. E. Schultz, *The Nader Report on the Federal Trade Commission* (New York: Richard W. Baron, 1969).

[12] Daniel Yankelovich, "The Real Meaning of the Student Revolution," The Conference Board, March, 1972.

[13] D. A. Aaker, and G. S. Day, "Corporate Responses to Consumerism Pressures," *Harvard Business Review* 50 (November-December 1972): 117.

[14] E. P. McGuire, *The Consumer Affairs Department: Organization and Functions, Report No. 609* (New York: The Conference Board, 1973), p. 2.

[15] R. T. Hise, P. L. Gillett, and J. P. Kelly, "The Corporate Consumer Affairs Effort," *MSU Business Topics* (Summer 1978): 17–26.

[16] Aaker and Day, "Corporate Responses," 1972.

[17] "Disgruntled Consumers Finally Get a Hearing," *Business Week*.

# CHAPTER 21  URBAN PROBLEMS

**PREVIEW**   Social awareness, sensitivity to community problems, and open communication with all segments of society must be part of the public relations objectives of any organization.

Public relations practitioners must be able to translate their organization's concerns and actions into messages that are meaningful for urban publics.

The urban poor must be recognized as an important public. Organizations must be responsive to the opinions, needs, and problems of the poor, whether or not this group includes consumers of their goods and services.

As the size and number of government programs designed to help minorities and the urban poor are reduced, business and other organizations will face increased responsibilities. This is especially true in the areas of unemployment and discrimination where substantial problems remain.

Public relations practitioners will be called upon by their organizations to assess the needs of cities in the 1980s and recommend appropriate responses.

**THE URBAN POOR AS A PUBLIC**

Today's organizations have come to understand the importance of responsible citizenship, and public relations practice has grown in stature and scope because of this heightened awareness. As we discussed in Chapter 18, public relations has become the functioning arm of most organizations with regard to their social responsibilities. One of the characteristics of modern society is the tremendous growth of urban centers. The movement of people out of rural America and into our cities in search of jobs is a continuing process. While many of these are highly educated young people seeking to establish a career, many more are uneducated, and unskilled and cannot be selective about employment. Today, even the promised-land cities of the Sunbelt are experiencing an influx of unemployable poor. This, coupled with the growth of immigrant, refugee, and illegal alien populations, is creating a scarcity of jobs, and increasing all of the problems associated with high unemployment.

Organizations of all types find themselves needing to understand and respond to these problems. Local, state and federal governments must monitor and help to relieve the problems caused by urban poverty. Charitable and health care organizations must serve the needs of these individuals on a continuing basis. As federal, city, and state welfare programs are cut back, private business must step in to see that necessary services are provided and that solutions to these problems are sought.

While the urban poor could not be considered a major market for many business organizations, they are an important public. Urban poverty is a negative factor in the business environment of any city. Business controls the distribution of capital and employment in our society and, therefore, the cycle of poverty cannot be broken without its help. In many ways good business environments, because they hold the promise of jobs, are responsible for the concentration of poor in our cities. This responsibility must be met by all organizations. Public relations must extend beyond those publics who are consumers or regulators. Public relations practitioners, because of their unique training, are the logical choice of most managers to monitor urban problems and recommend actions their organizations can take. The following mini-case describes the dawning of one executive's new awareness of a public too long overlooked.

**Mini-Case 21-1
Business and the
Urban Dilemma**

As James Roche sat in his presidential office in Detroit's GM Building one hot evening in July, 1967, he, like many of his colleagues, was shocked into an awareness of the crises facing most American cities.[1] What he saw was several square blocks of Detroit's inner city engulfed in flames. That summer similar occurrences were witnessed by business executives in several cities. Mass rioting, resulting in looting and fires which destroyed substantial portions of Los Angeles, Detroit, New York and Washington, D.C., produced a shock effect throughout our society.

Suddenly the attention of the entire nation was focused on the problems of urban decay and poverty that had been growing for decades. Even though business and government had always been aware of these problems and involved in attempts to solve them, the events of 1967 brought a new realization. The severity of these urban problems and their impact upon every phase of American life was suddenly clear. Businesses that had prospered for years with thousands of impoverished people living just outside their gates realized that they could no longer relieve themselves of responsibility by contributing to charitable organizations. A previously unrecognized public was making its needs known and it refused to be ignored. In this crisis American business and government responded in various ways, sometimes independently, sometimes in concert, attempting to provide equal opportunity employment, job training for the disadvantaged, aid to minority enterprises, and improved housing conditions.

Many of these efforts to improve conditions for those who live in the inner cities have been initiated and conceived by concerned business leaders who feel their organizations have certain responsibilities to the society in which they exist. After more than a decade of programs and policies designed to meet the needs of the urban poor, both business and government are beginning to evaluate their efforts. Such evaluations always uncover inadequacies, wastes, and misplaced emphasis. Yet in spite of some obvious failures on the part of both business and government, the past fifteen years have unquestionably changed the outlook and role of organizations in the United States. The need for sensitivity to community problems and open communication with many segments of society has not diminished, and as a result the role of those managers responsible for public relations has become a critical one. Public relations practitioners must be able to translate their company's concern and actions into messages that are meaningful for the publics involved. More importantly, the corporate public relations staff must be able to detect social problems in the community and make management aware of them. In its two-way communication role between the organization and its publics, public relations' function can be a critical key to the effectiveness of businesses' response to urban problems.

In this chapter we will examine some of the conditions of the inner cities that brought about the unrest of the mid 1960s, and attempt to evaluate the effects of various business and government programs designed to respond to these problems. Next we will take a critical look at the responsiveness of business and the areas in which this response appears to be most effective. Finally we will consider the role of public relations in discovering areas of need and in communicating the response to these needs.

**PROBLEMS OF THE**
**INNER CITIES**

**Urban Poverty**

Most of the problems that haunted our large cities in the 1960s could be traced to poverty in one way or another. Although statistics show that only about one-third of America's poor families live in the central cities, they are probably the best-known poverty group in our society. The urban poor who live in central city areas are more concentrated and thus more visible than other impoverished groups. The nature of the inner city itself makes the conditions of poverty even more devastating for the people who live there.

Concentrations of poor families have developed within most of our large cities. Minority groups are disproportionately represented: Although only eleven percent of the population of the United States in 1970 were black, thirty-four percent of the people whose income fell below the poverty level were black.[2] Similarly disproportionate statistics hold for Hispanics and other groups. The ghetto and barrio areas of our major cities have become centers of poverty, unemployment, pollution, crime, and are served inadequately by civic functions such as sanitation, police and fire protection, and transportation. Within these areas a cultural phenomenon develops which the economist John Kenneth Galbraith describes as "insular poverty:"[3] poverty that results from the environment. Many forces contribute to this cultural poverty in our inner cities: poverty itself—lack of income—contributes to ill health through inadequate diet, lack of medical care, and substandard housing, with poor sanitation and heating. These conditions, coupled with exceptionally high crime rates, create an environment that breeds poverty physically and psychologically.

**The ghetto is not just a place with many unemployed and subemployed persons; it is a place that saps motivation, erodes the capacity to learn, pulls young persons out of national mainstream acivities by overwhelming them with human temptation and risk. It is also a place where it is difficult, inconvenient, costly and risky to carry out economic activities.[4]**

In the late '60s and early '70s large corporations found themselves surrounded by these disabling conditions, and the civil unrest spawned in such environments made them realize that American business had a responsibility to help solve the problems of the inner city. Thus, the urban poor achieved recognition as a public with which business must maintain some relationship.

With encouragement from federal programs, corporate activities to combat poverty have increased substantially since 1967. Business is investing more money in programs to increase employment and training for the disadvantaged, to support minority enterprises, and to support city and regional planning and community health efforts.[5] Large sums of money from private industry are also being channeled into poverty areas through a variety of social-service organizations. One study reported that out of 247 businesses surveyed, 175 said they had revised their charitable contributions since 1967 to provide funds for organizations specifically involved with urban problems.[6] These organizations direct the corporate funds they receive into a wide variety of programs including drug rehabilitation, child care, recreation centers, youth counseling, help for the elderly, minority business assistance, and community health centers.

Government programs to combat poverty were stepped up in the 1960s and early '70s. The Area Redevelopment Act of 1961 provided special job training programs for workers in economically depressed areas. This was followed by the Manpower Development and Training Act of 1962, which provided training for workers whose skills had become obsolete due to technological and economic changes. In the same year, the Public Welfare Amendments set up federally financed training for unemployed persons whose families received Aid to Dependent Children. This era of antipoverty legislation concluded with the Economic Opportunity Act of 1964, a major piece of legislation that set a goal of helping the disadvantaged of our society to achieve greater participation in the country's economic activities by reducing the inequities in the distribution of income that existed then.

As with all government programs, there have been delays, charges of corruption, and inefficiencies, but progress has been made. In 1959, 22.4 percent of the population fell below the poverty mark; by 1970 this figure had been reduced to 12.6 percent—a decline of 14 million individuals in the poverty category. Table 21-1 shows the percentages of individuals below the poverty level for the years 1959–1970. A marked decline is present in all categories. Recent budget cuts have hit many of these programs especially hard, and the long-term effects of these actions are difficult to predict. But it appears certain, that past actions of business and government have been able to reduce poverty.

**Inadequate Housing**   In 1968 the President's Committee on Urban Housing summed up the problem of substandard housing as follows:

Life in the slums contradicts the classic picture of American democracy, a picture which includes equal treatment, free choice, and opportunity for a better life, full participation in the benefits of society. It is more and more apparent that life in contemporary American city slums does not accord with those promises.[7]

As early as 1934, in passing the National Housing Act, the Congress of the United States committed this nation to supply "a decent home" for every family. Yet more than 8 million families live in inadequate housing today. A 1972 study found that underhoused families are most likely to be living in rental quarters in the inner city, to be nonwhite, sixty-five or older, and have an annual income of less than $3,000.[8] For this reason most of the attention to problems of inadequate housing by both business and government has been directed toward the cities.

The problem of substandard housing, however, goes far beyond the slums in which it exists and the plight of the impoverished families that live there.

**Table 21-1**

Percentage of Persons Below the Poverty Level by Family Status and Race, 1959–1970

| | Percentage Below Low-Income Level (All Persons) | | | | | | | | | | | |
|---|---|---|---|---|---|---|---|---|---|---|---|---|
| | 1970 | 1969 | 1968 | 1967 | 1966 | 1965 | 1964 | 1963 | 1962 | 1961 | 1960 | 1959 |
| Total | 12.6 | 12.2 | 12.8 | 14.2 | 14.7 | 17.3 | 19.0 | 19.5 | 21.0 | 21.9 | 22.2 | 22.4 |
| In Families | 11.0 | 10.5 | 13.3 | 12.5 | 13.1 | 15.8 | 17.4 | 17.9 | 19.4 | 20.3 | 20.7 | 20.8 |
| Unrelated Individuals | 32.7 | 33.6 | 34.0 | 38.1 | 38.3 | 39.8 | 42.7 | 44.2 | 45.4 | 45.9 | 45.2 | 46.1 |
| White | 9.9 | 9.5 | 10.0 | 11.0 | 11.3 | 13.3 | 14.9 | 15.3 | 16.4 | 17.4 | 17.8 | 18.1 |
| In Families | 8.1 | 7.8 | 8.4 | 9.2 | 9.7 | 11.7 | 13.2 | 13.6 | 14.7 | 15.8 | 16.2 | 16.5 |
| Unrelated Individuals | 30.7 | 31.8 | 32.2 | 36.5 | 36.1 | 38.1 | 40.7 | 42.0 | 42.7 | 43.2 | 43.0 | 44.1 |
| Black and Other Races | 32.1 | 31.1 | 33.5 | 37.2 | 39.8 | 47.1 | 49.6 | 51.0 | 55.8 | 56.1 | 55.9 | 56.2 |
| In Families | 30.9 | 29.9 | 32.4 | 36.3 | 38.9 | 46.8 | 49.1 | 50.5 | 55.3 | 55.6 | 55.7 | 56.0 |
| Unrelated Individuals | 46.4 | 44.9 | 45.7 | 48.2 | 53.1 | 50.7 | 55.0 | 58.3 | 62.1 | 62.7 | 59.3 | 57.4 |

U.S. Department of Commerce, Bureau of the Census, *Consumer Income: Characteristics of the Low-Income Population, 1970.* Current Population Reports, Series P-60, No. 81 (November, 1971), p. 30.

Inadequate housing contributes to the problem of migration of the middle class from the cities, which erodes the tax bases needed to help solve the problems of the inner cities. "It is the source of many discontents among the millions of mishoused and dishoused families yearning to be rehoused. It affects family budgets, security, happiness, and stability. It is tied to the issues of segregation and neighborhood decay . . ."[9] The problems of housing are some of the most difficult and serious issues facing those who are attempting to repair the decay of the inner city.

In cities where land is dear and difficult to find the problem of providing housing is compounded. Although it is true that most of the housing industry concentrates its efforts on the upper one-third of the market, there appears to be very little they could do to solve this problem. Housing costs are a complex combination of materials, labor, land, and financing. All of these costs have escalated at such a rapid rate in the recent past that more and more people are being priced out of the market. Even though the home building industry itself is one of the largest in the country, it is composed mostly of small entrepreneurs confined to limited geographical areas. These businesses are almost always marginally-financed operations and are not often in a position to take the kinds of risks that other industries do to solve inner-city problems. In addition, it appears that there is no demand for the kinds of mass-produced no-frills housing that would provide the economies of scale needed to substantially reduce housing prices. Even if these problems could be overcome, there would still be difficulties in finding financing for affordable housing. In economic situations in which even the best risks are difficult to finance, it is doubtful that large sums can be found for investment in the high-risk inner cities.

Business has not been able to supply, on any large scale, affordable housing for lower income groups. Government subsidies and programs have failed to meet the problem as well. The Douglas Commission in a government report on housing needs summed up the situation as follows:

Despite the magnitude of needs and the interest in urgent action on housing and other aspects of the urban crisis, a complex of factors has inhibited the full implementation of the program:

1. Fiscal limitations
2. Congressional limitations
3. Administrative restrictions
4. Inhibitions at the community level
5. Limitations on private participation [10]

In spite of limited successes in dealing with substandard housing problems, there have been some notable efforts by private industry to assume abnormal risks and accept unusually low profits in attempts to fill some of the need for decent low-income housing. One of the earliest private efforts to provide adequate housing for low-income families was begun in 1943 when the Allegheny Conference on Community Development (ACCD) was formed. This joint business effort in the Pittsburgh area has been responsible for twenty redevelopment projects involving a private investment of $500 million in new buildings.[11] SmithKline started a community-development program in the Philadelphia area which integrated upgraded housing with job training, education, and information services. A group underwritten by RCA began a project to rebuild houses in inner-city areas and sell them to low-income families. Westinghouse became involved in building low-cost housing in 1969. Several large insurance companies agreed to combine to divert $1 billion from more lucrative investments to underwrite loans for inner-city residents.[12] Still other companies believe that the huge need for low-cost housing may represent an opportunity for substantial profits and are investing in research and development that may eventually lead to some solutions to the problems of substandard housing.

The failures (and successes) of past attempts to solve the housing problems of our central cities make it clear that cooperative efforts are needed: new technical developments to lower the unit cost of construction, more private investment in slum areas, elimination of obsolete building codes, and adequate government incentives and subsidies.

## Unemployment and Discrimination

Poverty, substandard housing and urban decay are directly related to the problems of unemployment and underemployment; to a large extent these problems result from the practice of racial and sex discrimination in hiring. Typically the unemployed or those whose salaries fall below the poverty level are members of minority groups. The unemployment rate among young black males is more than twice that of the nation as a whole. Discrimination against minorities takes two forms: direct discrimination because of race, color, religion, sex, or national origin, and systematic discrimination in which job requirements and recruiting are directed to white males.

Certainly racial prejudice still exists in all segments of our society, including that of business management. A number of government regulations and laws, however, along with an increased social awareness in management, have significantly reduced the incidence of direct discrimination in employment. The most significant legislation concerning discrimination is the Civil Rights

Act of 1964, which specifically prohibits discrimination in compensation, terms, or conditions of employment. This law is administered by the Equal Employment Opportunity Commission (EEOC), an agency whose policies and guidelines have had a tremendous impact of the employment practices of business and labor unions.

While direct discrimination in employment practices has been all but eliminated, the eradication of systematic discrimination is a more difficult problem. Even when direct references to race, color, religion, sex, or national origin were removed for hiring policies many organizations were found to still be systematically eliminating minorities through the use of requirements that were not relevant to the job. EEOC has filed suit and won rulings to prohibit employers from establishing educational requirements too high for the level of skill necessary to do the job and requiring applicants to pass tests which were not specifically related to the job. The courts have ruled that any employment practice which operates to exclude minorities and cannot be shown to be related to job performance is discriminatory.

People who live in the inner cities are often discriminated against by the location of plants and job sites. Inner-city land is difficult to find, expensive, and subject to unusually high taxes and numerous city ordinances. All of these factors make it unprofitable for businesses to locate production facilities close to where the urban poor live. Because public transportation to the suburban sites where jobs are available is generally inadequate, people in the cities are placed at a great disadvantage. Not only do they have trouble getting to the areas where businesses are located, but residents of ghetto areas also are uncomfortable and uncertain in the typically white, middle-class world of most personnel offices and employment agencies. Even when they are able to secure a job in a suburban setting, transportation difficulties make it difficult for ghetto residents to maintain a satisfactory attendance record.

In response to both direct and systematic discrimination, most companies, in cooperation with directives issued by the EEOC, have developed affirmative action policies and programs. These programs differ from organization to organization, depending upon the nature of the company and its environment. The underlying concept of all affirmative action plans is to bridge the gap between qualified minority applicants and the traditional job-seeking process. Targets are set and strategies developed to recruit and train minorities for jobs. Many organizations have underwritten transportation programs, such as car and van pooling, to overcome problems associated with suburban locations. Some companies have invested in inner-city locations even though suburban locations would mean significantly lower costs. For example, Aerojet General Corporation created the Watts Manufacturing Company in central Los Angeles to make tents on contract for the U.S. Army in 1965. Because inner-city plants generally operate at a competitive disadvantage, however, this solution has not been widespread and is not likely to be a viable alternative for most businesses.

Still, progress has been made to the extent that many of the "ingrained" forms of job discrimination for all minorities, including women, have been significantly reduced. Much of the credit for this must be given to determined business leaders who committed their organizations to nondiscriminative employment and promotion practices. An example of this commitment is the statement made by the chairman of the board of Xerox Corporation in support of his organization's efforts to place women and minorities in upper managerial jobs: ". . . a key element in each manager's over-all performance appraisal will be his progress in this important area. No manager should expect a satisfactory appraisal if he meets other objectives, but fails here." [13]

**Minority Enterprises**  Another factor which affects and reflects the plight of the urban poor is the relatively small number and poor success rate of minority-owned businesses. While most minority-owned businesses are concentrated in central-city areas, white ownership is still the controlling economic force in the ghettos and barrios of the United States. [14] Minority capitalism has been encouraged by many as a partial solution to the problems of the inner cities. If minorities in the inner cities could own the resources and control their use, it is argued, then the money spent by people who live in ghettos would filter back into the community and help upgrade the economic status of those areas. Many, including the federal government and several business leaders, have felt that if minority entrepreneurship could be fostered it would result in increased minority employment in the urban areas. It is believed that through increased minority capitalism the forces of the free market could be used to bring some degree of prosperity to economically depressed minorities.

Several government and private programs have been organized to help accomplish this goal of increasing minority capitalism. The Office of Minority Business Enterprise (OMBE) is the most ambitious of all these programs, administering several types of assistance to minority businesses including a program to stimulate deposits in minority-owned banks, the establishment of National Minority Purchasing Councils to encourage corporate purchasing agents to buy from minorities, educational programs to help minority entrepreneurs, loans to minority businesses, and helping minority businesses secure federal contracts. The Small Business Administration also is active in making loans to minorities. In the present era of federal budget cutting, however, more of the responsibility for this type of assistance may fall to businesses and foundations.

Many corporations have independently aided minority-owned companies. Mattel, Inc. extended initial financing and other forms of support to Shindana Toys even though the minority-operated business was in direct competition with them. General Electric, a pioneer in this area, started a black-owned aerospace company by awarding a subcontract to Progress Aerospace Enterprises. Many other organizations make special provisions to help minority enterprises through their purchasing policies. Eastman Kodak Company organized the Rochester Business Opportunities Corporation (ROBC) in 1967 to make private loans to minority businesses.

In spite of this effort the record of minority-owned businesses remains spotty at best. Only about three percent of the firms in the United States are minority owned, 95 percent of them have fewer than ten employees, and one-third of them have less than $10,000 in revenue each year. [15] While some

large corporations are still helping to build plants and sponsor minority
businesses in inner-city areas, many have been forced to withdraw because
of large losses. Even the aggressive programs of the federal government have
resulted in far more failures than successes. A study conducted in Chicago
showed that 80 percent of the black-owned businesses that were started in
1972 failed in that same year.[16] Most minority enterprises are small businesses
and are therefore subject to all of the problems of any small business. Finally,
logic and experience suggest that it is unlikely that a minority enterprise will
be able to prosper in inner-city environments that are not profitable for large,
professionally managed firms.

**THE ROLE OF BUSINESS IN SOLVING THE PROBLEMS OF CITIES**

While the record of business involvement in the problems of the inner cities
has not been overwhelmingly encouraging, there has been progress. After
two decades of activism, business needs to reevaluate its role in urban affairs.
It is time to learn from past mistakes and successes in order to plan more
carefully the next steps to be taken. In the 1960s government and business
were both shocked into action and reaction in an attempt to save the central
cities from further destruction. Many programs were begun that were doomed
from the start because of poor planning or hasty implementation. Now, as
both government and private industry slow the pace of many of these programs, business should begin a deliberate planning effort to continue its
involvement in the inner cities while learning from past mistakes.

Hay, Gray, and Gates suggest that if a company wishes to become socially
responsible in urban affairs, it should approach the problem using a systematic management model which includes the following steps:

**First, it must determine its company objectives, including its responsibility
to society in general . . . Second, . . . create an urban affairs department . . . Third, . . . cooperate with governmental units in the way
of tax incentives, contracts, and perhaps research and development.[17]**

A company following this plan, having determined its goals, would then
decide on the extent of its involvement with a reasonable knowledge of the
costs to be incurred. A cost/benefit analysis of such programs should be
conducted to be certain that limited resources are directed to the areas where
they will accomplish the most. Urban-affairs units should be designed into
all corporations of any size to help support societal goals. A department
specifically concerned with urban affairs could function within the overall
framework of public relations in the organization, reporting directly to either
the president or a vice-president in charge of such functions. The point of
such a plan is that a business organization can best serve society by determining its strengths and weaknesses and using its resources to help solve
those urban problems that relate to its expertise.

The record seems clear that even large corporations cannot make economically unfeasible enterprises work. Sadly enough, when they try they
often create more problems than they solve by raising expectation levels in
the community, only to have to lay off the workers who had come to depend

upon it when the venture fails. Business has also failed when it has attempted to duplicate or take over the function of government agencies. More cooperation between business and government would allow the private sector to supply financing and the things it does best while letting government function in its proper role.

**PUBLIC RELATIONS AND URBAN PROBLEMS**

The role of public relations in helping business respond to the problems of poverty, unemployment, inadequate housing, and minority enterprises is threefold: 1) Public relations practitioners in organizations must help management understand the problems of the inner city and plan the organization's response to them. 2) The public relations function must operate as a two-way channel of communication between the inner-city community and the organization to build mutual trust and understanding. 3) Those who manage the public relations function must also interpret the organization's actions and policies toward solving urban problems to society in general (including government) to gain support and credibility for these programs.

Burson describes the job of modern public relations executives with regard to the social responsibility of business as follows:

**The public relations executive provides a qualitative evaluation of social trends. He helps formulate policies that will enable a corporation to adapt to these trends. And he communicates—both internally and externally— the reasons for those policies . . . . One obvious objective for the public relations practitioner in the corporate environment is to make sure that business institutions perform as servants of the people.[18]**

The evaluation of social trends, as we discussed in Chapter 19, is one of the most important tasks of public relations managers in today's environment. Public relations executives must be able to help their organization select social issues for attention that are in harmony with its goals and resources and the opinions of various publics regarding the organization's responsibilities. Understanding what is expected of it by the various publics involved is crucial to an organization's success in urban affairs. Premature reaction to a problem that it is not expected to address may result in a competitive disadvantage due to the costs incurred and damage its relationship with an important public. If the organization is late in its recognition of public demands and response to related problems, however, it can also suffer losses in the form of poor community relations and legal and economic sanctions.

A recent study by Grunig helps identify some of the issues that various publics expect business to be involved with and those issues in which private-sector involvement is not expected. The results show that most publics feel corporations should be involved primarily in ". . . doing the things business was designed to do . . ."[19] The most important issues of social responsibility for business, according to the publics surveyed, were producing quality products and services and correcting negative consequences of the company's prior activities: combating pollution, holding down inflation, hiring minorities, and showing human concern for employees. Overall, the survey indicates that there is no general desire to see business be responsible for social programs not directly related to its function, such as charities, education, or decay of the cities. Even the most activist respondents did not believe business should be involved in social programs that were not related to its operations.

When such information about the demands of publics is related to a recent survey of 192 *Fortune* companies which revealed that the largest areas of corporate social investment were in charities and education, we see the need for adequate public relations information and analysis in such decisions.[20] If American business is spending most of its resources devoted to social responsibility on programs that are not deemed significant by the publics they are supposed to serve, public relations managers must begin to function more in these decision-making processes.

---

**CASE STUDY: THE DESERTED HOSPITAL**

**By Walt Seifert**
**Professor of Public Relations, School of Journalism, The Ohio State University, Columbus, Ohio**

---

You have been named public relations director of St. Christopher's Hospital. The facility has 500 beds at a downtown location in a major city.

You have your first meeting with your boss, the chief hospital administrator, Mr. Winston. Winston has been with St. Chris's for about two decades, and he is proud of his hospital's accomplishments. In the course of conversation you conclude that Mr. Winston has great confidence in his own conclusions. He gives you these "facts:"

St. Chris's recently built a highrise building on its inner-city site. Although the new building has been open two years, most of its rooms are unoccupied due to a lack of interest by physicians and a shortage of patients. The administrator attributes this to a fear of crime. "We are in the high crime area. Most people are afraid to come here," he says. "Also, a nurse was raped and murdered en route to this hospital. Although this happened quite far away, because she worked for St. Chris's most people think it happened right here."

On the positive side, he mentions that St. Chris's has an outstanding speech clinic and the only teen alcoholism program in the state. He says the hospital would be willing to give physicians free office suites on the top floors of the tower if they would come. NOW: Tell all you'd do in the next year.

---

**NOTES**   [1] George A. Steiner, *Business and Society* (New York: Random House, 1975), p. 281.

[2] U.S. Department of Commerce, Bureau of the Census, *The Social and Economic Status of Negroes in the United States, 1970,* Current Population Reports, Series page 23, No. 38 (July 1971), p. 7.

[3] John K. Galbraith, *The Affluent Society* (Boston: Houghton Mifflin Company, 1958), p. 326.

[4] Committee on Science and Astronautics, U.S. House of Representatives, *Science and Technology in the Cities* (Washington, D.C.: U.S. Government Printing Office, 1969), p. 93.

[5] John J. Corson, and George A. Steiner, *Measuring Business Social Performance: The Corporate Social Audit,* (New York: Committee for Economic Development, 1974).

[6] Jules Cohn, *The Conscience of Corporations* (Baltimore: The Johns Hopkins Press, 1971).

[7] The President's Committee on Urban Housing, *A Decent Home* (Washington: U.S. Government Printing Office, 11 December 1968), p. 45.

[8] Frederick E. Case, *Inner-City Housing and Private Enterprise,* New York: Praeger, 1972)

[9] Charles Abrams, *The City is the Frontier* (New York: Harper and Row, 1965).

[10] Douglas Commission, *Urban Housing Needs Through the 1980s: An Analysis and Projection,* National Commission on Urban Problems (Washington, D.C.: U.S. Government Printing Office, 1968), pp. 13–20.

[11] Steiner, *Business and Society,* p. 300.

[12] Robert D. Hay, Edmond R. Gray, and James E. Gates, *Business and Society* (Cincinnati: Southwestern Publishing Company, 1976), p. 199.

[13] *Fortune,* September 1972, p. 146.

[14] Allison Jennings, Suzanne Synott, and Edward Graham, "A Note on Black Capitalism," a report under the direction of Charles E. Johnson, Lecturer in Business Administration, Harvard Business School, 1969.

[15] Jennings, Synott, and Graham, "Black Capitalism."

[16] "Black Capitalism: Mostly an Empty Promise," *Time,* 9 July 1973.

[17] Hay, Gray, and Gates, *Business and Society,* p. 199.

[18] H. Burson, "The Public Relations Function in the Socially Responsible Corporation," in *Managing the Socially Responsible Corporation,* M. Anshen, ed. (New York: Macmillan, 1974), pp. 222–234.

[19] James E. Grunig, "A New Measure of Public Opinions on Corporate Social Responsibility," *Academy of Management Journal* 22 (1979): 738–764.

[20] S. L. Holmes, "Corporate Social Performance: Past and Present Areas of Commitment," *Academy of Management Journal* 20 (1977): 433–438.

# CHAPTER 22 INTERNATIONAL PUBLIC RELATIONS

**PREVIEW**   Multinational corporations are among the most controversial economic and political institutions of our time. Justly or not, they are accused of exporting jobs and capital; transferring scientific, technological, and managerial knowledge; and exploiting less developed countries.

U.S. business activities abroad generate an estimated fifteen percent of America's gross national product, thirty percent of corporate profits, and ten million American jobs.

Vast misunderstandings of multinational corporations at home and abroad give international public relations a ripe field in which to work. Public relations practitioners represent multinational corporations at home, informing public opinion and government officials; they help bridge the communication gap that exists between foreign operations and world headquarters; and they conduct all aspects of public relations in host countries.

In the 1950s we heard about "The Ugly American," cold-heartedly wheeling and dealing his way around the globe—ethnocentric, materialistic, insensitive. In the 1960s, American corporations were lambasted at home and abroad for the "complicity" with the war in Vietnam. Companies like Dow Chemical and the Bank of America were favorite targets.

In the 1970s, various U.S.-based multinational corporations (MNCs) were accused of overthrowing a government in Chile; corrupting government officials in Latin America, Belgium, and Japan; working against the United States' interests during the Arab oil embargo of 1973–74; supporting communist rebels in Angola; complying with South African apartheid policies; supporting the Arab boycott against Israel; manipulating international currency markets; and exporting American jobs to take advantage of cheaper foreign labor. The United States government moved to regulate and control the foreign operations of MNCs.

In this decade, U.S. MNCs find themselves at a crossroads. With stiff competition from MNCs headquartered in Western Europe, Japan, and even in such nations as Korea, Taiwan, Singapore, and Brazil, American MNCs face challenges at home and abroad. While the nature and extent of their impact is still debated, the American MNCs pursue business in a baffling variety of political, cultural, and economic circumstances.

The future of MNCs depends less on their economic power than on their abilities to influence and adapt to political social and cultural forces in both domestic and international markets. In this regard, public relations in its broadest sense is an integral component of the interdependent prosperity of MNCs and the world.

## THE DEVELOPMENT OF MULTINATIONAL CORPORATIONS

Although some have traced the beginnings of MNCs to the Dutch and English trading companies of the seventeenth century, it was only after World War II that corporations began to move away from their domestic bases and take on the structure we know today. Advances in communications and transportation made global management practical; developing economies, the economics of scale and the specific efficiencies of operating in various locales made global management profitable. The increasing interdependence of national economies made global enterprise imperative.

Strictly speaking, a multinational corporation is one that has direct manufacturing and marketing investments in a number of countries. These investments in foreign countries are made for essentially the same reasons the domestic investments are made—competitive cost conditions, reduced transportation costs, proximity to raw materials and markets, availability of labor, and of course, hopes for a good return on the investment. Corporations have gone abroad in search of greater opportunities than their home markets offered: greater growth and greater profitability.

Because MNCs operate in several countries simultaneously, numerous problems arise both for the corporations and the governments of home and host nations. That certain MNCs are larger than their host governments in terms of assets or even population (counting stockholders and employees as "citizens") exacerbates these difficulties. A lack of international political frameworks hamper the operations of economic concerns that are international in scope. Neil Jacoby sums up this situation by pointing out that "nineteenth-century political organization provides an archaic framework for a twentieth-century economy." [1]

For the thirty years following World War II, United States based MNCs dominated world markets. In the past ten years, however, German, Japanese, French, Dutch, British, Canadian and other nation's corporations have become increasingly active on a global scale. The devaluation of the dollar, the slowing of growth in these nations relative to United States growth, increases in labor costs, and the relative political and economic stability of the United States have been reasons for other nation's corporations to invest in places other than their homes. Like U.S. companies abroad, MNCs from other nations who establish bases in this country are experiencing criticism. Moves to restrict foreign purchases of American farmland, for instance, indicate that foreign MNCs have begun to experience public relations problems in the United States. Although American corporations are still individually and collectively the largest multinationals, they no longer have the field to themselves (*Table 22-1*).

The emergence of private multinational corporations is a powerful force for global social and economic change. The importance of MNCs can hardly be overestimated. In 1975, American business activities abroad generated fifteen percent of the country's gross national product, thirty percent of corporate profits, and an estimated 10 million American jobs.[2] Many of the most important corporations in the United States derive over half their profits from foreign operations (*Table 22-2*).

Indeed, it is in part because of their size and importance that MNCs are the subject of intense controversy. These controversies surround several aspects of multinational operations, and in the following pages we will explore the issues that critics have raised.

## CRITICISM OF MNCs

"The multinational corporation has become one of the most controversial economic and political institutions of our time." [3] Economic, political, social, and cultural disagreements have led to serious debates both in home and host countries. The underlying basis for criticisms of MNCs is the view that they are instruments of irresponsible private economic power, or agents of economic "imperialism." Charges of exploitation, plundering, and greed are often made.[4] Business philosopher Richard Eells maintains that large multinational corporations are perceived as relatively independent centers of

**Table 22-1**
The 25 Largest
Multinational
Corporations, 1978

| Rank | Company | Nationality | Foreign Revenues (Millions) | Total Revenues (Millions) |
|---|---|---|---|---|
| 1 | Exxon | U.S.A. | $44,333 | $60,335 |
| 2 | Royal Dutch Shell | Neth./Britain | NA | $45,246 |
| 3 | British Petroleum | Britain | $22,200 | $27,407 |
| 4 | Mobil | U.S.A. | $20,481 | $34,736 |
| 5 | Texaco | U.S.A. | $18,927 | $28,608 |
| 6 | Ford | U.S.A. | $14,985 | $42,784 |
| 7 | General Motors | U.S.A. | $14,172 | $63,221 |
| 8 | Standard Oil (Cal.) | U.S.A. | $14,150 | $23,232 |
| 9 | Phillips Gloeilampenfabrieken | Neth. | $13,592 | $15,096 |
| 10 | Unilever | Britain/Neth. | NA | $18,152 |
| 11 | IBM | U.S.A. | $11,040 | $21,076 |
| 12 | IT&T | U.S.A. | $10,023 | $19,399 |
| 13 | Gulf Oil | U.S.A. | $ 9,229 | $18,069 |
| 14 | Nestle' | Switzerland | NA | $11,798 |
| 15 | Bayer | Germany | $ 8,030 | $11,369 |
| 16 | Volkswagenwerk | Germany | $ 7,717 | $13,305 |
| 17 | Siemens | Germany | $ 7,294 | $14,443 |
| 18 | Compagnie Francaise des Petroles* | France | NA | $10,876 |
| 19 | B.A.T. Industries | Britain | $ 6,469 | $ 7,751 |
| 20 | Daimler-Benz | Germany | $ 6,321 | $12,066 |
| 21 | Renault | France | $ 5,717 | $12,684 |
| 22 | BASF | Germany | $ 5,447 | $10,710 |
| 23 | Citicorp | U.S.A. | $ 5,157** | $ 7,556 |
| 24 | Engelhard Minerals & Chemical | U.S.A. | $ 5,103 | $10,174 |
| 25 | Imperial Chemical | Britain | $ 4,474 | $ 8,701 |

*1977 Figures, Company would have ranged higher if 1978 results were available.
**Estimated

Adapted from *Forbes Magazine*, 25 June 1979, pp. 56–62.

power which appear to be unconcerned with social justice.[5] George Sawyer suggests that the basic conflict is between corporations' needs and desires to operate in many political jurisdictions and the ability of society to regulate effectively only within specific jurisdictions.[6] Again the questions of power and political allegiance are raised. We must not, however, overlook the fact that no corporation can enter and do business in any nation except by the permission of its government, and under whatever laws and terms it may dictate.[7]

Specifically, criticisms of MNCs fall into three major areas: job and capital exportation; transfer of scientific, technological and managerial knowledge; and exploitation of the less developed countries.

**Job and Capital Exportation**  Labor organizations, particularly the AFL-CIO, contend that MNCs export American jobs by increasing production overseas and then selling the product in the American market. The electronics and apparel industries are frequently

| | Foreign Revenue | Total Revenue | Foreign as % of Total | Foreign Profit | Total Profit | Foreign as % of Total |
|---|---|---|---|---|---|---|
| **Company** | | | | | | |
| Exxon | $44,333 | $60,335 | 73.5 | $1,947 | $3,434 | 56.7 |
| Mobil | $20,481 | $34,736 | 59.0 | $ 639 | $1,126 | 56.7 |
| Texaco | $18,927 | $28,608 | 66.2 | $ 436 | $ 853 | 51.2 |
| Standard Oil (Cal.) | $14,150 | $23,232 | 60.9 | $ 563 | $1,106 | 50.9 |
| IBM | $11,040 | $21,076 | 52.4 | $1,584 | $3,111 | 50.9 |
| IT&T | $10,023 | $19,399 | 51.7 | $ 799 | $1,461 | 54.9 |
| Citicorp | $ 5,157* | $ 7,556 | 68.3 | $ 645** | $ 827** | 78.0 |
| Chase Manhattan | $ 2,787 | $ 4,461 | 62.5 | $ 105 | $ 197 | 53.3 |
| Occidental Petroleum | $ 2,623 | $ 6,316 | 41.5 | $ 409 | $ 476 | 86.1 |
| Colgate-Palmolive | $ 2,441 | $ 4,312 | 56.6 | $ 233 | $ 374 | 62.4 |
| Pan American | $ 2,036 | $ 2,205 | 92.3 | $ 176 | $ 150 | 117.4 |
| CPC International | $ 2,031 | $ 3,222 | 63.0 | $ 214 | $ 295 | 72.5 |
| Coca-Cola | $ 1,983 | $ 4,338 | 45.7 | $ 460 | $ 732 | 62.9 |
| Johnson & Johnson | $ 1,506 | $ 3,497 | 43.1 | $ 285 | $ 546 | 52.2 |
| J. P. Morgan & Co. | $ 1,493 | $ 2,448 | 61.0 | $ 136 | $ 267 | 50.8 |
| Phillips Petroleum | $ 1,447 | $ 6,998 | 20.7 | $ 788 | $1,464 | 53.8 |
| Trans World | $ 1,398 | $ 3,720 | 37.6 | $ 123 | $ 174 | 71.0 |
| Manufacturers Hanover | $ 1,331 | $ 2,624 | 50.7 | $ 95 | $ 182 | 52.3 |
| Pfizer | $ 1,320 | $ 2,362 | 55.9 | $ 249 | $ 379 | 65.8 |
| ASARCO | $ 1,054 | $ 2,909 | 36.2 | $ 55 | $ 49 | 111.5 |
| Singer | $ 1,040 | $ 2,469 | 42.1 | $ 101 | $ 181 | 55.8 |
| Bankers Trust | $ 1,006 | $ 1,924 | 52.3 | $ 56 | $ 82 | 68.3 |
| Fluor | $ 987 | $ 2,866 | 34.5 | $ 76 | $ 151 | 50.5 |
| Gillette | $ 987 | $ 1,710 | 57.7 | $ 113 | $ 223 | 50.5 |
| American Standard | $ 978 | $ 2,111 | 46.3 | $ 123 | $ 241 | 51.0 |
| American Cynamid | $ 955 | $ 2,746 | 34.8 | $ 159 | $ 310 | 51.2 |
| American International Group | $ 922 | $ 1,981 | 46.5 | $ 148 | $ 266 | 55.6 |
| Getty Oil | $ 828 | $ 3,677 | 22.5 | $ 442 | $ 865 | 51.1 |
| Allied Chemical | $ 662 | $ 3,268 | 20.3 | $ 113 | $ 120 | 94.2 |
| Black & Decker | $ 545 | $ 960 | 56.8 | $ 43 | $ 66 | 64.5 |
| Hoover Co. | $ 482 | $ 692 | 69.7 | $ 29 | $ 56 | 51.5 |
| Richardson-Merrill | $ 473 | $ 945 | 50.0 | $ 77 | $ 133 | 58.0 |
| Smith Kline | $ 472 | $ 1,112 | 42.5 | $ 142 | $ 276 | 51.4 |

**Table 22-2** U.S. MNCs Deriving Half their Profits From Foreign Operations (All Figures in Millions)

*Estimated
**Pre-tax

Adapted from *Forbes Magazine,* 25 June 1979, pp. 56–62.

cited in this respect. Various studies have indicated, however, that foreign investment by American companies has expanded American employment. During the period between 1960 and 1970, MNCs increased their United States employment at three times the rate of the average increase in job rolls for all companies.[8]

Responding to the charge that MNCs sell their foreign-produced goods in the American market, James Cook wrote:

By and large, the U.S. multinationals did not go abroad in pursuit of cheap labor. Admittedly low-labor-cost countries like Taiwan, Korea, Hong Kong, Brazil and Mexico have prospered manufacturing transitor radios, toys, shoes and textiles on behalf of such U.S. companies as Zenith, Texas Instruments, RCA, and Levi Strauss. But the Commerce Department figures that only seven percent of the more than $515 billion in sales U.S. multinational affiliates generate each year comes back into this country.[9]

To ascertain the validity of the charge that multinational corporations export capital and create balance-of-payment deficits, *Fortune* asked 105 MNCs to calculate their own balance of payments for the 1972 fiscal year. Ten corporations had negative balances totaling $446 million; the rest had a positive balance amounting to $7.7 billion—a net surplus of $7.25 billion.[10]

**Transfer of Knowledge**

Congressional critics and others claim that multinational corporations are selling precious scientific, technological, and managerial knowledge abroad, thereby impairing the competitive position of the United States in world markets and working against the national interest. Computers, aircraft, advanced factory design, automotive technology, and oil drilling and refining technology are among the products and processes at which such criticism has been directed. Although these charges cannot be answered statistically, supporters of MNCs refute such criticisms in two ways. First, multinationals protect their own interests and their competitive advantages by guarding sensitive knowledge. Coca-Cola and IBM recently ceased operations in India rather than give in to that government's demands for trade secrets. Second, MNCs admit proudly to the role of international carrier of advanced managerial and technological know-how. As such, multinational corporations claim to improve conditions in the less-developed countries and to promote world harmony.

**Exploitation of Less Developed Countries**

The most prevalent and pervasive criticism has been the charge that multinational corporations cynically exploit workers, consumers and resources of less developed countries. The MNCs also stand accused of disrupting the social and cultural fabric of host countries and of corrupting host countries' leaders.

Actually less than one-fourth of all multinational corporations' investment has gone into less developed countries, most of it to countries that encouraged and welcomed the investment. About forty percent of total foreign investment in developing nations is concentrated in ten countries: Mexico, Brazil, Argentina, Colombia, Peru, Korea, Taiwan, Hong Kong, the Philippines and Indonesia.[11] Indeed, rapid development of these nations is a testimony not only to the resourcefulness of these nations and their people, but also to the potential contributions of MNCs and to the advantages of following relatively capitalistic paths. Although the proportion of multinational investment is smaller in the less developed countries, economic, political, technological, and cultural impacts are most striking in those countries. In such countries, investment usually means development, a process inevitably unsettling to a society.

In an effort to assess objectively the impact of U.S. multinational corporations on less developed countries, the National Planning Association sponsored twelve case studies over a fifteen-year period. These studies found that the MNCs play innovative and catalytic roles, founding new industries, transmitting technological and managerial skills in addition to providing investment capital. In many cases, MNCs create entire social infrastructures to support development, including schools, housing, health facilities, and transportation.[12]

Those who claim that MNCs are guilty of exploitation often point to the level of profit enjoyed by corporations operating in less developed countries. In their own defense, the MNCs point to the risks they take in searching for and developing new resources and markets in frequently unstable political, and social environments. Expropriation of operations and capital and the disruptions caused by civil wars are additional risks faced by multinationals, most recently in such countries as Iran and Nicaragua. The corporations also point to the large contributions they make to material welfare in host countries. The hosts, they point out, reap public income, private income, modern technology, and managerial skills without investing capital or taking material risks.

In the past, less developed countries have felt threatened by MNCs, fearing loss of control of national affairs, dependency on MNCs, economic exploitation, and depredation of traditional culture. These feelings were perhaps the result of the experience of colonialism. Increasingly, however, the world's developing countries have lost their fears. "To a considerable degree the officials of the poor countries are treating the multinational firms with more sophistication and pragmatism and less ideology," reports *The Christian Science Monitor's* David Francis.[13] The United Nations established a Centre on Transnational Corporations to help less developed countries deal with MNCs. N. T. Wang, director of the Centre's Information Analysis Division, said in *Forbes:* "Most developing countries now feel they would like to have foreign enterprises coming to their shores."[14]

**Corruption of Leaders: Bribery**   If you were playing a word association game in the mid-1970s and you said "multinational corporation," the almost inevitable response would have been "bribery." The corporations acknowledging pay-offs to foreign officials were a veritable "Who's Who"—American Airlines, Braniff, Gulf Oil, 3M, Goodyear, Northrop, Lockheed, United Brands, ITT, and over 200 others have admitted to bribery, pay-offs or political corruption. Such acknowledgments frequently became headline news. Congress was moved to pass the Foreign Corrupt Practices Act of 1977.

Foreign payoffs have a long history. In the 1600s the British East India Company won duty-free treatment for its exports by giving Mogul rulers paintings, carvings, and "costly objects made of copper, brass and stone."[15] Social commentators M. S. Gwirtzman and A. R. Novak explain the prevalence of what in this country is considered bribery:

The reasons multinationals must do business amid a profusion of outstretched hands go deep into the history and structure of the lands in which they operate. In much of Asia and Africa the market economy as we know it, in which the sale of goods and services is governed by price and quality competition, never has existed. What has developed in its stead are intricate tribal and oligarchic arrangements of social connections, family relations and reciprocal obligations, lubricated by many forms of tribute.[16]

In the Mideast, for example, "baksheesh" for government officials is comparable to tipping in American restaurants. Considered a gratuity for services rendered, it supplements salaries that are intentionally low in anticipation of such revenues. Baksheesh is involved in everything from getting a telephone installed to signing a multi-million dollar contract.[17]

"Bribery abroad is not exactly the corruption of innocents," say Gwirtzman and Novak.[18] It is often difficult to draw the line between legitimate gifts, reasonable payments, commissions, protection, extortion, and bribery. When the chairman of the South Korean ruling party promised to shut down the $300 million Gulf Oil operation in that country unless the company made a $10 million donation to the party, it could be argued that Gulf did well to negotiate the demand down to $3 million.

In Germany, Japan, France, Britain, Italy, Sweden and other countries, bribery payments by their multinational corporations seems to bother neither the governments nor the people. Raymund A. Kathe, a Tokyo-based Citibank senior vice president, notes that unbothered by antibribery laws, those MNCs are "laughing all the way to the bank." [19]

In the United States, however, the reaction has been dramatically different. When the facts came out about the $1.25 million bribe paid to the former president of Honduras by United Brands to reduce the tax on the production of bananas, the company's president committed suicide, its stock dropped forty percent, its holdings in Panama were expropriated and its tax and tariff concessions in Honduras were revoked.[20] Other companies experienced similar, if less extreme, upheavals. Top management at Gulf Oil and Lockheed were replaced, largely due to complicity in foreign payoff scandals.

The 1977 Foreign Corrupt Practices Act explicitly forbids:

1. The use of an instrumentality of interstate commerce (such as the telephone or the mails) in furtherance of
2. A payment, or an offer to pay "anything of value," directly or indirectly,
3. To any foreign official with discretionary authority or to any foreign political party or foreign political candidate,
4. If the purpose of the payment is the 'corrupt' one of getting the recipient to act (or to refrain from acting),
5. In such a way as to assist the company in obtaining or retaining business for or with or directing business to any person.

The penalty for the company involved can range up to a maximum of $1 million. Executives who willfully violate any provision of the act can be imprisoned for up to five years and be fined up to $10,000. According to a *Harvard Business Review* article, "it is to be expected that the directors of a company—especially those serving on the audit committee—will bear a share of the blame and liability arising out of violations of the act of their company." [21]

The two mini-cases in this chapter describe aspects of the foreign bribery issue. In one we see how Eaton Corporation's disclosure of questionable payments was covered by various media. In the other, we find that the inability to follow local practices caused AMF Corporation to divest itself of valuable subsidiary at a firesale price.

---

**Mini-Case 22-1**
**Eaton's Disclosure**

In early 1977, Eaton Corporation, the Cleveland-based multinational conglomerate, initiated its own investigation into its worldwide "questionable payments." [22] The investigation was supervised by the audit committee of Eaton's Board of Directors.

The results of the investigation were provided to the Securities and Exchange Commission and to the public via the media. The following four reports of the case, drawn from different newspapers, illustrate revealing differences in approach.

### Eaton Reveals Payments

Eaton Corp. today revealed that it made questionable payments overseas totaling $4.3 million from Jan. through Dec. 31, 1976.

The information was contained in an 8-K report filed today with the Securities and Exchange Commmission.

Commenting on the voluntary investigation and the report, Chairman E. Mandell deWindt said: "The investigation revealed no political 'slush funds,' 'unrecorded bank accounts' or hidden accounts of any kind."

The report said that at the request of some distributors and sales agents, the company paid amounts that were owed to them legitimately but outside the country of their business residence. These payments averaged $867,000 yearly.

The commission payments may, or may not have been, in violation of currency exchange or other laws of the recipients countries.

The report said that payments by foreign subsidiaries did not violate U.S. laws.

Subsidiaries outside the U.S. made payments during the five-year period of $2177 to employees of government-controlled customers and payments totaling $25,126 to employees of non-government customers.

In addition, $91,835 in commission was paid to agents, outside the U.S. Some portion of these payments may have been remitted by the agents to employees of government-controlled customers. Eaton said it has no evidence that such kickbacks were made.

In the U.S. Eaton's investigation discovered that an employee was reimbursed $100 in company funds for tickets to a political fund-raising dinner. The employee has made restitution, Eaton said.

Another employee was permitted a one-week leave-of-absence with pay while running for a state office. Two other employees provided clerical help to a political party. A value of $1100 was placed on this activity.

"The investigation revealed some situations where Eaton's corporate policy on ethical business conduct was not properly carried out. These practices have been stopped," de Windt said.

"Eaton Reveals Payments," *Cleveland Press,* August 6, 1977.

### Eaton Tells Dubious Payments of $27,000

CLEVELAND [AP]—Questionable payments overseas and in the United States have been reported by Eaton Corp. to the Securities and Exchange Commission.

The company said that from 1972 through 1976, subsidiaries outside the U.S. paid about $2,000 to employes of government-controlled customers and about $25,000 to employes of nongovernmental customers overseas.

Also, it said more than $90,000 was paid in commissions to overseas agents "under circumstances suggesting that some portion of the payment may have been remitted by the agents to employes of government-controlled customers." The company said it has no evidence the remittances were made, however.

Domestically, the company said, an employe was reimbursed $100 for tickets to a political fund-raising dinner. Also, an employe was given a paid, one-week leave of absence while running for state office, and two clerks spent office time working for a political party.

"Eaton Tells Dubious Payments of $27,000," *Chicago Tribune,* August 10, 1977.

## Eaton Probe Reveals Questionable Payments
### By John B. Harris

Foreign subsidiaries of Cleveland-based Eaton Corp. made questionable payments totaling $2,177 to employes of government-controlled firms and $25,126 to employes of non-governmental businesses between 1972–77, according to an internal investigation.

In a report filed yesterday with the Securities and Exchange Commission, the company added that an additional $91,835 was paid to sales agents in other countries, some of which may have been used for bribes.

Over the same five-year period, Eaton said that more than $4.3 million was paid to distributors and sales representatives at banks of convenience—banks in countries other than where the transaction occurred or other than the company's national origin.

These payments, usually commissions on export sales or undeducted discounts, may or may not have violated currency exchange or other laws of the foreign countries, the company said.

Eaton declined to reveal where or why the payments took place. It stressed, however, that none of the foreign payments violated U.S. law.

Domestically, the investigation also discovered several minor infractions linked to politics. One employee during the five-year period listed tickets to a $100 political fund-raiser as a job-related cost on his expense account. He has since paid it back, Eaton said.

The company also reported that one employee received a full week's salary while running for political office, and that two employes provided clerical assistance for a political party during office hours.

E. M. deWindt, Eaton chairman and chief executive, said the investigation showed "some situations where Eaton's corporate policy on ethical business conduct was not properly carried out."

He said these practices have been stopped.

Eaton Probe Reveals Questionable Payments," *The Plain Dealer,* Cleveland, Ohio, August 6, 1977.

## Eaton Study Shows Dubious Payments Were Relatively Small
### By a WALL STREET JOURNAL Staff Reporter

CLEVELAND—Eaton Corp. said an investigation turned up relatively small questionable payments overseas and in the U.S.

The company said in a report filed with the Securities and Exchange Commission that between 1972 and 1976, subsidiaries outside the U.S. made payments of $2,177 to employes of government-controlled customers and payments of $25,126 to employes of nongovernmental customers in countries outside the U.S.

In addition, the company said, $91,835 was paid in commissions during the period to agents outside the U.S. "under circumstances suggesting that some portion of the payment may have been remitted by the agents to employes of government-controlled customers.'' The company said it didn't have any evidence that such remittances were made, however.

Eaton also said the company paid about $867,000 yearly in legitimately owed money to distributors and sales representatives in countries outside the country of their business residence.

Domestically, the company said an employe was reimbursed $100 for tickets to a political fund-raising dinner. Also, an employe got a one-week leave of absence without loss of pay while running for a state office, and two clerical employes spent some office time providing clerical assistance to a political party, the company said.

The company said the investigation, which was supervised by the audit committee of the board and now is complete, didn't turn up any evidence of political slush funds or unrecorded bank accounts.

Eaton makes capital goods, auto parts, locks and other products.

''Eaton Study Shows Dubious Payments Were Relatively Small,'' *The Wall Street Journal,* August 8, 1977.

---

**Mini-Case 22-2 AMF's Divestiture**   Sasib was an Italian subsidiary of AMF Corporation, a manufacturer of cigarette machinery. In 1976 and 1977 AMF disclosed "questionable payments abroad" amounting to $3.4 million, stating in its reports "the termination of these payments may limit the ability of the company to compete in some foreign countries." [23]

AMF's biggest payments problems involved Sasib, whose customers were primarily state-owned tobacco monopolies. Its chief competitors were German, English, and Italian companies.

In September, 1977, AMF sold Sasib. Insiders suggest that without the ability to make payoffs legally, the subsidiary could not profitably compete. In 1976, the subsidiary had $7 million net income on sales of $59 million. Among the assets acquired by the Italian company C.I.R. was $7 million in cash. The selling price was $14 million in cash and securities—a price described as all but giving the business away.

AMF Director Rodney Gott speculated that Sasib's competitors "sat back and held their sides and laughed themselves sick—and went right on doing what has to be done in certain areas of the world."

Mauro Ferrari, C.I.R.'s Managing Director, reported that Sasib enjoyed increases in revenues and profits in 1978.

---

**PUBLIC RELATIONS FOR MULTINATIONAL CORPORATIONS**   Public relations for multinational corporations is a complex area of practice requiring all the skills discussed elsewhere in this book plus extraordinary cross-cultural sensitivities. The public relations function in multinational corporations has three distinct aspects. In one role, public relations practitioners represent multinational corporations at home, dealing with public opinion and governmental activities which relate both to specific corporations and to multinational enterprise as a whole. The second role of multinational public relations is to help bridge the communication gap that inevitably exists between foreign operations and top management in the world headquarters. Finally, public relations must be conducted in the various host countries of the corporation. William A. Durbin, who has directed public relations for two multinational corporations, recommends four actions to be taken by all corporations involved in multinational operation:

1. Conduct an audit of public relations assets and liabilities in each of the countries of operation;
2. Conduct a government relations audit dealing with specific political relationships, political history, and current or anticipated problems;
3. Analyze political and public trends in the host country;
4. Share information with other MNCs.[24]

**Domestic Public Relations for MNCs**     Multinational corporations have long recognized that their economic success abroad depends at least in part on their political success at home. There has been a long history in the United States of government support of multinational business, going back to 1801 when the U.S. Navy attacked the Barbary pirates to protect Yankee shipping. As Treasury Secretary Henry Fowler said in 1965, "The United States government has consistently sought . . . to expand and extend the role of the multinational corporation as an essential instrument of strong and healthy economic progress throughout the free world."[25]

George Steiner points out, however, that over thirty distinct governmental policy areas affect multinational corporations. Scores of domestic policies have international implications. Eight major agencies have clear authority over these policies and a dozen more assert some jurisdiction.[26] In short, the relation between U.S. multinationals and the United States government is extremely complex.

U.S. MNCs are currently constrained by the government in various ways not experienced by MNCs based in other nations: Antibribery and antiboycott legislation, taxation of corporations and their American employees, politically motivated trade restrictions, antitrust enforcement, and pressures brought by environmentalists. In many cases U.S. MNCs must compete abroad with state-owned or state-financed corporations. A *Business Week* special issue called the relationship between U.S. multinationals and Washington "a major disadvantage in a drastically changed world marketplace." The same article pointed out that U.S. multinational executives "almost unanimously . . . regard Washington's regulatory maze and an indifference to their interests abroad as key factors crimping their sales abroad and ultimately jeopardizing the security of their investments."[27]

Washington's "indifference" seems to derive from a lack of understanding of the true importance of multinationals to both domestic and international economies. Moreover, multinationals have not been particularly popular with certain potent political forces (e.g., organized labor) in this country, or with the general public. In 1973, Opinion Research Corporation found that by a margin of two to one, the American public favored federal discouragement of international expansion of business companies because such expansion, they believed, meant fewer jobs and a loss of tax dollars.[28]

The public's hostility and Washington's "indifference" to MNCs depends to a large extent on the effectiveness of their domestic public relations. According to Durbin, "This . . . will depend to a degree on the quality and persuasiveness of the facts and arguments advanced by the multinationals themselves."[29]

In order to improve perceptions of multinational corporations and ultimately to improve the regulatory environment of U.S. MNCs, public relations practitioners in their employ must make public the facts about MNCs. They must speak out whenever possible on behalf of the multinational concept and its benefits and correct inaccuracies, exaggerations and misapprehensions. Average American citizens have no idea how, if, or why the business of multinational corporations affects them.

## Bridging the Gap Between Host and Home

The effects of the intersection of national borders on the organization and administrative processes . . . may be classified as arising from four communication gaps—culture, nationality, environment and distance.[30]

Like the public relations practitioner who is concerned with operations in one political jurisdiction, multinational public relations people are paid not only to disseminate information but also to gather information for input into organizational decision making. The multinational communicator works under more difficult circumstances, though, because of the four gaps mentioned above.

As corporate citizens of many nations, multinational corporations daily confront conflicts between divergent national policies, economic and social systems, and values. Under these circumstances, public relations professionals explain to home management, and to publics and government at home, the attitudes and actions of the public and government in those countries where the corporation does business. Boddewyn makes specific suggestions in this regard:

1. Scan and study the nonmarket environment for relevant developments and to diffuse this information throughout the organization.
2. Assist in the education of line executives so that they can identify public relations problems and obtain staff aid.
3. Establish personal relations between line executives and appropriate government officials, labor leaders and others.[31]

The public relations practitioner may assist in interpreting not only linguistic differences, but differences in values, social mores, attitudes, actions and relationships. As Kean points out:

(multinational) public relations considerations begin with the marketing investigation and are not infrequently an important factor in deciding the

location of a foreign plant. . . . **Right from the start, good public relations can save the U.S. foreign operation considerable trouble.**[32]

**Public Relations in
Host Countries**

**The success of multinational corporations in operating in many countries
over long periods does not reflect an ability to escape control by governments. On the contrary, (they) owe their success . . . to their ability to
make flexible adaptations to national requirements.**[33]

The task of the public relations practitioner abroad is to adapt to the
particular audiences confronted abroad and to facilitate the overall adaptation
of the corporation to specific foreign environments. If there is hostility, the
public relations practitioner must seek to maintain legitimacy and accepta-
bility. Specifically, public relations abroad works primarily with three interrelated publics: governments, the general public, and the work force.

**Public Relations and Foreign Governments.** The importance of host government
relations for multinationals can hardly be overstated. Investment incentives,
price policies, employee relations, access to markets, indeed the environment
for business in a given nation is often largely a matter of governmental policy,
regulation, and administration. Moreover, as Sawyer points out, "Where many
corporate battles in the marketplace can be lost in one year and won in the
next, the losses in confrontation with political power tend to be more permanent."[34]

The first task of the MNC is to minimize the impacts of any conflicts with
national governments and to minimize any clash with nationalistic feelings.
This is being accomplished by:

1. Being responsive to the needs and sensibilities of host countries;
2. Scrupulously avoiding interference in the internal affairs of host countries;
3. Identifying the interests of the company with those of the host country
   in every possible way;
4. Conforming to local business practices whenever possible and introducing changes only in consultation with local authorities;
5. Decentralizing authority to local managers; and
6. Hiring local personnel.

Removal of conflict as a first priority does not suggest that attempts at
influence or defense against criticism are inappropriate. Influence by a multinational on a host government is usually most fruitfully pursued in one of
two ways. The indirect route is to persuade domestic constituencies to use
their influence on behalf of the MNC. The more direct route employs lobbying
or negotiation by the MNC's chief executive officer or other high-level personnel; Henry Ford II, for example, visited the United Kingdom in an attempt
to influence the British government to enact new and restrictive labor legislation.

When faced with criticism or actions which have negative consequences
(regulations, expropriations, strikes, boycotts and the like) it is appropriate
and imperative that MNCs defend themselves. Under these circumstances it
is important for the corporation to publicize its economic contribution to

the host country in terms of costs and risks assumed as well as benefits brought to the people. Practitioners should not assume, however, that tensions between MNC operations and host countries can be completely explained or resolved in economic terms. As Harvard's Raymond Vernon points out:

**In search of prime causes (for tension) one is pushed off economics into the political, social and cultural variables . . . The viscera prove more important than the cerebrum as the instrument of analysis.**[35]

Vernon's message to public relations practitioners is that they must be extraordinarily sensitive to noneconomic variables and prepared to act and advise line management based on these understandings.

**General Publics in Foreign Countries.** The practice of public relations must be tailored specifically to the cultural and social values of the particular sphere of operation. Of course in some aspects, as Kean states, "The basic principles of American public relations are quite exportable."[36] This is particularly true with regard to the mass media of developed Western nations. Cultural and social variations among countries under certain circumstances, however, can make American public relations practices useless, foolish or even destructive (see example #1 below).

Particular attention should be paid to variables of language, religion, cultural values and attitudes, social organization (class and kinship), education, technology, law, politics, and communication. Many nations are highly sensitive about language and how it is used. In the Canadian province of Quebec, for example, French is the language of public and business usage, despite the sizable English-speaking minority.

Religion, the mainspring of culture, is another extremely sensitive area. Great pains must be taken to avoid violations of belief, ritual, or religious law.

Values and attitudes taken for granted by Americans can be surprisingly different in various cultures. Efficiency, diligence, orderliness, punctuality, frugality, honesty, rationality, change, self-reliance, cooperation, time orientation, and achievement are differently defined and have different value placed upon them in western and nonwestern cultures.[37]

**Employee Publics of MNCs**

Guidelines for dealing with the general public, of course, apply to the foreign employees of the multinational corporation as well, and the same sensitivity to issues is called for. In relation to language, for instance, MNCs in certain countries hire workers who speak different languages in one manufacturing plant. Under these circumstances, bilingual workers are paid extra to serve as on-the-job translators.

The following scenes demonstrate the problems of cross-cultural communication that can arise between MNCs and their employees. The public relations staff, well versed in local culture, can help to avoid such problems to begin with, minimize or solve them once they have occurred, and handle any subsequent ramifications.

1. The managers of a U.S. firm tried to export the "company picnic" idea to their Spanish subsidiary. On the day of the picnic, the U.S. executives turned up dressed as cooks and proceeded to serve to their Spanish employees. Far from creating a relaxed atmosphere, this merely embarrassed the Spanish workers. Instead of socializing with their superiors, the employees clung together uneasily; whenever an executive approached a table, everyone stood up.[38]

2. Efforts to negotiate between American business executives and Greek officials were getting nowhere. The Greeks seemed resistant and suspicious toward the Americans. The Americans took pride in their outspokenness and forthrightness, qualities considered a liability by the Greeks. Furthermore, the Americans consistently attempted to limit the length of meetings and to reach agreements on general principles, leaving details to be cleaned up later. The Greeks considered these practices as devices designed to pull the wool over their eyes, as it was their practice to deal with all details taking as much time as necessary. No positive results came from the negotiations.[39]

3. A U.S. plant operating in the South Pacific had unknowingly violated the local status system and tribal arrangements in its hiring practices. The entire population of the island was seething because of the error. Since the Americans refused to see their error and mend their ways, leaders of local factions met to work out an acceptable reallocation of jobs. When they reached a solution they went en masse to see the plant manager, waking him up to give him the news. Unfortunately, since it was 3:00 A.M., the plant manager, who understood neither the local language nor the culture nor the situation, assumed he was under attack and called out a detachment of American Marines to quell the uprising.[40]

Various scholars who have observed the phenomenon of multinational corporations have concluded that despite the tensions and difficulties generated by these institutions, they represent a tremendous positive force in world affairs. Jacoby concludes:

**The spread of multinational enterprise will multiply the amount of international travel and contact between peoples, causing ancient myths and suspicions to decay. Cross-cultural experiences will gradually build understanding and trust. . . . Multinational business is the most powerful human institution in the forging of a world order.**[41]

The Brookings Institution's study determined:

**American multinationals generally contribute to both world welfare and the national welfare of the United States.**[42]

Public relations plays an integral role in the multinational business process, promoting understanding at home and abroad and facilitating management of world-wide enterprises.

---

**CASE STUDY:**  **By Thomas W. Zimmerer**
**PLASMA**  **Clemson University, Clemson, South**
**INTERNATIONAL**  **Carolina**

---

The Sunday headline in the Tampa, Florida, newspaper read:

"Blood Sales Result in Exorbitant Profits for Local Firm"

The story went on to relate how the Plasma International Company, head-quartered in Tampa, Florida, purchased blood in underdeveloped countries for as little as fifteen cents a pint and resold the blood to hospitals in the United States and South America. A recent disaster in Nicaragua resulted in scores of injured persons and a subsequent need for fresh blood. Plasma International had 10,000 pints of blood flown to Nicaragua from West Africa and charged the hospitals $25 per pint, grossing the firm nearly a quarter of a million dollars.

As a result of the newspaper story, prominent civic leaders and irate citizens demanded that Plasma International's licenses to practice business be revoked. Others protested to their legislators, seeking laws banning the blood sales for profit. One protester said: "What kind of people are these—selling life and death? These men prey on the needs of dying people, buying blood from poor, ignorant Africans for fifteen cents worth of beads and junk, and selling it to injured people for $25 a pint. Well, this company will soon find out that the people of our community won't stand for their kind around here."

Responding to reporters' questions, Sol Levin, president of the firm, exclaimed, "I just don't understand it. We run a business just like any other business; we pay taxes and we try to make an honest profit."

Levin was a successful stockbroker when he founded Plasma International Company. Recognizing the world's need for safe, uncontaminated, and reasonably priced whole blood and blood plasma, Levin and several of his colleagues pooled their resources and went into business. Initially, most of the blood and plasma they sold was purchased through storefront operations in the southeastern United States. Most of those selling their blood used the money to buy wine. While sales increased dramatically on the base of an innovative marketing approach, several cases of hepatitis were reported in recipients. The company wisely began a search for new sources.

Recognizing their own limitations in the medical-biological side of the business, they recruited a highly qualified team of medical consultants. The consulting team, after extensive testing and a worldwide search, recommended that the blood profiles and donor characteristics of several rural West African tribes made them ideal prospective donors. After extensive negotiations with the State Department and the government of a West African nation, the company was able to sign an agreement with several tribal chieftans to permit blood purchases.

As Levin reviewed these facts, and the many costs involved in the sale of a commodity as fragile as blood, he concluded that the publicity was grossly unfair. His thoughts were interrupted by the reporter's question: "Mr. Levin, is it necessary to sell a vitally needed medical supply, like blood, at such high prices especially to poor people in such a critical situation?" "Our prices are determined on the basis of a lot of costs that we incur that the public isn't even aware of," Levin responded. However, when reporters pressed him for details of these relevant costs, Levin refused any further comment. He noted that such information was proprietary in nature and not for public consumption.

**Questions**

1. Why should Mr. Levin be concerned about public response to Plasma International's business activities?

2. How should have Mr. Levin responded to the reporter's question?

3. How would you advise Plasma International to go about developing more positive public opinion toward itself and business in general?

---

**NOTES**

[1] Neil H. Jacoby, *Corporate Power and Social Responsibility* (New York: MacMillan, 1973), p. 98.

[2] M. S. Gwirtzman and A. R. Novak, "Reform of Bribery Abroad Involves U.S. Policy," in G. A. and J. F. Steiner, *Issues in Business and Society,* 2nd ed. (New York: Random House, 1977).

[3] C. Fred Bergsten, T. Horst, and T. H. Moran, *American Multinationals and American Interests* (Washington D.C.: The Brookings Institution, 1978), p. vii.

[4] Jacoby, *Corporate Power,* pp. 94, 102.

[5] Richard Eells, "Do Multinational Corporations Stand Guilty as Charged?" in G. A. and J. F. Steiner, *Issues in Business and Society,* 2nd ed. (New York: Random House, 1977), p. 314.

[6] George C. Sawyer, *Business and Society* (Boston: Houghton Mifflin, 1979), p. 364.

[7] Jacoby, *Corporate Power,* p. 122.

[8] George A. Steiner, *Business and Society,* 2nd ed. (New York: Random House, 1975), p. 445.

[9] James Cook, "A Game Any Number Can Play," *Forbes,* 25 June 1979, p. 52.

[10] "A Big Boost for the B.O.P.," *Fortune,* August, 1973.

[11] Cook, "Game Any Number Can Play," p. 54.

[12] *United States Business Performance Abroad* (Washington: National Planning Association, various authors and dates).

[13] David R. Francis, "Third World Loses Fear of Multinational Companies," *The Atlanta Journal and Constitution,* 13 May 1979, p. J-1.

[14] Cook, "Game Any Number Can Play," p. 55.

[15] Gwirtzman and Novak, "Reform of Bribery," p. 260.

[16] Ibid., p. 263.

[17] S. B. Prasad, and Y. Krishna Shetty, *An Introduction to Multinational Management* (Englewood Cliffs, N.J.: Prentice-Hall, Inc., 1976), p. 189.

[18] Gwirtzman and Novak, "Reform of Bribery," p. 263.

[19] Quoted in "How the Multinationals Are Reined In," *Business Week,* 12 March 1979, p. 76.

[20] Gwirtzman and Novak, "Reform of Bribery," p. 261.

[21] Hurd Baruch, "The Foreign Corrupt Practices Act," *Harvard Business Review* (January-February 1979); 32ff.

[22] Based on Richard S. Stoddart, "A Look from the Corporate Side," in C. E. Aronoff, *Business and the Media* (Santa Monica, CA: Goodyear Publishing Co., 1979), pp. 183 – 195.

[23] Adapted from "How AMF got burned on 'Payoffs,' " *Fortune,* 9 April 1979, p. 82.

[24] W. A. Durbin, "The Multinational Mentality," in Hill and Knowlton Executives, *Critical Issues in Public Relations* (Englewood Cliffs, N.J.: Prentice-Hall, 1975), pp. 200 – 201.

[25] Quoted in George A. Steiner, *Business and Society,* p. 445.

[26] Ibid., p. 446.

[27] *Business Week,* 12 March 1979, p. 73.

[28] *Business Week,* "Multinationals: The Public Gives Them Low Marks," 9 June 1973.

[29] Durbin, "Multinational Mentality," p. 195.

[30] John Fayerweather, *International Business Management* (New York: McGraw-Hill, 1969), p. 173.

[31] J. Boddewyn, "The External Affairs Function in American Multinational Corporations" in John Fayerweather, *International Business Government Affairs* (Cambridge, Mass.: Ballinger, 1977), p. 57.

[32] Geoffrey Kean, *The Public Relations Man Abroad* (New York: Praeger, 1968), p. 12.

[33] E. G. Collado "In Defense of the Multinational Corporation," in Steiner and Steiner, *Issues in Business and Society,* p. 306.

[34] Sawyer, *Business and Society,* p. 367.

[35] Raymond, Vernon, *Sovereignty at Bay* (New York: Basic Books, 1971), p. 230.

[36] Kean, op cit., p. 9.

[37] Vern Terpstra, *The Cultural Environment of International Business* (Cincinnati: South-Western Publishing Co., 1978).

[38] "The Spanish American Wars," *Worldwide P & I Planning,* May-June, 1971, pp. 30 – 40.

[39] Edward T. Hall, *The Silent Language* (New York: Doubleday, 1959), pp. 10 –11.

[40] Ibid., pp. 16 –17.

[41] Jacoby, *Corporate Power,* p. 262.

[42] Bergsten, Horst, and Moran, *American Multinationals,* p. 493.

# INDEX